MASCULINITIES
IN AFRICAN LITERARY
AND CULTURAL TEXTS

MASCULINITIES
IN AFRICAN LITERARY AND CULTURAL TEXTS

EDITED BY

Helen Nabasuta Mugambi
and Tuzyline Jita Allan

WITH A FOREWORD BY

Anthonia Kalu

AND AN AFTERWORD BY

Simon Gikandi

ayebia

An Adinkra symbol meaning
Ntesie Matemasie
A symbol of knowledge and wisdom

Masculinities in African Literary and Cultural Texts
Editors: Helen Nabasuta Mugambi and Tuzyline Jita Allan
This edition published by Ayebia Clarke Publishing Limited
Ayebia Clarke Publishing Limited
7 Syringa Walk
Banbury
Oxfordshire
OX16 1FR
UK
www.ayebia.co.uk

First published in the UK by Ayebia Clarke Publishing Limited 2010

ISBN 978-0-9555079-5-3

Distributed in Africa, Europe and the UK by TURNAROUND Publisher Services at
www.turnaround-uk.com

Distributed outside Africa, Europe and the United Kingdom exclusively by
Lynne Rienner Publishers Inc
1800 30th St., Ste. 314
Boulder, CO 80301
USA
www.rienner.com

Co-published and distributed in Ghana with the Centre for Intellectual Renewal
56 Ringway Estate, Osu, Accra, Ghana.

British Library Cataloguing-in-Publication Data
Cover Design by Amanda Carroll at Millipedia, UK.
Cover artwork by Getty Images.
Typeset by FiSH Books, Enfield, Middlesex, UK.

Available from www.ayebia.co.uk or email info@ayebia.co.uk
Distributed in Africa, Europe, UK by TURNAROUND at www.turnaround-uk.com

The Publisher wishes to acknowledge the support of Arts Council SE Funding

In fond memory of our fathers:
John M. Kyebasuuta and Joseph Koncheckma Younge
&
to all fathers, East, West, North and South
who teach their daughters to play in the sun and dance in the rain.

About the Editors

Helen Nabasuta Mugambi is a professor of comparative literature at California State University, Fullerton, where she recently served as acting coordinator of the women's studies program. She earned her bachelor's degree from Makerere University, Kampala and her PhD from Indiana University, Bloomington. Mugambi has published in the areas of gender, orality, popular song and postcolonial literature. One of her recent book chapters explores masculinity in Dangarembga's *Nervous Conditions*. She serves on the editorial board for *Jenda: A Journal of Culture and African Women Studies* and has received several awards, including a Stanford University Humanities Fellowship. She has held visiting professor positions at the University of California, Los Angeles and the University of California, Irvine.

Tuzyline Jita Allan is a professor of English at Baruch College (CUNY), she is one of three series editors of *Women Writing Africa*, a multi-volume collection of African women's writing through the ages. She has published a wide array of feminist and literary criticism. Recent publications include critical analyses of gender and modernism in Africa, the shorter fiction of Bessie Head and Ngugi wa Thiong'o and colonialism in Buchi Emecheta's *The Joys of Motherhood*. She is co-editor, with Chikwenye Okonjo Ogunyemi, of *Twelve Best Books by African Women: Critical Readings* (Ohio University Press, 2009) and has served as a guest editor of *Women's Studies Quarterly*.

Contents

PART II. Writing the Masculine

Acknowledgements

The resolve to produce this book has been constant through the years during which time we drew on a reservoir of support. First, we would like to thank the contributors who demonstrated the richness of their scholarly minds in these groundbreaking essays and patiently reaffirmed their confidence and respect for the project. We express deep gratitude to our publisher for being a pillar of strength as she worked tirelessly to ensure that the voices in the book enter the mainstream of masculinity studies. We are thankful for two of those compelling voices which are beautifully articulated in the Preface and the Afterword. The validations of Anthonia Kalu and Simon Gikandi are more than a conventional device; they speak to the book's ability to steer the subject in a new direction. We would also like to acknowledge the serious work of Bob Schwartz on the index. Many thanks.

In the end, our multitasking lives as teachers of literature never dulled the passion for this book. So, to each other, cheers!

Biographies of Contributors

Tuzyline Jita Allan (see *About the Authors* on page vi).

Austin Bukenya is a poet, novelist, dramatist, critic and translator. He has taught at universities in Uganda, Kenya, Tanzania and Scotland since 1968. He recently co-edited and contributed to an anthology of African short stories, *The Mermaid of Msambweni and Other Stories* (Nairobi: Oxford University Press, 2008). In the early 1970s Bukenya pioneered the establishment of the study of oral literature at Makerere University and with Pio Zirimu, coined the term 'orature' to describe oral genres. He has published and edited numerous anthologies and textbooks, in addition to serving as associate editor of *Women Writing Africa: Eastern Region* (New York: Feminist Press, 2007) and has worked extensively on French, Luganda and Swahili language translation projects.

Dominica Dipio is an award-winning filmmaker, a senior lecturer and Head of the Department of Literature at Makerere University, Kampala, Uganda. She has published widely in the areas of gender and film. She earned a Master's degree in literature from Makerere University and a PhD in film criticism from the Pontifical Gregorian University in Rome. Her first feature film is entitled *A Meal to Forget* and her current areas of research include film, orature, ritual performance and conflict resolution.

John D. H. Downing is a professor of media studies and director of the Global Media Research Centre at Southern Illinois University, Carbondale. He earned a PhD from the London School of Economics and Political Science and has taught at several universities, including Greenwich University in London and the University of Texas at Austin. His recent books include *Radical Media: Rebellious Communication and Social Movement* and *Representing 'Race.'* He is editor-in-chief of the *Sage Handbook of Media Studies* and has served as guest editor for a special issue of *Film Library Quarterly*.

Gwendolyn Etter-Lewis is a professor of English, women's studies and Black world studies at Miami University in Oxford, Ohio. She has published numerous articles and three books: *My Soul Is My Own*, *Unrelated Kin* and *Lights of the Spirit: The First Generation of Black Baha'is in North America*. She is the recipient of several prestigious awards, including a Fulbright Research Fellowship in the African Studies Institute at the University of Zambia, Lusaka, a Fulbright–Hayes fellowship to Ethiopia and Eritrea and a National Council for Black Studies Fellowship to Ghana.

Rangira Béa Gallimore is an associate professor at the University of Missouri, Columbia, where she teaches African francophone literature. She has authored two books and a number of articles and is co-editor of two special volumes of *Notre Librairie*, a journal devoted to francophone women's expression. She has also co-edited a volume of essays on the Rwandan genocide and is currently working on a book-length study of testimonies from women survivors of the genocide. Dr Gallimore has served as a consultant on gender equality and development for UNESCO and other international organisations.

Thomas A. Hale holds the Edwin Erle Sparks professorship in African, French and comparative literature at the Pennsylvania State University. A co-founder and former president of the African Literature Association, he has authored seven books on African and Caribbean literature. He is a specialist in West African oral literature and has conducted research on *griots* as well as on women's songs. He is currently working on several book-length projects, including a study of France, francophonie and Africa; an anthology and a collection of conference papers on women's songs from the Sahel region, with Aissata Sidikou and with Wendy Belcher, a collection of African literature texts from 3000 BCE to 1900 CE.

Peter Hitchcock is a professor at Baruch College and the Graduate School. He has taught at City University of New York since 1988 and as a visiting professor at the State University of New York at Stony Brook, the universities in Beijing and Shanghai. His criticism focuses on literary and cultural theory, twentieth-century film and literature (US, European, Asian and African) and the work of Mikhail Bakhtin. He is the author of four books: *Working-Class Fiction in Theory and Practice; Dialogics of the Oppressed; Oscillate Wildly: Space, Body and Spirit of Millennial Materialism;* and *Imaginary States: Studies in Cultural Transnationalism* (2003, University of Illinois Press). He has edited and introduced a special issue of *South Atlantic Quarterly* on Mikhail Bakhtin and has published many articles in journals such as *Modern Fiction Studies, Transition, Third Text, Rethinking Marxism* and *Research in African Literatures*, as well as in a number of anthologies.

Naana Banyiwa Horne is a poet and literary critic. She received her bachelor's degree from the University of Cape Coast, Ghana and her PhD from the University of Wisconsin at Madison. She has taught in the Humanities Department at Indiana University, Kokomo and currently, as an associate professor at Santa Fe College in Gainsville, Florida. She is a scholar of African women's writing and her books of poetry include *Sunkwa: Clingings onto Life*, which has already appeared in a second edition as *Sunkwa Revisited*. Her forthcoming poetry volume is entitled *Life Songs*.

Timothy Johns is an assistant professor of world literature at Murray State University, Kentucky. His work has appeared recently in the *Journal of the African Literature Association* and in *Atlantikos*. An essay on Phaswane Mpe's *Welcome to Our Hillbrow* will appear in the forthcoming edited collection, *Emerging African Voices* (Cambria Press).

Abasi Kiyimba is an associate professor in the Department of Literature and Deputy dean of administration and finance at Makerere University in Uganda. He teaches linguistics, African-American and European literatures. His scholarship focuses on folktales of the Baganda and masculine identities in the fiction of Ugandan women writers.

Siendou A. Konaté earned his bachelor's and master's degrees from Côte d'Ivoire (Ivory Coast) in West Africa. A recipient of a Fulbright Fellowship at the State University of New York, Binghamton, his areas of specialisation include comparative literature, translation theory and criticism. He writes poetry and as a critic, his areas of specialisation include the works of Léopold Sédar Senghor, Aimé Césaire, Léon Gontran Damas, David Diop, Birago Diop and Bernard B. Dadié.

Bernth Lindfors is a prominent pioneering Africanist. He is now professor emeritus of English at the University of Texas at Austin. He founded *Research in African Literatures*, a leading journal in African studies and initiated the Critical Perspective Series. A prolific writer, his books cover folklore, postcolonial and popular literature. He was awarded an honourary doctorate degree by the University of Umeå and has received many other honours, awards and prizes, including a Gold Medal from the English Academy of Southern Africa, an Outstanding Service Award from the African Literature Association, an Award of Excellence in the Criticism of African Literature from the University of Calabar, Nigeria and an honourary doctorate degree from the University of Kwazulu-Natal (then University of Natal), South Africa.

Daouda Loum is an associate professor in the English Department, Cheikh Anta Diop University, Dakar, Senegal, from where he received his master's degree and his PhD. He worked as a language assistant in London and was a Fulbright Scholar at California State University, Fullerton. He has published articles on Senegalese writers such as Leopold Sedar Senghor, Ousmane Soce Diop, Abdoulaye Sadji and Mariama Bâ, as well as American writers, including Mark Twain, William Dean Howells, Gloria Naylor and Frederick Douglass.

Helen Nabasuta Mugambi (see *About the Authors* on page vi).

Clement Okafor is a professor in the Department of English and Modern Languages at the University of Maryland, Eastern Shore, where he teaches African-American, African and world literatures. For many years, Okafor served as Chair of the Department of English at the University of Nigeria, Nsukka. He received his PhD from Harvard University and is the author of *Omenka the Master Artist: Critical Perspectives of Achebe's Fiction*. His numerous publications include criticism on Zambian folk narratives and the work of J. P. Clark.

Tanure Ojaide is the Frank Porter Graham Professor of Africana studies at the University of North Carolina-Charlotte. A renowned author and scholar, he has written over twenty books of poetry, fiction and criticism. He has won many national and international awards, including the Commonwealth Poetry Prize for the region of Africa, a BBC Arts and Africa Poetry Award, the All-Africa Okigbo Prize for Poetry, a National Endowment for the Humanities Fellowship and a Fulbright Senior Scholar Fellowship.

Ken Walibora Waliaula is a prolific Kiswahili fiction writer. Currently he is an assistant professor in the African Languages and Literature Department at the University of Wisconsin, Madison. His research covers African continental and Diasporic literatures, with a focus on anglophone and swahiliphone fiction. He has won numerous awards for his Kiswahili fiction and his English-language novel, *Innocence Long Lost*, was runner-up in the 2007 Jomo Kenyatta Prize for Literature. He has published a number of book chapters and articles in academic journals.

Marilyn Slutzky Zucker teaches in the writing and rhetoric programme at the State University of New York at Stony Brook. Co-founder of the Woolf Society Players, she has published and lectured on Virginia Woolf as well as on a range of women writers, including Ken Bugul, Jamaica Kincaid and Gloria Naylor. Zucker received a Fulbright lectureship to teach American literature in Portugal where she plans to return to teach and write on the subject of autobiography.

Preface

Anthonia C. Kalu

The arrival of *Masculinities in African Literary and Cultural Texts* during this period of self-reflection and reassessment in African literary and cultural production is timely. Dynamic in its conception, the volume points to the vitality of Africa's cultural heritage as its various contributors address the familiar, though vexing, subject of masculinity and call attention to the need to see African male identities from multiple perspectives. The volume also allows us to examine how far we have come in the past few decades of intense debate in gender studies and points to the culture work yet to be done for Africa to reassert itself globally.

The essays in this volume are accessible, illuminating and refreshing in their exploration of a variety of topics such as folktale heroines who defy cultural norms, challenges to contemporary forms of African political leadership, recreations of masculinity in popular culture and homosexuality in Africa. The collection is neither militant nor nationalistic. The contributors are part of a generation of scholars who understand Africa's place in the expanding global cultural economy. Both African and Africanist scholars bring to the volume rigorous research informed by indigenous and Western theoretical perspectives that illuminate the ways in which masculinity is negotiated in a range of texts from across the continent. The reader is made aware of new complexities in the relationships between men and women and ultimately, the fact that the gender debate continues as much in art as in real life. The editors have arranged the essays in coherent units that facilitate a comparative understanding of masculine traditions across genres, cultures and critical practices.

Like Achebe's *Things Fall Apart*, the texts examined here remind us of the sustainable qualities of the proverb, that ubiquitous verbal art whose formulaic structure provides moments of clarity in the daily commerce of African life. Invariably, each proverb has a counter-statement that provides the speaker–listener with another way of considering an idea or concept. In this book, the proverb takes pride of place as it wields authority in the analytical frameworks of many of the essays. For example, Okafor's essay opens with an Igbo proverb which encourages the guest in the man's *obi* to also visit the wife's dwelling not only because that is where food is prepared for family members and visitors. Not visiting this important part of an Igbo man's compound is likely to leave one with questions about what makes the man a man. For, since his food is a significant source of his physical strength undergirding all his other masculine attributes like status, virility, honesty, courage and wealth, failure to do so might jeopardise his honour and the will to sustained productive leadership. The proverb is notable simultaneously for its practical wisdom, its symbolism and its insight into gender complementarity.

As the contributors wrestle with past and present meanings of masculinity in these essays, they shed light on the particular and culture-specific environments that inform its multiple practices. International bodies are also aware of the implications of the changing climate of gender relations. When the United Nations Security Council adopted Resolution 1325 on 31 October 2000, for example, the event was hailed globally as a landmark achievement. The resolution '... reaffirms the important role of women in the prevention and resolution of conflicts, peace-building, peacekeeping, humanitarian response and in post-conflict reconstruction and stresses the importance of their equal participation and full involvement in all efforts for the maintenance and promotion of peace and security.'[1] What is important here is the fact that in the year 2000, the need to include women, even conceptually, in the movement towards peace and conflict resolution becomes part of a global effort to curb the reaches of self-assured masculinity. Hence one cannot overstate this volume's importance in drawing attention to the evolving states of male consciousness and the complex worlds of men and women in Africa. Readers who seriously engage these essays will discover many analytical possibilities to aid understanding of African sexual politics.

Introduction

Helen Nabasuta Mugambi
and Tuzyline Jita Allan

This collection of critical essays aims to expand and energise current research on African masculinities and the broader fields of gender and cultural studies. By giving prominence to African oral and written literatures as sites for articulating the masculine, the book brings a unique perspective to the emerging scholarship on African masculinities. Among a few pioneering studies, *Men and Masculinities in Modern Africa* by Lisa Lindsay and Stephan F. Miescher and *African Masculinities: Men in Africa from the Late Nineteenth Century to the Present* by Lahoucine Ouzgane and Robert Morrell are instructive in their deployment of an interdisciplinary approach that is germane to this study. Both provide an important socio-historical framework that illuminates the changing assumptions, attitudes and vocabularies of masculinity.

Like its precedents, *Masculinities in African Literary and Cultural Texts* draws on a variety of subject areas, including history, anthropology, gender studies and cultural studies to illuminate the processes by which masculinities are produced in orature, film and written literature. Its distinctiveness, however, lies in a critical strategy that opens up the literary-cultural terrain to scrutinize the nuanced and complex inscriptions of masculinity from a variety of African social contexts. Analyses of a range of oral, performative and written texts located in a broad spectrum of inter-regional and cultural environments point to not simply the structural, rhetorical and intertextual relationships of the genres, but also the role each plays in capturing masculine ambiguity.

The use of the term 'texts' in this book recognises the interplay between speech and writing, process and product, past and present states of historical consciousness and the events and contexts intrinsic to the creative process. These interwoven texts of Africa's oral and written traditions contain large elements of history suffused with the mythic and the prosaic. They bring a particular credibility to Terry Eagleton's notion that '[w]orks of art and culture are living experiences, not abstract doctrines.'[1] The narratives of proverbs, folktales, epics, song and cinema represented in this volume point to orality and film as formidable genres that bring into relief the creative effort of contemporary African novelists to make sense of the crises of our time. What Isidore Okpewho describes as the 'creative text[s]'[2] of African oral literature, for example, capture the pervasive orality of the continent's expressive traditions and the oral artist's ability to unlock the power of language in different settings. The 'texts' selected here for study are illustrative of the concurrence of various scripts and speech-acts—oral, performative and written—in the process of engendering meaning about masculinity in African societies.

'Men's studies' emerged a little over two decades ago from the growing undercurrent of discontent with the establishment of feminist gender critique as a force for social change in the 1960s and 1970s. Coming of age in the 1980s under the shadow of a decidedly female-driven sexual politics, the study of men and masculinity faced a crisis of confidence in its ability to engage a theoretical framework for challenging the intellectual arguments against male power and dominance in the social system. 'It has been suggested that many men were just too threatened to frame any coherent reply,'[3] David Cohen writes in his semi-autobiographical book, *Being a Man*. 'We had much to lose and were too afraid,' he adds.[4] Predictably, the first generation of books to break the silence heralded new models of manhood drawn from an expansive breadth of male experience. Three examples, *The Making of Masculinities: The New Men's Studies, Beyond Patriarchy: Essays by Men on Pleasure, Power and Change* and *Changing Men: New Directions in Research on Men and Masculinities*, all published in 1987, signal the depth of feminist influence on the emergent discourse. Recent developments, however, point to 'a complex and constantly shifting relationship,'[5] as noted by Michael Kimmel in the foreword to *Masculinity Studies and Feminist Theory*. It is a view shared by a number of contributors to this volume.

Practitioners of the new field of men's studies acknowledged from the outset that masculinity, like femininity, is socially constructed and like the environments in which they are produced, masculine identities are subject to change. The new configurations have placed an increased focus on the fluid, unstable and contradictory nature of masculinity, in opposition to the hegemonic view of an unchangeable and undifferentiated maleness. This development has been accompanied by the tendency to pluralise the term and to expand the historical, cultural and psychological contexts essential to its production.

Hence, the study of masculinities straddles not only the personal and the political but also a wide range of academic subjects, including biology, psychology, sociology, anthropology, ethnography, history, literature and cultural studies. R. W. Connell, in an early attempt to map the field's theoretical boundaries, sees the potential for valuable insight in these 'rival knowledges.'[6] 'To understand both everyday and scientific accounts of masculinity,' he declares, 'we cannot remain at the level of pure ideas, but at their practical bases.'[7] This approach, rooted in a cultural studies framework, has allowed for a concentration on those forms of masculinity precipitated by race, class, sexuality, ethnicity and other indicators of difference.

By situating the study of masculinity in the textual incarnations of the lived experience of ordinary and not-so-ordinary people, this book at once recognises and contributes to the democratisation of the study of culture in contemporary discourses of identity. The essays reverberate with the sounds and tones of cultural self-definition as the voices of traditional griots merge with those of contemporary writers and filmmakers to call up the the spirit of African manhood. Melissa Thackway captures the sense of continuity when she remarks that '[d]espite the profound changes that have taken place in contemporary Africa... griots continue to play a fundamental role, widely reflected in contemporary art forms, including film.'[8] This volume participates in what could be called an artistic adventure across genres as it tries to reframe the subject of African masculinity.

Overview of Chapters: Part I

The first two chapters in the Oral section present two epics: one from East Africa, the other from the Western region of the continent. In 'Staging Masculinity in the East African Epic,' Ken W. Waliaula explores conceptualisations of masculinity among the Waswahili peoples. He argues that although the Liyongo epic contains exaggerated elements of conventional masculinity, characterised by such attributes as virility, power, strength and domination, its unique—and thus far overlooked—characteristic is that the hero's masculinity is profoundly dependent upon female power. Describing this female power as the 'oxygen that ventilates masculinity,' Waliaula asserts that the Swahili epic constructs a form of 'masculine femininity,' a concept devoid of phallic or sexual connotations. The Liyongo epic, he concludes, exemplifies a masculinity that defies the usual masculine-feminine dichotomy.

In 'Masculinity in the West African Epic,' Thomas Hale expands the argument about male identity in the epic to include comparisons between medieval European and West African epic heroes. He contends that although the heroes from both continents possess the attributes of bravery, strength, loyalty and honour, unique family and social circumstances distinguish the characteristics of the West African hero. Sibling rivalry and the fluid dynamics of class, for example, complicate the heroic ideal and provide more nuanced models of nobility. Hale calls attention to current Eurocentric studies of masculinities and suggests that African notions of masculinity can be incorporated into Western scholarship to deepen perspectives on the subject.

Abasi Kiyimba's 'Men and Power: The Folktales and Proverbs of the Baganda' uncovers hegemonic forms of masculinity in the two oral genres. Kiyimba situates folktales and proverbs within the patriarchal ideology of male kinship and a hierarchical gender system. He argues that patriarchal ideology of dominance remains unchallenged because it is rooted in the culture's founding myth which permeates everyday life. The ascribed superior status of men, he insists, leads not only to male sibling rivalries, but also to a deadly competition among co-wives to bear male children.

Rangira Bea Gallimore's 'Ndabaga Folktale Revisited' examines the fate of a dutiful daughter who, in the absence of a male sibling, assumes a male identity to relieve her ageing father from military duty. Not only does Gallimore problematise the issue of whether masculinity in Rwandan society can be performed, but she also demonstrates how a feminist reinterpretation of the Ndabaga folktale in post-genocide Rwanda has resulted in the disruption of the indigenous patriarchal power structure. Furthermore, she points out that although the original version of the folktale ends in a reiteration of the privileged status of masculinity, its performance by women in post-genocide Rwanda has imbued it with a subversive power to appropriate attributes formerly reserved for men.

Tanure Ojaide, in 'The Man from Udje: African Oral Poetic Performance,' also explores masculinity in a male-centred society similar to the one described in Gallimore's chapter. In both scenarios, stories about war serve as a springboard for imagining and performing the masculine. Ojaide discusses Urhobo notions of masculinity expressed through oral poetic performance known as *udje*, an artistic contest in poetry, song and dance creatively staged as a battle of fighting words intended to 'annihilate' the opposition. Unlike the Rwandan example in which women subvert patriarchal structures in a performance of the masculine, *udje* is an exclusive male activity steeped in the actual history of the people. Ojaide highlights the irony that even though performing *udje* is a male tradition, many of the performers dress in women's wrappers and more intriguingly, the performance is dedicated to deities that are neither male nor female.

Helen Nabasuta Mugambi's 'Masculinity on Trial: Gender Anxiety in African Song Performances' underscores the critical contributions popular culture artists bring to current debates on class and gender formation. Mugambi explores reconfigurations of male identity through *kadongokamu* song which, like *udje*, contains exaggerated elements of manly attributes. She demonstrates how the masculine text in the two songs she analyses confirms that male identities predicated upon ambivalent cultural notions of the feminine are fated to crumble and collapse. Mugambi also asserts that within shifting ethnic and national identies, such masculine formulations are always already under threat of infiltration from the underpriviledged groups.

In 'Faces of Masculinity in African Cinema,' Dominica Dipio draws on Antonio Gramsci's theory of hegemonic masculinity to argue that in the post-colonial context powerful men cannot maintain total control over marginalised groups. She further examines ways in which African male filmmakers critique postcolonial governance by interrogating the propagation of 'dehumanising' myths, traditions and practices that cause untold suffering to subaltern groups.

John D. H. Downing's 'Masculinity in Selected North African Films' sheds light on prevailing images of maleness in North African and Arab cultures. Examining an array of films across North Africa, Downing starts by dispelling entrenched myths associated with Islamic cultures and goes on to discuss the complex ways in which masculinities are constructed within these cultures.

Bernth Lindfor's 'Penetrating *Xala*' is reprinted here as an instance of earlier attempts to critique the abuse of power in postcolonial contexts. Lindfor's analysis is in dialogue with the views expressed in several other chapters that highlight the role of metaphor in configuring the nation state.

Overview of Chapters: Part II

The centrality of proverbs in the first two chapters in this section links 'writing the masculine' to the discussion of the masculine in the orature and film section above. In 'Rapacious Masculinity and Ethno-Colonial Politics in a Swahili Novel' Austin Bukenya's interpretation of *Asali Chungu* (Bitter Honey) expands the critique of masculinity initiated in the previous section. He argues that issues of race, gender and class among Arabs, Creole Swahilis and Black Africans in the postcolonial Swahili island society of Zanzibar and Pemba undermine any monolithic idea of male identity in that culture. The protagonist's unbridled display of power and aberrant masculinity, Bukenya argues, is characterised by predatory practices directed at women and 'lesser' men and ultimately becomes a double-edged sword that destroys the victims and the practitioners alike. Bukenya sees the novel's utilisation of proverbs as an effective rhetorical strategy.

In 'Masculinity in Achebe's *Anthills of the Savannah*,'Clement Okafor explores the ways in which traditional beliefs about gender difference embedded in an Igbo proverb inform notions of masculinity in the novel, with tragic implications for the protagonist. His intertextual reading of *Anthills of the Savannah* and *Things Fall Apart* is especially illuminating in the light of the tremendous critical attention the latter has received. Okafor concedes that it may be difficult to dismantle systems of male domination, but that they are hardly the dominant force in the emerging postcolonial societies in which individuals compete in a wider socio-political terrain.

In 'Dark Bodies/White Masks: African Masculinities and Visual Culture in *Graceland, The Joys of Motherhood* and *Things Fall Apart*,' Etter-Lewis explores the interplay between word and image to point to 'alternative masculinities (including the forbidden domain of homosexuality) that co-exist uneasily and in constantly fluctuating positions of dominance and subordination.' She locates her analysis of *Graceland*, in which a Nigerian teenager performs Elvis Presley in 'white face,' against the backdrop of the images of masculine characters in two popular Nigerian novels by Achebe and Emecheta. The visual and verbal signs combine to create 'a space where opposing traits vie for dominance and expression.'

As the title indicates, Naana Banyiwa Horne's 'Sexual Impotence: Metonymy for Political Failure in Ama Ata Aidoo's Anowa' exemplifies the ways in which African writers use masculinity as metaphor to critique the nation state. Horne shows how Aidoo's play dramatises the powerful connection between sexual potency and hegemonic masculinity. Anowa, she argues, establishes a direct link between her husband's impotence and his callous exploitation of others and by extension, between male impotence and national inertia.

Siendou A. Konate's 'Virility and Emasculation in Ahmadou Kourouma's Novels' applies the sexual metaphor to the author's use of tcheyaa, 'a major cultural idiom of Manding society,' signifying simultaneously 'sword' and 'the force that produces manliness, virility and/or masculinity.' The male characters' fidelity to tcheyaa is said to be constantly undermined by the threat of emasculation embodied in the feminine ideal. Even '[t]hose who hold on to manhood are eventually emasculated.' As in Anowa, the woman in Kourouma's fiction becomes a powerful force for change.

In 'Women, Men and Exotopy: On the Politics of Scale in Nuruddin Farah's Maps,' Peter Hitchcock examines the relationship between space and gender in Nuruddin Farrah's Maps by tracking the novel's engagement with Mikhail Bakhtin's concept of outsideness or exotopy. He demonstrates how, in Farrah's Maps, the feminine and the masculine are not polarities but act as variable social markers. The 'misgendered' characters in the novel, Askar and Misra, Hitchcock argues, enact Farrah's vision of how Somalia can be fruitfully imagined, communicated and mapped, mainly as a spatial imaginary capable of the metaphorical transfer of meaning from received notions of gender and nation.

In 'Killing the Pimp: Firdaus's Challenge to Masculine Authority in Nawal El Saadawi's Woman at Point Zero,' Marilyn S. Zucker examines the author's depiction of masculine violence as it plays out in the life of Firdaus, a woman condemned to death for killing her pimp. The circle of abuse expands outwards from the protagonist's home to an uncle's home, through marriage and work and finally into a life of prostitution. Zucker proposes that Firdaus appropriates masculine narrative elements as a means of empowering the telling of her own story and concludes that El Saadawi gives authorial voice—traditionally reserved for men—to this most abused of women, who asks for no sympathy and understands the power she has usurped.

Unlike Woman at Point Zero, in which prostitution is presented as a dehumanising force against the female gender, the next chapter draws attention to prostitution's tenuous link with male homosexuality. In 'The Price of Pleasure: K. Sello Duiker's Thirteen Cents and the Economics of Homosexuality in South Africa,' Tim Johns opens his analysis with comments about the divisive debates over homosexuality in Africa. He concludes that South Africa is fighting for homosexual rights, unlike many other nations that consider alternative masculinities a polluting influence from the West. Johns suggests that anti-gay commentators privilege the idea of an aprioristic heterosexual man and overlook Duiker's convincing portrait of economically motivated choices that can be traced to pre-colonial times. Johns believes Duiker's vision offers as its subtext a striking condemnation of the ANC's failed neo-liberal policies and that homosexuality is becoming an acceptable sub-culture in Africa amid the changing social and economic realities of the continent.

Daouda Loum, in 'The Ambivalence of Masculinity in Gorgui Dieng's *A Leap Out of the Dark*,' links masculinity in the first Senegalese novel written in English with a plethora of images and definitions accumulated in the process of the society's evolution from rural to urban and from traditional to modern. He argues that the novel gains its power from its rootedness in the oral tradition of praise songs, tales, allegorical narratives and ancestral wisdom expressed in proverbs and aphorisms. At the same time, he points out the efficacy of applying deconstructive strategies to assessments of gender and sexual politics in Africa.

In a move that looks simultaneously into the past and the present, Tuzyline Jita Allan in 'A Retrospective' reflects on the significance of this volume by invoking *The Interesting Narrative of Olaudah Equiano* and the author's image as 'the African' – a term many in eighteenth-century Britain found unsettling. Allan believes that an important priority in the narrative is given to a hybridised European masculinity consisting of a cluster of masculine identities Equiano assumes in his rise to fame and fortune within British society. In the end, this hybrid strategy, Allan argues, enhances Equiano's manhood and eclipses his African identity. Allan believes the ensuing sense of disconnectedness has significant implications both in terms of the way identity is negotiated in the portraits of manhood presented in this volume and the current critical discourses of identity, such as hybridity, whose optimistic agendas of inclusion and diversity often fail to recognise historical and structural systems of inequality.

PART I

Configuring Masculinity in Orature and Film

1. Staging Masculinity in the East African Epic

Ken Walibora Waliaula

Mume ni mume hata akiwa gumegume

(A man is a man, however worthless he may be)—
Kiswahili Proverb[1]

This chapter examines the elements of masculinity staged in the Fumo Liyongo epic of the Waswahili people of East Africa. The eponymous hero, around whom the narrative revolves, is imbued with exaggerated masculinity; yet this masculinity makes profound statements about the conception of masculinity among the Waswahili. The hero's exploits and feats point to the extent to which, in the Swahili notion of masculinity, a premium is placed upon qualities such as virility, strength and intellect. Clearly, the Swahili idea of masculinity or manliness is in tandem with the traditional view of masculinity: vigorous activity, domination, power and strength.

Nonetheless, what is also implicit—but perhaps not often articulated enough in analyses of the epic—is how the hero's masculinity is either dependent upon or implicated with femininity. Therefore, I suggest that the Liyongo epic enacts what could be called 'masculine femininity.'[2] It is an amalgamated masculinity closely implicated in the (disputed) claim that the Swahili society is matrilineal in nature.[3] In other words, it is hardly fortuitous that an epic displaying the extraordinary deeds of an extraordinarily manly man such as Liyongo would link key moments of his failure and success to his mother's action or inaction, to her presence or absence. The gender dynamics staged in this epic tend to regard femininity as the oxygen that ventilates masculinity, enabling and enhancing its existence and survival. This chapter also addresses what Stephen Heath has curiously called the 'eternal problem of the phallus' as a symbol of masculinity.[4] The phallus is here characterised as an eternal problem because it refuses to go away in analyses and exegeses of masculinity and patriarchy. Following Lacan, Laplanche and Pontalis, I differentiate between the phallus and the penis: the former is the signifier or symbol of manliness; the latter simply refers to the male sexual organ.[5] In this regard the penis is one among any number of phallic symbols that are implicitly dramatised in this Swahili epic.

It is important to state at this point that although masculinity has something to do with what it means to be a man or manly, it does not preclude the possibility of females exhibiting masculine attributes. The converse is equally true—the male can be or can become feminine. Psychologists, such as Freud and Jung, have conceded that there is an inherent mixture of masculinity and femininity within each human psyche. Freud wrote that 'pure masculinity or femininity is not to be found either in a psychological or biological sense. Every individual on the contrary displays a mixture.'[6] Jung also recognised that men and women both have animus and anima, male and female attributes. It is imperative to mention this because, given its varied manifestations in different societies and epochs, masculinity defies universalising definitions or attributes. In other words, what it means to be manly does not always mean the same thing in all societies at all times. Even within a specific society there is not always a homogenised conception of masculinity. There is a need to heed Homi Bhabha's caveat, 'to speak of masculinity in general, *sui generis*, must be avoided at all costs.'[7] David D. Gilmore's statement that boys everywhere undergo tests or proofs of action to become men, whereas females rarely undergo such tests to become women, exemplifies the blind alley of universalising or homogenising masculinity.[8] To claim that tests are unique to boys is to elide geopolitical and cultural specificities. For example, it is common knowledge that even in African countries where there is an official ban on female circumcision, the practice is still widespread as proof of femininity, as recent studies among the Masai, Somali, Kalenjin, Meru and Kisii communities of Kenya demonstrate. The quotidian tests and proofs of femininity that women and girls undergo in Africa (e.g., elaborate initiation rituals and female circumcision) belie Gilmore's claims. In addition, stringent public virginity tests among girls attaining puberty in southern Africa are to be construed as significant thresholds into the world of womanhood. To the communities practicing these virgin tests, proof that one has maintained virginity into and beyond puberty is the defining feature of the process of becoming a woman. Like the male circumcision that Gilmore cites as an example of a test for manhood, female virginity tests are public and successful candidates are even issued certificates. Among the Waswahili, from whom the Liyongo epic emerges, the *unyago* initiation rites in which girls are instructed on the 'nuts and bolts' of womanhood testify to the tests and proofs of femininity that should not be elided or ignored. In the Swahili cultural universe, therefore, the *unyago* rites are socially mandated and recognised as the female counterpart of *jando* rites during which boys undergo tests in their passage into manhood.

The Liyongo epic makes possible some of the critical extrapolations of the meanings and manifestations of masculinity among the Waswahili that illuminate East African masculinity and retrieve masculinity from the parochial matrix in which certain critical inquiries have embedded it.[9] However, this is not to imply that there is an ecumenical notion of masculinity in East Africa, much less in the rest of the continent. What one notices are certain continuities and similarities that thrive alongside ethnic, regional and national specificities. Thus, when necessary, I will refer to other East African oral and written texts for purposes of comparison and/or clarification.

The native Swahili people have bequeathed East Africa not only Kiswahili, its *lingua franca*, but also a whole range of oral and written literature (e.g., proverbs and tales) that have enriched the region's ideological, epistemological, literary and linguistic heritage. Yet, as Alamin Mazrui points out, there is an interesting paradox regarding the relationship between the Kiswahili language and the Waswahili people: although the reality of the language as an integral vehicle for communication is taken for granted, the existence of the people is shrouded in mystery.[10] The cradle of the Waswahili is said to have been a place called Ngozi on the Kenya coast, from where they derived their original name: *Wangozi*. However, when the Arabs came to the East African coast they referred to them as *Suahel*, which means 'people of the coast.' It is from what Mazrui calls the 'Afro-Arab heritage' that Wangozi acquired their current nomenclature, with 'Waswahili' referring to the people and 'Kiswahili' referring to their language. Most Africanist historians dispute the Eurocentric view—i.e., Waswahili people and Kiswahili language are products of miscegenation between the Arabs and indigenous Africans then dwelling on the East African coast—insisting that although the Waswahili owe their nomenclature to the Arabs, their existence was not a consequence of or dependent upon the Arabic presence in the region. Nonetheless, it is worth noting that, as Mazrui has argued, the Arabs have had tremendous influence on the Swahili worldview, particularly through the Islamic tenets and ethos that suffuse Swahili oral and written literature. Mazrui writes:

> The beginnings of writings in Swahili literature can be traced to the Afro–Arab contact on the East African seaboard that goes back to antiquity. ... Recurrent waves of Arabian migrants were displaced by internecine wars in their own countries and found refuge in the East African City States. Over time, many of these settlers intermarried with the local population and Islam, which established itself in the area soon after it was founded in Arabia, became an additional force in the consolidation of this Afro-Arab heritage. It is out of this cultural intercourse that the Swahili written tradition was initially born.[11]

As Mazrui further illustrates, it is not surprising that not only did the earliest Swahili written literature adopt an 'Arabic alphabet akin to what is referred to as *ajami* in West Africa,' but this literature also had a significantly 'didactic and hagiographic thrurst.'[12]

The didactic and hagiographic thrust of this literature suggests a tremendous Islamic influence upon a wide spectrum of aspects of Swahili life, including notions of masculinity and femininity. But that is not the only influence that the Waswahili have encountered. The European encounter also left an abiding impact on Swahili culture, along with the Latin Italian script that competed with and soon superseded Arabic script in the Swahili literary landscape. As Mazrui concludes, the outcome was that the Waswahili, like most Africans, boast of a triple heritage: African, European and Arabic. At a local level, the Waswahili have bequeathed the East Africans the Kiswahili language and literature of which the Liyongo epic is an integral part. The transethnic property of the Kiswahili language is replicated in the Liyongo epic to which, as K. W. Wamitila, indicates other ethnic groups (e.g., Bajuni and Pokomo) stake a claim.[13]

Fumo Liyongo is a historical figure who lived and died in the city state of Shanga on the northern Kenyan coast. He is said to have lived under the reign of the Swahili King Mringwari in the Shanga city state around the tenth century C.E. Liyongo's centrality in the collective memory of the coastal peoples of East Africa accounts for the emergence of an epic that has both complemented and competed with his historicity over generations. In this respect, the Liyongo epic has striking resemblances to Son-Jara (or Sundiata) of West Africa, who inhabits both the historical archive and the world of the literary epic.

The Liyongo epic, like all epics, not only epitomises and dramatises the exceptional feats of its eponymous male hero, but also exhibits the heroism and masculine attributes of its female characters, without whom the hero's presence would amount to nothing. The story pits Liyongo against King Mringwari in what seems to be a power struggle for the control of Shanga. It is apparent from the outset that Mringwari is paranoid about Liyongo's rising popularity due to the latter's amazing physical strength and exceptional musical talent. At first, King Mringwari touts Liyongo's strength to the neighbouring Galla people as a way of intimidating them. Fearing that the Waswahili would easily vanquish them at war, the Galla give Liyongo a Galla wife in a hurried marriage alliance.

But relations between King Mringwari and Liyongo deteriorate quickly. At first the king plots to have Liyongo killed with an arrow in a palm-fruit-felling contest. When the first attempt on Liyongo's life fails, the king orders his arrest and execution. Aware that he will be executed in three days, Liyongo asks the king to arrange for a dance tournament at the prison house compound so that he may bid farewell to the people. Meanwhile, Liyongo sends a cryptic message to his mother through a slave girl, instructing her to bake a loaf of bread and hide a file inside it. On the day of the dance tournament, Liyongo entertains the audience with musical instruments provided for him (as he had requested) by the prison authorities. Those in attendance do not have any clue that he has used the music to muffle the filing away of his prison chains. Then, to their utter shock, they see him break out of the prison cell and using his mighty power, he kills dozens of the guards by smashing them against one another.

Having failed to conquer Liyongo in a frontal attack, King Mringwari uses Liyongo's own son, the product of his marriage to the Galla wife. He sends the son to investigate Liyongo's Achilles tendon, his most vulnerable spot. Liyongo unwittingly reveals to the son that the only way of killing him is to insert a copper needle in his navel. During the night the son picks a copper needle and pricks his father's navel, killing him. Liyongo continues to perform 'fantastic deeds' even after death. For instance, he refuses to remain dead in bed. He picks up his bow and arrow and takes a kneeling position at the communal well as if poised to shoot someone or something. So terrified are the people that they do not draw water in the well for some time. They beseech Liyongo's mother to talk to him so he can let them draw water from the well. When the mother approaches Liyongo, she sings to him a lullaby and upon touching him, his body falls to the ground. Only then does it become evident that he is dead.

The Liyongo epic is essentially an oral text for which precise dating is problematic and speculative, in addition to the rather superfluous claim that the hero predates it. But it certainly belongs to the classical period of Kiswahili literature and stands out as one of the most famous cultural texts in East Africa. Other works with similar prominence include Athuman Mwengo's *Utendi wa Tambuka* (1728), Mwana Kapona binti Msham's *Utendi wa Mwana Kupona* (1858) and Muyaka bin Hajji's countless *tarbia*, as quatrains are called in Kiswahili. Fundamentally an oral text, the Liyongo epic has been transformed into (or preserved in) prose form (e.g., Edward Steeres's collection, *Swahili Tales as Told by the Natives of Zanzibar* and Bitugi Matundura's novel *Shujaa Liyongo*), or transmuted into poetic form (e.g., Muhamed Kijumwa's *Utenzi wa Fumo Liyongo* and Sayyid Abdalla bin Ali bin Nassir's *Takhmisa ya Liyongo*). Moreover, the epic has engaged considerable scholarly attention with numerous theses and dissertations devoted to its explication.[14]

When Ruth Finnegan discounted the existence of the oral epic in Sub Saharan Africa in the 1970s, she still conceded, among other things, that the Waswahili people of East Africa, like the Hausa of West Africa, indeed had written epics.[15] For Finnegan the presence of the epic among the Waswahili, like their West African counterparts, was contingent upon the Arab influence, because she did not conceive of epic as autochthonous to Africa. Furthermore, Finnegan did not attend to the typical interplay between oral and written literature in Africa that as Wamitila has argued, makes the Liyongo epic both oral and written.[16] In any event, subsequent studies of African oral literature rejected Finnegan's initial negation of the oral African epic[17] to such an extent that Peter Seitel would claim that the issue has been settled for all time.[18]

Okpewho's definition of epic is both illuminating and potentially problematic. He states:

An epic is fundamentally a tale about the fantastic deeds of a man or men endowed with something more than the normal human might and operating in something larger than the normal human context and it is significant in portraying some stage of the cultural or political developments of a people.[19]

Okpewho's claim that an epic is definable through the fantastic 'deeds of a man or men' tends to suggest that this genre is typically a space for the enactment of male exploits and therefore a space where females are excluded. Although fantastic deeds are indeed the material with which epics are made, it is important to understand that masculinity is not defined solely by fantastic deeds, even within the epic. If that were the case masculinity would become an almost impossible ideal for both boys and men, on the one hand and girls and women on the other. On the contrary, the Liyongo epic exemplifies displays of manliness by both men and women in varied ways without all of them necessarily being forced to meet the criteria of fantastic deeds. Joseph Mbele posits that folktale scholarship has a tendency to downplay or ignore the heroic deeds of female characters. In this regard, I suggest an expansion of what constitutes masculine or heroic. Taking a cue from Mbele, I consider the female characters in the Liyongo epic as emblematic of unmistakable forms of heroism and masculinity.

To be sure, in the epic the 'fantastic deeds' of Liyongo are evident in both his life and his death. These are certainly not the deeds of ordinary men or women. In the beginning of the story King Mringwari brags to the Galla that the mere stature of Liyongo would make them urinate on themselves. And truly, as soon as Liyongo is brought to the palace, the Galla emissaries are seized by fright and trepidation and wet themselves. Thus, Liyongo possesses a somewhat exaggerated masculine physicality that induces both fear and admiration from both foes and friends, not to mention the involuntary physiological reactions in others. Liyongo's physical stature recalls the gigantic Philistine, Goliath, who was later felled by David's slingshot, according to the Judeo-Christian tradition. The king touts Liyongo's strength, not because he is a friend, but because it is expedient to showcase this kind of exaggerated masculinity in order to frighten what is perceived to be a neighbouring enemy. The Galla's frantic offer of a marriage alliance is equally an act of expediency against the possibility of annihilation at the hands of this epic character. But the marriage alliance scheme is also driven by a keen awareness of virility as a concomitant aspect of Liyongo's masculinity. (I will return to the question of virility below). The Galla ostensibly believe that the sexual liaison between Liyongo and a Galla woman would result in the birth of offspring with equally devastatingly masculine capabilities and thus neutralise Swahili claims to military superiority with Liyongo on their side. Put differently, with a Galla wife, the Galla believed the extraordinarily strong Liyongo would sire extraordinarily strong Galla children. The Galla military strength and warrior ethos would then match or supersede their Swahili counterpart. In a sense, the scheme seems to be successful because, according to certain versions of the Liyongo epic, it is the hero's son, sired with the Galla woman, who commits what Wamitila has called the

'Oedipal murder.' If King Mringwari rejoices at Liyongo's eventual murder, it would seem the Galla also rejoice because Mringwari no longer has Liyongo's exaggerated masculinity to brag about as a military advantage.

Liyongo's extraordinary masculinity is also demonstrated by his physical strength as well as his ability as an archer. In some versions of the epic, Liyongo refuses to climb the palm-tree to harvest palm-fruits, after realising there is a ploy to shoot him with arrows while he is atop the tree. Instead, using remarkable precision, Liyongo shoots the fruits with arrows and not only wins the kikoa contest but saves his life. Hence, in these versions of the epic, Liyongo's skill as an archer is shown to be a mark of his masculinity. However, in other versions, he refuses to climb the tree and instead of using the arrow, he merely shakes the tree trunk to fell the fruits. Hence, in this instance, strength, not skill, is the defining mark of Liyongo's manliness. Liyongo kills a huge number of prison guards by smashing their heads against one another. His physical strength recalls the case of the captive and blinded Samson of the Judeo-Christian tradition and how he pushed and crushed the pillars of his prison house leading to the collapse of the building, his own death and the death of many others. The difference between the two narratives is that, unlike Samson, Liyongo does not die with the enemy in a show of strength.

Beyond his skill as a marksman and his supernatural power, other masculine aspects of Liyongo's personality are centered upon his wit and musical ability. Liyongo is a man endowed with a near perfect balance of brain and brawn, a rare attribute in African orature. The hero of the Ghanaian trickster stories, Ananse the Spider, is miniscule in size and stature, as is the hare of the East African tales, which makes their survival contingent on ingenuity and wit, rather than strength. Liyongo's prison escape is a work of genius in which both his musical talent and his wit play a significant role. He composes a song that appears to be either self-deprecating or absolutely disrespectful of his mother. That putative appearance of self-deprecation or disrespect for his mother belies Liyongo's intent. Yet the guards misread the intent of the song by focusing on its tangential aspect. Liyongo states in the song:

> Ewe kijakazi nakutuma uwatumika,
> Kamwambia mama, ni mwinga siyalimka
> Afanye mkate, pale kati tupa kuweka,
> Nikeze pingu na minyoo ikinyoka,
> Ningie ondoni ninyinyirike ja mana nyoka,
> Tatange madari na makutano kuno kimeta.[20]

(You, slave girl, let me send you to my mother,
Tell my mother she is a simpleton [or: I am a simpleton], unaware of the ways of the world.
Let her bake bread and put files in the middle,

- 19 -

So that I may cut my fetters and unchain myself,
That I may go to the road and glide like a snake,
That I may scale the roofs and walls and look this way and that way).

It should be noted that it is not apparent in the song whom Liyongo refers to as a simpleton in the line 'Kamwambia mama, ni mwinga siyalimka' because there is no pronoun preceding the conjunction 'ni' (is). The question of whether the term 'simpleton' applies to the poet—hero or the poet—hero's mother cannot be easily settled and should not detain us. If anything, the confusion caused by the ambiguity of the term is precisely the point of the song. This distraction in the opening portion of the song helps camouflage the secret plot that lies hidden in the lines that follow. Liyongo's capacity to compose life-saving and life-affirming songs and to play entertaining but distracting music eventuates in his successful prison escape. These attributes reinforce the unique admixture of brain and brawn that sets his manliness apart from any ordinary man or woman.

I hasten to add that Liyongo's masculinity is not the quintessential masculinity of the Swahili people. More than anything else, the internal logic of the epic underscores the lack of autonomy in Liyongo's supernatural masculinity. For one thing, in spite of—or because of—his superhuman power, Liyongo still needs his mother's and the slave girl's intervention to successfully escape from prison. There is no evidence in the story that the mother and slave need Liyongo as much as he needs them. This subverts the quotidian enactment of the drama of the masculine as protector of the feminine. In the tale of Sela and Mwambu, from the Bukusu people of Western Kenya, for instance, Mwambu, the male protagonist, returns home from a hunting expedition to find his sister Selah swallowed by an ogre. His masculine warrior ethos plays a key role in his rescuing his sister and the entire clan from the belly of the ogre. Unlike Liyongo, Mwambu is the quintessential masculine character who protects the vulnerable female or effeminate characters.

What does this narrative tell us about what it means to be a man or, perhaps more accurately, to be 'manly' among the Waswahili? It is important to attend to the fact that there is no monolithic Swahili worldview. To be sure, Islam has had a tremendous influence on the East African coast for centuries and clearly informs perspectives on masculinity and femininity. Mwanakupona binti Mshamu, a devout Swahili Muslim woman, composed *Utendi wa Mwanakupona* on her deathbed as a roadmap to help her daughter Mwana Hashima binti Mataka on her journey to womanhood. In one of the most intriguing stanzas, Mwanakupona admonishes her daughter thus:

> Care for him as though
> He were a very young child
> Who could not yet speak;
> Anticipate his needs and desires.[21]

The long poem prescribes in detail how a wife must take care of her husband like an infant, indulge his whims and be submissive. It has been regarded as the defining statement on femininity in the Swahili world. What has not been said enough, however, is how Mwanakupona's apparent anxiety for her daughter to go to any lengths to please her husband should be seen as a parody and mockery of the conceptions of patriarchal structures that oppress and demean women and are as destructive to men as they are to women.[22] If, as Mwanakupona mentions in her poem, the man is in need of constant attention and care as a child is, the very ideal of a masculinity framed in patriarchal terms is itself being implicitly interrogated. In a way, Mwanakupona's poem unconsciously undercuts the very phallocentric and phallocratic structures it ostensibly sets out to support or endorse. The Kiswahili proverb that is the epigraph of this chapter—*mume in mume hata akiwa gume gume* (a man is a man, however worthless he may be)—also seems to lend credence to the conclusion that men are perpetual babies. At the superficial level, the proverb tends to call for the recognition of men's masculinity and the uncritical acceptance of the myth of male superiority over femaleness. Put differently, for a woman to have a 'worthless' man is still worthwhile and better than not having one at all because men are fundamentally special and superior. But implicit in the proverb is the caveat that some men possess foibles and weaknesses that may, at times, cast doubt on their masculinity. Hence, women are asked to accept such men (read: husbands) unconditionally despite—or because of—the doubts entertained about their masculinity, the same way vulnerable babies are to be unconditionally accepted. Liyongo's story seems to confirm this interpretive frame, given the fact that, like a baby, the hero is in constant need of his mother's intervention, including at the crucial moment of his escape from prison. Yet the idea that men are perpetual babies seems to be predicated on the erroneous premise that femininity and masculinity are biologically predetermined.

In any event, Swahili culture and language is acutely aware of what could be called the 'transgender' connotations of notions of masculinity and femininity that seem to be played out in the Liyongo epic. For instance, although not offering a blanket endorsement of male homoeroticism, the Kiswahili term that describes gay men is etymologically derived from the term *shoga* (female friend). The gay man is therefore a 'female friend': feminised because he occupies the space conventionally inhabited by females. In the same vein, the epic of Liyongo demonstrates that masculinity is not the preserve of men. Granted, Liyongo's virility, valour and strength account for his masculinity. But the epic seems to suggest that masculine qualities are not exclusive to men. Although clearly lacking in the masculine physicality associated with Liyongo, both Liyongo's mother and the slave girl exhibit tremendous temerity and courage. They intervene crucially in a scheme fraught with danger and ensure its success. Thus, Liyongo's mother and the slave girl can rightly stake a claim on being masculine or manly.

It may also be said that by contributing to Liyongo's escape from prison, the hero's mother stages a kind of second delivery by which the prison becomes the womb that pushes Liyongo, in a kind of rebirth, into the free world. As Martha Grace Duncan argued, 'Because it is imagined as an inward movement, an entrance into a great container, being incarcerated may unconsciously signify an entry into the mother's womb, which in turn, implies the possibility of rebirth.'[23] Liyongo is therefore reborn or 'born again' in the prison escape episode. Prison becomes a matrix of symbolic and spiritual rebirth. This second birth accentuates the way Liyongo's masculinity is inextricably tied to the maternal figure. But as with all births, Liyongo's symbolic second birth is neither an emblem nor guarantee of immortality. In effect, the moment of escape from prison signals the beginning of Liyongo's end because it is the initial step towards the ultimate severance of his attachment to his mother by a symbolic umbilical cord.

The free world into which his mother 'redelivers' Liyongo—with the help of the slave girl, who can aptly be taken as a symbolic midwife—has many subtle dangers. Liyongo's son colludes with the king to plot the hero's downfall. In seeking the secret of Liyongo's invincibility and using it to kill his own father, Liyongo's son commits Oedipal murder. It is significant that Liyongo's death is a consequence of the insertion of a needle in his navel, the point on his body where the umbilical cord was connected to the mother. The insertion therefore signifies the precise moment of the severance of the umbilical cord that joins mother and son. It implies that no longer can the mother's intervention meaningfully change the son's unstoppable journey to the grave; there is no possibility of the mother's protection and nurturing in the wake of the impending death of her son in the free world that awaits him. In other words, the free world is not free and is as much a place of death as the symbolic womb—the prison cell—would have become had the king succeeded in executing Liyongo. The hero's speedy progress towards his demise is equivalent to that of a terminally ill patient finally removed from his or her life-support machine. In a sense, the story of Liyongo becomes a narrative about mother and son and underscores the claim that Liyongo's masculinity is dependent on his mother. But if Liyongo's mother is the oxygen that ventilates Liyongo's masculinity in the mother-son relationship, there is still a familial rivalry between father and son that is inimical to Liyongo's own existence.

In referring to the patricide as Oedipal murder, Wamitila draws on Freud's psychoanalytic framework to extrapolate the masculine rivalry between father and son. What is remarkable about the conflictual masculinity enacted by the betrayal is the semiotic significance of the sharp objects involved. Liyongo's son kills his father by inserting a sharp needle in his navel at the anticlimactic stage of the narrative. In turn, Liyongo takes his bow and arrow and takes a combat position at the communal well. Both the needle and the arrow are sharp objects that no doubt symbolise the phallus. But these are phallic symbols that occur at the moment of the hero's demise, casting the shadow of violence and death over the masculinity they embody.

The phallus as a symbol of masculinity is not uncommon in East African oral literature. Andrew Michael Roberts has observed that 'the concept of the phallus is more or less inescapable in discussions of masculinity.'[24] More intriguing is Stephen Heath's characterisation of the centrality of the phallic symbol in conceptions of masculinity as the 'eternal problem of the phallus.'[25] Thus, this analysis of the Liyongo epic would be incomplete without addressing the 'eternal problem of the phallus.' In the Kibwana oral tale from the Haya people of western Tanzania, Kibwana is married to the Kaiser's naïve daughter. The Kaiser is eager to have a grandson who would become heir to the throne. The Kaiser has no clue that Kibwana has no penis, the sexual organ whose role as a phallic symbol of masculinity cuts across any number of spatial, temporal and cultural frontiers. Before the marriage, Kibwana had had his penis cut off after false charges of making sexual overtures towards his father's younger wife. Word soon reaches the Kaiser about the son-in-law's condition. The Kaiser orders all men to bathe in the river. An old woman moulds a penis from clay with which Kibwana hoodwinks the Kaiser that he is a 'man' like the rest. Later in the narrative, a tree under which Kibwana is resting miraculously converses with him and restores his penis. But the tree demands that when Kibwana sires a son he should donate it to the tree. The restoration of Kibwana's penis not only makes the long-overdue consummation of the marriage possible, but it also enables Kaiser's daughter to experience her first penetrative sexual encounter. It is interesting that, having not had sex before, she had been content with wedlock without sex, suggesting that in her view masculinity was not defined by the presence or absence of a penis on her husband's body. Kibwana's wife accepts her man as he is unconditionally, despite serious doubts being raised over his masculinity; she in effect takes a position that resonates with the proverb given at the beginning of the chapter—*mume ni mume hata akiwa gumegume* (a man is a man, however worthless he may be). To her, Kibwana is still a man with or without the male member. This contrasts with the view shared by the Haya and the worldly wise Kaiser: that the possession of a penis, fecundity and sexual performance are critical to being and becoming a man. In this view the restoration of Kibwana's penis makes him a man again.

There are obvious differences between the Haya narrative and the Liyongo epic. For example, although in the Kibwana story the focus is on the physical presence or absence of the male sexual organ, the Liyongo epic is preoccupied with phallic symbols that are merely implied (e.g., the arrow, the file, the needle). It is possible to speculate that although the narrator and audience in the Haya narrative may have to grapple with calling the penis a penis in certain contexts, the significance of the phallic symbols in the Swahili epic may be beyond some of its narrators and audience. Yet despite these differences, these two stories link the eternal problem of phallus with masculinity. In both narratives, virility is perceived as a salient mark of manliness and aggressiveness and violence are closely associated with this masculinity.

In sum, the Liyongo epic showcases a kind of exaggerated masculinity because the hero who dramatises this masculinity has a larger-than-life image and performs fantastic deeds in keeping with the epic genre. But beneath his supernatural feats he is a mortal man with a mixture of masculine and feminine attributes that ordinary men and women can also claim. Hence Liyongo's bravery, aggressiveness, ingenuity, fecundity and resilience are qualities attainable by ordinary people. The circumstance in which his mother and slave girl provide him succour imbues them with manly qualities and suggests the feminine nature of his masculinity. Their role in his life and death also point to their own inherent masculinity, which is not defined by the presence of a phallic symbol. Thus the Liyongo epic demonstrates how we should reject any and all fixations with a distinct bifurcation between masculinity and femininity, anima and animus.

2. Masculinity in the West African Epic

Thomas A. Hale

Masculinity is a notion that too often seems defined mainly by the West—from Greek epics to contemporary cinema. The strong, brave and intelligent man who will save the day for his family, clan, or nation incarnates our concept of masculinity. New interest in this seemingly timeless portrait has developed in part from the rise of Women's Studies, which has led to the wider field of Gender Studies. An area still very much in flux, Gender Studies calls for an examination of the subject of masculinity from a wider perspective. It is a basic lesson that many researchers in Women's Studies have already learned as they now take a more nuanced and global approach to the subject. But it is not evident that the more recent focus on masculinity, a major component of Gender Studies, has been broadened enough to include peoples outside the Western tradition.

For example, in Berger, Wallis and Watson's *Constructing Masculinity*, the emphasis is almost entirely on men in the Western world.[1] One reason for the Eurocentric perspective on masculinity is that, until recently, our understanding of this phenomenon in other cultures outside the Western tradition has been limited by inadequate knowledge of peoples whose ways and values are conveyed to outsiders only through stereotypes. How then, could one gain a more global perspective on masculinity? How would that new perspective modify our understanding of masculinity? Recent research on the African oral epic can provide preliminary answers to these questions with concepts of masculinity that are in some ways quite different from those found in the West.

The oral epic, a genre whose existence in Africa was contested until the early 1970s by some scholars,[2] has appeared on the African literary scene in the last few decades thanks to research by a diverse corps of researchers. By 1997, Johnson, Hale and Belcher were able to publish excerpts from twenty-five of these epics. One of the distinctive features of many of these narratives, in particular those from West Africa, is a set of heroic traits that are specific to the region, in this case the Sahel and the Savanna, where many of the epics are narrated. The purpose of this study is to offer evidence of those qualities that point to the need to frame our Western notion of masculinity in a wider global context.

African oral epics appear as "masculine" texts not only because the heroes are men but also because these narratives have been told almost exclusively by men known regionally as *griots*. Known by ethno-specific terms such as *jeli*, *jali*, *mabo*, or *jesere*, *griots* are the keepers of the oral tradition. The concept of masculinity that they convey is incarnated in the figure of the hero. The *griot* and the hero make up a couple who share a common focus. The hero assumes his role when, to an extreme, he manifests or performs the elements of masculinity and the *griot* tells the world about his deeds. But to understand the hero and the way the *griot* conveys his masculinity, one must examine the underlying values that contribute to shaping him.

On the surface, masculinity in many of the texts examined below is portrayed in what seem to be "universal" terms of strength, prowess on the battlefield and leadership. For example, there appear to be no differences between the French hero of *The Song of Roland* and his Mande counterpart, Son-Jara (known in different versions also as Sundiata, Sun-Jata, or Soundjata), as they battle the enemy. The hero must be strong, brave, intelligent and know how to inspire his followers. For the most masculine of them, honour and loyalty are more important than death. The pride and bravery of Roland, who volunteers to protect the rear guard of Charlemagne's army against the Moslem enemy, is matched by that of Son-Jara, who sets out to reclaim his homeland by attacking a non-Moslem invader. Roland's decision to hold off the enemy without calling for help reflects his deep-seated need to demonstrate that he is indeed a worthy successor to the generations of knights who have preceded him as well as a strong leader of those who follow him on the mission to protect Charlemagne's troops as they return across the Pyrenees to the Christian world they call home.

In the West African oral epic, these ancestral and contemporary values are etched in the minds of both characters in the epic as well as listeners today with much greater immediacy than one finds is the case in the West. This is because societies in many parts of the Sahel and Savanna are fundamentally different from those in Europe. The particularly African values that govern behaviour appear in a strikingly contemporary manner, not simply in the performance of the narrator, but in the diffusion of the epic on cassettes in the marketplace, on the radio and at a variety of live events, from installations of chiefs to weddings and naming ceremonies.[3]

Two distinctive features of these societies highlight the differences between the medieval European hero and his African counterpart: family structure and social structure. For families in the Sahel and Savanna regions, one distinguishing feature is the right to have more than one wife. The vast majority of the population is Moslem and lives according to guidelines contained in the *Qu'ran*. Another difference is that until recently, society was largely divided between those of noble or free origin and those of captive origin.[4] One's own status, or that of an entire village, could be transformed from free to captive overnight as the result of a battle between two rulers, with the winner taking all. Being of captive origin meant serving a different leader and did not normally imply chattel slavery as this practice is known in the West. But becoming a captive did lead to a change of status that might eventually be reflected in limitations on land tenure, possession of wealth and rights to marriage.

For example, nobles had rights to more land. Captives worked on that land in much the manner of sharecroppers. Those who could afford more than one wife—and this was more likely the case for those at the top of the social ladder—produced more children. Relations between siblings produced by the same father but different mothers were often marked by competition.

In the Mande world, a vast region composed of peoples in southern Mauritania, eastern Senegal, The Gambia, western Mali, northern Burkina Faso and the northern sections of several other coastal countries (e.g., Sierra Leone, Liberia and Côte d'Ivoire), all of whom claim roots in the medieval Mali empire (thirteenth and fourteenth centuries), this rivalry is conveyed by the term *fadenya* (father-child-ness). The individual is the rival of siblings born of the same father but of different mothers. In the Songhay world in eastern Mali, western Niger and northern Benin, a region that succeeded and dominated Mali (fifteenth and sixteenth centuries), that rivalry is called *baba-ize-tarey*, a phrase that also means "father-child-ness."

The children are rivals for many things, but above all for the role of succeeding the father. This kind of competition appears in the most widely disseminated version of the Son-Jara epic, *Soundjata ou l'épopée mandingue*,[5] narrated by *jeli* Mamadou Kouyaté, as well as in the more recently recorded linear version, *The Epic of Son-Jara* by *jeli* Fa-Digi Sisòkò.[6] In both versions, the hero becomes the rival of his half-brother for the kingship. The rivalry also appears in slightly modified form in *The Epic of Askia Mohammed*, narrated by *jesere* Nouhou Malio,[7] where a young man of mixed noble and captive origin, Amar Zoumbani, discovers much too late that in spite of the fact that he is the son of the ruler of Gao, Soumayla Kassa, he is actually of humble origin because his mother was a concubine of captive origin who had not been freed. He cannot therefore compete with the brother of Sagouma, born from another wife of Soumayla Kassa who is a descendant of the former ruler and therefore of incontestable noble origin. The brother, in fact, embarrasses Amar by offering him as a gift to the *griots*. After Amar Zoumbani offers ten horses to the group of *jeserey* who sing his praises, Sagouma's brother grabs his hand and shouts "I too, I have given you a captive."[8]

To assuage the anguish of Amar, who has just been treated as a common captive, Soumayla Kassa orders that the brother of his wife Sagouma be killed in a trap. This solution leads to the infanticide of the children of Soumayla Kassa and Sagouma by their mother, as well as a war between the city of Gao and the Moroccan-backed occupying army of Timbuktu.

The rivalry portrayed in this oral epic, recorded in 1980, echoes forms of sibling competition documented in the written Timbuktu chronicles,[9] two long narratives composed in Arabic by African scribes in the seventeeth century, which recount in much greater detail the rise and fall of empires of the Sahel. The focus of these accounts is the Songhay empire, which lasted from 1493 to 1591. In both the oral epic and the chronicles, the children of Askia Mohammed, the ruler who brought the Songhay empire to its apogee (1493–1528), engage in murderous rivalry among themselves for several generations over the issue of succession.

For example, one of the sons of Askia Mohammed, Askia Daoud, had to prove himself to his brothers by killing two lions before he could assume the position of leader of the empire.

> Line 522 The two lions are on the road to Gombo
> Anyone who has not killed these lions will not have the paternal throne in the Songhay.
> Line 564 He pierced the first one with a single throw of the spear.
> He cut off the head of the other.

When Daoud reported his deed to his brothers and demanded the throne, they at first did not believe him and told him again "that a child cannot have the throne of Songhay" (line 574). Only the evidence of the dead lions convinced them.

The requirement that Daoud kill the lions might first be interpreted as simply a routine test of bravery and skill. But from what we know of the period in the Timbuktu chronicles, it is clear that the two older brothers were simply seeking a way of eliminating their younger rival. Subsequent rulers, all brothers, tried to kill each other off in more direct fashion. For example, in 1586–1588, the Songhay commander of the army in the Timbuktu area, a man named Sâdiq, who was the brother of ruler Askia Bâni in Gao, attempted to join forces with another brother, Sâlih, the governor of Tendirma, a city southeast of Timbuktu. Sâdiq suggested that the two overthrow their brother Askia Bâni. Sâlih became suspicious of Sâdiq, then attacked and killed him. Sâlih then marched south with his army to attack brother Askia Bâni, who mounted an offensive against Sâlih. Askia Bâni died en route from Gao to Timbuktu, but other brothers took over and succeeded in putting down the revolt.[10]

All of this rivalry, attested in the chronicles and echoed in the oral epic, undermined the stability of the empire, leaving it ill-prepared to repel a Moroccan-led army that defeated the last Askia in 1591 and brought an end to the period marked by the three great empires of Ghana, Mali and Songhay.[11]

This kind of synchronous rivalry helps construct a form of masculinity that is in some ways highly dangerous for society, as Bird and Kendall have pointed out in their essay on the Mande hero.[12] The hero is welcome when there is external danger, but on other occasions, the rivalry inherent in his relationship with others in his family is not appreciated. To succeed, the hero must not only outdo with his deeds his half-brothers and fend off enemies from without, but in some cases he may have to go to war against his siblings in order to achieve some sort of temporary internal stability.

The same kind of rivalry tore apart the much earlier Mali empire as well as the later Kaarta and Segou kingdoms. The well-known competition between Son-Jara and his half brother Dankaran Tuma led to the departure of Son-Jara, the weakening of the kingdom after the death of their father and the attempt on the part of their common enemy, Sumanguru, to take control of the region.[13]

In the lesser-known *Epic of Sonsan of Kaarta*, narrated by *jeli* Mamary Kuyatè, Sonsan, the favourite son of his father, must face competition from six other young men from a different mother who envy his status. The eldest of the six calls a meeting. He said

> There is something for which we must find a remedy.
> That is Sonsan. [. . .]
> All the strangers who come and go,
> They stay at the house of Sonsan.
> The father is not yet dead.
> But if it is like this when he lives,
> When he dies, Sonsan will surely become head of the family.
> Let us go after Sonsan and kill him.[14]

The hero survives the assassination attempt and manages to escape to become a respected ruler in another town. This is the fate of many heroes from the region. They are only invited back when the community is faced with extraordinary danger or if they can conquer local rivals.

In the nearly 8,000-line *Epic of Bamana Segu*, narrated by *jeli* Tayiru Banbera, one of the many heroes, the late eighteenth-century ruler Monzon Jara, comes to power after the death of his father Ngolo, but the refusal of his younger brothers to accept his leadership and their insistence that the kingdom be divided up leads to a fratricidal war. It is only after a series of battles between the brothers that peace is restored.

> Line 2645 Oh, the two armies met between Sebugu and Sekura.
> . . . The forty companies fired their muskets, *wuu!*
> . . . The five companies fired, *wuu!*
> They engaged forces two times.
> At the third time the younger brothers put their hands behind their backs: "They said, 'Older brother, we submit to you'" (line 2653).[15]

In addition to the synchronous rivalry described above, however, the hero must measure his own masculinity against that of his ancestors. In the case of the version of Askia Mohammed narrated by Nouhou Malio, the competition between ruling uncle and nephew begins before birth because Sonni Ali Ber, founder of the Songhay empire and known in the epic as Si, decides to kill all of the male offspring of his sister Kassaye because he has been warned by seers that one of those children will overthrow him some day.

Line 10   The seers have said "Listen" they told Si, it is Kassaye who will give
        birth to a child who will kill him and take over the throne of Gao.
        It is Kassaye who will give birth to a child.
        That child will kill Si and will take the position of ruler.
        Si also heard about this.
        All the children that Kassaye gave birth to,
        As soon as Kassaye delivered it, Si killed it.[16]

That rivalry between the generations, here presented in the most extreme case, normally appears in a somewhat less violent fashion, with the child attempting to accomplish deeds that will overshadow those of the father. Rivalry between past and present is inflamed by *griots* who know about the accomplishments of the ancestors and who seek to incite those in the present to surpass their parents. With songs about heroes, the *griots* inspire soldiers setting off to battle. During the battle, the *griots* participate as officers, urging the troops on and after the conflict they mark the deeds of the combatants by citing them in genealogies and by composing praise songs.[17]

Thus, the need to succeed is immediate, not simply because the *griots* are there to observe the successes or failures of the warriors, but also because of the great social pressure caused by the family structure. This form of societal influence led to the deaths of large numbers of soldiers engaged in battle who would rather die than risk the humiliation of dropping out of the family chronology. Unlike Roland, who is inscribed into the history of France precisely because he failed to hold off the attackers in what is widely viewed by the French a noble fashion, for the heroes of West African epics, failure may lead to erasure from the verbal record. Losers are not remembered.

In *Sundiata: An Epic of Old Mali*, the English translation of the reconstructed prose version of *Soundjata ou l'épopée mandingue* narrated by *jeli* Mamadou Kouyaté to Djibril Tamsir Niane in 1958, the hero's *jeli* asks warriors about to go off into combat what he will have to report about their performance on the battlefield the next day. Balla Fasséké extolled the heroes of Mali. To the king of Tabon he said: "You whose iron arm can split ten skulls at a time, you, Tabon Wana, king of the Sinikimbon and the Djallonké, can you show me what you are capable of before the great battle is joined?"[18]

The *jeli* goes down the list, calling forth names and asking "what will I have to relate of you to future generations?"[19] In other words, if a warrior does not distinguish himself tomorrow, he will not find a place not simply in the history of the battle, but more importantly in the genealogy of his own family.

This phenomenon of historical erasure is documented on a broad scale in the comparison between the genealogy of rulers of the Songhay empire described in the Timbuktu chronicles written by Moslem scribes, texts that include everyone, the successful rulers and those who failed and the same genealogies in the oral epic, where one finds references only to the most notable Songhay rulers.[20] If an individual has not made a mark in the minds of the *griots*, then there is normally no reason to waste memory on him.

The truly masculine hero, therefore, finds his world framed in the present by peers in general and half-brothers in particular and in the past by ancestors from his own clan. A great deed in a major battle is sufficient to mark the oral history forever. But those who have acquired a reputation as incarnations of masculinity cannot rest on their laurels. Each day offers a new challenge. And the *griots* are the key to those challenges, even when there are no battles to fight.

If a noble from a long line of heroes is confronted by a *griot* who begins to sing the story of the subject's ancestors, the individual, as Hoffman has pointed out, is placed in an extremely uncomfortable situation.[21] If there is no occasion to demonstrate one's bravery in the near future, there is always time today, as in the past, to reveal another dimension of nobility, a synonym in many ways for masculinity in patriarchal societies of the Sahel and Savanna. That trait is generosity. At the moment of the encounter between the *griot* singing the praises and the subject of those flattering verses, a tense drama plays out. Will the noble be able to offer rewards that match those given by his ancestors, who gave cattle, gold, slaves and clothing? If not, his masculinity and social status will suffer publicly by comparison.

Beneath the fear of not measuring up to the ancestors—or to other nobles who may have offered greater rewards—lies an even deeper fear, that of the occult power bound up in the words of the *griots*. Although there is much debate about the nature of that occult power, there is enough data to suggest that artisans—blacksmiths, weavers, *griots* and others who make up this special category of people known as *nyamakala* in the Mande world—are widely believed to possess an ephemeral but pervasive occult power known as *nyama*. Subjects of praise appear to believe that only by giving the *griots* appropriate rewards can one protect oneself from the *nyama* rooted in the words that are pronounced. Thus, the threat to one's status and to the masculinity bound up in that public image is invisible but, judging from the intense reactions reported by Hoffman, nearly palpable.

Beyond this fundamental difference between Western and West African societies rooted in the family and social differences found across the Sahel and Savanna regions, one finds a variety of more culturally specific nuances that cannot be ignored when considering the forces shaping masculinity.

For example, Kelefa Saane, a mid-nineteenth–century warrior from The Gambia, never succeeded in conquering a kingdom. But *jali* Bamba Susso's version of the epic recounting his life continues to be popular today, long after the narrator's death, precisely because of Kelefa Saane's personal qualities. He incarnates the widespread princely ideal of courage in battle. But he also reveals a sense of loyalty and generosity by his willingness to respond to an appeal for help without any desire for personal gain. For example, when the King of Niumi asked him to help in a war, he responded not only by setting off to raise an army, but more importantly by refusing the offer of gifts from other chiefs through whose territory he must pass and whom he tries to enlist in the creation of an army. They attempt to dissuade him from aiding the King of Niumi by promising slaves and other forms of wealth. For example, at Sun Kunda, the leaders declare:

If it is wealth that you seek,
We will give you a hundred slaves.[22]

The king of Wuli also announces,

If it is a desire for wealth which draws you to war,
    I will give you a hundred slaves
That is the gift you will receive as a visitor and when you leave,
    I will give you a gift for the journey.[23]
The king of Niani asks, "Is it just a desire for wealth that draws you to war?
I will give you all the wealth you could want."[24]

In these and other cases, Kelefa Saane replies that if he accepts the gifts, a spear should strike him dead. Kelefa Saane's refusal of gifts as inducements to weaken his sense of loyalty to the king who has requested his help underscores the significance of this element of masculinity for the peoples of the Mande today who often call for *griots* to narrate this epic.[25]

Other variations are rooted in more fundamental cultural differences. For example, in Fulani epics, masculinity is reflected not only in great deeds and competition between rivals, but also in cattle raiding.[26] Cattle are the traditional measure of wealth among the Fulani. Taking another man's cattle is one of the most feared ways of demonstrating one's power. For example, in the *Epic of Silâmaka and Hambodedio* narrated by *mabo* Boubacar Tinguizi, Silâmaka and his companion Poullôri, two legendary figures in the Fulani epic tradition, go to visit Hambodedio but are insulted by his servants who treat them as individuals who do not amount to much. To demonstrate their power, they kill five of Hambodedio's seven herdsmen, repel an attack by the king and his warriors and then escape with 700 of his cattle.

> Line 116 Silâmaka told Poullôri to collect all the cattle, as many as there were,
>   The cattle of the seven herdsmen
>   And to take them away,
>   To go a bit farther,
>   And to stay with them.
>   He should make a big corral.
>   He should wait there with them.

It turns out that the stolen cattle belong to the wife of Hambodedio and she sends a Fulani *mabo* to negotiate the return of the animals. Silâmaka and Poullôri return the cattle eventually, but only after Hambodedio has learned his lesson. The message of this episode is that when a Fulani steals another man's cattle, even temporarily, he is inflicting on his victim a lesson about masculinity and in particular about how to treat other people.

Finally, in the Wolof *Epic of Lat Dior* narrated by Bassirou Mbaye,[27] the masculinity of the hero emerges not simply from his ability to fight battles and conquer territory, but more importantly from his fierce resistance against French colonialism. Although the story of his many successes and failures in the highly complex political arena of late nineteenth-century Senegal is convoluted, what emerges today for the people of that country who have marked him as their national hero is the tale of a man who stood up to the French. Heroes manifest masculinity in a variety of ways as kingdoms rise and fall, but to do battle with the French, who could claim an overwhelming superiority in firepower, was to manifest a kind of superheroism that would echo down through the generations to the era of Senegalese independence today. From the evidence conveyed by these oral epics, it is clear that masculinity in the Sahel and Savanna embodies not simply the traits of strength and courage, but also other qualities such as the ability to overcome fraternal rivalry and the extent to which the individual's deeds stand out from those of the ancestors. It is a complex concept that cannot be separated from its social and historical contexts. One is masculine only by comparison, it seems, to others who might play the role of challengers. Masculinity, ultimately, is not static but dynamic, the product of constant interaction and competition between rivals, living and dead, for a permanent place in the history of a family. In this sense, the values of masculinity are individual on the surface but, fundamentally collective. *Griots* and their female counterparts, *griottes*, who sing the praises of heroes to audiences today are mediators and translators of masculinity. If we want to understand the nature of masculinity in the particular regional context that produces these oral epics, we need to read these narratives and compare them with counterparts from other parts of the continent and the world. Only then may we be able to arrive at a more textured and global understanding of this fundamental concept.

3. Men and Power: Masculinity in the Folktales and Proverbs of the Baganda

Abasi Kiyimba

The negative stereotypes of women in African oral literature have attracted considerable scholarly attention and some scholars have as good as accused men of creating the literature as a means of subjugating women.[1] However, although strong arguments have been made in defence of this position, the question of what it means to be male in African oral literature has not been sufficiently explored. The portrayals of the man as a husband, father and societal-political leader need to be examined more closely to highlight how they work as part of a broader mechanism that perpetuates a legacy of male dominance. This chapter looks at the question of masculinity in African oral literature, drawing illustrations from the folktales and proverbs of the Baganda people of central Uganda.

The central argument of the chapter is that the folktales and proverbs of the Baganda greatly contribute to a process that constructs the male in the dominant role because they derive from powerful ideologies of male superiority that permeate the different forms of the oral literature of the Baganda, starting with the Kintu myth. It is in the Kintu myth, the founding myth of the Baganda, that the gendered identities that are so often taken for granted are premised. Kintu, the first Muganda man, marries his wife Nambi in heaven. On their way to earth, Nambi's brother Walumbe (Death) follows them as a result of Nambi's disobedience to her husband and starts killing their children. Kintu then lays down the rules that will govern the way men relate to women in the Baganda society. The rules are the *de facto* constitution of the Baganda, which places the man in a position of authority and advantage. He is the undisputed head of the family, the children belong to him and his word is law. The other narratives within the oral literary tradition of the Baganda cover a broader social and political spectrum, but the gendered identities within them derive from this myth. In broader terms, the literature is a general reflection of the social lives of the Baganda people, but as works of art, the folktales and proverbs are a means of construction and articulation of the social psyche of the people from whom they originate. Although the literature also deals with other concerns, the construction of people into male and female roles is so central to the action that it constantly plays itself out within it. The discussion of notions of masculinity in folktales and proverbs in this chapter is prompted by the belief that an exploration of the male character in the narrative genre would greatly enrich our understanding of the construction of masculine identities in this cultural setting and beyond. This in turn will contribute to a balanced appreciation of gender as a phenomenon. The proverb, like the narrative, is a key medium of expression among the Baganda and the two genres interact closely in their dialogue with the sociocultural processes that produce the gendered identities under discussion. In both genres, the portraits of the powerful male as husband, father and political leader are cumulative social constructs that have absorbed many factors and are part of the various mechanisms that the system of patriarchy uses to sustain notions of masculine superiority. It is these notions that make it possible for the male to remain the head of the family and the undisputed leader of society, even after he has been portrayed as greedy, irresponsible, inconsiderate and brutal.

The Baby Boy

When a Muganda man marries, one of his principal expectations is that he is going to get a son to perpetuate the lineage of his forefathers. It is therefore not surprising that a lot of pressure is put on women to bring forth baby boys. If a woman should have only baby girls, both the male and female relatives of the man and other members of society, hold the woman responsible for 'not giving the man an heir.' The woman and her family are also anxious to produce a baby boy so as to secure their positions in the man's family. This anxiety runs through the various forms of oral literature. In many folktales among the Baganda (and elsewhere in East Africa), 'hated' women redeem themselves by producing a baby boy.[2] This pressure often causes the woman to do inhuman things. A folktale entitled 'A Cow for the Mother of a Boy' features a woman who is in competition with her co-wife to produce a boy for the husband. The husband offers a cow to the woman that will produce a baby boy for him. When she produces twins, she decides to leave the girl in the banana plantation and takes only the boy home.[3] There are several variations on the theme. In some, the woman must choose between abandoning the boy or the girl when caught in a situation where she can only take one. She decides to abandon the girl. In other tales, women go to the extent of stealing their co-wives' male children in exchange for their female ones.[4] Tales like those above show the importance the Baganda attach to producing a baby boy. What the stories in this group say overall is that a boy is a treasure, whereas a girl is not. In the story of the woman who 'voluntarily' abandons the girl in the bush, it might appear as if she takes the decision without any direct pressure, because no prize has been offered, as in the other tales. However, it should be kept in mind that the patriarchal structures in this society make life extremely difficult for a woman who does not have a son. Thus, the decision to abandon the girl is dictated almost as directly, as in the tales where the men promise to reward women who produce a baby boy.

Like the folktales, many Luganda proverbs idolise the woman who produces a baby boy within the clan and consequently impose a feeling of guilt upon the woman who has produced only girls. The following proverb is probably more blunt than most, but its spirit is shared by many others: *Anaaganja, asooka ddenzi* (The one who will become a favourite [wife] begins by giving birth to a baby boy).

The word *kuganja*, from which the first part of the proverb above is derived, is loaded with all that a woman would like to become to her husband and his family—the dear one. In order to achieve this, she must produce a baby boy. But even the language used to signify 'baby boy' is expressive. The ordinary term for baby boy is *mulenzi;* the form *ddenzi,* as used in the proverb, is one of endearment, leaving no doubt that he is a treasure. The message of this proverb is even grimmer than that in the folktales reviewed above. Whereas the folktales stopped at the idea of producing a baby boy, the proverb stresses the importance of *beginning* with one. The producing of a baby boy therefore goes beyond the physical act of bringing forth a child of the male sex. It is a statement about the power and destiny of the particular individual that has been born, *vis-à-vis* her female counterpart.[5] Proverbs in this category suggest that the woman's position in society can only be guaranteed if she makes a natal alliance with the male sex.[6]

The producing of a baby boy is the most potent 'ammunition' that the woman has at her disposal in this deeply patriarchal society. She can use it to score a 'victory' against her co-wife, or to fight her way to a better position in society. Thus, it is not surprising that women like Kaddulubaale in the tale cited above are prepared to go to the extent of exchanging their daughters with someone else's male child. The next proverb further highlights the power wielded by the mother of a baby boy: *Bakidambya, kye kizaala eddenzi* (The woman that is despised is the one that ends up producing a baby boy). At this level, although his power can be felt even before he is born, the focus is more on his maleness than on masculinity as a social notion. It is implied that there is power in producing a boy, even before it is known how he will turn out as a social being.

In other proverbs, the boy is projected into the position of the parent, as in the following proverb: *Ssenkuzaalenkuzaale ng'omwana ow'obulenzi* (When your son comes of age, he becomes your father). Merely being born male places him in the same position of power occupied by parents in society and this is in great contrast to his sister. This near glorification of the baby boy is central to the understanding of what it means to be male among the Baganda.

Long before he emerges into the adult world, the boy already has a head start over the girl, by virtue of being born a boy. The understanding of the baby boy as a phenomenon among the Baganda is also interlocked with the patrilineal system of succession in which the individual Muganda descends from the ancestors through the father and is identified with the father's clan at every point. This process starts with the elaborate naming system that continues to be one of the most conspicuous features of the society of the Baganda today.[7] When a girl marries into a family of higher social status, she raises the fortunes of her immediate family and clan by giving them access to economic and political power; but this power is never firmly secured until she has produced a baby boy. It is therefore not unusual for a folktale about a lucky girl that marries the king to conclude that after some time she produced a baby boy. The tale of Nannono in Buganda is particularly significant. She was a practical woman who managed to occupy the king's seat after her husband Nakibinge had been killed in a battle with the neighbouring tribe of the Banyoro. She was able to do this because there was hope that the child she was carrying would be male. She would then rule in his name until he came of age. As fate had it, the child turned out to be a girl and Nannono had to give up the throne.

The lack of a son is as near to a social death as a man can get. Girls may be praised for their beauty, but we do not have cases of rewards being offered for a woman who will produce a baby girl, even though it is logical to imagine that there are men who may have only baby boys. The scenarios featured in the folktales also extend to real life among the Baganda, where there is overwhelming evidence that a male child is still considered more valuable than a female one.[8]

In real life, the boys still learn the trades of their fathers. They go fishing, learn bark-cloth making, hunting and other occupations that they practice in their adult days. However, they do not get as involved in the domestic routine as the girls do and the folktales capture this clearly. The girl's absorption into the mother's domestic work routine enables her to receive thorough instruction in the social and cultural norms and taboos of the society, some of which actually exclude the boy from this work by defining him as different from the girl.[9] The boy, on the other hand, is not completely absorbed in the father's life routine. When they're not at work and the father has gone to visit the neighbours or to drink, he is rendered redundant, while his sister is busy helping her mother with preparing the evening meal. This gives him a certain sense of independence and confidence that prepares him to be the leader of the home and of the wider society.[10]

As a direct result of the above, the folktales of the Baganda consistently characterise boys and girls differently. The boy is the true leader of society; he is brave, confident and enterprising. In the many tales in which the boy and the girl have to look after themselves without elders, the boy emerges as the natural leader in the situation and dutifully protects his sister. In a folktale entitled 'Kayima and his Sister in the Forest,' the father abandons his children in the forest because he has nothing to feed them. Through the hardships they experience, which include facing wild animals and the danger of starvation, Kayima, the boy, leads in finding solutions, even though he is the younger of the two. He is always innovative, as seen in his making 'spears' out of pieces of stick and he constantly reassures his sister. This story also features the sub-theme of the irresponsible father, which is discussed later, but the bravery of the boy in protecting his sister is what is highlighted. The girl, on the other hand, is frightened and dependent on her brave younger brother.[11] Tales in this category vindicate those who argue that African oral literature both originates and consolidates stereotypes of male superiority.

The contrast between boys and girls is also powerfully captured in proverbial idioms. The boy, among the Baganda, is idiomatically referred to as *Naatuukirira* (I will persevere to the end), whereas the girl is called *Gannemeredde* (I cannot go any further). These expressions are commonly used in everyday language, in effect telling the boy that he has to persevere to the end, for the social consequences of not doing so are great. On the other hand, the girl need not persevere, because she is 'only a woman,' and the society will forgive her many failures that it will not forgive a man.

The Man as a Husband

The craving for the baby boy discussed above is an early signal of the gender power balance and the outstanding feature of the relationship between men and women as husbands and wives.

Discussing the relationship between men and women in a broader context, John Stuart Mill observes that:

> Men do not want solely the obedience of women, they want their sentiments . . . They have therefore put everything in place to enslave their minds. The masters of all other slaves rely, for maintaining obedience, on fear; either fear of themselves, or religious fears . . . All women are brought up from the very earliest years in the belief that their ideal character is the very opposite to that of men; not self-will and government by self-control, but submission . . . [12]

Mill's view is shared by other scholars, such as Kabira and Schipper. The argument is that the man is able to dominate various areas of social and political life because he has 'put in place' forms of control, including oral literature, that enable him to psychologically overwhelm the woman into believing in the superiority of the man as a species. The suggestion that it is the man who has 'put this literature in place' is problematic and raises issues that go beyond the scope of this chapter.[13] But literature does provide important clues to what it means to be male in this society.

The creation myth of the Baganda serves as a framework of social reference for many Baganda and its legacy still dominates many aspects of their social structure. As discussed above, Death (Walumbe) is a brother to the first Muganda woman and mother of the tribe (Nambi). Descending from her abode in the heavens, Nambi forgot the millet for her chicken and returned to collect it (despite her husband's protests) . Her dreadful brother (Walumbe) followed her to earth and started killing her offspring, the Baganda. This myth lays down several 'dos' and 'don'ts' that define the relationship between man and woman as that of master and subject, favouring the man. The myth also blames the woman for the several forms of evil in the society of the Baganda—in particular, death. Meeting a woman while on a journey is a bad omen. Apolo Kagwa records it in the following words:

> If a man was going on a journey and he met a woman before he had travelled a long distance, he would take the decision to return home because meeting a woman was bad luck. If the distance he had covered was big and he could therefore not go back, he would be worried throughout the whole journey, wondering whether the purpose of his journey would be achieved at all, since he had met with bad luck in the form of a woman.[14]

Kagwa suggests that the reason why women were regarded as symbols of bad luck was because it was Nambi who had brought her brother Walumbe to earth, as narrated in the Kintu myth. The belief that the woman is a symbol of bad luck and evil permeates many other forms of literature and is actively propagated by both men and women. And though there is no evidence that this literature was 'invented' by men, there is no doubt that it helps to promote notions of male superiority.

The general picture of maleness is fairly uniform throughout the different forms of oral literature of the Baganda. The male, starting from his days as a boy, must present the picture of a brave, strong individual qualified to lead society. In this context, masculinity has to be attained and defended, which is significantly different from the acquired maleness of a baby boy who simply had to be born male in order to be a potential heir to the power reserved for him by the system of patriarchy. The process of attaining masculinity begins when the male is a young boy and continues into his time as a man. The most 'innocent' act, such as that of a boy killing a monster, is a step towards the attainment of masculinity, using the inherited maleness as a threshold.

It is also significant that many Luganda proverbs sound like general praise songs for men. Among them the following are particularly striking: *Nkolola nsajja, egoba engo* (The cough of a man frightens away a leopard) and *Basajja kye balya, tekifa bwerere* (What men eat is not wasted). These proverbs, along with several others, occur regularly in the speech of the Baganda and are powerful social signals.[15] The suggestion that the cough of a man frightens away a leopard, however idiomatically conceived, loudly proclaims the notion of male strength and invincibility and is intended to contrast the natures of man and woman. These proverbs are an integral part of the cultural construction of masculinity among the Baganda, especially because they function as originators of social authority.

It was observed earlier that the creation myth of the Baganda serves as an important frame of social reference because its legacy permeates most of the structures of society. In the marriage institution, it is important that there should be harmony. Harmony can only be maintained if both partners know their responsibilities towards each other. The man is the leader of the home and this is not debatable. But the society makes certain demands of him, because of his being male. He must be strong and able to hold the home together. This demands intelligence, physical strength and courage. Likewise, the obedience of the wife to her husband is one of her responsibilities to the marriage and her husband. The notions of the strong male figure and the subordinate female figure derive from the Kintu myth referred to above, but it is also stressed in various other forms of literature. Indeed, several proverbs of the Baganda suggest that it is not necessary for the man to be handsome; what matters is that he should be strong and take charge of the system. That is why, although it is important for the woman to be beautiful, the 'beauty' of a man is ridiculed, as in the following proverb: *Bulungi bw'omusajja, buzaala obunafu* (The beauty of a man degenerates into laziness). In the folktales, the wife's obedience is taken for granted and it only becomes an issue if she withholds it. There are many tales in which the woman is the silent host to the man's visitors. She does the cooking and generally sees to the comfort of the visitors. For as long as she does this well, she goes unnoticed and even her name often remains unknown. In the words of Helen Mugambi, she is effectively silenced.[16]

The literature also endorses the principle that a woman may be beaten to enforce compliance. A folktale entitled 'The Man and the Cock' features an episode that is domestic in its setting, but that actually deals with questions of power dynamics in the relationship between men and women. A man called Moja has learnt the secret language of animals, but the medicine man who helped him to do so warned him that he will die instantly if he tells another person this secret. Then, one day, his wife catches him laughing at something the animals have said and she threatens to leave him if he does not tell her what he is laughing at. The man knows that if he tells his secret he will die instantly;

but he is on the verge of doing so because he does not see any other way out. Then his cockerel comes to his rescue by retorting, when the dog mentions the impending death of its master:

> Let him die, after all he is dying because of his own stupidity. For, you look at me, I rule over eight women in this home alone and I roam all over the village and rule over those living there. Then how can he fail to rule one woman? How can a woman make me say my secret when I do not want to say it? As for me, if she bothered me as much as she has bothered him, I would simply get my stick and teach her who is the boss in the home.[17]

On hearing these words, the man gains courage, gets his stick and gives the woman a good beating; he continues to beat her until she promises not to bother him again and to always obey his will. This simple action cements the power order between the two of them and by extension, between men and women in general. When the woman in the tale 'learns to obey' she is presented to the audience as a 'good woman' and the man is a 'tough man.' This tale is only one of a type and although it features a power struggle between the man and the woman, its significance, especially as a demonstration of the dynamics of male control, goes beyond the home. It provides the philosophical framework for the division of power in other social and political scenarios.

There are many other tales in which women are beaten to enforce compliance. The beating they get and the silence it enforces, is the ultimate warning to women who might have wished to 'answer back.' This is 'perfect' advice to young girls. In the tale of 'Naluggya and Sempala' it is significant that this advice is given by a wise old woman in the neighbourhood, thus underlining the complexity of the process that silences women and compels them to accept male authority as the natural order of things.

These tales are part of the mechanism that society uses to create and entrench notions of femininity and masculinity and to make statements about the power relationship between men and women. The overall message of these tales is that a 'real man' must demand the obedience of his wife, even if this means beating her. For the definition of power in its simplest form is 'the ability to exercise control or authority over others.'[18] The man's right to use instruments of coercion to bring the woman under control is presented in the oral literature of the Baganda as part of the basic understanding of masculinity. This literature is able to project its message this graphically because it occurs against the background of a supportive social system.[19] The proverbs, like the tales, also legitimise the practice of wife beating. One proverb says, for example, that: *Akaggo akakubye muka balo, bwokalaba kasuka wala* (When you see the stick that has been used to beat your co-wife, throw it far away). This one is even grimmer: *Omukazi birenge bya ddiba, bw'otobikunya tebigonda* (A woman is like the tough ends of an animal skin, if you do not squash them with a great force, they will not soften). Luganda proverbs on this subject generally present as desirable a situation where the woman obeys the man without question. They also explicitly state that this obedience can be enforced by physical coercion, if the woman does not voluntarily offer it. Some proverbs even suggest that it is shameful for a woman to exchange words with her husband in an attempt to present her case. The good woman keeps quiet and does what her husband says. This is one of the most powerful methods of enforcing male authority.

The philosophy of the man as 'lord' chimes with the fact that the system allows and even encourages husbands to marry more than one wife. Indeed, the system operates a structured polygamous lifestyle. In a home with more than one wife, wives have special names that define their status.[20] What is perhaps more significant about the institution of polygamy is the role it played in underlining the social worth of the man, as suggested in these proverbs: *Ow'omukazi omu, ye Ssabaddu w'abawuulu* (The man with one wife is a chief among the unmarried); *Zikusanze, ng'ow'omu alwaaza* (You are in trouble, like a man with one wife who has fallen sick); and *Nsekedde mukikonde, ng'omuwuulu asikidde abataano* (I am laughing in my fist [due to excessive joy], like an unmarried person inheriting five wives). The man who had two wives or more was regarded as more masculine than the one who had one. The literature presents a continuous debate on the merits and demerits of having more than one wife, but there is no doubt that the institution of polygamy is a celebration of superior masculinity.[21] The third proverb, in particular, is located within the sociocultural setting of the Baganda, which firmly conceived the woman as a material possession.[22]

Although the husband is generally powerful, certain images of him are comic and contemptible, on account of his excessive greed, selfishness and irresponsibility. In one tale, the husband and the wife visit the in-laws, but the man fails to contain his desire for a fatty part of the goat. So he leans over the curtain that separates the men from the women to remind his wife Nambi that she should preserve *ennuuni* for him. The curtain breaks and he falls into the food on the female side of the curtain where his mother in-law is sitting. The man returns home covered in shame. And in the tale 'Our Husband went to Singo' a husband tells his wives that he is going on a journey to Singo, one of the counties in the old Buganda kingdom. He hides in the chickens' house, comes out every day after they have gone to work, eats the reserve food and goes back into hiding. He does this repeatedly until the women work out a plan to catch the thief. They pretend to have gone to work but hide instead and catch him in the process of eating the reserve food. There are many other tales that feature aspects of male greed, with husbands starving both their wives and children. He is either caught in the act by one of the children or he cuts his tongue while cutting the stolen meat. As a result, he loses the moral authority to govern but retains the social power that derives from the patriarchal system. Together with the loss of moral authority, he loses the emotional attachment to his children, who develop stronger bonds with the mother who shares with them whatever food she is able to acquire. Tales in this category are backed by proverbs, such as: *Omusajja nkoko mpanga, tetakulira baana baayo* (The man is a cockerel; it does not fend for its children). In other tales, the man makes direct attempts to starve his wife. In one such a story, a wife loses her parents in an arson attack and the husband decides to take advantage. Whenever it is time to eat, he refers to the parents who perished in the fire; when the woman starts crying, he eats all the food. This goes on until the woman's friends advise her to ignore him and eat her food.

In some stories, the man is presented as both greedy and murderous. In a tale entitled 'The Husband that Killed His Mother During a Famine' a man suggests to his wife that they should kill their mothers because of the scarcity of food. The wife agrees, but hides her mother, leaving the man to kill his. And in another tale, the man hides and cuts off the ears of his mother-in-law to stop her from frequenting his home to collect food during famine.

When the man is not greedy or beastly, he is stupid, ridiculous and irresponsible. There are several tales in which it is the woman who is innovative and the *de facto* leader of the home in situations of danger. In 'Wazzike, Nalongo and the Stupid Husband' the man is lazy and stupid, whereas the woman is practical and enterprising. The family, looking for food, ends up in the territory of a monster gorilla that has eaten all the people of the village and now has plenty of food in its village. When the monster gorilla returns and finds these uninvited visitors, it instructs them to start cooking themselves for his meal. Where the man might have cooked one of his children for the gorilla to eat, the enterprising woman devises a way of killing the gorilla and saving the family.[23] The people who the gorilla had swallowed earlier are liberated and the village is repopulated. It is significant, however, that although the woman is the undisputed master of the situation in this story, it is her husband who is made chief of the liberated village and she does not dispute it. It was inconceivable for a woman in Buganda to formally rule over men and the literature conforms to this.

Tales and proverbs like this are, of course, entertaining but they popularise stereotypes of the man as greedy, brutal, irresponsible, stupid and ridiculous. Many men will enjoy the powerful roles into which the folktales and proverbs generally cast them, but they will resent the negative stereotypes. The image of the man who kills his mother during famine will be particularly upsetting, as men generally love and revere their mothers.[24]

The Man as a Parent

The other aspect of male power enshrined within the social structures is the understanding that the man is the 'owner' of the children and the ultimate source of social legitimacy for them. The society of the Baganda is patrilineal and therefore accords an elevated position to the father as the provider of the line through which a child descends from the ancestors. Even when the father is poor and makes no material contribution to the upbringing of the child, it is still of great social importance that the child should be acknowledged by both the father and his family. The concept of *Ekika* (clan) among the Baganda really refers to the identity of a person in the social system. Everyone is identified in accordance with who and what his or her father is. It rarely mattered where one's mother came from, provided one was able to prove one's ancestry on the father's side. This is what made one a *bona fide* member of the society of the Baganda. If the father denied paternity of a child or disowned him or her for some reason, that child became a 'nobody' in society, regardless of the social status of the mother or the material well-being of the child itself. It is for this reason that the Baganda believe that the only grudge a child is allowed to permanently hold against its mother is that of not revealing the 'correct' father. If she reveals the father, then the child should be able to forgive her everything else. Two proverbs emerge from and promote this philosophy: *Nnyoko abanga omunyoro, n'akuzaala ku kika* (Your mother Munyoro's ethnicity is irrelevant as long as she produces you in a [Ganda] family) and *Ab'oluganda baagalana, nga kitaabwe waali* (Brothers and sisters love each other when their father is alive). The father is perceived as the spirit of unity in the family. On the strength of the philosophy of these proverbs, the children are able to look at one another as brothers and sisters, even when they have different mothers.

The power of the father, however, is not just abstract power, in terms of him being a gateway to the clan and society. As noted above, he is also 'the owner' of the children in the social system of the Baganda and he takes the important decisions in their lives, such as when and who one marries. This understanding of child ownership leads Baganda men to look at women as 'gardens' where the man, on behalf of the clan, 'plants' seeds. This thinking is expressed in this proverb: *Omukazi omuzadde kinnanga kya lumonde; buli kwekyusa ojjamu ogutuuse* (The child-bearing woman is like a potato patch; every once in a while, you harvest a potato that is ready).

Because of his position, power and ownership rights, the pleasure or displeasure of the father can determine one's social destiny. Thus, you must avoid ever giving the father reason to raise his voice against you in society. You are also advised to treat your father's close friends with care because they may know something sensitive about him, metaphorically expressed by the following proverb: *Ekiku ekisula mu kisenge kya kitaawo, kikumanyaako ekyaama* (The bedbug that sleeps in your father's bedroom will know a secret about you). The proverb could be used as a general warning to treat with care anyone close to one's roots. But the use of the image of the father is a significant symbol of masculine power.

The power of the father is so subtle that it extends to one of his sons after his death, as noted in a proverb cited earlier in another context. From the point of view of the sisters, this is lamentable and the proverb might even seem to contradict those that suggest that the father is irreplaceable. But the proverb has a social significance that goes beyond the act of mourning an individual biological relative. It is part of a general social mechanism that vests the father with the power of the patriarchal system and the system provides for the power to be handed down from one male to another. The sisters may lament this situation, but they would feel lost if they did not have a strong male figure to symbolically take over from the father and offer them the social security they need.

The aforementioned background constitutes part of the context within which the personal and social plight of a childless man in Buganda should be understood. He has no children to keep him company in life, protect him in old age and ensure the continued remembrance of his ancestors. Above all, he falls short of society's expectations of him as a man. Although a woman's childlessness is equally painful, it is an individual concern. For a man, childlessness is seen by society—and is represented in oral literature—as a betrayal of his forefathers' lineage, as captured in the following proverb: *Nabazaaya, omufiirwa azaaya bajjajjabe* (I will exterminate you, the way an impotent man exterminates his ancestors [by not begetting heirs for them]). This proverb specifically refers to instances where the childlessness is due to impotence, but also applies to other circumstances.

An impotent man commits a 'crime' far worse than that of a barren woman, because, for the Baganda, the impotent man is 'a non-man,' 'a non-person,' something to be scorned by men, women and children.[25] Even in private, impotence is always described in metaphors—and there are a variety of them. An impotent man is referred to as *omufiirwa* (the bereaved), *eyatomerwa endiga* (one who was knocked down by a sheep), *eyaggala amatu* (one whose ears are blocked), *atalima* (one who does not dig), *atayitaba* (one who does not answer when called), *eyetisse ekirevu* (the one sporting a beard), *oweffumu eryamenyeka* (one with the broken spear) and many others.[26] The image of the impotent man that emerges from this veiled language is that of one tormented and makes impotence appear worse than death.[27] Social decorum prevents the transmission of these tales and proverbs to mixed audiences of men and women.[28] The oral literature in which they are used becomes a nightmare and torture chamber for the impotent man. For example: *Naku z'ekirevu, n'eyatomerwa yetikka* (The beard is very unfortunate, even the impotent man sports it); *Byamufiirwa, Walumbe y'agaba* (The property of the impotent is distributed by death). In 'Kalasa the Impotent' a man chooses to live alone, for undisclosed reasons. Members of society automatically assume that he is impotent and stories to this effect begin to spread. Girls even coin a song about his assumed incapacity. Finally, one of the more adventurous of them decides to go to his home to tease him. As she discovers, the man had chosen to live alone for reasons other than impotence. Unfortunately for her, she learns the hard way: she loses her virginity. In another story entitled 'Lukomwa's Children', a woman marries a man who turns out to be impotent. She reveals this to her mother-in-law and her mother-in-law advises her to stay and secretly have children with her husband's brother. Both stories communicate the great sense of shame associated with impotence. In 'Kalasa the Impotent' even young girls can freely sing about an adult with this problem. In 'Lukomwa's Children', it is even suggested that if the news of Lukomwa's impotence should leak out, his brothers will find it difficult to get wives.

These tales and proverbs ultimately define masculinity among the Baganda. It is not enough to be biologically male; in order to be accepted by society as a real man, one must be sexually potent. For impotence is the most bitter potion of maleness and the single circumstance that would make a man wish he were a woman.

Men, Women and Political Power

The philosophy of male dominance, out of which domestic power arrangements grow, plays itself out even more clearly when it comes to political power. The Baganda generally believed in kingship as a system of social and political governance. In the day-to-day life of individual monarchs, the wishes of those in authority often had to be physically enforced.[29] Sometimes this force was even used to decide who succeeded who in the system, though there was a fairly elaborate succession mechanism. The real political power among the Baganda was exercised at two levels—at the level of the king and at the level of the chiefs subordinate to and appointed by him. Both positions could only be occupied by men. By signalling in unequivocal terms that the man was the ruler, the political system reinforced the general perceptions of what it meant to be male or female in this society. Wives, mothers and sisters of the king and the chief shared in this power and often influenced him, but the symbolic and real power was in male hands.

The overwhelming impression that one gets about political power from the oral literature of the Baganda is one of brutal force. The man, as represented by kings and chiefs in the folktales and proverbs, uses it to suppress others and to enforce his will. The woman, on the other hand, is one of those who suffers from this power, even though she exercises or moderates part of her husband's power when she is the wife of a king or a chief. In the majority of cases, however, the woman not only suffers as the direct subject of the broader political order, but also becomes the soft target to which the frustrated husband turns to reassure himself that he is 'still a man.' Records of the experiences of the Baganda confirm the chronicle of royal brutalities featured in folktales as well as occasional changes of heart.[30] Even the marriage to the beautiful young girl, which the king does as of right in many folktales, is often an act of suppression and self-preservation. The beautiful girls constitute a threat to the king's authority, because they divert some of the public's attention from the king. Once they are married, however, they have to operate within the confines of the married woman's space, as defined by the patriarchal order. These confines include restrictions on their movements and freedom of association.

The proverbs about the king communicate the same sense of power and danger that the king symbolises in these folktales. They bring to prominence his male form, even though it would be known to all that as the supreme ruler in Buganda, he must be male. In the following proverb, the king is conceived as a cockerel with command over all the hens: *Kabaka seggwanga, bwekookolima ensenyi zibundaala* (The king is a cockerel, when he crows all hens cower before it). The image of the cockerel also has a broader social relevance, because the Baganda also conceive him as husband of all men.[31] It is images like these that put the final seal on political power as far as women are concerned because they cannot fit into these masculine images.

Even princes enjoy the king's glorified status as a symbol of menace, as in the following proverbs: *Omulangira ngo, bwekula evuuma* (The prince is a leopard, when it grows it growls' and *Omulangira muliro, ogwoota ogweesamba* (The prince is fire, you enjoy it from a distance). Although the prince is conceived in such terms, his sister, the princess, is not and the reason is understandable: she can never become king and is therefore not as great a threat. However, she does enjoy some kind of power, especially if she is on good terms with the male establishment.

The chief, who is the king's representative in every locality, is given almost as much reverence as the king himself, except of course in the king's presence. For the ordinary Muganda, who might never even see the king in his lifetime, the chief is the most real authority that he knows. The point is that this power is exclusively male. Indeed, the word for chief in the Luganda language (*Mwami*) also means 'husband.' This has the psychological impact of further entrenching male authority in the home. This is because, for the married woman, the first 'chief' is the husband. But he is only the first because he is followed by a succession of others, all of whom are identified by the symbols of the power that is familiar to her—the power of the husband. Thus, it becomes a vicious cycle of male authority. The literature that results from this socio-political set-up either ignores the woman completely or presents her as a speechless spectator in the events that affect her life. Here are two proverbs that glorify the chief: *Akaami akatono okagayira mitala wa mugga* (A small chief can only be despised from across the river) and *Obukyala bwami: akawala kaatuma Kyabaggu omuliro* (To be a wife is to be a chief, a [slave] girl sent [King] Kyabaggu for fire). These proverbs glorify masculinity and implicitly compare it with femininity with inevitable results. The second proverb is particularly striking. When its socio-historical context has been understood, its irony strikes one with force. The terms *obukyala* (womanhood/wifehood) and *obwami* (manhood) have opposite meanings, but in this proverb, their attributes are invested in one person to make a strong socio-political point. The state of being a 'wife' is praised because it enables a young girl who has just given birth to send King Kyabaggu for fire. She has just given birth to his child and he is the only one available to help. The social system regards it as an achievement for the woman to send a man and a king at that, for anything, even during conditions such as those described. In this context, *bwami*, which comes from *mwami* (man/husband/chief), is a power symbol to be coveted by women not as fortunate as the one who sent Kyabaggu for fire.

Conclusion

The subject of masculinity in the oral literature of the Baganda is broad and complex, but three general trends emerge. First, the literature presents a glorified image of the boy child and assigns him a more elevated social position than that of the girl. He is the more welcome child at birth and he is the leader even when they are children. Second, the system assigns the man enormous power over the woman in marriage, politics and parenthood. Also, the man has superior physical strength and society sanctions his use of it to beat the woman, especially in the relationship between husband and wife. In some tales, the man is presented as ridiculous, greedy, inconsiderate and brutal. But even when the man is clearly in the wrong, he remains the head of the family and the worst that the woman can do to him is to leave him. If she chooses to remain, she must still be under his authority, his faults notwithstanding. This image of the greedy, irresponsible, inconsiderate, but all-powerful male featured in folktales and proverbs is a cumulative social construct and has benefited from a steady process of socialisation that uses the inculcation of the Kintu myth as the basis of life among the Baganda. But certain pictures of the man as a father, although showing him to be socially powerful, are also pathetic. For example, the father has a lot of social power but loses out as an individual human being when compared with the mother, who is shown to be caring and to have strong emotional bonds with her children. Likewise, the portraits of male tyrants in the home and in general societal leadership also largely negate the assumption that the man is favourably presented in this literature. Therefore, although the notions of masculinity that emerge from the folktales and proverbs of the Baganda promote male dominance, they also pose enormous challenges for the male members of society, the advantages that the patriarchal system gives them notwithstanding.

4. 'Ndabaga' Folktale Revisited: (De)constructing Masculinity in the Post-Genocide Rwandan Society

Rangira Béa Gallimore

The search for identity is one of the most pressing preoccupations of the human condition. Even more pressing, however, is the female quest for equality in a male-dominated world where self and social status are narrowly defined by culture-bound gender roles. From the ancient times of oral tradition to our modern era of high-tech communication, the story of a woman disguising herself as a man in order to participate in the significant circles of power from which society excludes her is told and retold.

Cultural portrayals of this theme can be seen in the award-winning movie *Shakespeare in Love*, in the Walt Disney movie *Mulan* and in the film *Men Don't Cry*. In these films, women assume a male identity in order to enter the exclusively masculine world where they indirectly disturb the patriarchal order.

Susan Faludi also explores the issues of identity, power and gender inequality by placing them in the precise cultural context in which they are constructed. In *Stiffed: The Betrayal of the American Man*, Faludi exposes the problems of men trying to be masculine in a culture where the definition of manhood is undergoing radical change. She argues that as men struggle to free themselves from their identity crisis, they need to realise that their masculinity lies not in their utility to society but in figuring out how to be human.[1]

The Rwandan folktale 'Ndabaga' describes and reiterates the privileged status attributed to masculinity in a universe where femininity is given a coefficient of negativity. The story is about a young woman named Ndabaga who disguises herself as a young man in order to take the place of her ageing father in the military, because he and his wife are unable to produce a son.

Accounts of the search for identity, whether ancient or modern, continue to captivate us, because we each have a personal interest in the outcome of this unresolved critical controversy. We study 'Ndabaga' to explore the timeless problematic construction of masculinity and to show how masculinity was deconstructed and the folktale subverted in post-genocide Rwandan society.[2]

The Ndabaga character has become legendary in Rwanda. Ndabaga's act is understood by the traditionally patriarchal society of Rwanda to be a symbol of feminine rebellion, one that must be suppressed at all costs. This interpretation of Ndabaga's tale is encoded in a popular Rwandan saying: 'Things have reached Ndabaga's stage.' This saying is often uttered in times of crisis. In post-genocide Rwanda, however, Ndabaga's attempt to acquire masculinity is viewed as an act of bravery and temerity and the Ndabaga character is seen as a 'feminist' before her time. The folktale has been adapted into plays; one of the dramatic adaptations was presented on Rwandan radio in celebration of women's liberation. The tale also serves as encouragement to women to assume roles that were traditionally reserved for men.

The first part of this chapter is devoted to answering the following two questions in relation to this folktale: Can gender identity be constructed through performance in Rwandan society? And how is gender identity perceived in the Rwandan cultural context? I will attempt to answer these questions by considering Ndabaga's performance, using both an existentialist and an essentialist approach. In the existentialist point of view, emphasis is placed on the comportment of the character in the process of constructing a masculine edifice. From this perspective, the performance and the accomplishments of the individual are considered decisive determinants in the definition of masculinity.

The second part of the analysis considers the question of masculine identity from an essentialist perspective. In this approach, gender is a given—it is a biological construct. Masculinity is essentially built on an unalterable and fixed premise, a sufficient and necessary condition: the phallus. Thus, any performance, no matter how 'masculine,' is automatically considered inferior and pathetic if the performer lacks this essential male member. I will go on to present different social and political mechanisms that allowed the new Rwandan woman to subvert the patriarchal order and to deconstruct masculinity in modern society.

Before entering into the analysis of the folktale, it is best to give a quick summary of Ndabaga's story using the structural semiotic model in order to show where the conflict resides and how the main character tries to overcome obstacles in her quest for masculinity. Algirdas-Julien Greimas argues that a narrative text is built upon a profound narrative structure composed of actantial functions.[3] The main actantial role is played by the subject. The *subject* is always a subject in relation to an *object* of desire. However, the quest of the *subject* is triggered by the *sender*. The *sender* motivates the *subject* to desire an *object* for the benefit of a *receiver*. In other words, although the *sender* triggers the action, the *receiver* is the beneficiary of the action undertaken. In its course, the *subject* is assisted by an *adjuvant* and contested by an *opponent*. The *opponent* creates an obstacle to the acquisition of the *object* of desire. The *opponent* is in competition with the *subject* for possession of the same *object*.

This model, applied to 'Ndabaga,' shows that the *subject* of the story is a young woman whose *object* of desire is masculinity. She wants to become a boy because there is no male child in the family. Sexual categorisation is a fundamental element in this plot, because a male child would have replaced his father in the military and spared his mother the burden of excessive farm work.[4] It is this lack, a mark of deficiency and affliction (*sender*), that confers humiliation on the family. The lack also triggers the action of the young woman and defines the nature of the desired object. This fact is revealed during the moving dialogue between the protagonist and her father:

> 'Come, I have something to ask you.' He came and she said to him: 'I
> have often asked my mother where you were and she always hid it from
> me; when I finally learned your whereabouts, I started learning all kinds of
> [male] exercises. Do you recognise my sex now?'
> 'You are a boy.'
> 'You are right, I am a boy, I wanted to become a boy; I was in fact a girl
> but I suppressed my breasts so that I could replace you.'

Ndabaga does not, therefore act for herself. The beneficiaries (*receiver*) of her quest are her parents. If Ndabaga acquires masculinity, her father will be able to go back home to his wife and will be spared the humiliation and ignominy associated with death in the military. Her mother will also benefit. She will be discharged from excessive farm work.

The young woman disguises herself as a man and goes to the military camp to serve. In her quest, Ndabaga garners early success by performing very well in male exercises. She is ranked first in the high jump. Her military performance proves excellent as well. She learns how to shoot with a bow and arrow, even competing for the target. Finally, her clothing and physiological disguise allow her to alter the public's perception. She starts with the suppression of her breasts so that no one can tell that she is a woman. This painful physiological disguise is further masked by the donning of men's clothing (*adjuvant*).

Nevertheless, the female genitals (*opponent*) of Ndabaga, the operator subject, become a permanent threat to her successful quest for the acquisition of masculinity. Thus, 'she built herself a small shed [*adjuvant*] in the compound where she lived and it is there where she went to urinate [in privacy] each morning.'

Ndabaga's behaviour shows that the object of value in her quest is the acquisition of masculinity without ambiguity. The protagonist is ready to destroy all obstacles in her quest for masculinity. It is a choice she imposes on herself. In this instance, Ndabaga confirms the existentialist view of gender. She has made her choice and takes actions by which she constructs a male persona. And society accepts and interacts with Ndabaga based on this public persona, which surpasses perception and becomes reality.

The contribution of Jean Paul Sartre's *Existentialism and Humanism* and existentialist philosophy is the belief that the individual is defined by his actions. According to this philosophy, the essence of a human being is never pre-existent to her or his existence. 'The existence precedes the essence.'[5] A human being exists first before he or she can create his or her own identity; in other words, before he or she can establish his or her own essence. A human being is not a given static, immutable and definitive entity. He or she is under perpetual construction. He or she is a product dynamically generated by acts he performs. A human being is, therefore, perceived as a being potentially afflicted *ab initio* by the problem of identity. Through choices and actions, a human being can realise her or his identity. Because identity categorisation cannot be established *a priori*, the determination of gender, like all identity is therefore the result of a series of experiences.

Simone de Beauvoir illustrates the issue of gender construction through the maxim, 'One is not born, but rather becomes, a woman.' According to De Beauvoir, 'no biological, psychological, or economic fate determines the figure that the human female presents in society: it is civilisation as a whole that produces this creature, intermediate between male and eunuch, which is described as feminine.'[6]

In the existentialist view, one is not born a man or a woman but *becomes* one or the other. De Beauvoir shows that a woman is not a 'completed' reality, but rather a 'becoming' reality and 'it is in her becoming that she should be compared with man.' In other words, her possibility, her potential, should be defined during this process of 'becoming.'[7]

However, the construction of individual identity always requires the approving gaze of others to validate it. From this perspective, the construction of masculinity can be reduced to a series of acts and accomplishments that are perceived and recognised by the general public as generators of masculinity. A person is never born a man or a woman but becomes one or the other because the person has accomplished a performance that the society identifies with a specific gender. It is important to point out that in this existentialist perspective a tacit and subtle break divides sexual identity from gender identity. Gender, unlike sex, is not biologically determined, but is a product of social conditioning. For the existentialist, the masculine or feminine gender is a social construct.

If masculinity can be constructed, what then are the important stages and diacritic signs towards its construction in 'Ndabaga'? In the folktale, the protagonist's desire for masculinity is born from a feeling of lack, absence and deprivation. It is because of these feelings that Ndabaga asks her mother: 'Where does my father live?' The mother's answer reinforces the daughter's lack of masculinity: 'What good would it bring to you since you are a girl? If you were a boy, then I would tell you!' Ndabaga's mother tells her indirectly that because she lacks masculinity, she cannot be of any help to her parents or to

– 53 –

herself. The mother projects her guilt onto her daughter. Unable to have a son, she resents her daughter for not being male. 'In Rwanda, the strength of a family is measured in the number of its boys.'[8] The female birth has somehow robbed Ndabaga's family of its well-being and strength: masculinity. It is therefore this phallic infirmity that triggers Ndabaga's actions and establishes the construction of masculinity as her priority.

Ndabaga's plan of action constitutes an initiatory itinerary, an initiation rite to fulfil a phallic absence, to be cured of her essential phallic infirmity. She does so by disguising herself as a man. Thus, will and determination are the main ingredients in the construction of masculinity. The important role played by the individual in the quest for masculinity is expressed explicitly in the narrative. Ndabaga indicates to her father her desire to become a boy. The will of the protagonist is therefore an important aspect in the construction of masculinity. Once the volitional basis is established, the female character proceeds towards the realisation of the desired masculinity. In this process, Ndabaga performs a series of actions to negate and eliminate her social handicap: her femininity. She is determined to hide the physical signs of her femininity in order to accomplish what the female Ndabaga would not have been able to accomplish. Here, Ndabaga offers an excellent example of the subversive woman.

Ndabaga's subversion or construction of masculinity by 'detour' finds its justification in modern psychology. Lacanian psychoanalysis is built on the dichotomy of 'a fundamental lack or absence [*manque à être*]' and a forever unattainable 'object of desire [*objet de désir*].' According to Jacques Lacan, this lack can be either feminine or masculine. The phallus is 'the universal signifier,' not the male sexual organ and is rather a 'metonymic presence' that is indicative of the *manque à être*.[9]

Ellie Ragland-Sullivan shows that Lacan argued that a person becomes male or female by identifying, or not identifying, with the phallic signifier, rather than by any innate mechanism. In Lacanian terms, female is defined as 'not' being male and all other identifying characteristics derive from this primordial definition. By this dialectic movement, the male both 'is' and 'has.' Man is the being who possesses the standard of measurement: the phallus. Two processes are therefore important in postulating masculinity. The first is a literal and explicit exhibition of the penis. But when this physical exposition is impossible, when the subject is deprived of a penis, masculinity can still be constructed by a dialectic movement. This movement consists of denying and rejecting any female characteristics.[10]

Ndabaga uses this technique of detour to construct 'her' masculinity. In the narrative we are told that Ndabaga flattens her chest so that her breasts will not grow and ultimately betray her. By dialectic movement, the presence of breasts would signify that the penis, the iconic representation of the phallus, is not present. Breasts are promoted to the rank of a defining vector. They are the primordial defining element of femininity. But it is important to note that identity is ascribed based on the absence of the phallus, rather than on the presence of breasts.

The suppression of breasts projects to the outside gaze a masculine image and constitutes an important element in the construction of a masculine identity. By suppressing her breasts, Ndabaga eradicates the cumbersome and compromising feminine signifier. It is by this process that she is able to project her masculinity to the validating gaze of others. From that moment, her association with femininity becomes inconceivable and even undesirable. This explains why, in the military camp, she conceals her sex by building a little shed within the compound where she can urinate in privacy. As such, she continues to project the image that she is a man. This projected appearance, reinforced by the concealment of her breasts and by her military exploits, encourages the validating gaze to accept 'her' masculinity.

The protagonist in this folktale first stresses a physiological construction of masculinity. This is not surprising because from the existentialist perspective, the *paraître* (appearance) determines or defines the *être* (being). The body is a medium on which cultural meanings are inscribed. The pertinence of the performance and the accomplishments are only affirmed in the identifying process. When Ndabaga's lack (*manque*) has been supplied and the object of desire is within reach, she undertakes a series of performances to embellish 'her' masculinity. As emphasised in the tale, she learns and participates in all 'male' exercises and activities 'instead of weaving little baskets like other girls.' Basket weaving was exclusively a female occupation in traditional Rwandan society. Gender roles were dominant too and they are still prevalent today. One recent observer noted that, 'from a young age, the education that girls receive from their mothers initiates them into their future lives as wives and mothers. A woman will take care of the house as well as work in the fields.'[11]

According to a 1995 Rwandan government report prepared for the UN Fourth World Conference on Women, '[t]he ideal image of a woman is still generally viewed through the perspective of her maternal role. The woman must be fertile, hard working and reserved. She must learn the art of silence and reserve.'[12]

By rejecting roles assigned to her gender and by submitting herself to an education generally reserved for men, Ndabaga slowly but surely crosses gender boundaries. Not only does she acquire and assert men's roles, but she assumes their physical appearance too. On her way to camp, she puts on men's clothing. This dress code allows her to integrate fully into the masculine arena. It is important to point out that the military camp encodes important symbolic social values. It is a place and a space traditionally assigned and reserved for men only. No woman was admitted into the military camp, where masculinity supposedly reaches its zenith. Ndabaga's performance is therefore a heroic act that can be compared to an ascetic pilgrim's journey to the Holy Land. During her initiatory journey, Ndabaga, like a pilgrim, endures and survives all kinds of obstacles imposed by the patriarchal society.

From the existentialist perspective, a separation must be established between biological sex and socially constructed gender. Lacking male genitals, Ndabaga is able to acquire a masculine identity through her actions and to find acceptance as a man. At this point in the story, genetics seems to count less than socialisation in the making of a man. This first part of Ndabaga's tale appears to confirm the basic argument of existentialist feminism, which asserts that 'gender and sexuality, whatever the biology that helps to inform these, are created culturally and socially; they are not immutable givens.'[13] Ndabaga's performance shows that 'one is not born a man but rather becomes one' and that the body is 'a situation,' not a passive medium, but a 'becoming.'

Ndabaga's story does not end there, however. It surprises us with a Cinderella ending, which interjects an essentialist viewpoint into the story. As the days go by, Ndabaga's peers become suspicious of her stubborn need for privacy. They follow her during her frequent disappearances to the little shed and discover that the seemingly formidable military man is in fact a woman, unable to urinate in a standing position. This is humiliating for Ndabaga. De Beauvoir points out that for females to urinate, 'custom generally demands that women sit or crouch, while the erect position is reserved for males. This difference constitutes for the little girl the most striking sexual differentiation. To urinate, she is required to crouch, uncover herself and therefore hide: a shameful and inconvenient procedure.'[14]

Urinating continues to convey masculine overtones of power and autonomy. 'Pissing straight' is considered a mark of competence and desirable performance even among men. Being crouched and uncovered puts a person in a vulnerable and powerless position. No man, it can be argued, wants to 'get caught with his pants down.' But Ndabaga is discovered in this most shameful and humiliating position. It is a discovery that abruptly destroys 'her' masculinity and all the efforts she has undertaken to construct it.

Ndabaga's shameful secret is also revealed to the king. The chief of the military camp tells the king that 'that man, the one who beats us in the archery, is in fact a woman.' The king is surprised and sceptical to learn that Ndabaga is a woman. The tale recounts that:

> The king was very surprised and he laughed a lot. To verify their information, the king wanted to engage her in a wrestling match in such a way that he could find out if she was really a woman. But she was so strong and courageous that the king couldn't put her down. They wrestled and wrestled. Days passed by and the king couldn't get what he wanted.

In the end, Ndabaga asks the king what the challenge is about. When the king tells her what he has heard, she decides to reveal to him her true identity and the motives that triggered her disguise. The king is impressed and congratulates her. However, instead of rewarding Ndabaga for her skills and performance, he asks her to leave the military camp. The king says: 'This is extraordinary! Leave, go and get married; women, they get married; no woman goes to war!' But Ndabaga fears that she cannot marry because she is a woman without breasts. Her ultimate symbol of femininity is now missing. But then the king decides to marry her.

In one of the recent dramatic adaptations of the folktale, upon hearing about her exploits, the king shakes Ndabaga's hand and says: 'This is extraordinary, you are a man!' This added line introduces another element of gender identity that is deeply embedded in Rwandan culture. Just like the saying that 'Things have reached Ndabaga's stage,' evoked in times of crisis, Rwandans use the saying *uli umugabo* to acknowledge and praise notable performances. *Uli umugabo* means literally 'you are a man.'[15] This phrase is used to congratulate both men and women for their performances. This linguistic convention embodies the patriarchal order of traditional society that survives even today.

In recognising worthy performances as explicitly male performances, the Rwandan language, the primary indicator of cultural identity, reinforces the societal inequalities embedded in gender roles. By using *umugabo* to compliment a woman, the unstated and more powerful, subconscious message is that some acts and accomplishments can only be performed by a man. The language itself robs women of the possibility of equality. It takes away their potential by denying that worthy acts can be performed by women. By calling the successful female performer a man, the society symbolically strips her of her feminine identity. In granting her the honourary status of a man, the patriarchal order also says noteworthy and worthwhile performances are out of the reach of women.

The king never doubts Ndabaga's strength, or her military prowess, but he dismisses her from the military, stating that 'a woman doesn't go to war' and in doing so, he rejects her masculine performances. For the king, masculinity is an essentialist entity. According to the essentialist approach, no distinction is established between gender identity and sexual identity. These two categories overlap and are perceived as products of the same reality. For essentialists, masculinity needs its phallic pillar to have credibility. Without a penis, no masculinity exists. This is why essentialists establish a separation between 'being' and 'doing.'

At the end of Ndabaga's tale, the young woman marries the king. But, 'once pregnant, she could no longer jump. When she took her bow and tried to shoot, the king saw clearly that a woman cannot go to war.' Ndabaga's pregnancy is a milestone in the process of feminine domestication. It is not surprising that she can no longer uses her bow because weapons and martial arts were the monopoly of men in traditional Rwandan society. No exception is allowed. Ndabaga cannot be anything else but her true self, which is a woman, a simple woman whose essential role is to conceive. She is subjected to all kinds of taboos that put an end to her quest for masculinity. Nature eventually imposes its law and femininity surfaces. Marriage can be understood as a subtle means by which the patriarchal society aborts any tentative feminine rebellion, any menace to the established patriarchal order.

Certainly, the story has a 'happy ending.' By marrying the king, the protagonist achieves a social ascension. However, in the process, her masculine persona is discarded. In the end, the military community in which she lived refuses to give her credit for her unusual accomplishments and does not consider her performance as a defining factor in the identification of 'her' masculinity. No one doubts her military superiority, but the only thing taken into account is her biological sex. The validating gaze refuses to see her as masculine because she does not have a penis. This means that in the Rwandan popular conscience, masculinity or femininity cannot be constructed. That is why Ndabaga's encounter with the king can be understood as a crisis of identity, a conflict whose terms are defined by nature and culture. Ndabaga wanted to suppress her natural identity and assume a constructed one. The admission of her true identity to the king can be interpreted as the victory of the natural over the assumed identity.

The folktale shows that performance is not a crucial factor in the construction of identity. Ndabaga undergoes a symbolic masculine initiation rite and is successful. She first subjects herself to physical suffering. In some popular versions of the folktale, Ndabaga has her breasts removed and not just suppressed. In one version, Ndabaga asks a blacksmith to cut off her breasts.[16] This self-mutilation is even more painful than the circumcision without anaesthesia that adolescent boys endured during their initiation into manhood in many traditional African societies.

Ndabaga competes in male exercises and activities and she excels. She undergoes all kinds of social and military tests and passes all of them. She faces difficult ordeals and survives them and yet her masculinity is constantly subjected to doubt and in the end, is destroyed. Despite her formidable exploits, the members of the camp refuse to acknowledge her masculine identity. They disassociate the masculine performance from the feminine être (being). For them, individual identity cannot be determined by actions.

Contrary to the views of De Beauvoir and existentialist humanism, the folktale seems to assert that one is born a man or a woman and remains as such. Ndabaga's story argues in favour of a fixed and immutable identity. It is an affirmation and a reaffirmation of the essentialist conception of sexual identity. It shows that in Rwandan society, sexual identity is intrinsic and fixed at birth. Identity cannot in any way be constructed. Individual performance is simply an epiphenomenon in the identity process.

When the encoded saying from Ndabaga's tale—'Things have reached Ndabaga's stage'—is uttered in modern Rwandan daily life, it is simply to call attention to a crisis situation requiring immediate attention. The English equivalent of the saying would be that something has 'gone to the dogs.' When a Rwandan says that 'Things have reached Ndabaga's stage' it is usually with a tone of regret and fear—fear that something dreadful has happened or is about to happen.

To understand the role played by the post-genocide Ndabaga within the modern Rwandan context, one needs to look at the beginning of the Ndabaga folktale. At the beginning, we learn that there is a political crisis in Rwanda. Political relations are not good between the Rwandan kingdom and the Ankole kingdom situated at the north of Rwanda and south of Uganda, respectively. According to the original account: 'For a long time, the Ankole had been attacking Rwanda and raiding its cows until the day the king decided to establish a military camp at the border. He set up a camp where every man was required to serve until he was replaced by his son. If he had no son, he would serve there until his death.' This political crisis causes a social crisis. Men have to be away from their families. The nuclear family is fragmented and truncated. Ndabaga's father and many other fathers are forced to remain in the camp until their death. Married women become husbandless and children fatherless. The head of the family is missing. The absence of a man in the household, or rather the absence of masculinity, is the main cause of this chaos. It is from this chaotic atmosphere that the main character of the tale evolves. Her identity is therefore given an important focus. It is this identity that allows Ndabaga to give structure to the nuclear family in chaos. Ndabaga's performance allows her to tear herself away from a linear relationship with her mother and to build a triangular relationship that includes her father. In her quest, she attempts to create order from chaotic family life and at the same time, is confronted with the problematic of her being. Ndabaga unites her family by gaining access to her father. And once this unity is accomplished, the original chaos is replaced by family unity. At the end of the folktale, the king revokes his law and dismisses everybody from the military camp so that gender boundaries will not be violated. The king says, 'When a woman goes to war that means things have reached Ndabaga's stage; I dismiss everybody, go!' Each man in the camp rejoins his family to form a nuclear family unit.

Although the family unity Ndabaga seeks is accomplished, she realises that she is a woman without breasts. During the quest for masculinity, their suppression was a major asset to the project. They allowed Ndabaga to disguise herself, subvert the validating gaze and acquire male physiology. But when she is discovered and revealed to be a woman, Ndabaga is haunted by the anguish of impending celibacy. She asks, 'Since I suppressed my breasts, who will marry me?' Without marriage, Ndabaga would be a total failure in traditional society. It is necessary to recall here the torments, anguish and humiliation that unmarried women endure in traditional African society. The question Ndabaga asks the king transcends the simple desire for a husband. It raises an existential problem. Once her 'masculinisation' fails, she is no longer a man or a woman. She is instead trapped between a masculine identity she cannot acquire and a femininity that she has denied, rejected and compromised. She is now living the ambiguity of an asexual being. Pierre Smith explains that in the traditional Rwandan society, 'women whose [chest] breasts were not developed were, like unmarried mothers, considered as real calamities and a menace to the well-being of the whole country. They were sentenced to death or forced into exile on the decision of the court.'

Without breasts, Ndabaga would have been considered a cursed and dangerous being to be excluded from society. Her marriage to the king is then very significant. It allows Ndabaga to redeem her identity, a necessary condition to her socialisation. It removes her from the margins and places her at the centre of society. She becomes a woman and as such she is assigned a social functionality. Ndabaga's marriage puts an end to her identity crisis and to her androgyny. It allows her to regain her femininity and indirectly, her ontological identity.

The marriage to the king reinforces the notion that Rwandan society is essentialist. The Ndabaga icon and the popular saying embedded in the collective conscience demonstrate the powerful notion that gender is an intrinsic and immutable conception determined by physiological sex at birth. One is born a man or a woman and remains such in Rwandan society. It is clear that Ndabaga's performance was not fundamentally a subversive act. Ndabaga's abandonment of her quest for masculinity and her acquiescence to the traditional female role of marrying and childbearing are an ultimate reification of the old order.

Like the Ndabaga from the original folktale, the new Ndabaga woman was born shortly after the genocide in Rwanda that claimed about a million lives. Most of the victims were from the minority Tutsi group, but others were sympathisers from the majority Hutu group. The country was economically, politically and psychologically devastated by atrocities committed during the genocide. It is in this atmosphere of chaos that the modern 'Ndabaga' woman emerges to acquire the new roles that were traditionally reserved for men, even up to a few years after the end of the genocide.

During the 1994 genocide of the Tutsi, most of the killing was done by Hutu men, although some Hutu women participated by helping their husbands, brothers and fathers. But overall, the percentage of women who participated in the genocide is said to be very small. Elizabeth Powley stated that:

Women represent only 2.3 per cent of genocide suspects in Rwanda (3,442 of 108,215 imprisoned). For the most part, they were not planners or perpetrators of the genocide. Importantly, women are an important symbol of moderation in Rwanda today. They are trusted in the tasks of reconciliation and reconstruction in part because they have not been implicated in the violence to the same extent as men.[17]

This lack of men in Rwanda led to a drastic change in the traditional patriarchal structure of society. Shortly after the genocide, 70 per cent of Rwandan households were headed by women. Many Tutsi women were widowed by the 1994 genocide, which took more men than women. Many Hutu women were husbandless because a large number of Hutu men were imprisoned for their involvement in the genocide as perpetrators and accomplices and also because some Hutu men went into exile in neighbouring countries, fleeing possible reprisals from soldiers of the Rwandan Patriotic Front (RPF), the predominantly Tutsi army, which put an end to the genocide in July 1994. Rwandan women, Tutsi as well as Hutu, were left to raise their children alone. Some women had to take care of the many orphans whose parents and relatives were exterminated during the genocide, along with the children whose parents left them behind when they fled the country, as well as their own children.

It was during this absence of a dominant male presence, the general lack of masculinity, that the patriarchal order was shaken. Although they were victims, women refused to become passive and instead became active social agents, playing an important role in the reconstruction of the country. In the aftermath of the genocide, Rwandan women have been engaged in tasks that were traditionally reserved for men, such as burying the dead, building houses and roads, working as mechanics and even running businesses such as import and export companies. Women are also known to be the best healers in Rwandan society. Many women's associations have transcended the ethnic conflicts and are now working together to transform the culture of violence into a culture of peace.

Fourteen years after the genocide, the percentage of Rwandan men has risen but women still represent about 54 per cent of the population. Despite the increase in the male population, Rwandan women continue to participate in significant numbers in the rebuilding and running of the country. The 1994 genocide caused social change not only in Rwandan society, but has also initiated new, non-traditional roles for women in politics. Female organisations, along with constitutional set-asides, have catapulted women into political power in unprecedented numbers. After the genocide, the Rwandan government understood that ignoring the importance of women in the reconstruction of Rwanda would be a step backwards. The new Rwandan Constitution, ratified in May 2003, called for female participation in important decision-making positions. The Constitution requires women to have at least 30 per cent of the seats at all leadership levels. In October 2003, women won 45 per cent of the seats in the general elections, including thirty-nine of the eighty seats in Parliament and six of the twenty seats in the Senate.

President Paul Kagame appointed women to nine of the twenty-eight ministerial posts, making Rwanda a world leader in gender balance in political representation and decision-making. It is also important to note that these percentages have increased over the years. In looking at the Rwandan executive branch, one can see that there is a remarkable increase in the number of women after each ministerial cabinet reshuffling by the president. In the March 2006 cabinet reshuffle, the percentage of women increased from 28 to 30 per cent. In the March 2008 reshuffle, female representation increased from 30 to 36 per cent. This progressive increase speaks to their leadership qualities and the undeniable government commitment to gender balance.

The post-genocide Ndabaga woman has also acquired a new leadership role in the military. As shown through the analysis of the Ndabaga folktale, Rwanda had no tradition of female conscription during the pre-colonial era. Traditional Rwandan law stated that women did not go to war. A July 2001 report by the Rwandan female association Haguruka stated that; 'in the military structure of the Rwandan Kingdom, all Rwandan men belonged to the army... At the beginning of each reign, a new army was formed. At that end the King required all his clients to bring their sons (never daughters) who were not members of the army.'

During the Rwandan colonisation, neither the Germans nor the Belgians modified this exclusively masculine military structure. No women were admitted into the military when the colonial army was formed. For a long time after Rwandan independence, no women were admitted into the national army. It was only after the coup by the late President Juvénal Habyarimana that a few women entered the army. Since 1990, a significant number of women, Tutsi as well as Hutu, voluntarily took up arms alongside men to assume military responsibilities. Christopher Taylor writes:

> During the genocide itself, women were important as both agents and symbols and this can be seen in different ways. As agents, women played important roles on both sides during the conflict. In the Rwandan Government Army, for example, there were many female Hutu soldiers. Although no woman to my knowledge was involved in actual combat operations against the Rwandan Patriotic Front, in the Hutu extremist militia groups, there were women who engaged in the killing of Tutsi civilians. Other extremist women acted as neighbourhood informers keeping note of Tutsi individuals and families who resided in their section. After the onset of the violence on 7 April 1994, these informers indicated where Tutsi families lived to bands of Hutu extremist youth, the Interahamwe. Informers of this sort were often rewarded with the property

of their victims. On the other side, the side of the Rwandan Patriotic Front, composed of about seventy to 80 per cent Tutsi, women were active in fund-raising activities and in the preparation and dissemination of RPF literature.[18]

Before the 1994 genocide, the RPF army aggressively recruited men and women among the Tutsi exiles through different forums in different countries. The most common were cultural forums in which young people, male and female, were invited to learn about Rwanda, their country of origin, its songs, dances and traditions and also to be educated about the RPF cause. At some of these forums, the Ndabaga folktale was adapted to a play to make women aware of their military responsibilities in helping the Tutsi people return to their country of origin. After the genocide, high-ranking female leaders from the RPF army moved into political positions in Rwanda.

After the war and the genocide, there was a demobilisation process and the Disarmament, Demobilisation and Reintegration (DDR) commission was established. However, many female ex-combatants rejoined civilian life without identifying themselves as ex-combatants. They therefore were not receiving benefits from the DDR commission's demobilisation package.

During this process, women noticed that gender was not taken into account. In 2001, a group of Rwandan female ex-combatants decided to unite all female ex-combatants from the various opposing military groups under the name of 'Ndabaga.' Like the Ndabaga of the folktale, their objective was to bring unity and reconciliation in a country that had been torn by war and to provide solutions to challenges as Rwandan women, regardless of their military affiliation. 'What matters is that many of us have many children to look after, some are single mothers and others are widows. We want to work together to overcome poverty and unemployment.'[19]

During the DDR process, Hutu and Tutsi ex-combatants had to face the harsh life of poverty in Rwanda. 'It is at this point that Ndabaga has put itself to the task of identifying these ladies so that together with the DDR commission, these women shall benefit from the commission as the others.'[20]

By banding together in the Ndabaga Association, these women decided to become advocates of the female ex-combatants and to help each other find or create possibilities for work. They were able to show that female ex-combatants face numerous obstacles that male ex-combatants do not, because there are physiological needs specific to women that are not taken into account. Thus, the Ndabaga Association brought a gender perspective to the DDR process in Rwanda. Ndabaga was also the first female ex-combatant association in the Africa Great Lakes Region.

In 2004 Ndabaga's voice went beyond the national boundaries when the Rwandan government decided to become a part of the regional peacekeeping missions by sending troops to Darfur, Sudan, to help the African Union monitor ceasefires in the region. Ndabaga women requested inclusion in these missions because of their experience in warfare and as female ex-combatants they believed they could enhance the success of the peacekeeping mission by including a gender perspective. Ndabaga's president stated the importance of female ex-combatants in the following terms: 'If female ex-combatants took part in regional peacekeeping missions, they would alert the world of any abuses committed against women and children and particularly lobby for more humanitarian aid for the victims of war.'[21] She added that in the case of African conflicts, many women face similar problems and would be more comfortable telling their stories to other women.

In the Ndabaga folktale, sexual identity is like the force of gravity that confines the individual in a narrow or limited space. This patriarchal immobilisation of women has been deconstructed by the mobility of women at all levels of modern Rwandan society. In post-genocide Rwanda, the name 'Ndabaga' and the maxim associated with it have completely lost their essentialist meaning, thanks to the Ndabaga association. However, this change did not happen overnight. The Ndabaga of the folktale benefited from social reintegration by approval of the king, who reinstalled the old order by redeeming the socially unfit Ndabaga and reintegrating her into patriarchal society by way of marriage. Unlike the folktale character, women of the Ndabaga association had to fight their way to their social reintegration. They did not get their reintegration from a benevolent male but demanded and required it as a right—equal to male Rwandan ex-combatants—while arguing that their inclusion in the demobilisation process was a particularly important female right in the army because women are affected differently by violence than men.

Since the creation of their association, the women of Ndabaga have also used their rights to help other civilian women who were victims of violence. They have thus committed the ultimate feminist act by seeking to empower other women. Today, there are many Ndabaga women in different districts of Rwanda and they play important roles in the community and in political leadership, including the female ex-combatants who were elected to the Rwandan Parliament and Senate. The subversive act of the Ndabaga association reached even greater spheres of power when its members requested to be a part of the UN Peacekeeping mission in Darfur. Using the UN Security Resolution 1325 clause on peace and security from a gender perspective, they defended their position and their demand was honoured.

As I have demonstrated in this study, the Ndabaga of the post-genocide society has gone beyond where the Ndabaga character was able to reach. The association has dismantled the patriarchal society and its reification of differences and has rejected the conventional and conservative norms in which the character of the folktale was entrapped. As they say, 'Every cloud has a silver lining.' From the chaos caused by the 1994 genocide emerged another Rwandan woman who was able to find a sense of dignity as individual and not as someone else's appendage.

5. Deploying Masculinity in African Oral Poetic Performance: The Man in *Udje*

Tanure Ojaide

The Urhobo people of Nigeria are renowned for their *udje* dance-song performance. Although *udje* is mainly associated with Arhavwqrien, Ewu, Okparabe, Olomu, Udu and Ughievwen clans, it is the latter two that are popularly known in Urhobo as the 'kingdom of songs.' In its heyday *udje* was also practised in Agbon, Ogor and Uvwie (Effurun) clans, with master poets and performers hired from Ughievwen and Udu to teach *udje* poetry composition and its performance. The Urhobo people, a Pan-Edo subgroup, live mainly in Delta State, but there also is a substantial number living in Bayelsa, Edo, Rivers, Ondo, Osun, Lagos, Plateau, Borno, Kano and other states of Nigeria. Many Urhobo currently live in Ghana, Liberia, Côte d'Ivoire, Britain and the United States. Although the Urhobo share a common identity and ancestry, they have close neighbours in the Edo (Bini, Ishan, Ora and Owan), Isoko, Ukwani (Igbo), Itsekiri and Izon (Ijo). However, none of these neighbouring groups practise *udje*. *Udje* is thus an exclusively Urhobo people's oral poetic performance tradition.

As a patriarchal society in which men are privileged over women and the customs and traditions have been established to favour men at the expense of women, the notions of manliness, manhood, or masculinity are not limited to being male by gender. Masculinity is a conglomerate of virtues and characteristics built around the traditional expectations of being a man and the glorification of virile values. These qualities, sometimes related to warrior virtues, are not only integral parts of the culture but are also seen by the people as meeting established rules of behaviour/conduct and the action of men. In this chapter, I intend to discuss Urhobo notions of masculinity as deployed in the oral poetic performance of *udje*. Masculinity in many African societies is a heightened form of human behaviour and action that is the antithesis of femininity. In the *udje* poetic performance, masculinity assumes an even more heightened form, not only in poetry, music and dance, but also in its being geared towards extolling those virtues that the Urhobo hold to be admirable in men.

Udje is a unique type of Urhobo poetry-song, composed from often exaggerated and sometimes fictional materials about a rival side of the community and performed with dance by rival quarters, towns or villages on an appointed day during festival time, with large audiences in attendance. In a given year, it is the turn of one side to sing about the other and that side uses materials it gathered to compose songs that exaggerate the other side's foibles and frailties. The following year, the side that sang the previous year listens to and watches the response of the opposing side. Each song is either a response or a counter-attack; each side responds and springs new surprises. The tradition is seen foremost as a form of entertainment, despite the fact that the poetic composition is, as in battle, aimed at 'wounding' and even destroying its target.

Udje is a male performance tradition. The composers of the songs (*irori-ile*) and the performers/cantors (*ebo-ile*) are all men. Women stay at the periphery in *udje* dance-song performance. Their role is limited to clapping to the percussive rhythms of the drumming, fanning the male dancers and chanting praises of the drummers and dancers. Ironically, the men involved in the performance, especially the dancers, dress in women's wrappers. Also significant to the *udje* sense of masculinity is the fact that the performance is dedicated to Uhaghwa or other local deities that are neither male nor female. Despite some of these aspects of *udje* performance that incorporate female and androgynous qualities, *udje* in its conception and execution deploys masculinity in a variety of ways to achieve moral, ethical and aesthetic goals.

The setting of Urhoboland where *udje* is performed is crucial to the understanding of the masculine ethic. The performers of *udje* live in the riverine area of the Niger Delta, which is made up of mangrove swamps and rainforest vegetation. The Ughievwen and Udu clans that perform *udje* live in small rural towns and villages, where fishing and farming are the main occupations. In addition, the men tap rubber trees and also produce palm oil, two rigorous means of livelihood in the rainforest environment. Nobody takes to performing *udje* full-time; rather, it is combined with fishing, farming or some other work. In keeping with the dominant values of the rural environs of Urhobo, *udje* aims to promote communal harmony and peace. The songs are meant to deter individuals from crossing the line of decency and morality and breaking the communal cohesion. These rural values are seen as the opposite of those held in urban areas such as Warri and Sapele, where morality is lax and where aggressive individualism is at the expense of the communal spirit.

Udje is conceived and practised as *ofovwin* (war) in which one party uses all the poetic and theatrical resources at its disposal to 'annihilate' the other side.

War is often a masculine art in which physical prowess is displayed to assert the twin manly qualities of courage and power. Chief Jonathan Mrakpor of Edjophe explained this link between war and *udje* performance:

> Wars and fights led to disputes and the accompanying judgement led to *udje*. When there was a war or fight, one side won—the victorious group rejoiced with songs. In the process, the victorious sang songs about the defeated—they boasted about their prowess and mocked the weakness of their opponents. Stung, the defeated got angry and retaliated with biting songs of their own about the other group. *Udje* was the result of abusing the one who abused you.[1]

Chief Dozen Ogbariemu, a veteran of the art of *udje*, confirms that '*udje* songs are used to destroy or praise.'[2] In this context, the songs are used to praise one's group and vilify one's rivals. War or war-like action is thus a mark of masculinity among the Urhobo people, in their real lives and in their poetic performance traditions. Men seek to assume positions of leadership, whether in a war or in a performance competition, to defend their side and make it proud. In so doing, they are also boosting their egos in the society.

To all concerned in the tradition, *udje* is an artistic contest framed as a battle or war (*ofovwin*) between two parties and in the fiercely competitive spirit each side avails itself of all the 'big guns' in the verbal arsenal and theatrical repository to sing the opponents to a fall. Images and motifs of battle or war fill *udje* songs and their performance activities. Often, the *obo-ile*, the chief performer, projects himself as the leader of an army and calls on his followers to put in their best in singing and dancing to ensure victory in the artistic battle. Here is an Otokutu song that, like an opening salvo in battle, is meant to exhort his group and to intimidate the other side:

> The time has come at last.
> The chimpanzee boasts it will break the gorilla's back.
> If the civet cat cries all night, there must be cause for it.
> The akpobrisi tree says it is tough,
> but people bypass it to make offerings to the iroko tree.
> The boast of prowess between strong and weak
> will only be settled after a hand-to-hand encounter.
> The time has come at last.
> Now that our *udje* dance is out,
> will you still contest our superiority?
> It is sheer delusion, sheer delusion;
> if not, who will beat his chest
> that he is everything in the world?

The river god says he will dance,
says he will dance himself to madness.
The ocean god says he will clap for him.
When the waves rise in mad turbulence,
who dares set in, in a canoe?
The time has come at long last![3]

Here, the Otokutu men project themselves variously as gorillas, the fierce mythical akpobrisis tree and ocean waves, respectively, stances that the opposing side cannot contend with in the battle of songs ahead. Although the Otokutu group is strong, the rival group is weak. It is a metaphorical display of physical and mystical power meant to intimidate the other group into submission even before the 'battle' of songs begins. The akpobrisi tree is imbued with mystical power in Urhobo mythology. No two akpobrisi trees are found in the same vicinity and only low brushes grow around it. It thus stands alone in defiance of other low shrubs around. In the *udje* songs, masculinity involves physical and mystical dominance as well as artistic superiority in poetry composition and performance.

The leader of a particular side often encourages his men to put in their best in the 'battle of songs.' In a song, Akanabe, 'respected for his strength,' exalts his men:

My people, stand close to me;
help me gather more clubs.
If you laze about
when the battle is being fought,
we shall all be enslaved.
We can defend ourselves if we are together.[4]

It is significant to put these songs in the historical context of the Urhobo people. Tired of intra-ethnic wars, they resolved in the middle of the nineteenth century to channel their violent energies into artistic competition rather than real battle, which often led to senseless bloodshed. *Udje* is, thus, a manly oral poetic performance that brings out the competitive spirit of war without its negative realities. To Urhobo men, physical war is destructive and should be avoided if at all possible. They opt instead for the artistic war that elicits the poetic and performance talents they have to entertain themselves.

Udje is a satiric genre and the entire performance is meant to generate laughter. Laughter is expected from the abuse of a rival or opponent in a poetic narrative that is meant to be humorous, sarcastic and highly metaphorical. However, there must be an element of provocation to make laughter or the poetic assault of *udje* justifiable to the audience and the tutelary gods, especially Uhaghwa, for whom the songs are composed and performed.

A man should not attack somebody else without being provoked. Masculinity entails holding back one's endowed strength until provoked to fight back; once incited, one is bound to retaliate. Masculinity, as manifested in *udje* performance and Urhobo culture, has to do with character and attitude, the ability to defend oneself or one's side in a battle for honour, especially when piqued by a rival.

Many *udje* songs show the element of provocation before a satirical onslaught is unleashed against one's rival. One of the fiercest rivalries in *udje* is between the neighbouring villages of Iwhrekan (whose *obo-ile* is Oloya) and Edjophe (whose *obo-ile* is Memerume). Oloya's famous song 'Gbogidi' is based on a provocation by the Edjophe people and is his justification, on Iwhrekan's behalf, for unleashing the scathing attack on Gbogidi, a great performer from Edjophe:

> Gbogidi it was who first smeared me with the image of poverty.
> Unless there are performers, there will be no spectators.
> The idiot acted in ignorance.
> You saw a lion asleep and tampered with its tail.
> Gbogidi, we have brought the war to you.

Calling Gbogidi 'the monarch of paupers,' Oloya goes on to paint a devastating image of a wretch. Often tinged with rivalry, the provocation involves earlier songs and the assertion of self-pride as shown in the epic duel between Iwhrekan's Oloya and Edjophe's Memerume, singing against each other. Memerume begins one of his songs with 'Oloya talks ill of me behind me.'[5] In a similar vein, Oloya begins another song with: 'Memerume, the time has come. / Never at any time / will a goat's challenge worry the leopard.[6]

The Ekrejegbe quarter of Orhuwhorun in its song says: 'Ughere ward it is who brought about / this warfare; spectators take note.'[7] Once one is attacked, one is honour bound to retaliate. In 'Eshamredje,' 'Eshamredje boasted around / that he would destroy me with songs.'; hence the attack on him.[8] 'Shame on Ekrabe' also cites provocation before attacking the rival or opponent:

> A goat has asked a leopard for a duel;
> and as the world waits for the great spectacle,
> the goat prays that it leave the scene alive.
> Boasting accompanies heavy drinking;
> and bad jokes are fraught with danger.[9]

The poet-performer is the 'leopard' challenged by a 'goat' to a duel that the goat is bound to lose. Once there is provocation, there are no boundaries in the response and counterattack. The rival party can base its song on so much falsehood that that itself becomes a provocation to be responded to.

The disabled are exempt from being satirised, unless seen as assisting others in the 'battle.' Wives of poets and performers are constant subjects of songs, because in Urhobo society a man is expected to protect the honour of his wife when assaulted. It is the height of unmanliness for one to ignore anybody saying negative things about his wife. Thus, picking on a person's wife becomes an easy way of insulting and provoking the person.

Sometimes blood affinity to a great poet or performer makes one, irrespective of circumstances, the subject of acerbic songs. Okpoto, Okitiakpe's brother, is represented as a violent sex maniac from whom women flee. Likewise, all of Kpaeban's children, including Gbogidi, the performer, are verbally assaulted and described as the worst of the poor:

> Gbariemu and his brothers formed a team
> Poverty and Misfortune made up the other team
> A draughts game
> Come and watch, the appointed day is due
> Oloya began advising:
> *Brother, play this, play this*
> *Maybe we can avoid Poverty.*
> Diisi began advising:
> *Brother, play this, play this*
> *Perhaps we can escape from Poverty.*
> Poverty set him one trap
> Gbariemu escaped it.[10]

In the song, Gbogidi's brothers are all abused by virtue of being related to him. At the same time, the tradition establishes borderlines that should not be crossed in making fun of others. Crossing such borders results in poor taste and could generate, not only disgust and revulsion from the audience who are judges of the songs and their performance but also provoke retribution from angry gods against the transgressors. Thus there are limits to laughter. Although the Urhobo code of masculinity demands retaliation when provoked, it is unmanly to attack the innocent or the helpless.

Closely related to the concepts of provocation and retaliation is the principle of honour in Urhobo men. The concepts of honour (self-pride) and shame (disrepute) among the Urhobo people are embedded in the *udje* tradition, whether the genre of the song is satire, panegyric, dirge, or religious invocation. The songs are intended to be sufficiently devastating metaphorically to destroy the opponent or rival. An Orhuhworun song, for example, describes this objective: 'Behold the fire the gods lit in the human mouth / It does not emit smoke / Yet it causes destruction.'[11] As R. C. Elliott puts it, 'the more a person dreads shame, the more he will avoid situations which might bring him the bad name conveyed by public mockery.'[12] *Udje* involves public mockery of individuals, families, quarters, villages or towns by rival groups, as well as assertion of self-pride and honour by the singers.

Every Urhobo man wants to avoid shame. To be publicly shamed is to lose one's manliness. In an Orhuwhorun song, 'Whenever songs are to be composed,' a family expresses the shame they suffer, a condition that inevitably reduces their standing in the town:

> Farmers, who once grew enviable yams,
> now grow petty cocoyams;
> we can see the change.
> When we, the renowned Ekrabes, sang,
> everybody moved;
> but we bewitched ourselves,
> and now make Ekrejegbe singers
> taunt their seniors and betters
> in spite of themselves.[13]

Here, the Ekrabe family members bewail their plight in the song contest because 'we bewitched ourselves.' Shame, as expressed in this song, erodes masculinity in an Urhobo community in which pride and honour are manifestations of one's greatness.

Sometimes it is incumbent on the *udje* performer to mock himself rather than wait for the opposing side to do so. Thus, the principle of *iten*, masking, becomes a strategy to deflect one's weakness and avoid embarrassment. Once you have mocked yourself, others will not see the need to do so; or if they do, it will be regarded as an overkill in a tradition in which one is meant to spring fresh surprises. In the use of masking in *udje*, masculinity employs wit and self-mockery to forestall insults from others. This means that no human being is perfect or flawless, but it is a mark of manliness to laugh at one's self.

A good example of masking is Memerume's 'Amonomeyararia,' a song seemingly directed at a woman in the rival Iwhrekan village, but generally interpreted as relating to the Edjophe poet-performer himself. A talented and renowned poet and performer, handsome and dignified, Memerume had many wives and concubines but no child. Because he knew rivals would use this deficiency in a song about him, he first sang about barrenness as a pre-emptive gesture. Amonomeyararia, the subject of the song, conjures the real person, Onomeyararia, in one's mind. Although there was an Onomeyararia in Iwhrekan at the time, there was no Amonomeyararia. The poet apparently used the fictional name that easily evokes an actual person as a cover to sing about his own barrenness and the misfortune of not having children. In Urhobo, not having a child is seen as a serious masculine deficiency; hence Memerume chose self-ridicule rather than give rivals the opportunity to mock him. The courage to pre-empt deprecating is one of the ways of deploying masculinity in Urhobo society.

Chief Dozen Ogbariemu, a practitioner of *udje* in his young days and 89 years old in 2008 when I interviewed him, describes *udje* as songs used to bury heroes, a fact that explains the dirge aspect of many of the songs. What is significant here is the deployment of masculinity in such an egotistical manner by the poet-composer or the cantor-chief performer to create a hero of himself at the expense of his rivals. Many Urhobo men have Ivwri icons in their homes. Ivwri is the god of toughness and revenge and is fabled to put psychological and physical pressure on enemies to surrender. Chief Ogbariemu has an Ivwri statuette in his bedroom and he pours libation on it regularly. It is thus the practise of many Urhobo men, especially those who face competition, to invoke the Ivwri spirit. Ivwri is the divine personification of masculinity in Urhobo culture and *udje* exponents or practitioners often invoke the spirit to defeat their rivals.

In *udje*, the principals indulge in glorification of virility by self-projection at the expense of rivals. Okitiakpe of Ekakpamre, who died in 1979, was one of the best known *udje* poets and performers.[14] He practised *udje* for decades and was a pain to his rivals who saw no other way to insult him than to sing about his ugliness. In the famous song, 'Me vwen Odjelabo' (I am the Invincible Wrestler), Okitiakpe turns his so-called age and ugliness against his rivals:

> Uto is all bush.
> Its people got wind of my grey hair
> and are gleeful.
> Since they are gloating around,
> have the old been driven from town?
> The talk about my so-called age
> Is more publicised than the first head tax.
> The fuss is unbelievable:
> it is the head that grows grey hair;
> it is not a dress I choose to put on.
> This year we will see.
> Gin may be tasty,
> but palm wine makes it so . . .
> I am Odjelabo, the invincible wrestler.
> Like Uvwiama, I am ageless.
> Even when life is hard for a king,
> he still has coral beads on his neck.
> When it comes to performing *udje*,
> I am the peerless star;

First, like Eni among the gods.
Uto folks call me an old man;
but do they see age in a flying bird?[15]

To counter his rivals' jibe at his age, Okitiakpe sings of his experience as a poet-performer in the light of the ageless town of Uvwiama, long settled before Udu and Ughievwen towns sprang up and yet still 'ageless.' He is the king of *udje* songs, who remains rich by virtue of the expensive coral beads he wears at all times. And above all, he remains athletic despite his so-called age. The poet-performer's rhetorical question, 'Do they see age in a flying bird?' underscores his superiority over his Uto rivals.[16]

Boasting is an expressive mode of masculinity in *udje* songs and performance. Each *ororile* (poet) or *obo-ile* (performer) deploys metaphors to extol his talent and skill while insulting his rivals. In 'Osokpro,' the poet boasts: 'I, a diamond, they mistake me for silver.' In the same song, the poet says: 'The words of my song are the iroko tree / An iroko tree can never be dwarfed by others.'[17] Oloya in 'Gbogidi' boasts: 'I am governor of *udje*' to show his supremacy in composition and performance of *udje* poetry. In 'Mienka, the Prisoner' the singer says, 'Ughere's songs are a snake ever dreadful,' and goes on to praise himself as 'the fountain of songs.'[18] In an Orhuwhorun song, the poet calls himself 'the dictionary of Udunvwurhie ward,' whereas his rival, Arite, is 'the monarch of ugliness.' In 'Odaro' the poet boasts: 'I am the bitter head of *okpeyin* yam: / it's neither good when roasted / nor good too when boiled' to emphasise the masculine qualities of ruggedness and resilience in Urhobo society.[19] In 'Krekpe' Memerume says, '*erha* and the leopard look alike, / but the leopard still feeds on its meat!'[20] Here, the poet says that he is superior to his rival poet. In other words, among the poets, some are far better than others.

From the songs one can deconstruct the values and virtues that affirm masculinity and those that negate it. Praise elements are masculine, whereas insults render one unmasculine. Toughness and intimidation are masculine. Wealth is a masculine virtue. In song after song, poverty, deprivation and debt are denounced. In 'Gbejeriemu' the thoughts of a poor man are compared to a river and 'the boats that ply it / are boats of miserable tales.'[21] Inono's only dress is compared to the only child of a parent and the devastating loss. This song paints a damning picture of poverty. Inono has only one dress, which is used as both a work dress and an outing dress. When a falcon snatches it as it's drying outside after being washed, the poor man, naked, runs after the bird, pleading for his only cloth to be returned to him. In another song, a poor man is not allowed to talk; he only sits at meetings and listens to what the rich people say. Oloya says, 'Gbogidi is an interest on a loan / An interest makes a loan longer forever / It consumes one's entire earnings.'[22] In the same song 'The pauper's thoughts are like a spider / Ever unsure whether to move forward or backwards.'

Udje songs condemn all forms of excess, including rigidity, being over-sexed, miserliness, theft and other traits that the Urhobo society abhor.

Often the content of the songs speak to the influence of masculinity in the relationships between men and their wives or concubines. It is expected that a man marries into a good family to maintain his prestige, honour and dignity. Okitiakpe of Ekakpamre, the renowned poet-performer, praises his wife's street, Ekenewhare, as 'Oboye k'Ingla' (Her street is England). To the Urhobo, England is a beautiful place. By saying that his wife comes from a place as beautiful as England, the poet is enhancing his prestige. It is manly for a performer to praise his wife's family home, affirming his faith in her. Likewise, a man's wife is expected to be clean and neat at all times and properly dressed to make the husband proud. On the contrary, a dirty woman brings shame to her spouse and erodes his masculinity. For instance, Oloya's filthy wife, Revukperi, is described thus:

> The lump of filth on Revukperi's back juts out like a hillock
> Like the charge office building
> Where people obtain summons in Warri
> Witness her pulp-tissued belly like that of Ahwin
> With doughy muscles like a decayed *aligun* fish
> She trudges back and forth like a huge worm
> With an undulating back like Ilaje landscape . . .
> With greasy hair like wrappings of chestnut
> Oloya's filthy wife stinks
> Like the beast called donkey common at Burutu port.[23]

The woman is a specimen of ugliness. Her skin is rough, she's fat and she doesn't wear make-up. She also stinks. Oloya is a celebrated poet-performer who brags about his artistic skill. He also represents his quarter of town in the 'battle of songs.' Such a distinguished man is expected to have a befitting wife, but in this case he does not. His filthy wife thus diminishes his stature in a society which places importance on marrying a 'good' woman. Masculinity must possess social propriety, which involves the good conduct and neatness of a man's wife. In other songs, a man is judged by his wife's conduct or actions. Okpoto, who was brother to a great performer and was himself a performer, had a wife who was known to be a bad cook. The fact that Okpoto's wife could not prepare good food reflected badly on her husband.

Sex is meant for married or adult men in Urhobo. Because traditionally men are allowed to have many wives, sex is often a tool of domination. A man who cannot marry is ridiculed and so the number of wives a man has enhances his masculinity. This is even more apparent as marrying multiple wives is connected to wealth. Only the rich can afford to have many wives and concubines and the poor remain unmarried or married to just one wife. In one of the songs, Ubiogba remains a bachelor for too long and becomes an embarrassment to himself and his family. In Urhobo society, men are expected to marry at about the age of twenty-five years and those who remain unmarried after that time are looked down upon. It was after Ubiogba's marriage that he could sing 'I am now free of insults.'[24] In another case of being single for too long, Majotan, an *obo-ile* (poet/composer) remained a bachelor into his late forties, which was unusual for a healthy Urhobo man. He laments the misfortune of remaining single and doing what his wife should do for him:

> It's time again
> for singers and dancers to meet
> and go to the lead singer's.
> Should they get there
> and find the leader alone by the fire
> preparing his own meal,
> wouldn't you be shamed?
> Uhaghwa, give thought to my plight.[25]

In many songs, wifeless adults are ridiculed and parents keep their young daughters from them to prevent assaults on them.

Impotence is a serious negation of masculinity in *udje* songs. Memerume's 'Kpojiyovwi' is about a man who loses his potency and his wife revolts by leaving him. The greater tragedy in Urhobo culture is that 'The particles that fall from the wind / get lost in the current / and the name is forgotten.'[26] By being impotent, Kpojiyovwi will not have children to perpetuate his family name.

Self-restraint, especially as it affects married men, is also an expression of masculinity. For example, a night watchman who returns from work in the morning and makes love with his wife is ridiculed for being unmanly. In Urhobo culture, adults are supposed to make love only at night and in the privacy of their bedrooms. However, this guard who works during the night has no other time to sleep with his wife. Still, he is portrayed in the song as lacking self-control because he violates the ethics of mating in Urhobo.

There is another example in a song in which a woman comes from the cassava farm in the late afternoon and the man is so aroused that he tries to have sex with her. She protests that she is sweating and needs to bathe, but the man drags her to bed and makes love to her. The man is supposed to be disciplined enough to wait for his wife to be ready before making love. In addition to his indiscipline and impropriety, the man is guilty of coercion. The sex act between husband and wife should be mutual, not coerced by the male. In the *udje* tradition, masculinity demands discipline, restraint and patience to ensure the continuity of social norms that promote harmony.

Udje performance is physically expressive of masculinity. *Udje* performers are expected to be handsome and perform with bare chests. Memerume, perhaps the greatest *udje* performer, was a tall man with athletic ability. A celebrated embodiment of masculinity, he exuded grace and dignity. There are extant reports of women rushing to embrace him before and after his performance. Not surprisingly, he had several wives and many concubines. Oloya, his main rival and perhaps the greatest *udje* poet, was also very graceful and dignified. The Urhobo people have at various times in their history chosen men with a magnetic personality to be their kings. Kingship in Urhobo embodies masculinity at its most heightened form; hence handsomeness, gracefulness and a dignified personality are major factors in occupying the throne.

As a window into Urhobo socio-cultural life, *udje* performance reveals that not all men possess masculinity. Debtors, wretches, cowards, layabouts and others that fall below the Urhobo measurement for success may be men but lack masculinity. Despite the patriarchal nature of the society, every man is not masculine. Individual male attitudes, response to life, conduct and deeds are used to judge masculinity. Women are not expected to possess these masculine qualities and those who do are not seen in a positive light. There are *udje* songs in which women who assert themselves or possess strong personalities are condemned. Women are supposed to be feminine, unlike men, who are expected to be masculine. Men who lack masculinity are therefore seen as effeminate and falling short of their roles as men.

Udje masculinity dramatises toughness, honour, propriety, the capacity for revenge or retaliation and the projection of self-pride, all of which are the values the community has embraced for harmonious living. Masculinity demands cleanliness, restraint, patience and the discipline of a partner. A man should not be self-centred but should be generous to others, especially the less fortunate in society. Furthermore, a man should not abuse his freedom and rights. Above all, in the Urhobo communal society, the code for masculinity involves distinguishing oneself in established positive terms.

6. Masculinity on Trial: Gender Anxiety in African Song Performances

Helen Nabasuta Mugambi

Bikongoolo tebitta nnume
(Unseen contempt and mockery do not kill a billy goat)
Traditional proverb[1]

Can a man, deceived and flouted by his family, impose himself on others? Can a man whose wife does not do her job well honestly demand a fair reward for his labour? Aggression and condescension in a woman arouse contempt and hatred for her husband. If she is gracious, even without appealing to any ideology, she can summon support for any action. In a word, a man's success depends on feminine support.

Mariama Bâ, *So Long a Letter*[2]

The above epigraphs point to a precariously constructed form of masculinity, one that is contingent upon female action. The Luganda proverb suggests that if a man suspects that his wife holds him in contempt (*kukongoola*) he will not mind so long as she keeps it to herself. The second quotation extends that logic, stating that a wife's perceived public indiscretions tarnish the husband's name and place his status or success—and by implication, his masculinity—in jeopardy. Although they belong to different genres and come from opposite ends of the continent, these statements speak to the interconnectedness of the genders and encapsulate the anxiety that characterises expressions of male identity embodied in the two *kadongokamu* song performances, *Nakakaawa* and *Kayanda*, analysed in this chapter. But first, it is important that I describe *kadongokamu* in order to establish its critical role in the formation and transmission of masculine identities at the ethnic and national levels in Uganda.

Kadongokamu, a genre of Ugandan popular song, originated as a solo narrative sung performance accompanied by a single guitar, hence the rather derogatory nomenclature *kadongokamu*, meaning 'solitary miserable little guitar.' Traditional multi-instrument music performers, from whom the *kadongokamu* pioneers adopted the drum-based rhythms and narrative lyrics, regarded performances on a solo guitar as an impoverished genre. However, the flexibility—in composition and performance—of *kadongokamu* resulted in the singular mobility and adaptability of the genre, enabling its speedy growth in rural and urban environments.

Despite the persistence of the nomenclature, this music form has evolved into one of the most popular multi-instrument performance genres and functions as a central vehicle for disseminating gender and socio-political histories in contemporary Uganda. Complex compositions can be labelled as minimusicals or dramatic comedies. In urban and semi-rural locations, these are frequently staged in theatres as operattas in which song and dramatic scenes are interwoven. Their captivating comedic power makes them potent stage entertainment. But even when disseminated through radio or audio cassettes, the rhetoric is striking. One needs only board public transportation, for instance, to experience a mobile 'classroom-cum-theatre' as newly created songs fill the airwaves and a receptive audience searches for a message of individual or social significance. Carrying many varied themes beyond those discussed here, the performances are often set against expressed or implied proverbs. Melodrama is usually peppered with satire, parody and metaphor to create an ingenious genre that defies simple categorisation. Nevertheless, structurally, *kadongokamu* can be classified into two broad categories: songs that, like folktales, narrate stories with single or multiple plots and those characterised by complex plots structured as theatrical mini-dramas.[3] *Nakakaawa* and *Kayanda*, belong to this latter category.[4]

With the proliferation of frequency modulation (FM) radio stations, *kadongokamu*, besides today's popular dance music of the younger generation, remains one of the most important genres broadcast on the country's airwaves. In the 1970s and 1980s, in particular, the radio broadcasting medium was supplemented by the boom in what Peter Manuel, in his study of technologised popular music in India, has termed the 'cassette culture,' a phenomenon that allowed access to popular music through cheaply produced audio cassettes.[5] I must point out though that most mass distributed songs, including those of the *kadongokamu* genres have a very short lifespan as audiences are always hungry for new compositions. Taking their place among the oldies, the subject songs of this discussion retain their place as archetypal embodiments of the dynamic nature of masculinities during Uganda's turbulent political times. Furthermore, a cursory look at this nation's political history sheds light on the troubled male identities that characterize these songs.

An East African country created by the British (who forced an assortment of ethnic groups on the western shores of Lake Victoria into one nation), Uganda has been plagued by all sorts of identity crises since its establishment. The names commonly used to refer to 'Uganda' (the nation), 'Baganda,' (the ethnic group), 'Luganda' (the language) and 'Kiganda' (the things belonging to Baganda) are indicative of the kinds of problems encountered in discussing Baganda's interconnected ethnic and national identities. Uganda is derived from the largest ethnic group, the Baganda, in whose region and language (Luganda) the *kadongokamu* dramas are performed. Nevertheless, the country is made up of more than thirty indigenous ethnic groups and a large immigrant community, especially from Rwanda and Burundi. The British colonialists, who forced these disparate groups into a 'protectorate' which they ruled between 1890s and 1962, allied themselves with the Baganda and used them to govern the other ethnic groups during most of the colonial occupation. This was largely because the Baganda already had a well-organised and strongly centralised society, built around their king (*Kabaka*). Thus, the contemporary Uganda nation evolved around the nucleus of the Baganda community, hence the challenge of discussing creative works operating simultaneously astride ethnic and national identies. The capital city and the central government were located in the Buganda region. The Luganda language in which *kadongokamu* songs are composed is widely understood across the nation today because it was instituted during the colonial era as the medium of instruction in schools and churches. Taking advantage of their colonial status, the Baganda developed a powerful social identity, building a prosperous agricultural economy, dependent partly on hired labour from other ethnic groups and migrants. But Baganda supremacy and the accompanying force of masculinity, rooted in the *Kabaka*, became unhinged and increasingly untenable as the country moved towards independence in the early 1960s.

Buganda is a patriarchal society in which masculinity is held in the highest esteem. In the traditional Kiganda body politic, the *Kabaka* (king) was the epitome of masculinity. All power was derived from him the 'arch-man' or 'super-masculine one' (*Ssaabasajja*), whom all Baganda, men and women, refered to as 'husband' (*Bbaffe*). The men not only knelt before the *Kabaka*, like women knelt before them, but they were required to prostrate themselves. In feudal times, hierarchical gender relations seemed to work conveniently, if not satisfactorily, because they were connected to other factors sanctioned by myth and history. However, at the dawn of the new nation, the kingdom found itself on unstable ground and male dominance was seriously threatened. The *Kabaka* was exiled by the British in 1955; in 1966 he was driven out of his palace and fled for his life under the rule of Milton Obote, the then head of state of the new multi-ethnic nation. Obote's subsequent abolition of all the other kingdoms in Uganda intensified the sense of slipping feudal identities. These political developments not only created political insecurity for the Baganda, but also severely challenged the group's ideals of masculinity. With their feudal structures in tatters, the Baganda found themselves without a point of reference and retained only declining influence in the emerging multi-ethnic community. Political strife ensued in the 1970s and 1980s as other ethnic groups struggled to claim a larger share in the emerging nation, culminating in a bitter civil war that became the backdrop for profound social, cultural and political upheaval.

When the civil war ended in the late 1980s, the survivors found themselves desperately searching for new orientations, not only in politics but in gender relations. At this time, *kadongokamu* performances took centre-stage in re-telling the troubled ethnic and national histories that reflected the civil unrest of the times. In the process, the songs unveiled elements of distressed and ambivalent masculine identities. After the guerrilla war of the late 1980s, for example, nationals who had been scattered to different parts of the world, or those that suffered internal displacement within Uganda, returned to their homes. In many instances, traumatised families would gather for hours to exchange their experiences of the war. Such storytelling sessions were often punctuated by radio broadcasts or cassette-generated songs narrating horrifying war experiences and the drastic changes in the nation. More specifically, the songs sometimes commented on the emasculating impact of the brutal military rule which rendered men increasingly incapable of protecting their families. Song artists thus played an important role as the nation's historians as well as 'oratherapists' who employed humour to help the nation cope with individual and national trauma.

This postwar environment of dismantled gender structures increasingly inspired a kind of tragi-comic meditation on the challenges to masculine power. Playing at restoring gender balance, many songs strategically lauded male prowess while simultaneously exalting women's bravery in the guerrilla war. Michael Kimmel identifies the ability to 'theorise masculinity as a system of power relations *among men* as well as a system of power relations *between women and men* as characterizing new directions in gender discourse.[6] Against the backdrop of public declarations of women's heroism, *Nakakaawa* and *Kayanda*, in particular, betray an overwhelming anxiety about relations of power among men and textualise male/female relations as envisioned by Kimmel.

Structured like operattas, as mentioned above, with sequences or movements that may be performed individually, the two performances also reveal a power progression with the relatively self-assured masculinity in the first song, *Nakakaawa*, becoming gradually challenged until it disintegrates into the uncertainty and radicalism of *Kayanda*. Ssepiria in the first performance enacts the eventual triumph of male power while Kayanda, the featured servant in the second performance, exemplifies the 'contradictory locations experienced by men not priviledged by class, race, ethnicity...(creating) a world of contradictory filaments of power and privilege.[7] It is instructive that masculine power in *Kayanda* is tested, not only through female individual and group revolt, but also through the rise of the marginal man, the migrant worker whose ethnicity and status as a servant lie outside the privileged majority. Complexity in these perfomances is achieved through staging the performances as actual 'court trials' thus putting the gendered identities of men of class, ethnic privilege and power on both real and symbolic trial. Furthermore, within this textual landscape, masculine identities are precariously cast against ambivalent and shifting female identity constructs.

The central argument in this analysis is that when masculine identity is predicated on ambivalently constructed femininity, the resulting masculinity is riddled with anxiety. Furthermore, such masculinity is always already under threat from women's proclivity and ability to challenge oppressive masculinities and opt for alternative forms more conducive to female survival. In present-day Ugandan society, notions of manhood undergirded by anxiety of the feminine and the exclusion of gender complementality are fated to crumble and collapse. Similarly, masculinities predicated on controlling men considered effeminate or of lower class exist under constant fear of subversion. They cannot withstand the rapid changes taking place as shifting socio-political national boundaries defy the constraints of ethnic traditions within Buganda's indigenous patriarchal hegemony. The two performances that I examine here bear out these assertions. Proverbs and related indigenous discourses which help to decode the songs' embedded notions of masculinity provide contexts as well as theoretical grounding for this discussion.

Although a considerable number of Luganda proverbs highlight harmonious relationships between men and women, a good number, such as those employed in this discussion, are characterised by antagonism and dissonance. I present a cluster from this latter category as a means of providing an interpretive framework and capturing the diverse sentiments interspersed in the songs' account of anxious masculinity. A single proverb could easily capture the general spirit of this discussion. However, the polyvocality of the selected cluster provides deeper insights into the complex cultural base from which the explored male apprehensions emanate.[8]

In line with the opening proverb which implies that a man is hurt only if a woman's contempt for him is made public, the crisis in both performances is triggered when insubordinate wives publicly expose their husbands' shortcomings. Such betrayal is also set against the cultural construct summed up in the saying *Ebyomunju tebitottolwa* (Domestic matters are not for public consumption). Proverbs such as *Omukazi mmese: ne bw'ekulira mu nnyumba ekubba* (A woman is a rat: even the one raised in your house will steal from you) betray the anxiety produced by an endemic male distrust of women. Betrayal always seems to be anticipated and engenders the antagonism encapsulated in proverbs such as *Omukazi birenge bya ddiba: bw'otobikunya tebigonda* (A woman is rough-hide ends: they do not soften unless you squeeze them hard), which points to a masculinity contingent on a man's ability to control the woman. Such references to the assumption that women are insubordinate unless they are treated harshly or ruled with a heavy hand tends to keep a man ready to talk or beat the wife into submission. Furthermore, *Omukazi ngabo: gy'otonnakwatamu gy'otenda okwanguwa* (A woman is a shield: it is the one you are not carrying that is presumed to be light) characterises women as unpredictable while hinting at the man's constant search for feminine submission. The 'shield' reference connotates the male-female relationship as a war of the sexes.

The performances hint at the notion that all women are liars. Mukaabya's wife unabashedly denies and then confesses to her affair with the servant. This notion figures in *Omukazi talema kulimba: ajja enjuba ewanze, nti 'nkedde bukeezi'* (A woman never fails to lie: arriving late in the morning she says, 'I came at the break of day'). Again, the masculine assumption that women are a cause of discord among men is indicated in: *Omulungi atava ku kyalo: aleka emisango* (The beauty that lingers too long in a village: causes disputes among the inhabitants). The *mulungi* (beautiful one) in all these sayings is a synonym for woman, an admission of the irresistible attractiveness of woman.

However, even when a woman looks perfect, expectation of imperfection pervades the mind, again signalling persistent suspicion: *Omulungi tabulako kamogo: bw'atabba awunya akamwa* (No beauty is without a defect: if it is not being a thief, it is foul breath). Finally, the woman as an 'object' of contention among men, however powerful they might be, is represented by this proverb: *Omulungi ng'oma mpunde: emala abagabe* (A beautiful woman is a decorated drum: it finishes off the rulers). *Abagabe* can be commanders or kings (*Runyankole*), thus connecting the winning or losing of a woman with the attainment or loss of power. This is what befalls the protagonist of *Kayanda* when he is deserted by his wife in the second song under discussion. It also characterises Ssepiria's desperation in response to his wife's desertion.

The portion of the *Nakakaawa* series discussed here is made up of four movements through which we can trace the husband's sometimes-veiled struggle to hold on to a beleaguered masculinity put on trial by a wayward wife who publicly humiliates him. The main characters are the husband, Ssepiria and the two wives, Kaddulubaale and the titular heroine, Nakakaawa. Many themes run through this complex performance but I will limit the summary to those structured around a masculinity plot. The initial movement contains an affirmation of Ssepiria's masculine supremacy. It opens with a jubilant Ssepiria (the hero) announcing his intentions to take a second wife (Nakakaawa) despite the protestations of Kaddulubaale, his first wife of fourteen years. After the wedding festivities, the second movement dramatises the husband's struggle to assert his power in the face of his rebellious new wife who adamantly refuses to live by the accepted norms of family decorum. In the third movement, matters escalate forcing the self-proclaimed indomitable male to summon his relatives and elders to mediate the disintegrating marital situation.

Instead of humbly acknowledging her misdeeds, Nakakaawa publicly humiliates the husband declaring him impotent before the assembled community. This declaration is the ultimate act of contempt a woman could commit against a husband. Thus Nakakaawa boldly defies masculine authority and amid jeers from the assembled mediators, victoriously storms out of the marriage. At this juncture, a voice from the assembled mediators declares: 'Nakakaawa, you are a man.' This gender destabilising moment is followed by the fourth movement, in which masculine power appears to be rescued. Ssepiria has secretly coaxed Nakakaawa back into the marriage. The movements included here culminate in an epilogue that reinstates Ssepiria's authority over his wives and celebrate his selection as a leader at the national level. (Space constraints, prevent inclusion of the subsequent movement). If control of a wife is a prerequisite to success within the nation, then the epigraph from Mariama Bâ's novel is validated: a man's attainment of public stature is contingent on his ability to keep his wife in check. Nevertheless, by cleverly disguising a masculinity that is losing its footing, the *Nakakaawa* saga enables a reading that identifies distinct stages in the validation of a masculine edifice.

Nakakaawa opens with Ssepiria, the performance's phallocentric figure, singing a boisterous oration in which he declares that his masculinity is natural, biological and hereditary. He casts himself as the indomitable bachelor for whom the feminine exists only to affirm an indisputable masculine power. Martial Frindethie explores a parallel phenomenon in the Francophone literary tradition and states that the continuous compulsion among postcolonial writers and critics to find inspiration in an ancient African order of discourse is aimed at writing out women's agency.[9] Ssepiria thus resorts to his geneology as he parades his successful courtship of the teenager Nakakaawa, a conquest that symbolises his virility. With great pride in his ripe age, the sixty-year-old Ssepiria boasts:

> The blessings of my paternal grandfather were awesome
> Those blessings are my inheritance
> Young women flock to me for the picking
> Well into my sixties, my charisma is unabated
> Picking Kaddulubale [his first wife] out of the numerous eligible girls
> Posed great challenges in selection
> So it is, with Nakakaawa, [the bride he is about to marry]
> My inherited blessings are my invaluable asset
> Here I am arriving at Nakakaawa's home...

A belief in an indelible masculinity has the potential to guarantee a secure male identity. Hence, Ssepiria strategically recounts his manly characteristics as inherited and embedded in his DNA!

The claim to this biologically constructed maleness, a central feature of conventional masculinity, sets the scene for the ideology of dominance that characterises Ssepiria's interactions with his wives. The proverb describing woman as 'hard hide-ends that do not become supple unless squeezed hard' is particularly pertinent here. The performance dramatises Ssepiria's triumph over the first wife. He shrewdly and resolutely defies her protestations as he cajoles her into accepting a co-wife. Ssepiria's request for Kaddulubale's permission to marry Nakakaawa is an empty gesture—he has already made the wedding preparations and is about to set out on the journey to bring the new bride home. Furthermore, embedded in Kaddulubale's objections is the revelation that this scenario has been played out many times previously and that her husband is once again imposing his will over her futile protests. It is significant, however, that Kaddulubaale does protest against Ssepiria's excesses:

> What are you looking for that you never had?
> It has been many years since you brought me here
> You keep heaping woman after woman upon me
> It is they who have led to my becoming so frail . . .
> You use the money raised from my farm work
> To collect women to dump on to me like litter
> No, sir, I am tired of this overcrowding
> I am tired, sir, of the patches you slap upon me
> I am tired, sir, of your endless wife additions on to me.

Kaddulubaale's remonstration indicates that even the supposedly subservient traditional woman is not always as compliant or acquiescent as the guardians of masculinity would like to believe. Her outspokenness forces Ssepiria to at least offer an explanation—or an excuse—for his intentions. Most probably the pleas have triggered in him a sense of insecurity even though his plans to bring the second wife are not thwarted.

In subsequent actions, the logic of the performance makes it clear that masculinity triumphs only after it has successfully overcome obstacles. Hence the honeymoon with Nakakaawa is short-lived. To restore indomitable male power, Ssepiria must re-assert his power by taming the insubordinate younger wife. The first confrontation takes place when Nakakaawa publicly shows contempt for her husband. She rudely responds to his call to discuss her disruptive behaviour. Instead of the customary polite response, *wangi ssebo* (yes sir) expected of a wife, Nakakaawa blurts out a subversive *yaaaa*, to the shock of her husband and co-wife. Such a public display of insolence knocks masculinity off-balance because as the opening proverb states, it is only concealed contempt that leaves a husband's image unscathed. Unfortunately for Ssepiria, even if Nakakaawa had responded with the expected etiquette, he would still have been in no position to gauge her submission. A contrasting proverb—*Okuyitaba wangi si bufuge* (Responding with grace is no proof of subservience)—complicates Ssepiria's position.

A wife's defiance against a powerful husband is symptomatic, not only of her unwillingness to accept a subservient position within the family but it also symbolises her potential to erode the community's patriarchal power. Thus the devastating impact of Nakakaawa's insubordination on Ssepiria's public image has far-reaching implications beyond wounding his ego. Even Kaddulubaale who is shocked at her co-wife's insolence tries to shield her husband from public disgrace. She comforts him: 'No, that insolent response comes not from Nakakaawa, but from one of the children.' The mortified Ssepiria replies, 'No, I know Nakakaawa's voice, that is indeed her [defiant] voice.' Such lingering trepidation over the challenges of real or perceived female subversion hovers over most of this performance. As mentioned ealier, the man's unwavering persistence in defining himself through power over the female gender amplifies his nervous tension.

Ssepiria's struggle to recover his tarnished image intensifies. At all cost, he must bring the errant young wife back into an acquiescent position. Before any such restoration can occur however, the fire of the wayward woman's words must try his much-vaunted masculinity. Standing before the summoned mediation elders, Nakakaawa invalidates the core attributes of Ssepiria's proclaimed hereditary dominion. She, for instance, mocks his assertions that the power of his magnetism belies his age. In a long litany of disparaging declarations, she sings of his imperfections. She sings of how only blindness drove her into marrying a decrepit old man who is in fact, impotent. With this decisively humiliating insult, Nakakaawa storms out of the marriage apparently to join Tony, her former young lover. As the proverb goes, it takes an acquaintance to free one from 'widowhood.'

However, the performance must still insist on male triumph. Nakakaawa's victory over male dominance must be short-lived and more importantly, it must appear superficial. Consequently in the episode that follows, Ssepiria has inexplicably lured the wayward wife back into the marriage. Once Nakakaawa realises that she cannot escape the force of Ssepiria's masculine dominance or rescue herself with her own feminine ideals, she no longer protests her subjugated position and ceases to subvert masculine power. Her return restores Ssepiria's idealised polygamous status and with the two women under control, he can regain his stature in the community.

Again the bliss is short-lived. Ssepria feels overcome by the challenge to keep the wives under submission. Although one proverb denigrates monogamy, stating that a monogamous husband is only slightly better off than a bachelor, its wisdom is contradicted by Ssepiria's proclamation subsequent to Nakakaawa's return. Addressing the men in the audience, he sings:

My fellow men,
This is my discovery
Marrying more than one wife
Places you in a perilous position
It banishes tranquillity from your life

Once again, the stability of masculine power is not guaranteed as embedded subtexts in this story further indicate. The drama of naming, for example, which is fairly common in most African narratives, functions as a pre-existing threat to an otherwise comfortably celebrated masculinity and precludes easy conclusions about a masculine triumph in the *Nakakaawa* performance. 'Ssepiria' is an adaptation of 'Cyprian,' a Western Christian name. 'Kaddulubaale' is the traditional title of the first wife in a polygamous family in which the second and third wives would be named 'Kabejja' and 'Nassaza.' 'Kaddulubaale' (little slave girl of the ancestral spirits) is of dubious honourific value. Although it has been claimed that the name is derived from the first wife's important role in worship rituals at ancestral shrines, the 'slave' aspect of the designation cannot be ignored. 'Nakakaawa' (which is coincidentally the real name of the performer) is derived from the name list of the *kkobe* (*bud-yam*) lineage. Its literal meaning is 'the sour little one.' Thus, in this *ménage-à-trois* we have a handful of implications played out in the performance. The contradictions inherent in the protagonist Ssepiria, a 'Christian' who is not averse to polygamy and a 'Westernised' man who would like to maintain a traditional family, complete with little slave girls for the ancestors, point to his internally flawed individual identity, as well as to his ambivalent and untenable position in an increasingly Westernised nation.

Male ambivalence about women's ascribed spiritual power furthers apprehension about the destabilising potential of the female. During the period after Nakakaawa storms out of the marriage, for instance, Ssepiria claims that her desertion has tampered with the very laws of nature. In a long exposition to the community, he sings of how 'the community is besieged by strange and inexplicable occurrences—cocks crow at midnight, people are haunted by ominous dreams and destructive hailstones have replaced normal rain.' The most cogent implication of these observations is that if masculinity is natural, its violation must lead to unnatural occurrences.

Furthermore, the power of the performance is amplified in its demonstration that female rebellion against patriarchal control effectively becomes a threat to the existence of the entire community. Ssepiria declares that his livelihood, indeed the entire community's well-being is in peril. He tellingly sums up Nakakaawa's desertion in a single, apprehensive declaration: 'We are on the brink of extinction.' Such an alarming declaration inadvertently ascribes an invincible power to the female—power that goes beyond destabilising individual masculinity. I discuss this issue extensively in the aforementioned feminist analysis of this performance in the 1994 issue of *Research in African Literatures.* However, the anxious Ssepiria is no longer a lone victim as he has strategically transformed his personal trial into a community challenge. If he fails, the community fails.

As Mariama Bâ's character Ramatoulaye states in *So Long a Letter,* a man derided by his wife cannot retain his status in the public arena. Because Nakakaawa has publicly dethroned Ssepiria's phallocentrism, she must subsequently function as the tool for its reinstatement. Furthermore, she must return—if the laws of nature are to stabilise. However, how can the man control this female power on which his identity is pegged when women appear to have control over the supernatural laws that govern nature and by implication, govern men? Yuliyana, Ssepiria's sister, represents an instance of this dreaded power as she is credited with the ability to control rain, as demonstrated in Ssepiria's compliments:

> Yuliyana struggled to prevent the rain
> Without her intervention
> Rain would have drenched the wedding guests.
> To neutralize that power, another character,

Koloneli (Cornelius), recasts Yuliana's powers:

> Ssepiria, your sister is a potent witch
> She cast a spell over my lawn
> It withered instantly

This comic rendering of the woman's presumed power notwithstanding, the performance's attempt to nullify any possible infiltration into the patriarchal monopoly on power is obvious. Despite this disguised fear, another threat of feminine power appears to have been nullified and masculinity can continue in its pursuit of stable supremacy. *Nakakaawa* so far details the course by which conventional masculinity is formulated, propagated, put on trial and reinstated, however tenuously, within ethnically constructed gender constructs.

The epilogue dramatises how the ethnic man must devise new strategies to reinvent himself if he is to survive on the national stage, where concepts of hereditary masculinities are insignificant within a multi-ethnic postcolonial milieu.The astute Ssepiria is able to retain his biologically constructed ethnic attributes while striving for the socially constructed achievements of the postcolonial world. In another characteristic boast, which parallels his claim of inherited masculinity, he lays claim to new attributes he has constructed as prerequisites for leadership in the new nation. These include proficiency in the English language and the possession of Western symbols of affluence. However, should the new postcolonial male retain the anxiety of the feminine from the precolonial times, his survival will remain precarious particularly because of the rapid changes in women's participation in the military and in national governance.

In Buganda's pre-colonial military history, 'femaleness' symbolised cowardice and weakness, as the postwar rituals, documented by ethnographer John Roscoe, indicate:

> The men who were made prisoners but were to be spared were also taken to the Prime Minister's house, where they were stripped of their war garments and dressed in bark cloths, which were fastened around them as though they were women. They were required to wait upon the others at the meal. . . . After the meal was over, the prisoners' garments were padded to look like women with child. They were placed on bedsteads and carried about the capital for the crowds to ridicule.[10]

Such gender constructions were challenged during the civil wars of the 1980s. Women's successful participation in the guerrilla war that liberated the nation (these were women from various ethnicities including Baganda) transformed them into symbols of military heroism valorised in conversations around the country and in many *kadongokamu* performances.

Moreover, the community was now multi-ethnic and national identity had replaced Baganda identity. For the Baganda, this historical factor meant that femininity could no longer symbolise masculine cowardice. The change also underscores the fact that feminity, against which masculinity appears to define itself, is itself a hodgepodge of impositions on women made in the interest of patriarchal ideology. Among the Baganda, women are socialised in the early stages of development not only to regard themselves as inferior to men but also to be totally subservient to them. The culture ensures this compliance through a barrage of injunctions, taboos and practices, even in the use of language. Girls and women are repeatedly told never to talk back to a man, never to raise their voices, never whistle, never climb trees, never squat and to always obey without questioning. The taboos include a wide range of forbidden food (mainly delicacies reserved for men) including chicken, eggs and mutton.

The self-effacing behaviour of women is encoded in the social practice that requires them to kneel when addressing men or are being spoken to by men. It is not unusual, even today, to see a dignified elderly woman sinking to her knees on the pavement of a busy city street in order to greet a male relative or acquaintance. The enjoyment of such exaggerated subservience is what Baganda men regard as the essence of their masculinity. A special term is reserved for this phenomenon: *kusajjalaata* (exercise rampant manhood) which is derived from *musajja*, the word for man. The performances embody this notion. On the surface, Baganda men, as they revel in this precariously constructed power, might not realise that the women on whose subservience they thrive might not always remain as acquiescent or cooperative as they appear. *Kayanda* dramatises this possibility. Women in Buganda today are no longer required to strictly adhere to the indigenous taboos and public demonstrations of subservience. It is no wonder that the insistence on impermeable masculinity in the first part of *Nakakaawa* gives way to a destabilised, wobbling masculinity at the mercy of female agency in the opening segment of of *Kayanda*.

The main characters in *Kayanda* are a middle-class husband (Mukaabya), his wife and their servant (Kayanda). The performance opens with traditional masculinity in crisis. It dramatises Mukaabya's agonising failure to enforce his authority over his wife. Above all, it dramatises the struggle and eventual failure to regain lost masculinity, thus subverting the concept of immutable conventional masculinity implicit in *Nakakaawa*. A distraught Mukaabya discovers that his own servant, Kayanda, a migrant worker, has usurped his masculinity when he overhears a conversation between his wife and the servant in which the latter claims the fatherhood of Mukaabya's presumed daughter, Nakiyimba. Mukaabya immediately summons the Resistance Council (RC), an arbitration body.[11] During the hearing, Mukaabya's wife initially denies any wrongdoing and instead, accuses her husband of tyrannical rule. She charges him with domestic abuse and neglect. However, when the servant is threatened with expulsion from the home, the wife publicly declares her affection for the servant and humiliates Mukaabya, accusing him of irresponsible sexual behaviour and sexual neglect. She then sings a praise song to Kayanda, extolling him as the embodiment of real manhood: a true friend, helper and compassionate companion. She implicitly admits that Kayanda, embodying a compassionate masculinity, has indeed usurped her husband's position. This is a critical moment in the performance as it signals an alternative, non-hegemonic masculinity. The servant and the wife, both expected to hold a subservient position, appear to have joined hands and overthrown hegemonic masculinity.

Within the second movement, Mukaabya's public image ends up in total ruins at the hands of his rebellious wife and his fatherhood is dealt a severe blow. The movement opens with Kayanda, as husband to the wife of his former master, returning to the RC to establish paternity of Nakiyimba. Further shattering Mukaabya's manhood, the wife publicly declares that Kayanda is not only the father of the young girl Nakiyimba, but that he is also responsible for the pregnancy she carried prior to leaving her husband's home. Unlike Ssepiria, who succeeds in regaining his status in the *Nakakaawa* performance, Mukaabya attempts but fails to regain his lost public image. Instead, an alternative masculinity triumphs. It is a masculinity based on male-female complementarity exemplified in Kayanda's relationship with Mukaabya's wife.

In both *Nakakaawa* and *Kayanda*, the crisis in male identity is triggered when the women bring their defiance and contempt (*bikongoolo*) for their husbands into the public arena. Mukaabya's public humiliation becomes excruciating when his wife divulges the true paternity of her daughter before the assembled arbitration court and blames their lack of progeny on Mukaabya's infertility. (In traditional Buganda, blame for a couple's lack of offspring is always placed on the woman). Thus, *Kayanda* completely inverts the traditional masculine plot to reveal an unstable male identity.

The fear of women's potential to subvert masculine power materialises in *Kayanda*. The performance affirms that masculinities are precarious and susceptible to subversion because of their extraction from flawed depictions of an outdated femininity, overtaken by a new spirit of female power. An anti-genealogical performance, *Kayanda* counteracts the phallocentric performance that precedes it, whose main purpose was the maintenance of a genealogy of morals based on male domination. As such, *Kayanda* explicitly re-enacts the 'male anxiety' contained in *Nakakaawa* as the very condition of its being. Ssepiria's self-aggrandising monologue in the first part of *Nakakaawa* has given way to Mukaabya's heart-rending cry of betrayed masculinity as the outraged husband appears before the RC to reclaim control over his errant wife and to expel Kayanda. At first, the humiliation of publicly confessing to his compromised masculinity renders Mukaabya speechless. However, arbitrators finally prod him into stating his case. Mukaabya's anxiety at the discovery of the alleged infidelity is represented in the extracted statements below:

> Today I will kill you ... [addressed to the wife and the servant]
> You must disclose to me today . . .
> The roots of this ongoing contempt [towards me . . .]
> How will the public hear, my fellow men
> How will the public hear, my fellow men
>
> This is pressing me ...
> It is killing me ...
> It has destabilised me ...
> Warnings about her [the wife's] insolence
> Fall on deaf ears
> I am stunned my kinsmen
> I am distressed to no end ...
> I am dumbfounded at women in this world
> [To his wife]
> Now what could have driven you to an affair with Kayanda? ...
> A man who carries on an affair with your wife
> Walks all over your manhood
> Oh! My kinsmen ...

Mukaabya's focus on the tragedy of public humiliation cannot go unnoticed. Despite his convincing argument and the wife's confessed transgressions, the arbitrators (consisting of men and women) do not decide the case in Mukaabya's favour. Instead, they brand him a neglectful husband who deserves what has befallen him. This explanation draws attention to the most unsettling threat to contemporary hegemonic masculinity: women's ability and inclination to reject rigid culturally imposed forms of male authority in favour of benevolent relationships more suited to their needs. Kayanda's caring male presence, as already pointed out, triumphs over Mukaabya's aggressive, domineering and presumptuous masculinity.

This triumph again finds its roots in the indigenous discourse that appears to authorise alternatives to the patriarchal dictates. For instance, in the case of a widow's inheritance, wherein a dead man's wives may be taken by his brothers or cousins, the women's coping mechanism is encoded in the cryptic saying: *Eyali akumanyi y'akuggya ku mwandu* (It takes a well-cultivated acquaintance to take you from the widows' line-up). In the performance, Kayanda rescues Mukaabya's wife from the absent husband's domineering yet neglectful marital grip. (In the case of *Nakakaawa*, Tony, a former boyfriend rescued Nakakaawa from Ssepiria's grip, however temporarily). The implication is that a woman probably has more choices in her relationships than is officially or publicly admitted. The next sequence of the performance substantiates this point. Mukaabya's wife has moved out and is living with Kayanda. They are expecting a second child.

The status quo is completely reversed. The wife has elevated the status of the man who infiltrated her husband's rightful place. The council now addresses Kayanda, the former servant, as *Mwami Kayanda* (Master Kayanda) instead of the diminutive address, *ka-Kayanda*, employed at the beginning of the performance. Publicly addressed as Master Kayanda, the former servant is now the respected husband of Mukaabya's former wife and the legitimised father of both Nakiyimba and the expected baby.

The precariousness of a claim to a naturalised masculine ascendancy and domination is revealed because Mukaabya, like some men, can never really know if his children are biologically his, he loses custody of his daughter to the servant. The finale leaves Mukaabya stripped of his presumed power and incapable of wielding any social authority.

Kayanda also represents mutable notions of masculinity. His triumph at the end of the performance implies that masculine identities that adapt and integrate with balanced, flexible perceptions of femininity will create new, more secure gender relationships. Nevertheless, the security of male identity remains implicitly threatened by concurrent subtexts.

As in *Nakakaawa*, understanding the play on names in the performance emphasises this point. 'Mukaabya' means 'one who terrorises others' (literally:

'one who uses his power to make others cry'). By coincidence, Mukaabya happens to be the composer's real name. Nevertheless, the name is satirised as Mukaabya laments, 'What makes me cry is the usurping of my masculinity, the usurping of my position.' In a figurative and literal sense, Mukaabya's position as head of the household and a figure of authority has been thwarted, leaving him in a space of indistinct boundaries. His fate is controlled by his wife's feminine ideal and he finds himself deserted by the new postcolonial male power structures.

Women now play a significant role in monitoring the abuse of power on the national stage. In the final sequence of the performance, a group of women exercise their power to storm a meeting presided over by a corrupt RC chairman who detains other men's wives on frivolous grounds. That is how Kayanda's wife becomes a prisoner in the chairman's home, setting off a series of actions that culminate in this women's revolt and *coup d'etat* against the RC's dictatorial regime. The women strategically invade the chairman's house during a court session. The council members are seized with trepidation at the sight of the approaching women. Before a mesmerised male court, the women interrogate the chairman and find him guilty of using his political office to imprison and dominate women. In a sense, they put the chairman's unbridled virility on trial. Subsequently, they liberate the women detainees and effectively dismantle the male judicial power structure invested in the RC leadership.

Once again, male power within the postcolonial space has been turned on its head, a conclusion borne out in yet another scandalous episode in which Kijjambu accuses his wife of defying his authority and of having an affair with the family chauffeur. Like Mukaabya before him, Kijjambu has lost his wife to a member of the servant class. Driven to tears (like Mukaabya), Kijjambu laments his wife's desertion of him, leaving him with all the domestic responsibilities, including the care of their children. Despite her acknowledged guilt, Kijjambu's wife erupts in a subversive song that simultaneously appropriates and exposes the ridiculousness of patriarchal power:

> It would be best if we [women] took the men into marriage
> If he messes up—you simply expel him
> The next day you replace him . . .
> Thus they will realise our equality . . .
>
> Indeed, I can order you to wash my feet and to bathe me
> And pay you no wages for your household chores . . .
>
> You had better know that we are all equal
> We sit on the Resistance Councils
> We hold cabinet and ministerial posts

> We hold positions at district levels
> Men are no match for us at military skills.

The woman skilfully justifies her freedom to have two husbands in the same way that men justify polygamy. Most significantly, although her eloquent declamation masquerades as a desire for hegemonic male power, it is in effect an indirect manifesto in favour of equitable gender relationship. The woman's satirising and mirroring of an oppressive masculine ethic indirectly serves as a call for gender complementality.

She thus critiques the overbearing nature of hegemonic power and provokes a rethinking of rampant masculine identity formations in the family as well as in the nation. Although the two performances may not provide conclusive answers to the crisis of African masculinity, they reveal that the survival of any type of male identity is likely to depend on women's accommodative or subversive potential. Most significantly, these texts evidence the contribution that popular culture artists bring to current gender discourses within postcolonial contexts. Their trademark is the successful deployment of satire to focus society's gaze upon masculinities perpetually on trial.

7. Faces of Masculinity in African Cinema: A Case of Dani Kouyate's *Sia, Le Rêve du Python*

Dominica Dipio

Masculinity is best understood in relation to femininity, its implied counterpart. Both are concerned with power relationships that influence the division of labour between the sexes and the social construction of sexuality. As constructions, both are contingent and unstable. The process of constructing and deconstructing gender is ongoing, sustained by social institutions that are considered unquestionable and natural.[1] Although there are dominant traits of masculinity within a given society, it is not possible to speak of masculinity as a faceless block. As a facet of culture that is itself never static, masculinity is influenced by factors such as epoch, class, age, education and sexuality. Fictional representation is one way of reproducing and deconstructing masculinities. There are men who are considered, often pejoratively, feminine and women who likewise are viewed as masculine. Masculinity is a pillar of hegemonic culture in many traditional societies. Nonetheless, there are variations of masculinity that exist alongside hegemonic masculinity and at times, challenge it. In order to sustain itself, hegemonic masculinity is constantly on the 'look out' for threats against the status quo—and adjusts the balance of power to keep situations under control.

In this chapter I will examine how masculinity is represented in African cinema. My discussion will focus on Dani Kouyate's film, *Sia, Le Rêve du Python* (the film will be referred to in subsequent references as simply *Sia*), a metaphoric film that uses the past as a platform to reflect on contemporary power relations in Africa. The past and the present, especially in the exercise of power and in the relationship between men and women, are linked: there are continuities and discontinuities in these power relationships. I argue that hegemonic masculinity does not have total control over marginalised groups.

Although it reasserts itself at the end of the film with a 'new' hegemony in place, there are uncertainties and questions in the minds of the people about the 'new' order. Nothing has fundamentally changed: hegemonic masculinity has only recycled itself and dominant features of it remain unchanged as root paradigms. Resistance to this 'new' hegemony is implicitly beginning to form on the day of its inauguration, showing that power and resistance go hand-in-hand. The chapter also examines how the people react to the hegemony, how the filmmaker cues the audience to perceive dominant masculinity and how it continues to reproduce itself in spite of resistance to it. Antonio Gramsci's theory of hegemony will be used as the framework for examining the power relationships presented in the film.

The Plot and Context of Dani Kouyate's *Sia, Le Rêve du Python*

Dani Kouyate, a Burkinabe filmmaker with a background in theatre and cultural studies, comes from a family of *griots*. The role of the *griot* as a communicator, historian, guardian of tradition, musician and sometimes community poet, occupies a significant place in his filmmaking. Kouyate sees himself essentially as a *griot*, using the principal attribute of the *griot*: a storyteller who uses stories full of fantasy and metaphor to reveal morals. He sees cinema as a fabulous tool with which to perform, using a different medium of expression and at times subverting the role of the traditional *griot*[2] His first feature film, *Keita, L'Heritage du Griot* (1995), is a celebration of the educative role the *griot* plays in the traditional community, a value that is quickly disappearing and is neglected in the modern educational curriculum. The *griot* is also featured in his second film *Sia*, which is an adaptation of the play, *La Légende du Wagadu Vue par Sia Yataber*[3] by the Mauritanian playwright, Moussa Diagana. Talking about the reason for this film, Kouyate says:

> I have applied myself to the reasons for the inner battles which have bloodied Africa, looking for the causes (not again slavery and colonialism) but going well beyond, questioning our foundational myths. Myths which, sometimes, contain pernicious closes of totalitarianism, have their share of responsibility to assume. *Sia, Le Rêve du Python* comes from the legend of Wagadu, the founding myth of the pre-Nandingue people, to become a universally political fable.[4]

The Wagadu myth tells how the most beautiful virgin girl in the land is, from time to time, selected by the Python god and ritualistically offered in exchange for prosperity for the entire community.[5] The will of the Python god is mediated through the institution of the priesthood. The priests are a privileged elite social group whose esoteric rituals have the blessing of the state. To criticise the priests is tantamount to blasphemy and is punishable by death. This ritual sacrifice has come to be accepted as necessary for the well-being of the community and has continued unchallenged for generations. If there are questions in the minds of some in the community, they are kept muffled. The family upon whom the honour of finding the beautiful virgin falls is considered noble and heroic for not resisting the will of the Python god and is consequently rewarded, either with bags of gold equivalent to the weight of the virgin or some high-ranking office. Sia Yatabere, a young woman with a strong desire for life and the betrothed of Mamadi, a young soldier leading an army in battle, becomes the honourable virgin found worthy as a sacrifice to the Python god.

Mamadi's uncle, Wakhane, the commander of the army, whose own daughter, 'Little Mother,' had previously been sacrificed to the Python god, proposes that another virgin be found because Sia is already betrothed. In his view, it would be like robbing Mamadi of what has already been promised him; if this is not possible, to let Mamadi come to bid Sia farewell. The priests vehemently refuse Wakhane's suggestions, accusing him of blasphemy. They refuse to alter what the oracles have dictated. Kaya Maghan, the emperor, endorses whatever the priests have said in the interest of the state, before which all private interests must bow. When the news of Sia's choice is delivered to the Yatabere family, Sia overhears the conversation between her parents and Balla, the *griot* and bolts off into the night. It is significant to note that the message is principally delivered to Yatabere, the father of Sia. Sia's and her mother's views have no significance, for this is male hegemony and complicity. The women are positioned in these power politics on the lowest ranks of the subaltern group. Gender is seen as a product of the 'various social technologies,' which includes the socialisation process and 'institutionalised discourses' that make women accept their position in the community.[6]

The rest of the narrative is the search for Sia and involves unleashing coercive state apparatuses and handing her over to the priests. The coercive and ideological state apparatuses are both activated to get the people to cooperate, but nobody does so willingly. As the narrative progresses, we see on the one hand, the state's threats to punishment of all those suspected of being accomplices and on the other, the resistance of the subordinate groups. Sia cannot escape the law. However, although the hegemony appears to be winning the battle, it is significant to note that throughout the search, subversive actions that challenge the establishment take place concurrently with actions that reinforce the status quo. Wakhane, one of the key functionaries, is the first to challenge the orders of the priests. Responding from the depth of his humanity, he secretly arranges for Mamadi to leave the front in order to take leave of Sia before she is sacrificed. Although he knows that Sia is hidden in Kerfa, the madman's house, in complicity with one of the soldiers, he defers her arrest until Mamadi comes to see her. He does not, however, foresee that Mamadi will rebel to the point of wanting to kill the Python god to liberate Sia. Wakhane, who is a core member of the hegemony and propagates dominant masculinity, is constrained to imprison Mamadi even though he is his nephew. Wakhane considers himself first and foremost, a statesman who cannot tolerate blasphemy of any kind. He considers it madness for Mamadi to think of killing the Python god that has been honoured for generations. To underline his dominant masculinity, the director occasionally inserts his wife's attempts to persuade him to be more humane towards both Sia and Mamadi, who are related to him after all. Wakhane's wife is often framed behind her husband to undercut her husband's dominant masculine stance. As expected, he continually ignores her and shuts her up.

However, notwithstanding his faithfulness to the state, he and Mamadi are accused of planning a *coup d'état*. This unfounded gossip leads to a split in the army. Wakhane realises that the priests are going too far with their 'authority' when they implicate him in sabotage. As Sia is being handed over in a solemn procession to the seven priests who ritualistically rape her, Mamadi and his army are coming to rescue her. They arrive too late to prevent the rape, but in time to rescue her from being taken into the cave where she would be left to die like several virgins before her. This is the point of rupture of the Python god myth, a myth that has been put in place to mystify power and make it cryptic so that a few men can control it.

This situation is similar to that portrayed by Malian filmmaker Soulaymane Cisse in *Yeelen* (1989). The problem of totalitarianism and abuse of power is prevalent on the African continent. African filmmakers often resort to myth to expose these problems and to propose more inclusive and humane forms of governance. In *Yeelen*, the conflict is mainly generational: between father and son, although it is the mother who gives the son the key to the more relational (i.e., inclusive) approach to governance. These filmmakers continually indicate that the neglect of feminine principles in governance is the cause of so much suffering. Dominant masculinity is represented as exclusive and destructive.

Under the adept experience of Wakhane, a new hegemony is formed, once again on the basis of lies. In order to make Mamadi the new hero the slayer of the Python god—and for a new myth to emerge to replace the old one—more massacres are committed. The secret of the non-existence of the Python god must be kept at all costs to perpetuate the mysterious nature of power. This can only happen if it remains in the hands of a few. For political expediency, those valiant soldiers who together with Mamadi, try to liberate Sia must die because they know the truth. Power must remain mysterious and esoteric. As the 'new' order constructs its own myth, the feelings and trauma of Sia, the victim of the rape, have no political importance. It is, in fact, relegated to the private sphere as Wakhane advises Mamadi to persuade her to cooperate. The new myth catches up with the naïve masses' enthusiasm for celebrating heroes: they are not critical enough to question things. Driven mad by the state's insensitivity, Sia nonetheless, remains a threat to the new hegemony. She refuses to be gagged by accepting the title 'queen' in exchange for living a lie. The director ends the film in a subversive, mind-probing manner that jolts complacent audiences into reflection. Sia's emergence from the royal chambers, as the crowd waits to applaud her as queen, is a deconstruction of the state's version of the truth. She presents herself to the public as Balla, the *griot*, a lie she invents to explain her failure to come out to greet the people as their queen. When Sia strips out of her regal attire and walks away from the palace, into the streets of a modern city naked as a madwoman, the audience questions whether they have reason to celebrate the 'new' regime.

Key Tenets of Antonio Gramsci's Theory of Hegemony

Antonio Gramsci's theory of hegemony modified the traditional Marxist understanding of how the ruling class maintains control over subordinate classes, which Marx believed was solely through the use of force and coercion. Gramsci underlines that there are two basic ways of exercising control. The first is domination, which is physical and direct in its employment of force; the second, which is more pervasive, is ideological and elicits the consent of the subordinate groups. This is what he refers to as 'hegemony,' in which the relationship between the dominant and the subaltern groups keeps shifting. This concept is more useful for analysing cultural products such as literary and film texts. Hegemony stipulates that the exercise of power by the dominant social group over other classes is maintained not so much by force or coercion, but by consent. Carl Boggs explains his theory thus:

> By hegemony, Gramsci meant the permeation throughout society of an entire system of values, attitudes, beliefs and morality that has the effect of supporting the status quo in power relations. Hegemony in this sense might be defined as an 'organising principle' that is diffused by the process of socialisation into every area of daily life. To the extent that this prevailing consciousness is internalised by the population it becomes part of what is generally called 'common sense' so that the philosophy, culture and morality of the ruling elite comes to appear as the natural order of things.[7]

For the dominant social group to continue to exert control, it seeks the complicity of subordinate groups who 'willingly' accept a view of themselves that is orchestrated through political, cultural and spiritual institutions. These are the ideological state apparatuses that make them see things as natural and objective. Winning the consent of these subordinate groups therefore, involves incorporating some of their interests into the hegemonic interest in order to pre-empt revolt and for the subalterns to identify with the values of the hegemony as objectively interested in their welfare.

Institutions and intellectuals within hegemony play a significant role in sustaining the status quo. In Gramsci's view, all people are intellectuals, though not all may perform the role of intellectuals in a society. This awareness is important because it shows that ordinary people can form a counter-hegemonic bloc that can challenge the status quo. He identifies two categories of intellectuals in society, both of which are identifiable in *Sia*. The first group is made up of the traditional intellectuals who appear to be autonomous and independent. They also appear to be stable and eternal even when social upheavals are experienced. This sense of independence from the ruling class is however, an illusion, because their function assists the ruling class in maintaining power.[8] This is the role the priests play in the film.

The second group is made up of the 'organic intellectuals' who are the result of a socialisation process; their function is to sustain the hegemony. In the film, they include Wakhane the army commander, the army, the council of elders and Balla the *griot*. It is in this respect that Gramsci refers to intellectuals as 'functionaries.' They are 'the dominant group's "deputies" exercising the subaltern functions of social hegemony and political government.'[9] Institutions such as schools, the police, the army and religion all appear to be impartial and representative of everybody's interests; they are also the producers of meaning and sense for the community. The dominant hegemonic bloc in *Sia* is masculine, which is typical of many traditional societies. Enshrouded in ideology, the kind of violence the hegemonic bloc commits on subordinate groups, such as beautiful, young virginal women, is what Pierre Bourdieu refers to as 'symbolic violence.' The victims are made to construe being chosen by the Python god as a kind of 'nobility.'[10]

In hegemony, what Gramsci refers to as 'power blocs' are formed through alliances between the hegemony and various social groups, including those from subaltern groups. Whichever group perceives its interest is accommodated in the hegemonic interest becomes part of the hegemonic bloc. The hegemony is thus perceived as dynamic and always recruiting new members from various social groups in order to strengthen and sustain itself. This alliance is the authority that sustains the hegemony. On the other hand, counter-hegemonic groups or alliances may also form to challenge the dominant hegemony. Continuity and discontinuity occur hand-in-hand in the theory of hegemony. Oppositional consciousness is always present and the process of change is, therefore, always immanent, though this change is not necessarily a revolutionary one.[11] This is the attraction of the theory of hegemony in cultural studies: that resistance to hegemony and change as a process is always at work in social institutions. Kouyate's *Sia* is set at a time when tension between the hegemonic and counter-hegemonic blocs is beginning to build.

The Dynamics of Power and Resistance in the Film

This powerful fable presents several points of tension between the hegemonic and subaltern blocs. There are ongoing intra-bloc tensions. The power of this legend lies in its timelessness. The director temporally achieves this by interfacing the traditional-cultural setting of pre-colonial with postcolonial days when, in the final shot, we cut from the past to the present. The story is rich with the contemporary—and universal—relevance of power relations. Commenting on the character of Sia, the director says she is as universal as Antigone, who stands against the state, or Iphigenia, who refuses to be sacrificed to the gods. His choice of a familiar myth and metaphor to comment on a contemporary situation enables his African audiences to appreciate the message: in any case, metaphor is richer and preferable to realism. African politics is still predominantly shrouded in mystery and crimes against the people are still committed with impunity by politicians. This is particularly so because of a lack of viable public opinion. Subordinate groups are gullible in the hands of their unscrupulous political leaders.[12] There are key characters whose roles accentuate the power question, as discussed below.

Kerfa the Madman

In African cinema, the figure of a madman (or outcast) turned hero, is common. The role Kerfa plays in this film can be compared to that of Kabebe the madman in Haile Gerima's *Harvest* 3000 (1976), whose main goal was to awaken the sleeping masses and inspire them with revolutionary spirit. Like Kerfa, though Kabebe does not achieve his objective by the end of the film, when he is hunted down and killed, there is at least, a boy who begins to see things differently as a result of his influence. When Kerfa is introduced in the narrative he is immediately seen as one whose values juxtapose and subvert those of the hegemonic group. As a 'madman' he represents the extreme periphery of the subaltern groups, yet he is also the symbol of the artist and visionary who can dare to raise his voice and say what others cannot. The first time he appears, he is framed in a low camera angle that gives him power and dynamism in relation to the women washing clothes in the stream. He is brisk and bold as he addresses and sympathises with the women as representatives of the suffering people of 'Koumbi.' He prophetically announces that although things look normal and peaceful, doom is impending: they are, in fact, trapped in this doom! He sees the regime of Kaya Maghan as a monster and the Python god as a perverse god that devours its own children. The camera frames Sia with two young women, who could be possible victims for the Python god, listening attentively to Kerfa. The rest of the women simply laugh at him as though he were a madman. Kerfa is like the spirit that challenges the entire land to wake from its lethargy: he moves around and boldly declares his message to counter the official pronouncements of the hegemonic bloc. Dressed in a 'kingly' robe, he is like a subversive king. He tells everyone that the rule of the emperor is built on falsehood and prophetically declares that such a miserable rule will reap only penury. Though the state sees in him more than just a madman and is scared of him and would like to silence him permanently, the rest of the community simply takes him for a madman: they are not bothered by his cryptic messages. No amount of harassment by the army can stop Kerfa from uttering his unpalatable insights. He uses his license as a madman well and he guards it jealously as a gift that he cannot barter for any kind of power.[13] He tells Sia, 'Not just anyone can be mad! You must earn it!' Kerfa is the symbol of truth and in a repressive government such as this, only mad people can proclaim the truth without fear of consequences; they alone can 'say things that cannot be said by normal people,' for the truth cannot be marginalised in him.[14] This is indeed, power with authority. The greatest sign of hope in the film, according to the director, is Kerfa's transfer of the power of truth (i.e., madness) to Sia at the end of the film, when she chooses madness over being part of the hegemonic lie. In a paradoxical way, truth survives her.

Kerfa can also be looked at as a foil for Balla, the court *griot*. At times Kerfa speaks lucidly, at times his language and manners are clouded and abstruse just like that of the priests. Presenting him as one of the biggest challenges to the state, his warnings to the people to hide from 'the cruel feast of Kaya Maghan' (from Sia) interfaces with the official spokesman's announcement of the approach of the honourable hooded priests. Kerfa, in spite of being openly against the state, is least suspected of hiding Sia, the fugitive. His abode is searched only because the regime wants to be thorough. Up to the time he is eliminated, he remains the one viable force rocking the state, until Sia replaces him. The rest of the people have been beaten, harassed and made to accept the status quo. It is clear though, that the state cannot control the feelings and conscience of the subordinates. Part of their torture is to force them to memorise the 'catechism' of the Python god under the surveillance of one of Wakhane's strong men:

> Kaya Maghan the benefactor!
> Python god the saviour!
> They give us rain!
> They give us gold!
> They protect us![15]

It is worth noting that the panning camera reveals that, among the arrested men and women, not all repeat the above words. Control indeed has its limits.

Kerfa disturbs the emperor with the lashing of his tongue. The rest of the state functionaries, like Balla the *griot* and the army, would have eliminated him long before for not toeing the line. It is also a surprise to the emperor that, for all the insults he hurls at the state, Kerfa's head has not yet rolled. Wakhane, the master statesman, advises the emperor that 'Kerfa would be more of a nuisance dead than alive. As long as he speaks he's but a madman, keeping the people amused. But any violence unto him will make him a martyr.' What is politically expedient is to accommodate him, 'crazy' as he may be. Power in order to survive must be flexible. Kerfa is ironically and subversively powerful. He is eliminated only when Sia is ready to replace him, showing the principle of continuity in resisting oppressive regimes.

It is after the queen's challenge that Kaya Maghan realises he is surrounded by opinionless and spineless councillors. It is at this point that he invites Kerfa into the palace to persuade him to become one of his functionaries. Inviting a madman to the palace for a conversation with the emperor is unimaginable from the point of view of the court officials. Kerfa's insubordination before the king remains unchallenged: he refuses to go on his knees as is the custom. He tells the king: 'Is your rule on its knees? If it is upright, I will remain upright!' The king's helplessness is seen in the ensuing conversation, which takes place before the king's officials:

King: (Restraining his functionaries who want to roughen Kerfa up) Let him go. Lay not a finger on him! If he wishes, let him stand and let him speak!

Kerfa: (Sarcastically) Speak? Me? It is for you to speak. I didn't ask for an audience.

King: I'm giving you the chance to repent. If you don't I shall offer your life to the priests for having blasphemed.

Kerfa: (Laughing in his face) Kill me? I am not afraid of death! I know how to wake up when I die (laughs). Kaya Maghan, you are not like me if you die ... If you die, you do not know how to wake! In fact you are already dead because you are asleep. Sleep does not govern (the king listens ponderously).

The best the king can do to minimise this loss of face is to ask to be left alone with Kerfa, the madman, a request that looks like perversion itself. When the two are together, the king literally and symbolically undresses before Kerfa: he puts on a friendly and benevolent façade to obtain Kerfa's good will and co-operation. He tells him that in spite of Kerfa's antagonistic attitude towards him, he is willing to accommodate him if he becomes his mouthpiece: he wants to become close to his people. He confesses that he is tired of the brood of complacent 'yes men' who surround him. He wants an independent 'dreamer' like Kerfa to dream for him. He goes to the extent of removing his crown and robe and attempting to give it to Kerfa to become his agent. During this dialogue, Kerfa's words and attitude oscillate between sarcasm, surprise, ridicule and outright rejection of the king's offer. Throughout most of this dialogue, he stands with his back half-turned to the king, to underscore his oppositional stance. When he realises that he cannot persuade Kerfa, the king resorts to threats and violence:

King: (Pleading) Take the throne and dream.
Kerfa: Me? Never! Keep your throne! My dreams belong to me alone!
King: (Throwing the robe and crown down and angrily confronting Kerfa) Nothing is anyone's! All belongs to me, even you and your madness!
Kerfa: Leave my madness alone! Hands off! (The two face each other at close range: Kerfa points a finger at the king's eye). Let me seek myself. Me. I seek myself! (He moves around the baffled king chanting) He is already dead! Kaya Maghan is dead!
King: (Angrily) Kerfa! (Kerfa stops and they face each other) I will kill you (points a finger at Kerfa's eye). I will wipe you out!
Kerfa: (Laughing sarcastically) Kill me? But I am already dead! Dead but awake! Every day I die! If you cannot die and wake you are nothing! Believe me! (He walks away, leaving the king totally stunned. In a medium shot, the king is left alone with his own shadow before him).

The dialogue between the king and Kerfa brings the question of the role of the *griot* and court councillors into focus. In the film, Balla plays the classical role of the traditional *griot*, a singer of praise who is the echoer of royalty and the chronicler of the official history. Using Kerfa as a foil to Balla, the director invites audiences to reflect on the role of the *griot* in the context of contemporary times. Surely, a progressive king does not need an echo or a shadow of himself, but an intelligent person as advisor. Ideally, the *griot* should be a mouthpiece for the king, a kind of 'buffer' between him and his people uninterested in power. Over the years, this role has been impoverished: *griots* have tended to be more singers of praise of power and royalty than mediators. Commenting on some of the themes of the film, Kouyate says: 'Si je dénonce le dieux qui mangent leurs enfants, je dénonce aussi dans ce film les griots qui trahissent leur société.'[16] But the *griot* is a creation of royalty; he is denied individuality; he has no independent opinion; when his opinion is asked, the king does not expect it to differ from his. It is too late when the king realises that he has surrounded himself with a group of sycophants who are not helpful for the construction of his kingdom. The *griot* in this film is a clever and slippery character who, as a survivor of political regimes, identifies with the winning side. When it is clear that the tide has turned against Kaya Maghan, he changes allegiance to Wakhane and begins to sing his praises. Although he is involved in the scheme to eliminate Kaya Maghan, there is no evidence that his role is going to be different in the 'new' hegemony: his survival lies in doing exactly what the state wants. As an opportunist, he finds himself a niche in the institution that created him. Kerfa, in his subversive way, is a better *griot* than Balla. He truly acts as a mouthpiece and mediator between the two blocs.

Kerfa is seen again after the arrest of Sia: he is telepathically connected to her as the women prepare her for the sacrifice. From a distance, he hears the familiar sound of the tam-tam, announcing the hour of the sacrifice. A cross-cut shot and the sound link the two who are in different locations. The sound of the drum makes both feel deranged, as both block their ears against it. Sia must go through with the ritual: she is trapped as the tight framing indicates. Simultaneously, in another location, a high camera angle, a tracking shot and a tight frame reveal the unbalanced state of Kerfa as he restlessly moves up and down, blocking his ears in protest against what must inevitably happen to Sia:

Never does the vulture sing! Never does the hyena dance! (Cross cut to Sia as Kerfa pronounces these words; she too blocks her ears against the sound of the tam-tam; she hears the voice of Kerfa over the drum-beat.) People of Koumbi, you are cursed! I hate your song and dances. They stink! (Cut back to Kerfa who still blocks his ears as he speaks.) Blind tam-tams! Deaf tam-tams! (With blocked ears, he runs away shouting these words; the tracking shot follows him, giving the impression of him being chased; all emphasising the inevitability of the sacrifice).

The telepathic connection between the two symbolically shows how Kerfa and Sia protest against this sacrifice, but nobody can hear them: the sound of the familiar celebration and ritual overwhelms their feeble cries of protest. The rest of the community does not have the level of consciousness that Sia and Kerfa have. The elimination of Kerfa comes as something unexpected. When Wakhane plans the mutiny against Kaya Maghan, he orders the killing of Kerfa as if it has come from the king; partly to further tarnish the king's image, but also because he knows Kerfa's 'blaspheming' tongue will not spare the new regime. After his death, his earlier challenge to the king that, when he dies he will rise up from the dead comes true when Sia becomes the new 'Kerfa.' She has rightfully 'earned her madness,' as Kerfa would say. The spirit of resistance, however dominant a regime may be, cannot be totally silenced and change does not necessarily come by revolution, but also through small subversive actions. This is what inspires hope in the film: alongside the predominantly naïve masses, there are always one or two people to fan the flames of resistance. The resistance of Sia and Kerfa is even more dramatic, not because it demystifies power, but because it demystifies myth itself.[17] The image of the mad person corroborates what the poet Niyi Osundare says about what it means for an artist to work in the context of a repressive political regime. In this context, insanity becomes the dynamic stance to show the way out for society. He observes:

> Freedom is vital for the creative enterprise as oxygen is to a living organism. That enterprise can only flower and flourish when the creative spirit has the liberty to dare, venture, argue, make mistakes, lose and discover itself in the rapture of being and becoming. It can only flourish when it has the liberty to contemplate (for the spirit that can contemplate is the one that can anticipate), ruminate, brood, dream, navigate the threshold of madness (not sanity!), develop inner eyes for seeing and apprehending unborn possibilities, cultivate the audacity to keep telling the emperor: 'Your Majesty, thou, indeed, are naked.'[18]

This aptly describes Kerfa's function in the film: he plays the role of the authentic *griot*, the visionary, the artist.

The King's Court

Kaya Maghan has a chain of institutional functionaries: priests, a *griot*, councillors and the army that make him almost invisible yet omnipresent. This hegemonic conclave is an all-male one, reflecting the male predominance in the exercise of political power in African society. The king, the absolute ruler, remains remote while the entire land is rife with a tight spy network that lets nothing escape his ears. This is seen at the barber's shop when the men who express opinions about Sia's escape are among those rounded up for torture the next day. Through these officials, the king's rule appears objective and dedicated only to the common good of the community. By and large, the people have come to see their interests in sustaining and cooperating with the hegemonic group. This is what Gramsci refers to as:

> The 'spontaneous' consent given by the great masses of the population to the general direction imposed on social life by the dominant fundamental group; this consent is 'historically' caused by the prestige (on consequent confidence) which the dominant group enjoys because of its position and function in the world of production. [19]

The priests are the most powerful and honourable instruments for sustaining the hegemonic ideology and myths. They wield special ritual powers as mediators of the oracle of the Python god; and they exist to affirm the fundamental traditions and customs of the land. The Python god's gift of prosperity for the community is sought through them; the king is in total accord with the wisdom of the priests. Priesthood, the highest office, which links the mundane world with the spiritual world of the gods, is accorded great respect and the priests are not to be antagonised. The *griot* is the one who announces, in flowery language, the wisdom of the hegemonic group and through the artistry of language ensures that the community accepts these creeds. The council of elders is there to be consulted when delicate issues that affect the life of the community are to be resolved. Where there is resistance in accepting the dictates of the hegemony, the army is there to repress all subversive elements. Though the power structure is exclusively male, it is ostensibly representative and interested in the well-being of the entire community. Whoever stands in opposition is therefore seen to be acting against their common sense.

The fate of Sia Yatabere, as the sacrifice for the Python god, is ideologically interpreted for the people as a rare honour bestowed upon a chosen 'noble' family. The *griot* presents the news to the Yatabere family as 'honour knocking on their door.' For their acceptance of this honour, the king offers the family a gift of gold corresponding to the weight of Sia, as if to underline that she is as much an object as a bag of gold. It is evident that in the silence of their hearts, the people feel there is something wrong with this ritual sacrifice, though they dare not openly express it. The song of the *griotess* expresses how appalling human sacrifice is. Song, as artistic form of expression, has its poetic license and the singer, as an artist uses this license to voice the concerns of the community.[20] Likewise, when Balla announces the verdict of the oracle to the hearing of the king's court, the reaction of the councillors does not indicate that all are happy about the oracle's demand. The news is received with some foreboding, though the councillors must agree to it as part of the tradition. There is a reaction shot of three elders, framed together as they nod their heads in approval; but there are also pensive faces among them. As for Sia's father, sad as he may be, his fatalistic response is that the ritual must be carried out because Sia is not the first, nor will she be the last, sacrifice. Whatever doubts and questions they have about this ritual they keep muted. Only a madman or madwoman would step out and dare to challenge it.

When Sia disappears, the state uses different methods, ranging from threats to bribing with gifts, to get the people's cooperation. Throughout this search, the director uses cross-cutting shots to contrast Kerfa's views with that of the state. Kerfa makes a fool of the state functionaries with his sarcastic, subversive and blasphemous pronouncements about the Python god. He obliterates the façade that Balla's oratory creates: he insults the Python god for all to hear: 'Python god most misshapen! Deep in your stinking cave what do you know of beauty? Be gone! All our daughters are beautiful. In fact, all is beautiful in Wagadu!' Kerfa cannot be avoided; Balla and his entourage run into him repeatedly. When Balla announces that the king will reward with gold whoever finds Sia, Kerfa confronts them directly with a counter pronouncement that is a prophecy against the king and his nearing doom: 'Informers! May you be cursed to damnation! Kaya Maghan. Master of the universe! No need to hurry. You shall soon drown in the misery of your people like this cat; completely drown (dangling the dead cat he has just found for his day's meal)!'

Balla and his entourage are not only baffled and enraged by this madman who cannot be ignored, but they are powerless to stop him. As Kerfa's words continue to follow and disturb the hegemony, Balla and his team no longer look as confident as before. All they can do is threaten Kerfa with death and Kerfa subverts their death threats because he is fearless, because he 'knows how to rise from death!' Balla's official announcements are juxtaposed with the challenging statements/songs of the subalterns. In the sequence in which men and women with sad faces gather at a drinking place, the voice of the *griot* sings:

> Do not fear death!
> Death spares no one.
> If you are afraid, you will die.
> Even if unafraid, you will die just the same.

Death is what the regime threatens whenever someone expresses a different view. The camera pans the sad faces as the song is sung. This is a song of protest by the subordinate group of people who look helpless and vulnerable, demystifying death. Fearlessness against the regime—fearlessness against death—is itself a form of protest. This is interfaced with Balla's message of eighteen kilos of gold for whoever finds Sia. The silence and the expressionless faces of the people in close up juxtaposed with this announcement, is suddenly interrupted by another song by a *griotess*, protesting human sacrifice:

> Sacrificing human beings,
> How appalling!
> Human life is sacred!
> I declare it most appalling!

The king, the man behind the goings-on, cannot be readily described as oppressive because his orders are executed through well-established and traditional institutions that have come to be perceived as objective and standing for the common good. His unflinching authoritarianism however, is seen when Sia's disappearance brings him face-to-face with the fact that there are saboteurs in the land. When Sia cannot be found, the queen and later the councillors, advice him to take a practical course: pick another one of the several beautiful and noble virgins in the land. But the king is inflexible: for him, flexibility means slighting or bargaining with his authority. He sees negotiation as loss of face and a sign of weakness. This is the dominant masculine stance. The queen warns him that authority that is not flexible cannot survive and challenges him to wake up to see beyond appearances—his *griots* and councillors are men without individuality, who merely echo him and who will turn against him when the tide turns. This reminder jolts the king into seeking audience with Kerfa to explore the possibility of negotiation. But the king, the masculine *par excellence*, is not really intent on negotiation, for he cannot take a different view. He invites Kerfa to his palace partly in contempt of his *griots* and partly to manipulate him. His true colours show when Kerfa cannot be manipulated. Even with other officials like Wakhane, the king is self-confident and believes that without him they are nothing. It is because of his arrogance and self-confidence that he is taken by surprise when Wakhane, whom he trusts as the ideal functionary, stages a *coup* against him.

The irony of the king's desire to have absolute control is seen when subversive actions take place right under his nose without him realising. That Sia's whereabouts cannot be revealed, even after one of the soldiers sees her in Kerfa's abode, shows that the state can never have absolute control. Indeed, a counter-hegemonic group begins to form around Wakhane as he reveals humane tendencies. When his request to have Mamadi come from the front to bid farewell to Sia is rejected by the priests on the grounds that 'a soldier does not leave the front for his fiancée,' he goes ahead and secretly arranges for the meeting between the two. He orders Sia's arrest after Mamadi has tendered his farewell. From the dominant masculine hegemonic point of view, what he has done is less manly: he has let sentiment influence his judgement. The king tells him he has acted more as an uncle to Mamadi than as head of the army. This is not a compliment. One who responds to the emotive dimension of his nature and to family ties is rated as less manly and ignoble. Wakhane, who has been the perfect model of manliness and nobility, is now the one who lets his feelings get the better of him when faced with a conflict of interests. He has on many occasions told his wife, who keeps reminding him about his family ties and responsibilities, that the interests of the state come before that of the family. However, under her gentle but persistent pressure, he becomes progressively uncertain. Beyond appearances, Wakhane is a traumatised man, haunted by a deep sense of guilt that he covers by an excessive show of manliness. As a key instrument in the state, he only challenges those orders that do not rock the system. He has Sia arrested and delivered to the priests, because he also believes her death is as noble as that of any soldier dying in defence of the empire. When Mamadi cannot see the sense in Sia's death and swears he will kill the Python god to liberate her, Wakhane arrests Mamadi because he still believes and sustains the system. As far as he is concerned, Mamadi must be crazy for speaking such blasphemy and so he must be locked up.

The turning point in terms of Wakhane's psychological state occurs when, in spite of his unflinching defence of the state, he is accused of sabotage against it. This leads to his defecting with Mamadi and a handful of soldiers. It is at this point that one sees a crack in the strong edifice that is Wakhane. He makes a moving confession to Mamadi about what has troubled him for years. It is the story of his insensitivity towards 'Little Mother,' his own daughter, whom he 'nobly' consented to be sacrificed to the Python god. Since then, he has been distressed by the fact that, in the name of manliness, he denied her the one favour she had asked of him before she faced the Python god. Confessing with a tremulous voice, one cannot help pitying the vulnerable Wakhane, who has been living the lie of being a tough and mechanical instrument of the state. The binary oppositional system of socialisation, which emphasises psychological differences between men and women, makes Wakhane deny a significant aspect of his humanity. In him we see clear evidence of what Sylviane Agacinski says about gender relations and human nature being essentially mixed.[21] There is no purity in being male or female: men and women each have a bit of the other sex in themselves. Now we see Wakhane, the perpetuator of the system, is as much a victim as the young virgins that have died in the Python god scam. He is a victim of the male dominance that has destroyed his very humanity.[22] He explains to Mamadi the story of 'Little Mother':

Wakhane: ...At 16, they delivered her up to the Python. I will never forget the look on her face that day. Her distraught antelope eyes, begging (his voice trembles with emotions that he tries to keep under control)..
Mamadi: (Moved to pity, gently pats him on the shoulder) My poor uncle...
Wakhane: Let me speak! (He stops him and moves away) There is time for everything. Do not console me; I am not to be pitied. I am an unworthy father (his voice breaks again). You know what 'Little Mother' said to me on the day of the sacrifice? Do you know? (Mamadi listens empathically) She said: 'Father! You always told me that death was invisible. I am not afraid of death. It is the serpent that I fear...I beg you father, blindfold me, I don't want to see the Python!' Do you know what I did that day? Do you know? I refused! I closed my eyes so not to see her tremble...I sinned out of sheer pride. I didn't want to see a girl of my flesh and blood tremble before death.
Mamadi: Uncle, for 'Little Mother' and for Sia, we must kill this monster.
Wakhane: Kaya Maghan named me head of the army to console me for her loss. But it is impossible to forget. My only reason to live is to take revenge upon myself. Mamadi, listen well, what I am about to tell you is capital. Tomorrow, I will make you Kaya Maghan.

'Virility' is the battle cry of masculinity and it goes hand-in-hand with violence. This is reflected in the psychological state of Wakhane. What drives him is the desire to prove that he is not a weakling of a man, even if it means committing violence against his own beloved daughter. Such masculinity as his is, of course, is rewarded and celebrated as 'nobility.'[23]

Although Wakhane regrets his insensitivity towards his daughter, he does not fundamentally change or challenge the political order. His actions and schemes do not change anything for the other victims of the system either: he simply avenges himself. Mamadi, who he propels to power, does not deserve the fame now accorded to him as the slayer of the Python god, for no such god exists. Wakhane has been a victim of a system built on lies and now he helps to set up another, built on a new set of lies and intended to keep power secretive and mysterious. He is the master manipulator exploiting the gullibility of the people. When the army massacres Kaya Maghan, he announces that power in the new regime belongs to the people, yet he is totally insensitive to Sia's trauma as one who had been raped by the priests of the Python god—the same experience his 'Little Mother' had gone through. He now wants Sia silent and to celebrate the lie of Mamadi's 'heroism'—which she knows is a lie. Here we see crude, insensitive power and masculinity having the same face. Wakhane now warns the uncooperative Sia, 'It is we who saved your life. We can reduce you to silence.' He has learned nothing from his experience.

Mamadi, the fiery young man who a moment before swore to defend Sia against the Python god, is now won over to the side of falsehood. He does not want Sia to live in the truth as he pleads with her not to 'wreck our hopes.' All he can think of now is the hope of being king and he is ready to sacrifice his fiancée. When Mamadi kills Wakhane, his political mentor, for trying to arrest Sia, it does not mean he sees things differently; it simply shows he has quickly learned to play politics which involves eliminating even those who are closest to you. In protest at the tenor of this new regime, Sia disrobes before the community gathered to celebrate their 'heroism.' She now assumes the role of Kerfa the madman. She laughs sarcastically in the face of the new king, who is literally trembling. She uses the same words that Kerfa had used to challenge the Kaya Maghan: 'The new Kaya Maghan is dead! Dead in the well of endless falsehood! Dead from the very beginning.' Mamadi then uses the same words that are used to describe all subversive elements: he orders his army commander to take the 'madwoman' out! But there is something invincible about this madwoman who scares the 'hero' trying to order her out. The hegemony dares not touch her as they watch her undress and leave the palace naked to go into the modern streets. She stands apart from the naïve masses. She now has as much subversive power as Kerfa had; the mad people in this regime are those who know better and the tragedy is that the easy-to-fool community does not take them seriously. As Kerfa tells Sia, 'All stories have their madmen, but madmen never have stories.' To have a story, one must have an audience: this does not happen in the case of the mad, like Kerfa and Sia and this is the tragedy of society. However, paradoxically, although the community does not listen to these mad people, they cannot be ignored. The hope for change, which is a gradual but ever-present factor, is that beside Sia and Kerfa there is a growing number of potential mad men and women in the film: people who are beginning to question the status quo. Sia's challenge to the state, to a certain extent, raises the consciousness of the predominantly naïve masses.

The Resistance of the Subalterns

There are various forms of resistance represented in the film, ranging from silence, songs and secret schemes to an outright oppositional stance and the taking up of arms. Even when the people are predominantly reduced to silence, there is always a 'mad' person or two who shout out. The men at the barber's shop are a case in point. The atmosphere here is tense and shrouded in silence: the men do not trust each other, for one cannot tell who is friend or foe. Nonetheless, the barber expresses his opinion about the brutality of the state and hopes that Sia succeeds in evading its clutches. For him what the state is committing is a heinous crime that he can never support. Later, when the barber and one of the men are arrested and whipped for their subversive comments, the former is not deterred. The barber neither cries nor pleads for mercy as he is being whipped. On the other hand, his colleague, whom he refers to as 'lily-livered,' pleads for mercy like a clown. In the anti-hegemonic bloc, the barber is read as manly, both for holding out against the whips and for boldly challenging oppression. After the arrest of Sia, an ominous sadness and silence grips the barber's shop once again. He still risks his life when he voices what the others dare not say: that they must take to the streets and protest against Kaya Maghan and his priests. The others are in sympathy with him, but dare not raise their voices for fear. In the face of state tyranny, it is expedient to keep silent, but silence does not mean consent. The people detest the regime and their sympathy is with Sia.

One can draw another level of resistance by comparing the way men and women respond to the same issues. The example here is the way Sia's father and mother take the news that their daughter is the chosen one for the Python god. Sia's father is rather quick to rise to the 'honour' bait and taking it as a 'man,' he agrees in the name of honour and nobility. He tells his wife, who is crying beside him, that she must not cry because their daughter's death is honourable and besides all will die one day. He succumbs without resistance to the dominant ideological view. Before Sia runs away, he pleads with her to cooperate with the state. As a man, he is more of an insider in the hegemonic practice of this myth, where young virginal women are constantly positioned in the role of 'victim' glamorised as an honourific position. The mother sees things differently. When the state mounts a search for Sia, terror is unleashed upon the entire land. Balla warns Sia's father: 'If she vanishes, sparks will fly for you and for me; but much more for you.' At this point the state does not pretend to be persuasive, but is openly coercive.

During the search for Sia, the women characters are represented as more challenging to the status quo than the men in the subaltern groups. These challenges range from body language (e.g., when Sia's mother jeers at the men coming to search), to spitting contemptuously (as Sia's grandmother does), to lashing out with insults or even refusing to take a subordinate posture in front of authority (as Sia's friend Penda does). When Penda is arrested and brought before Wakhane as an accomplice, she refuses to go on her knees, as is customary and she insults the soldiers as a 'bunch of cowards': an insult that challenges and hurts their masculine egos. Shocked and angry as they may be, they are powerless to do anything to her. When she is brought before Wakhane as a difficult case, she refuses to go on her knees: she stands and looks him straight in the eye and offers herself to be sacrificed in place of Sia, instead of tormenting innocent people. This fearlessness before death is itself an oppositional stance. She challenges the commander that even if those arrested were accomplices, they would never confess. They would rather die than shame themselves with confession. She refers to all those innocent people arrested as having 'balls,' whereas their tormenters 'have none!' Manliness and masculinity are deconstructed by female characters.

For men whose yardstick of power is dominant masculinity, Penda's insult is too much for the commander and his officers to bear. The most they can do to cover up is to dismiss her and lock her up as a possessed girl who is not in her right mind. When Sia's parents are brought before Wakhane, the father is much more acquiescent: he goes straight onto his knees before the commandant, whereas Sia's mother wrenches herself free from the rough grasp of the soldiers. She drops to her knees slowly. The father confesses more readily that they have no reason to hide Sia, for she is not the first, nor will she be the last, to be sacrificed. The father cowers and looks quite diminished from the slightly high camera angle, whereas the mother, with her challenging words, is captured in a higher position, looking more empowered. Like Penda, she swears that if she were an accomplice, she would never own up and she challenges the men around her: 'In this land, bastards have a name. We ought to find one for unworthy fathers!'[24] Sia's father pleads with the commander to treat his wife's words as those of a madwoman. Even when she protests against being considered mad and challenges Wakhane that he knows exactly what she is alluding to, the latter, to the surprise of the other officers, reacts by ordering both to be released. This is a most unmanly reaction from Wakhane, who is known for his toughness. He releases the woman because he understands the significance of her challenging words.

Hegemonic masculinity tries to adjust the balance of power among the men themselves. It is the complicity of the men that is required, negotiated and rewarded for handing over the destined virgin. The women do not count as subordinates; they are not even expected to have an opinion on this power issue. The men who express views contrary to the hegemony are viewed as less manly and dishonourable. Dominant masculinity in this film involves sacrificing one's own sensitivity (i.e., humanity) in order to be an effective state instrument, such as with Wakhane. In the subalterns' camp, the man who is afraid of the state is referred to as 'lily-livered'; a real man would protest the brutality committed against women and innocent people; he would rather risk his life to change things for the better by saying 'no' to absolutism and oppression than keep silent and let oppressive regimes continue. Masculinity, in this respect, is constructed differently by the two groups. The rhetoric of each group speaks for itself: the audiences realise how miserable dominant masculinity must be, if it leads to being insensitive to the cries of the vulnerable.

The hegemony sustains itself through socialisation as well. Throughout the narrative, the little prince keeps close to the king and follows the issues of state with keen interest. Each time court officials and priests come for important discussions he stops playing (with an ordinary child) and rushes into the palace so that he misses nothing. It is significant to note that in the encounter between the king and Kerfa, after the king has demanded to be left alone with him, the young prince hides behind the curtain and eavesdrops on the drama between the two. The king realises too late that his son is behind the curtain. Hearing his father discuss serious issues with a madman and seeing him disrobed before the madman might demystify the king's absolutism and invincibility to his young son, who symbolises a new generation of leaders. It is a clever way of puncturing the king's supremacy before his own son whom he is mentoring to succeed him.

As a motif that runs throughout the film, anybody who expresses or stands for different views, or who challenges the hegemonic posture, is accused of subversion and made to repent. Whoever sticks to his or her guns and cannot be controlled by the state is dismissed or locked up as possessed or mad. It is the gullible masses that take these people to be mad; the state takes them seriously as threats to its hegemonic establishment and this is its way of frustrating them or protecting itself against further attacks. The filmmaker, however, makes it clear that these people cannot be ignored. The subtle power and hope in this film lies in its representation of absolute power as powerless once the people begin to wake up to and challenge it. Dani Kouyate, the *griot*, tears the veil from the face of power to reveal how vulnerable it is when exercised without authentic authority.

Conclusion

Hegemonic masculinity is portrayed as repugnant and crumbling. It makes victims of and dehumanises the very men who uphold it, yet it is an entrenched value that is difficult to change. It is too late when the emperor realises that his regime needs more humane touches. Wakhane, at the moment of crisis, seems to have regretted his insensitivity towards his daughter, but he does not learn from his experience, as he is indifferent to Sia's traumatic experience. He still wants to perpetuate the mystification of power though it has cost him his daughter's life. Mamadi, who has grabbed power, has also proven to be quicker to use the sword than reason and has begun his reign on the same foundation of lies. The inner circle of men keep the secret of this power. It is clear that the filmmaker challenges this order, but it is also evident that he presents dominant masculinity as far from changing, however undesirable that may be. By exposing this regime, Kouyate challenges the predominantly masculine parameters that characterise African politics. Political regimes often have bloody ends because the men in question are not eager to negotiate with and accommodate oppositional views. This is often seen in the endemic exiles and elimination of opponents. At the end of the film, the viewer feels the pointlessness of the emperor's murder and the exile of the royal family. As the queen and the little prince are being escorted to the border of the neighbouring country, the community is gripped by sadness watching their departure. This is particularly poignant for the little boy who has been the playmate of the prince, an innocent victim of a bad regime. Although the people can do nothing to prevent this exile, it is clear that they question a form of intolerance that exiles its citizens. The film ends with a question mark: it is time for self-examination and conscientisation among the masses. The responsibility for the continuity of the system is a collective one, just as the responsibility to challenge it should be. Kouyate represents the myth of power and the power of myth as challengeable.

Male African filmmakers increasingly question dominant masculinity by exposing myths, traditions and practices that not only diminish the humanity of its advocates and practitioners, but also cause untold suffering to subaltern groups in society. The sensitivity of these filmmakers in portraying such practices, as in Idrissa Ouedraogo's *Tilai* (1990) and *Yaaba* (1986), Cheick Oumar Sissoko's *Finzan* (1987), Jeanne Pierre Dikonge-Pipa's *Muna Moto* (1975) and Ousmane Sembène's *Xala* (1973)[25] are signs of hope that change is gradually affecting cultural practices that at one time seemed eternal and unshifting.

8. Masculinity in Selected North African Films: An Exploration[1]

John D. H. Downing

Before beginning this exploration of masculinity in selected North African films I will dispense with certain preliminaries that demand attention. They are the notion of masculinity itself; stereotypical Western discussions concerning masculinity in Africa and Islam; notions of the 'Third World,' 'Africa' and the 'Maghreb'; academic discourse around the film director as *auteur*; the analysis of acting in cinema, because much of my commentary will address the characters in these narratives; and distinctions between Egyptian and Maghrebi cinema. This will not be a lengthy discussion, but simply indicates where I stand. In particular, however, I hope in this review of films to poke some holes in trite Orientalist stereotypes of North African and Arab cultures.

Masculinity. It is hardly news that masculinity has been under deconstruction. Anthropologists such as Andrea Cornwall and Nancy Lindisfarne have been able to demonstrate the emptiness in the actual social practice of dualistic definitions of gender: their fluctuations, their subtle inflections, their contradictions. Although masculinity has traditionally been defined in binary terms, as signifying a blend of determination, endurance, tenacity, moral strength, courage, intelligence, rationality, vision and the capacity to be solitary, whereas femininity has been viewed as the mirror-opposite of these, contemporary perspectives are more attuned to the variability of such traits expressed in gender roles. Film criticism has joined this wave (cf. Bingham, *Acting Male*) and seeks to disentangle the various strands of masculinity and femininity within cinematic discourse, rather than simply identifying patriarchal stereotypes.

There is a danger of over-simplifying, of taking masculinity as a generic metaphor for socially diffused power in a roughly Foucauldian sense and femininity as a metaphor for weakness, or, likewise, simply identifying masculinity with violence. This latter dimension is where terms such as 'masculinism' or 'misogyny' (the latter term I take to be a more ideologically waterproof and aggressive version of masculinism), are appropriate. 'Social' masculinity and femininity are the terms I will use below to refer to the more generic cultural and social forms that characterise all societies, though they are realities independent of physical difference; albeit in practice they are ideologically recategorised under the same terms, as with 'race.'

Masculinity, Africa and Islam. The subject of masculinity is unavoidable, because all the films I shall discuss are set within African nations with an overwhelming Muslim majority. The continent of Africa has been endowed, in the imagination of the general Western public, including its more highly educated circles, with a particularly large dose of masculinism and misogyny. Enlightened attitudes towards women are perceived as rare, with the practice of female genital cutting— widespread in certain regions and districts of West and East Africa—being perhaps the most routine example cited of harsh and barbarous masculinism.

The documentary *Warrior Marks* (1993), on female genital cutting, directed by Pratibha Parmar, inspired by novelist Alice Walker and shot by Nancy Schiesari, attracted considerable attention from standard Western critics and pro-African commentators alike. For the former group, the fact the film showed older women themselves to be the cutters and for cutting to be akin to their profession, seemed to prove the ultimate depths of ethical degradation: How could these women lend themselves to such cruelty against their younger 'sisters'? A number of US pro-African critics, by contrast, felt the film played into the hands of racist ideologues through its failure to contextualise the practice and by seeing it in purely moral terms. These critics, arguably, had fallen prey to the need to deny or mitigate all negative aspects of the continent in order to combat White racism at home. It could be argued, though, that the majority of Western interpretation had fallen into the snare of the 'noble savage' myth, reframed as 'the African woman' and that the cutters' demolition of that myth was then taken to connote its obverse, namely that African women are enthusiastic reproducers of their own patriarchal suppression.[2] As a result, for the most politically correct of reasons, Africa becomes constructed—once more—as culturally and morally inferior. The rich differences throughout the continent, the struggles for justice that pervade it, including the struggles against misogyny and female genital cutting, are obliterated. It is akin to the historical treatment of foot-binding in China and *sati* (suttee) in India, a negative that somehow siphons off every single other facet of the culture and leaves the West feeling rather pleased with itself.

Likewise with Islam: the West is typically only too ready to homogenise more than 1 billion adherents, not least in the realm of gender relations.[3] Yet this perspective is entirely blinkered in regard to national and regional variations within Islamised cultures, the meld between Islamic practice and older cultures and the energetic challenges that women—and a number of men—in Islamic cultures are mounting to patriarchal codes. This point has been effectively argued by Barbara Callaway and Lucy Creevey for Senegal and Northern Nigeria and by Elizabeth Warnock Fernea, Soraya Duval, Wilhelmina

Jansen, Marjo Buitelaar and Evers Rosander in Karin Ask and Marit Tjomsland's book *Women and Islamization* in relation to Egypt, Tunisia, Algeria, Morocco and Senegal. Even though the label 'feminism' is one that they are uncomfortable with—as, unfortunately, to break another stereotype, are many American women—their actions and agendas frequently overlap with core feminist agendas. Moreover, as demonstrated by a number of the films we shall examine (and a considerable number of North African novels that are not part of this discussion), a variety of cinematic and literary challenges to traditions of subordinating women have been visible for some decades.

'Third World,' 'Africa,' 'Maghreb.' Without going into detail, it is also the case that these categories have considerable problems as containers in which to place films from Africa. Insofar as they homogenise and flatten out the diversity in place and insofar as they carry with them a colonialist and neo-colonialist contempt, they must be rejected. If they are used for brevity's sake, it is important also to signal their shortcomings. Words are struggled over.

Auteur Theory. Given this warning not to homogenise regions or binarise gender, the compass needle in film studies could well veer towards the notion of director as *auteur,* simply because these categories—Africanity, Islam, Third World, Maghreb, male-female—are so deconstructed and so dissipated that the director of a film represents an empirical reality to which we can gratefully hang. At least we can speak of Youssef Chahine, Merzak Allouache and Ben Lyazid without them melting into air. I want, however, to avoid this move to the *auteur,* not entirely and absolutely, but as a knee-jerk over-reaction to false categorisation. I do so in the name of cinematic, literary, theatrical and popular cultural intertextuality, in the name of the intertextuality of the Ouagadougou and Carthage biennial film festivals, in the name of Islamic cultures and French colonial and neo-colonial cultures (and in the case of Egypt, just a little bit, British colonialism and neo-colonialism), not to mention the industrial sociology and political economy of cinema. A substantial swing to the *auteur* would divert attention from these important dimensions.

Acting in the cinema. James Naremore and Dennis Bingham are two authors whose work is helpful in conceptualising the roles of acting within the ensemble of films. Naremore proposes that:

> Western culture as a whole, from at least the Renaissance onward, has [prompted us] to think of ourselves as unified, transcendent subjects of experience who express an innate personality through daily activity, ultimately becoming star players in our personal scenarios... In fact... the self is more like an effect of structure—a crowd of signifiers, without any particular origin or essence, held in place by ideology and codes of representation... By analysing the paradoxes of performance in film, by

showing how roles, star personae and individual 'texts' can be broken down into various expressive attributes and ideological functions, we inevitably reflect on the pervasive theatricality of society itself.[4]

This formulation of the contribution of acting meshes well with the nuanced understanding of masculinity I have been proposing, an understanding evinced interestingly by Bingham's discussion of James Stewart, Jack Nicholson and Clint Eastwood.[5]

Egyptian and Maghrebi cinemas. There is a distinct difference between most Egyptian cinema, with its star system and films from the Maghreb. Sabry Hafez suggests that Maghrebi films 'may share certain traits with . . . Egyptian cinema, from the relative size of frame, lighting techniques, camera movement and close-up on human gaze, to narrative flow and other salient features of the canonical format; but their montage, syntax and rules of codification are different.'[6] Maghrebi features have been produced in a very different institutional setting from Egyptian features. The former have generally been closer to an *auteur* cinema than an industrial model, except for the signal third case of Algerian state productions that have, for years, contented themselves with praising the heroism of the nationalist struggle.

Selected Films

I have not selected these films as a random representative sample of North African cinema. For example, there is no Egyptian musical or Algerian national struggle epic. I have chosen them because they are interesting texts and artworks in a variety of ways, given the focus of this book, but also because most are accessible in the United States in a subtitled form.[7] Moving from the course and the classroom to scholarly discussion in print to professional film critics is an important initial step in the diffusion of North African and Arab cinema in the Anglophone world, as is the awareness of both the audience and the distributors. This region is one of the last to reach the Anglophone world, though it has been well established in the francophone world for a long time, as the bibliography demonstrates.

I shall explore, to varying degrees, four Egyptian and five Maghrebi movies. From Tunisia: *The Flight* (*Al-Hurub*, dir. Atef al-Tayeb, 1991), *Dreams of Hind and Kamilia* (*Ahlam Hind wa Kamilah*, dir. Mohammed Khan, 1988), *Terrorism and Barbecue* (*El Erhab wal Kebab*, dir. Sherif Arafa, 1992), *The Band and the Bracelet* (*Al-Tawq wal-Iswiran*, dir. Khairy Bishara, 1986), *Silences of the Palace* (*Samt al-qusur*, dir. Moufida Tlatli, 1996) and *Aziza* (dir. Abdellatif Ben-Ammar, 1980); From Algeria: *Omar Gatlato* (dir. Merzak Allouache, 1976) and *Bab el-Oued City* (dir. Merzak Allouache, 1994); and the Moroccan *A Door On The Sky* (*Bab al-Sama' Maftuh*, dir. Farida Ben-Lyazid, 1988).

The Flight presents a mixture of melodrama, detective and social realist genres, with a strong critical element of police corruption.[8] It centres on a petty criminal in a Cairo migrant labour visa racket who finds that his latest assignment is to hoodwink, not strangers, but desperate people from his native village in Upper Egypt. He finds he cannot do business as usual and is determined to do right by his village, namely to get them properly forged passports and visas that will pass scrutiny on arrival. This will cost his boss considerably and most likely cancel out any profit from the transaction.

His boss, enraged, plants drugs in his room, shops him to the police and thereby gets him wrongfully thrown into jail for his pains. His girlfriend takes up with his boss while he is serving his term. The rest of the film follows his attempts at revenge on those who betrayed him, including his girlfriend. He kills his boss but then accidentally kills two other individuals and becomes Public Enemy Number One. Most of the film is preoccupied with portraying his daring escapes and his battle of wits with two levels of the police force: the Cairo police chiefs and the local police chief from his village.

The film can be read as a classic portrayal of social class and village clan loyalty, even as a celebration of the virtues of village life as opposed to the heartlessness of the capital city, but it particularly centres on male bonding. In its action-police movie dimension, it mostly foregrounds the relationship between this essentially decent and even brave-hearted petty criminal and the resolute police chief from his home village with whom he grew up. Their paths diverge, only to reconnect with ultimately tragic consequences. They end up gunned down together, dying in each other's arms, by order of a cynical and despotic Cairo police chief who wants them both silenced and sacrificed to boost his image as tough on law-and-order. Clan and village solidarity (and the masculine bond that is an essential element of that solidarity) repeatedly battles with the demands of law and order, with the official representatives of the latter portrayed as mostly corrupt, despicable and brutal—the village police chief being a shining exception. What is interesting here is the centrality of bonding between the local police chief and the criminal, for both of whom honouring a promise and family loyalty are central.

Compared to those values and the relationship between the local police chief and the criminal, the criminal's emotional relationship with his new girlfriend, a professional nightclub singer, takes second or even third place once he is out of jail. Tenderness between the couple is restricted to very brief moments indeed. She seems to be there solely to underscore his masculinity. Indeed, we see them in bed together early in their relationship, complaining that she cannot handle any more sexual activity. Through this scene his superior virility is established early. She is also there to confirm that underneath the killings, for which he is (mostly inadvertently) responsible, he is a good person, lovable in fact. The girlfriend is a supporter only; her most active role is to engage in a screaming catfight with her female neighbour to divert the police's attention while he escapes.

The fact that these masculine values and the male bond are doomed in the film does not subvert them, but rather enthrones them. The film leaves the audience with the memory of numerous close-ups of the solemn, determined faces of the two protagonists, 'real men' tragically set apart and fated to die in each others' arms. Warmth and toughness die hand in hand and Egypt is the loser.

While *The Flight* is a conventional piece in many respects, structured almost like a weekly soap opera, *Hind and Kamilia* presents a different picture. It is the story of two women friends in Cairo and how their mutual support carries them through many trials and tribulations, all imposed on them by the men in their environment.

Here, there is no male character to applaud or even for whom to feel sorry. Kamilia has been rejected because she is childless. Her fat and distasteful husband requires food and sex on demand and flies into a violent rage if neither is supplied as and when he wants it. Hind's boyfriend, played by Ahmed Zaki, makes a pass at Kamilia, literally behind Hind's back in the cinema where they are watching a movie. He later brings his petty thief friend to burgle the apartment where she is employed as a cleaner and the low-life friend actually threatens her with a knife when she protests. Later the boyfriend makes Hind pregnant. Then, through his petty thieving, Hind's boyfriend gets thrown into jail so he cannot support her or his daughter. The only point where the women are happy is when they are on their own. This lifestyle is especially displayed in the climactic scene at the beach in Alexandria where Hind plays with her baby daughter Ahlam, the only dream left to them.[9] The film also underscores the constant support women offer each other, which is so alien to the relationships between themselves and males, who represent a constant threat to their peace and security.

The depiction of masculinity is, in sharp contrast to *The Flight*, unrelievedly unappealing, as it is in the village of *The Band And The Bracelet*.[10] This film, based on a novel of the same title by Yahia Al-Taher Abdullah, is set in the period from 1933 to 1948 and examines recurring tragedies in three generations of one family. The family members are, in the first generation, a mother (Hazina), her brother (Mostafa) and her husband; the second generation is their daughter Fahima and her husband, Haddad; and finally the third generation is the daughter's daughter (Farha). These names, as Ghada Helmy emphasises in 'The Plight of Women in Filmic Text and Literary Adaptation,' are emblematic of their roles: *hazina* means 'the grieved or mournful one'; *fahima* means 'understanding'; *farha* means 'joy'; *haddad* means 'blacksmith' (but here with perhaps a sour twist, because the firmness of the iron with which he works in his smithy does not carry over to his sexual behaviour). Helmy provides a good analysis of the film as a whole, but I will focus solely upon its representations of masculinity.

The males, generation after generation, are a sorry group: paralysed and dying (the grandfather, played by the director himself); absent for nearly two decades (Mostafa, the brother); sexually impotent (Al-Haddad, the daughter's husband). Farha's young lover impregnates her and leaves her. Mostafa is brutal in the enforcement of the virginity code for his niece, burying Farha up to her neck and refusing her water or food until she names the father. Another young man, her would-be lover, rescues her then kills her. Mostafa, shouting at him rather than killing him, asks 'Did you think my stick was too soft?' There is no need to subscribe to all of Freud's research in order to read *that* remark as evocative. Fahima, despite having herself conceived Farha in a mysterious night-time temple ritual, seemingly constructed by the village to cope secretly with infertility, is so rigidly entrenched in the ideology of sexual shame that she informs Mostafa of Farha's pregnancy and does nothing to help her escape. The suffocating masculinist ideology the film critiques has women as well as men in its stranglehold.

Like *The Flight*, the action is meant to be redolent of Upper Egypt, albeit in the 1930s and 1940s, so that urban-rural and social class sentiments play both a part in the production of the film's narrative and in its reception. However, *The Flight* portrays clan life rather sympathetically, whereas *The Band and the Bracelet* takes no prisoners. The visual contrast is extremely powerful between Farha's spontaneous dancing joy when her uncle Mostafa, whom she has only ever heard of, finally turns up after twenty years away and when he later beats her up and buries her, half-conscious from the beating, once he finds she is pregnant. And the impotent Haddad, Fahima's husband, is often seen playing with or twirling a stick.

Although the women have some strength imputed to them, for good (when the women join the men in stoning an unpopular local entrepreneur) or for ill (Haddada, Haddad's unrelievedly vicious and grasping sister), the destinies of the Hazina, the grandmother of Fahima, the daughter who dies in childbirth and the granddaughter, Farha, whose fate we have seen, are those of the absolutely powerless. Hegemonised, Hazina says she would bury her granddaughter herself if she had the strength. As the opposite term to what we have called 'social masculinity,' these 'feminine' roles seem to accentuate the untrammelled agency of the males—except that the males, too, are demonstrably puppets of their own circumscribed destinies. Mostafa is away in Palestine, which is in the process of shifting from British to Zionist settler rule and comes back with little or nothing to show for his years of labour. How far the film ultimately is intended as a parable of the modern Arab struggle against both history and the international system would be an intriguing topic for further exploration.

In some ways the film has echoes of *The Ballad of Narayama* (dir. Shohei Imamura, 1983), set in the mountains of northern Japan in the late nineteenth century and even of *Babette's Feast* (dir. Gabriel Axel, 1987), set in a remote fundamentalist village in Denmark in the same era. For all three, rural life is suffused with idiocy and is nasty, brutish and short. Cinema-going in Egypt is, even today, far more an urban than a rural phenomenon and multi-faceted cinematic portrayals of farming communities and rural culture have been rare.[11] The stereotypification of rural life is also a dimension of these portrayals of masculinity.

In *Terrorism and Barbecue*, a comedy with a sharp edge, Ahmed, a middle-class office worker, tries to get official permission to transfer his two small children to a school near their home. He goes to the Mugamaa, the semi-circular tower block in Cairo that serves as a major government building and there his frustrations begin to mount. He is told that the official who can solve his problem is nowhere to be found and the two others in his office are a secretary endlessly chatting to her friend on the phone and a bulky Islamist who seems to be preoccupied with saying prayers rather than working. At one point in a sequence of events (which would take too long to detail here), the police are called in on him and he accidentally takes hold of one of their automatic weapons. He suddenly finds himself defined as a terrorist. The building is evacuated almost entirely and he faces the acute dilemma of how to extricate himself and the others without being gunned down by the anti-terrorist detachments sent to the scene.

Social masculinity in *Terrorism and Barbecue* figures in a different way than in the films reviewed above. In the overall narrative of the film, the depictions of the state's and public's social masculinity are set in an intriguing dialectic. Let us first address the state. The outward signs of state power are definitively socially masculine: the menacing anti-terrorist shock troops, armed to the teeth with automatic weapons, with sinister black helmets and visors, marking quick time with their boots; the general in the Mugamaa enjoying himself rebuking the private assigned to his office; and the interior minister pontifically announcing that his ministry deals in deeds, not words and striding self-importantly out of the Cabinet meeting without regard for the prime minister or his colleagues.

Yet, when we first see the minister as he gets the news that the Mugamaa has been occupied by terrorists, he complains about being disturbed just as his ministerial colleagues have had a chance to sit around and listen to the radio. This response is hardly a flattering commentary on the demands of their jobs, or their fulfilment of them. When Ahmed accidentally seizes the automatic rifle, the other soldiers with automatic rifles instantly drop them and flee and a whole swarm of state bureaucrats, mostly male, flee the building in abject fear like sheep.[12] The perpetually praying fundamentalist bureaucrat proposes that a group of the captives rush Ahmed and his handful of allies—a high-class call girl, a farmer repeatedly denied elementary justice by the courts and a Nubian[13]—but the other bureaucrats tell him 'After you!' And he relapses into silence. A child is called upon to take a two-way radio into the building to Ahmed, when he returns his mother shouts to the interior minister, the generals attending him and the surrounding media: 'He's faced the terrorists, he's only a child, *he* has no uniform or epaulettes!'

The state is thus presented as having the power to prevent—perhaps—but not necessarily the power—or even the will—to take initiatives for the public good. Three powerful symbolic moments occur to underscore this. One is when Ahmed is in the Mugamaa toilet calling out for Mr Medhat, the elusive bureaucrat he has been told can solve his dilemma. A stereotypically camp gay man waltzes out and eyes Ahmed up and down while saying to him winsomely, 'I could be Medhat if you want, I can be incredibly Medhat.' The second is when the minister begins to talk on the walkie talkie and Ahmed deputises the call girl to answer for him. The minister is shocked that it is 'a feminine voice, a tender voice; I was expecting more of a man's voice.' The third is when the minister sends some troops up in a fire truck hoist to enter the building by a window and Ahmed turns a fire hose on them, drenching them and provoking the hoist's rapid detumescence. These three moments, I would suggest, are significant because of their play with social masculinity in the narrative. The powerful, but always invisible, decision-making Medhat is momentarily transformed in our imagination into someone who can be imagined as quasi-feminine, even cottageing in the men's toilet. Satire, social gender and sexuality combine. In the minister's imagination, terrorists and the interior ministry are formally akin, socially masculine to the core, hence his shock at the woman's voice. Yet the macho minister is in fact being confronted by the powerless, whose simple waterpower (urination?), without wounds or guns, can shrink the state's phallic might.

By contrast, about a third through the narrative, just after Ahmed has been physically thrown out of a neighbouring government building and is about to give up his fruitless quest, he spots an elderly man at whom he had smiled when first heading to Mugamaa. The man, crisply attired in suit and tie, had been preaching loudly to travellers on the packed bus that they were letting themselves be pushed around and failing to insist on their rights. He had gotten off the bus after a final peroration and had continued walking down the sidewalk still expostulating out loud and waving his arms. That is when Ahmed, disillusioned with bureaucracy, sees the old man again, still walking down the street and *still* expostulating. His resolve is resurrected and intensified and he goes back into the Mugamaa, ready to do battle. It is shortly after that that he accidentally finds himself holding the soldier's weapon.

The elderly man has a pivotal role in the narrative. It suggests that social masculinity is something to be associated with the elderly, as we have seen it already associated with a small child and yet by implication it is absent from the middle-aged group conventionally expected to have the most agency. Is this a shaming device? Is masculinity here being used to try to galvanise agency? Is the character of Ahmed—variously humorous, reasonable, conflict-avoiding, irritated by idiocy, stunned at the turn of events he has accidentally let loose, tactically shrewd—perhaps an amalgam of the socially masculine and the socially feminine? Does he represent an ideal of the Egyptian nation?

Silences of the Palace is set in Tunisia in the postwar period, during the nationalist movement's agitation against French colonial rule. It is set in one of the Beys' palaces. It focuses principally upon the women's lot, constrained to stay in the palace, used as sexual and domestic slaves and condemned to suffer in voiceless silence. The two principal women characters are Khedija, the mother and Alia, her daughter by a Bey. The narrative mostly covers the coming of age of Alia and her mother's frantic efforts to protect her from the abuse she herself has not had the resources to resist.

The first film by a woman director in this discussion constructs masculine characters, with two partial exceptions, rather like in *Hind and Kamilia* or *The Band and the Bracelet*. That is to say, they are rapacious, harsh and self-obsessed, with the exception of Chérif, a drunk and foolish comic foil. Admittedly the male leads, with the exception of the teacher, are representatives of the old feudal order, glad to be assimilated into French colonial culture. To that extent, their version of masculinity can be slightly distanced from a hypothetical present, perhaps making the film's message about women's silencing more assimilable to unreconstructed males in the audience.

It could be argued that Khedija's silent and fatal miscarriage following her use of abortifacients, beyond its intercutting with the theme of anti-colonial revolt, represents a socially masculine response. The message is: endurance of suffering and death without complaint suggests a superordinate level of self-control of the kind that masculinism prides as its own (think of all those ludicrously gallant dying heroes on film battlefields).[14] Except that Khedija's martyrdom is in no way ludicrous and is waged out of desire to protect her daughter, not in the clash of military weapons. It contrasts starkly with the craven males, whose aggression is turned inwards on Tunisian women, not against the colonisers.

The teacher seems to be more 'modern' and more sympathetic than the feudalists for much of the narrative. The film begins with his depiction later in time than the bulk of the action, as someone who has insisted Alia, the female lead, abort any children they have conceived together. The result of her repeated abortions has been the deterioration of her health and the collapse of her singing voice, which is both how she earns her living and her rupture of women's silence. The teacher's different generational political culture does not seem to alterered his masculinism one jot.

There are two symptomatic moments in the film's discourse concerning masculinity. The first redefines fatherhood from biology to social reality, when Khedija upbraids Alia in response to her daughter's anger about the identity and 'absence' of her father. She says, 'Is a father simply a name? A father is sweat, pain and joy. An entire life. Daily caring.' The second moment equates colonialism and patriarchy, when one of the women, maddened by the French curfew and its all-too-gross parallel with the Beys' harem, screams: 'Our *lives* are like curfews. We don't belong to ourselves. We have nothing to be afraid of. I want to go out in the street, naked, barefoot ... without being stopped ... to scream and shout out loud. Only their bullets can shut me up, as they pass through me as if through a sieve.' She collapses in tears, the fact staring her in the face, in the midst of her passionate rhetoric, that she is facing two immensely powerful and utterly ruthless enemies. Colonialism and patriarchy are twinned in this film, as are femininity and nationalism. At a key juncture, Alia sings a Tunisian nationalist song, scandalising many of her listeners, but the songs of the legendary Egyptian chanteuse Umm Kulthum are her stock in trade.[15]

Aziza, also from Tunisia, shows the female lead asserting herself strongly and once again constructed male characters, not least the buffoon-like Gulf Arab role, that could hardly be regarded as sympathetic. Ben-Ammar has said explicitly that he wanted to:

> ... show that women are more and more to be reckoned with, that half of the Tunisian population can't be left out of account. Even if women like Aziza are in the minority, they have a demeanor and an attitude which forces us to take account of them. Victims yesterday and still sometimes so today, tomorrow they will be pushing forward a genuine renewal.[16]

Omar Gatlato, which marks a sharp break with the heroic tradition of Algerian cinema and which was nearly suppressed by the government, focused on a young denizen of the working-class suburb of Algiers that is featured in the other Allouache film discussed below.[17] Omar is torn between masculinist rhetoric and paralysing shyness in the face of a potential girlfriend. We see his character and his numerous frustrations exemplified in a number of scenes in the film. The film has him address the audience directly on several occasions, an effective device for encourageing us mentally to join in dialogue with him and see the world through his eyes.

This close-up is telling, when his male friends are egging him on and the young woman who finds him attractive is waiting for him (not knowing he is just out of sight) he still cannot bring himself to walk the fifty or sixty metres that lie between them. Allouache, amongst other things, seems to suggest that social space for people such as Omar is extremely limited. The mores insist on male aggressiveness and have no space for someone whose personal psychology cannot support the masculinist rhetoric they reiterate.[18]

However, Mouny Berrah has an important observation to make. He identifies the core values of the *rejla* which have often been inadequately translated as 'machismo' by Western commentators, as 'the respect of others, the given promise, faithfulness in love, unbreakable friendships.'[19] Omar confesses to the audience at the beginning of the film that these core values are killing and suffocating him. These values, which are constantly celebrated in the popular songs that he adores, bind Omar and his close male friends together. These values parallel the values celebrated in *The Flight*.

In his later *Bab el-Oued City*, Allouache identifies masculinism closely with fundamentalist Islam. Boalem, who works an early shift in a bakery, cannot sleep because of the loudspeaker from the local mosque that has been placed on top of his apartment block. He cannot cope with the disruption of his sleep any longer and unobserved by anyone except Yasmina, his admirer, rips down the loudspeaker and disposes of it. This creates consternation among the young male members of a fundamentalist group, who take it as their mission to find and punish the blasphemous thief. The film depicts the developing confrontation.

In the character of Said—who is also Yasmina's brother—we see a concentration of hatred, aggression and ultimately self-hatred. He fights physically with Yasmina. He calls in his four cronies to beat up Boalem when he himself cannot overcome him in a fair combat. He tells his own mother not to watch a television soap opera. He bursts in on another woman in the neighbourhood, Ouadja and terrorises her with his pistol (which is unloaded, a phallic allusion?) and he polices the streets, strutting through them aggressively with his little gang. One of his groups is seen boasting in one scene about his own (probably imagined) experiences as a *mujahid* in Afghanistan. Another indicates he is actually desperate to return to France, where he feels he really belongs, but is part of the group for the moment. The young men are at their most aggressive when together, seemingly in need of each other to prop up their phalluses. Apart, their personas are less obnoxious, with the exception of Said. However, Said himself is in reality taking orders from some well-heeled hoods. Masculinism takes some frontal assaults in this text.

Masculinity, however, is more variably constructed. Boalem, his friend and workmate Mabrouk, their boss the baker and the *imam* in the local mosque are all presented as reasonable human beings. The three secular men are neither especially good nor especially bad and the imam voices his heartfelt dismay at and condemnation of the violence perpetrated by the fundamentalists. However, when Mabrouk is being beaten up by Said and his followers, the scene is intercut with a totally different one, of the women in the apartment block standing on the roof and enjoying themselves as a highly camp male denizen of their block entertains them with a humorous skit of familiar television characters. The gender statement could hardly be blunter in its contrast.

And then there is a final character, Amar the postman, who abruptly interjects into the conversation that he hates both fundamentalists and women. His role seems more to round out the picture, to indicate the out-of-the-blue misogyny that will voice itself in casual conversation rather than to contribute to the narrative as such. The source of Amar's dual frustration is that he is unsuccessful in his attempts to engage with women amorously and the young fundamentalists despise him.

In *A Door on the Sky* the storyline concerns principally the journey to self-awareness and mature self-assertion of Nadia, who returns in a hurry from France to her father's deathbed.[20] It focuses centrally on masculinity, inasmuch as it traces the struggle to establish a spiritually authentic space in which women can function, a space that masculinism and misogyny deny in many cultures and by a variety of means. Including, as the film portrays, through some women. Nadia ends by transcending gender roles.

The film traces Nadia's transformation through two phases. The first transition is from a strident, two-colour dyed hair, miniskirted and booted young secularist to someone who has rediscovered the resources of Islam, at least in one of its Sufi variants. The second is her need to have a mutually respectful relationship with her male lover, which collides with the growing separatist sectarianism of the women's shelter she helped found. From having excluded only abusive men, the majority of the women move to excluding all men, including her lover. She is forced by this to make the second transition and leave the commune she herself brought into being. Their absolutism appears as the mirror image of masculinism.

One of the film's two sharpest notes of asperity in gender relations seems to define neo-colonialist culture as the most corrosive and dangerous masculinism of all. It arises in the early depiction of Nadia's relationship with her French boyfriend. Their exchange has the force of a cataclysmic break-up out of the scriptwriter's own experience: 'I don't need Western guilt over the supper table!' rages Nadia. The fact that in the beginning she cannot even react to her father's death is tribute to the film's perception of the numbing impact of the culture from which we see her, in this rage, gradually shaking herself free. Yet Driss, her brother, albeit loudly proclaiming his right to dispose of the family house regardless of his sisters' preferences, is constructed as a rather insubstantial presence in the narrative.

Gender relations are presented in a utopian fashion in a number of scenes. The old house caretaker, a Sufi devotee and mystic, is constructed as an altogether benign character, returning to Nadia in a vision after his death to bless the women's shelter project. At the Sufi celebration, men and women celebrate side-by-side and dance in each others' presence, but not as a spectacle to each other. Non-abusive men are, initially at least, allowed into the shelter. In the final sequences of the film, Nadia and her boyfriend are seen in shot after shot in idyllic equality, wrapped up in each other's love, absorbed in each other as human beings. Perhaps the film calls upon us to make our own the Italian students' challenge of the 1970s: 'Be realistic! Demand the impossible!'

Two Final Comments

Quite often in these films, males are presented as highly subject to external control, deprived of autonomy yet insisting on depriving women of their autonomy too. This is a rather well-known phenomenon, whether we are thinking of Afrikaners in South Africa, militant Zionists in Palestine/Israel, or even just the ritual torments that senior members of institutions typically impose upon new initiates. Yet it suggests a common thread in these cinematic critiques of masculinism and misogyny. A number of postcolonial writers have proposed that colonialism and neo-colonialism and their accompanying poverty and powerlessness, have prevented men from exercising their role as providers for women and children in their extended families. This is an immensely powerful shaming experience in cultures in which shame and honour are central.[21]

As for the much-debated topic of *auteur* theory, two observations: first, the majority of these films are by male directors, often with an all-male crew. Only two are by women directors and in both instances they wrote the screenplay too. This suggests that although patriarchal forces have greatly reduced the number of women able to be active in these spheres, their extrusion has not been paralleled by any across-the-board refusal to address seriously the issues discussed in this chapter. Second, this further suggests that the partly subterranean movement of women in the Islamic world noted earlier is having an artistic impact in the world of cinema. Certainly a considerable number of modern North African and Arab films and novels by women and men foreground questions of masculinity and the rights of women.

9. Penetrating *Xala*

Bernth Lindfors

Interpreters of Ousmane Sembène's *Xala* tend to agree that El Hadji Abdou Kader Beye's sexual impairment operates metonymically to signify a much larger systemic malfunction in the political economy of postcolonial Africa. That is, a part—in this case El Hadji's flaccid private part—represents the wholesale public emasculation of Africa's petite bourgeoisie, who are seen as a sterile class of corrupt, parasitic entrepreneurs incapable of engageing in productive activities. The impotence with which El Hadji is cursed is thus far more than an embarrassing individual affliction, being in addition a symptom of something gone devastatingly awry in the entire body politic.

Françoise Pfaff has made the interesting observation that:

> Sembène implies that Africa, in order to grow and truly assert itself, should be fecund and nurturing like a woman...[He] intimates that the African woman is earth/land and 'Mother Africa' the genetrix of a new Africa...El Hadji is impotent (inability to 'plough' through the 'earth'/penetrate the woman) because he has misused the fecundity of Africa/woman to assert his social and male ascendancy. A true example of the 'rapacious bourgeoisie' denounced by Fanon, El Hadji first robbed a peasant (the beggar) of his land and then diverted tons of rice (another fertility symbol) to his own profit. Africa and N'Gone are fecund but El Hadji is unable to impregnate them because of his socioeconomical/sexual impotence, thus causing the barrenness/sterility of Africa.[1]

Without wishing to belabour an argument so pregnant with seminal ideas, I fear that Pfaff, by conflating N'Gone with Mother Africa, may be pushing the fecundity issue to a point where it is in danger of miscarrying, for N'Gone, at least as presented in the novel, could hardly be construed as a nurturing genetrix. Indeed, her own mother and aunt are eager to marry her off because they recognise she is stupid and suspect her of being immoral. They 'dread the month when she won't be washing her linen at nights' (6)—i.e., when she has been made pregnant by one of the unemployed young 'loafers' who take her to movies and dances. Described as a 'child of national flags and hymns' (7), N'Gone clearly represents another type of postcolonial profligacy and degradation. She certainly is not a symbol of anything wholesome. Her fecundity is viewed as dangerous because it could bring shame to her family.

And there is no other Mother Africa anywhere in sight, for all the rest of the women in the story have serious flaws of character too. The matchmaker Yay Bineta, described as 'a dumpy woman with a large behind' (5), is calculating, devious and materialistic, as well as being fundamentally unattractive. Oumi N'Doye is jealous, possessive and demanding, 'a volcano' (75) of emotion who abandons her husband when life gets tough. Even Adja Awa Astou, though presented somewhat sympathetically as an exemplary Muslim wife who manages to maintain her dignity despite numerous annoyances and disappointments, is shown to be addicted to religion and not much fun in bed; she lacks the earthiness essential to a Mother Africa. And Rama, El Hadji's liberated daughter who at first glance appears to be enlightened and uppity enough to challenge patriarchal privilege, later is revealed as a reactionary upper-class pseudo-revolutionary, one who cannot endure the company of the truly oppressed proletariat and tries her best to protect her father from the ritualised humiliation of an exorcism through lower-class spit. No, none of these flawed women could bring about a regeneration of Africa.

Perhaps a more sensible way to approach Sembène's *Xala* is not by means of a feminist or gyno-critical hermeneutics, but rather through a straightforward phallocentric exegesis. Impotence, after all, is a peculiarly masculine malady and we may be missing the point if we search too assiduously in the text for hidden recesses of meaning when all the pertinent figurative paraphernalia requiring attention may be up front and visible, dangling there within easy reach.

To take the most obvious example first, El Hadji himself can be considered a rather blunt, even protuberant phallic symbol. A member of the Chamber of Commerce and Industry, he rises and falls, becomes swollen with self-importance and then shrivels up, wants to extend himself beyond his capacity and cannot perform as required. In a sense he is a classic tragic hero, an over-reacher who does not recognise his own limitations and plunges recklessly into a void of self-destruction. But because his fatal flaw is represented as a physical shortcoming rather than as a psychological, philosophical, or spiritual weakness, El Hadji also serves as a comic hero, one who wilts ignominiously instead of tumbling precipitously. The emphasis is not on his hubris but on his pubis.

Sembène reinforces the bathos of El Hadji's situation by repeatedly playing on polarised images of expansiveness and isolation, movement and stasis, projection and retraction. Philip Rosen has called attention to the importance of journeys and spaces in Sembène's work, noting how 'journeys echo and inflect one another, while tracing . . . core-periphery geographies.' Of *Xala* he says:

...there is a point where the film elaborates the journey of El Hadji Abdoukader Beye *to* the countryside in search of a marabout who can lift the cure of impotence laid on him by a band of beggars. The beggars themselves have converged *from* the countryside on his place of business and home in the city, in order to wreak the revenge of the impoverished swindled out of their just share...[2]

One can push this comparison further by noting not only how core-periphery geographies function in the characterisation of El Hadji and his beggar adversaries but also how journeys traversing these geographies offer ironic insights into the power relationships that are of central concern in Sembène's narrative. El Hadji's honourific title (i.e., one who has made the Hajj or pilgrimage to Mecca) is a clear indication that he is someone who has travelled long distances. Not a religious man, he nonetheless has made a holy pilgrimage, using 'his growing affluence' (3), much of it from ill-gotten gains, to enhance his reputation and prestige. El Hadji also practices long-distance trade, his import-export shop being 'a large warehouse, which he rented from a Lebanese or a Syrian. At the height of his success it was crammed with sacks of rice from Siam, Cambodia, South Carolina and Brazil and with domestic goods and foodstuffs imported from France, Holland, Belgium, Italy, Luxemburg, England and Morocco' (60). El Hadji evidently is a worldly sort of man, having interests that extend around the globe.

And before he falls victim to the curse, he has unlimited mobility, for he owns a Mercedes, employs a driver, has acquired a minibus for transporting his children to school and has just purchased a two-seater car for his third wife. That these vehicles are emblematic of his potency is apparent from the intramural squabbling that goes on within his tripartite family over access to these resources. Oumi is aggrieved because she has not been allocated a car; the children do not enjoy sharing the minibus; Yay Bineta insists that N'Gone be provided with a chauffeur who can teach her to drive. These are demands on El Hadji's manhood, on his ability to provide satisfaction to all the women in his life. This is highlighted when, imagining that Oumi may have been the one to afflict him with the *xala*, he almost brings himself to beg, 'Please, if you are the cause, release me. I'll buy you a car' (67). He is willing to bribe his wife with shared mobility if she will only allow him to get moving again, presumably at his accustomed speed.

Once the curse is on him, El Hadji experiences severely reduced mobility. He is willing to go long distances to consult *marabouts* reputed to have the power to cure him, but he can go only part of the way by car and must finish the journey in a donkey-drawn cart or on foot. In the end he suffers the humiliation of having all his vehicles repossessed; at this point two of his wives desert him, for in his diminished state he no longer commands their respect.

Now he is almost completely isolated, having been cut off from the rest of the world and reduced to a single nuclear family unit. As he stands on a table to serve as the target for the beggars' spit, he is absolutely motionless. El Hadji, who had once driven furiously in the fast lane of life, heedless of others, has finally been brought to a dead stop. The final frame of the film freezes his immobility into a tableau of total paralysis.

The beggars, by contrast, start out immobile and end triumphant after a long and difficult trek to El Hadji's villa. They still have impaired mobility and the last line of the novel suggests that they too are about to be brought to a dead stop, but in the film version they are allowed to get their full revenge on a representative of the petite bourgeoisie, the class in society that has brought them low and kept them underfoot. The reversal of power relations between the rich and the poor, the able and the disabled, the quick and the slow, is now complete; the revolution has succeeded, albeit only in a limited sphere. In the unwritten chapter that may be presumed to follow, the beggars are not likely to inherit the earth or extend their own territory significantly. If they survive, they will remain an immobile underclass, despite their momentary advance at El Hadji's expense.

The remainder of the petite bourgeoisie, on the other hand, will continue to thrive, for they have mechanisms in place to guarantee their own safety. If a member of the Chamber of Commerce and Industry misbehaves, as El Hadji does, he can be expelled and another thief put in his place. In attempting to defend himself from complete commercial castration, El Hadji tries to confront his colleagues with evidence of their own economic impotence:

> Who owns the banks? The insurance companies? The factories? The businesses? The wholesale trade? The cinemas? The bookshops? The hotels? All these and more besides are out of our control. We are nothing better than crabs in a basket. We want the ex-occupier's place? We have it. This Chamber is the proof. Yet what change is there really in general or in particular? The colonialist is stronger, more powerful than ever before, hidden inside us, here in this very place. He promises us the left-overs of the feast if we behave ourselves. Beware anyone who tries to upset his digestion, who wants a bigger profit. What are we? Clodhoppers! Agents! Petty traders! In our fatuity we call ourselves 'businessmen'! Businessmen without funds (92–93).

El Hadji goes even further and accuses his accusers of bouncing cheques and selling quotas just as he has. To him it is a matter of the pot calling the kettle black, but to his colleagues in the Chamber El Hadji's counter-charges smack of class treason. He must be cut off in order for their own corrupt, exploitative practices to continue unabated. El Hadji thus is quickly expelled. His penetration into the charmed circle is abruptly terminated. He does not withdraw voluntarily; he is forced out, ejected, banished for good once and for all. In this foreshortened condition, a virtual social amputee, El Hadji loses all semblance of prior potency.

The story is told well in both book and film, but in the visual medium Sembène is able to reinforce his message by presenting contrasting scenes focusing on modes of locomotion. The opening motorcade ferrying members of the Chamber of Commerce and Industry, one member per Mercedes, through the busy streets of Dakar to El Hadji's wedding reception is nicely counterpointed with the concluding collective procession of beggars, some limping, some on crutches, some crawling or heaving themselves along dusty dirt paths. At the wedding reception itself, guests gracefully stroll in the garden, dance to slow music or sit in comfort and chat while the beggars and onlookers stand outside the gates silently gazing at the guests or fighting for the coins El Hadji throws on the ground. In another scene, where the beggars squatting in front of El Hadji's warehouse are rounded up by the police, they are hustled into a police van and efficiently carted away, but when El Hadji's Mercedes later is impounded, the policemen, not knowing how to drive such a vehicle, push it slowly down the street. These scenes help to underscore social and economic disparities by graphically depicting differences in locomotion, privilege and access to space and goods. In such a lopsided world there can be no doubt about who occupies the vital core and who the periphery. By pairing such scenes Sembène very effectively projects memorable images of a divided society.

Xala thus may be viewed as an exercise in concordial contrasts: virility versus impotence, mobility versus paralysis, centrality versus periphery, wealth versus poverty, decency versus indecency, love versus money, etc. The primary peg on which the story hangs remains El Hadji's unreliable penis, but Sembène enlarges and extends this protean tool in so many interesting directions in both film and novel that we are left with an unforgettable impression not just of one man's private life but also of the problems peculiar to unproductive postcolonial societies in which socialism is merely a bankrupt slogan. Ousmane Sembène's Xala thereby points with mock priapismic insistence at the real curse afflicting much of modern Africa.

Part II
Writing the Masculine

10. Rapacious Masculinity: Gender and Ethno-Colonial Politics in a Swahili Novel

Austin Bukenya

Asali Chungu (Bitter Honey), the text discussed in this chapter, is the earliest of Said Ahmed Mohamed's novels, which include *Utengano* (Separation), *Kiza Katika Nuru* (Darkness in Brightness), *Dunia Mti Mkavu* (The World Is a Dried Up Tree), *Babu Alipofufuka* (When Grandfather Came Back to Life) and *DuniaYao* (Their World). Mohamed is also a poet and dramatist, with poetry collections including *'Sikate Tamaa* (Despair Not), *Kina cha Maisha* (The Depth of Life) and *Jicho la Ndani* (The Inner Eye) and plays such as *Amezidi* (Beyond the Limits) and *Kitumbua Kimeingia Mchanga* (Sand in the Doughnut) to his name. He is also an eminent literary scholar whose critical and theoretical work, e.g., *Kunga za Nathari ya Kiswahili* (Fundamentals of Swahili Prose) commands considerable respect among his colleagues. His writings are therefore a good entry point into the intricacies of the 500-year-old corpus of Swahili writing.[1]

Mohamed's creative writing is characterised not only by a striking balance between traditional and innovative stylistic and structural techniques but also by an incisive and critical questioning of the institutions and assumptions of his postcolonial Swahili island society. Thus, in *Asali Chungu*, he takes to task the race-based class divisions among the Arabs, Creole Swahilis and Black Africans of Zanzibar and Pemba, as well as the injustices of a male autocracy that regards women as objects at the disposal of the feudal and colonial rulers. In the process, he exposes the unsustainability of such a system and the inevitability of the historical 1964 Revolution, against whose background the narrative of the novel ends.[2] Because the system is patently patriarchal, the narrative is bound to be a critique of the masculine presumptions that underpin the ruling class.

The tantalising taste of honey (*asali* in Kiswahili) and its elusive availability are common images in Swahili orature and literature.[3] Among the popular proverbs, for example, several of which are actually quoted in the novel, we have *Fuata nyuki ule asali* (Follow the bee and you will eat honey), *Mchovya asali huchonga mzinga* (the honey taster disturbs the hive), *Chovya chovya humaliza asali kibuyuni* (One little dip after another empties the gourd of its honey) and *Nta si asali: nalikuwa nazo si ufugaji* (Wax is not honey: long lost cattle do not mark a herdsman). Thus the title of Said Ahmed Mohamed's novel, *Asali Chungu* (Bitter Honey), is easily recognisable to Swahili readers as a coded riddle that the narrative is expected to help in unravelling. The author lives up to this expectation and this chapter suggests that the riddle of the honey losing its expected sweetness is the gradual crumbling of a masculine hegemony into a heap of horror and revulsion. Because the text is not readily accessible to non-Kiswahili speakers, a synopsis of the narrative may be appropriate before proceeding with the discussion. For the same reason, there will be a slightly more liberal presentation of translated excerpts from the novel than might be expected in a chapter of this length.[4]

On the face of it, *Asali Chungu* is the narrative of an intricate web of sexual and incestuous depravity set in motion by Bwana Zuberi, an 'Arab' colonial district commissioner in Zanzibar, who rapes one of his young African domestic employees some twenty-five years before the Zanzibar Revolution.[5] Semeni, the victim, flees from his house pregnant. Pili, the friend with whom Semeni seeks asylum, informs Zuberi of Semeni's pregnancy, but the district commissioner refuses to accept responsibility and throws Pili out of his office. Pili, who has a daughter, Baya, shelters Semeni and Dude (pronounced 'do-day' meaning 'Thingummy or nonentity'), the son that she eventually has. But the two women are forced by need into prostitution and their children, taking a cue from what they see, get sexually involved with each other at a tender age. Semeni eventually dies and her son, Dude, uneducated and ghetto-bred, drifts from one petty job to another, eventually getting into trouble with the law.

On his release from custody, he is introduced by an acquaintance to Amina, a middle-aged lady 'who wants some company and comfort' in return for some material benefits. Dude thus becomes her young gigolo and this lady just happens to be the (now former) district commissioner's wife and the mother of his two daughters. She is so taken up with Dude that she even persuades her husband to hire him as the family's business manager. Bwana Zuberi, who is now ageing and ailing agrees and takes a certain liking to the boy, seeing in him the son he 'never had.' Dude's chance encounter with his former companion, Baya, Pili's daughter, in the company of the district commissioner's wife, arouses the latter's jealousy so much that Dude is forced to abandon his 'employment' and distance himself from Zuberi's family.

Dude, however, reappears eventually, having started a relationship in another East African city with Zuberi's elder daughter, Shemsa, who insists on marrying him. The mother, for obvious reasons, is adamant that this should not happen. But she is overruled by Zuberi and the marriage goes ahead. Soon afterwards, while Shemsa, Dude's wife, is expecting their first baby, Dude seduces her younger sister,

Latifa and makes her pregnant too. More trouble erupts when Shemsa's baby turns out to be 'Black' (with predominantly African features), unexpectedly, because both her parents are apparently 'Arabic.' The scandals become the talk of the town, even inside Zuberi's own house. He is just about to pick up his cane to go and chastise the gossiping serving women when he has a stroke and dies, to the raucous chorus of the crowds that usher in the 1964 Revolution.

A brief comment on the setting of the narrative may help to highlight the significance of these events. The East African coast, from Kismayu in Somalia to Lindi in Tanzania and the islands adjacent to it, is called 'Uswahilini' (the home of the Swahilis) by its inhabitants. Of the islands of Uswahilini the best known is Zanzibar, the main Spice Island, where *Asali Chungu* is set. This region has for many centuries had close interactions—commercial, cultural and political—with the countries of the Arabian Gulf. Trade boats (*dhows*), following the patterns of the monsoon winds, have always plied the Indian Ocean, carrying goods, practices and people between the two regions. On the East African coast this has resulted in the rise of a nation, the Swahilis (or Waswahili), with an intricate blend of African and Arabic characteristics. Kiswahili, their language, for example, although recognisable structurally as an African Bantu language, has about 30 per cent Arabic-derived lexical content. Ethnically, one may claim that most Swahilis are of mixed African-Arabic descent, but that would be an oversimplified generalisation, because people who identify themselves as Swahili range from apparently full-blooded Arabs through Creoles to pure African indigenes of the coast. Indeed, Zanzibar was originally called 'Unguja' (land of the Blacks). Swahili is thus more of a cultural and linguistic identification than an ethnic one. Hence the absurdity, exposed in *Asali Chungu* (87, 199–201), of trying to identify and treat the people, especially discriminatively, according to their assumed ethnicity.

Unfortunately, that kind of racial and racist stratification was the official policy of Zanzibar's rulers up to the time of the Revolution. The island's population was classified and administered along racial lines: European, Indian, Arab and African, with mixed-race people caught between Arab and African. Racial discrimination in the school system, for instance, is referred to directly in *Asali Chungu* (77), with the mention of the 'All Hindu Brothers Madresa.' The story (which actually occurred) is told, for example, of Zainab Himid, a dark-skinned Swahili who had to disguise herself as an Arab in order to be admitted to the first girls' school in Zanzibar, because Africans were not allowed to attend.[6] The fact that she could 'pass' for an Arab and eventually became a teacher at the same school shows the naïveté of the policies.

Yet these practices were deeply grounded in the sad and curious history of Zanzibar and the East African coast as a whole. Arabic involvement with the region always had a disturbing ambiguity about it. The interracial relations with the Arabs, for example, had a one-sided aspect to them in the sense that initially only Arab men travelled to the region, marrying African women and starting Swahili families yet, in most cases, keeping their other families in their home countries. The relationships between the itinerant Arabs and the communities they gave rise to through their African liaisons were never easy and indeed, frequently exploded into conflict. The Arabs, especially from Oman, eventually gained the upper hand over the *Sahawwal*, as they called the region and in the 1840s Seyyid Said bin Sultan of Oman decided to move the Sultanate's capital from Muscat to Zanzibar. This may have been out of the Sultan's enchantment with the island or the political convenience of being more centrally placed within his vast domains, or possibly a mixture of both. But it should be noted that the timing of this transfer was at the height of the Indian Ocean Slave Trade in the region and Zanzibar was host to the largest market for African slaves.

Indeed, the Slave Trade issue was the excuse for the British invasion and annexation of Zanzibar a few decades after Sultan Seyyid's own colonisation of the islands. Under the pretext of abolishing the trade, the British put the islands under their 'protection,' establishing their own administration over and above that of the Sultan and admittedly, curtailing slavery and freeing large numbers of the African victims of the trade. But of course the British had ulterior motives for occupying Zanzibar, such as their need for a base from which they could (and eventually did) penetrate and colonise East Africa.

Of more direct relevance to our discussion, however, is that British colonisation in Zanzibar complicated the social situation in two main ways. First, instead of abolishing the Arabic feudal system, it only overlaid it in its so-called 'indirect rule' approach, wherein local magnificos (e.g., Bwana Zuberi of *Asali Chungu*) were co-opted to administer the land on behalf of the British. Second and closely related to the first complication, is that although British rule granted legal freedom to the slaves, it did nothing for the vast majority of ordinary citizens, who were reduced to living either as serfs on their ancestral land, seized and divided into vast estates claimed by the Arab colonists, or as ghetto-folk in the *Ng'ambo* (other side) of the cities. The British failure to address these issues, even up to the time of political independence in 1964, played a major role in the radical politics that led to the Revolution.[7] With reference to *Asali Chungu*, the feudal land system (*umwinyi*) lent itself easily to all sorts of abuse, including sexual exploitation, as we shall see. The *Ng'ambo*, on the other hand, was the breeding ground for totally alienated characters (e.g., Dude) who, knowingly or otherwise, were to prove a thorn in the flesh of their oppressors.

Interacting with these complications of the colonial political setting of *Asali Chungu* is the social factor of masculinity: the presumptive and assertive construction and assignment of qualities, characteristics and roles to the man. Masculinologists (as I think scholars who study this phenomenon should be called) repeatedly remind us that there is no general, universal template for masculinity and it would be safer to speak of masculinities as they manifest themselves in various cultural contexts. In the Swahili context addressed in *Asali Chungu*, for example, the expected attributes of a man are power, possession, ambition, command, strength, pride and virility. Apparently the 'manliness' of a person will be measured according to the number of these qualities that he exhibits and according to the degree to which he exhibits them. Thus a 'real' man is expected to exercise unquestionable authority and command over his household, estates and all those women and 'lesser' men who come under his sphere of influence. A show of physical strength is central to the process. Towards the opposite gender, this strength is manifested in presumed virility, the urge to sexually exploit women at every opportunity. The man must aspire and struggle to widen that sphere of influence and to strongly—even ruthlessly—resist any challenge to it. Pride of rank, descent, class and race are a driving force in this enterprise.

These presumptions of masculinity are, however, subject to several complications, many of which are addressed or suggested in *Asali Chungu*. Three related complications that are highlighted in *Asali Chungu* may be labelled as 'perversion,' 'victimisation' and 'challenge.' Perversion refers to the misperception and misunderstanding of the attributes of masculinity, whereas victimisation is the negative impact of the exercise of the misconceived attributes and the challenge that comes, often in unexpected ways, from the victims of that exercise.

The main argument advanced in this chapter is that the kind of rapacious, imperious and opportunistic masculinity practiced by characters like Bwana Zuberi is destructive, not only to other people but also ultimately to its practitioners.

The misconception, misperception and perversion of Swahili masculinity presented in the novel seems to stem from a basic problematic inherent in all masculinities. This is the realisation that masculinity is not only presumptive but also presumptuous. Unlike a systematic revolutionary approach to gender relations (e.g., feminism) or masculinism when it finds its feet, masculinity is generally not a set of rational concepts but a vague assumption of conceits generated, sustained and propagated by cultural hegemonies for the convenience of their own survival. Thus in Swahili society, the attributes of masculinity mentioned above are generated by its patriarchal structures as contributions to their perpetuation. But these attributes, though frequently reiterated and constantly reinforced through speech and practice, are hardly ever defined with clarity and precision. This renders and subjects them to misconception, misperception and indeed, wilful and opportunistic distortion. In *Asali Chungu*, for example, it is easy to see that the masculine assumptions are constantly perverted and distorted by the leading characters, especially Bwana Zuberi, for what they consider to be their benefit but what turns out to be their destruction. Power, for example, is taken as a license to oppress and ride roughshod over the powerless, consistently referred to in the text as *wanyonge* (the powerless ones). Thus, early in the novel we see Zuberi, always called *Bwana* (master), grossly abusing his office as district commissioner by refusing to attend to the crowds of petitioners who throng his office with urgent needs and grievances. Zuberi also uses his powerful position to shield himself from accepting responsibility for his own misdoings, as we see from the mistreatment to which he subjects Pili, who tries to get him to accept paternity of Semeni's child (5–6). Thus power (and likewise command) is not seen by the powerful men in the novel as an opportunity to serve society but as a chance to oppress and exploit ordinary people. This perversity permeates the system even to petty officials, such as Mukri, the recruiting clerk at the labour office (77–78), who uses his office to benefit only those who are close to him or those who bribe him.

One of the most disgusting instances of the misuse of power in the novel is when Bwana Zuberi demands that *Mzee* (Elder) Omari, a poor serf who has been seeking audience with him in vain for days on end, should send up his daughter to him for his pleasure. Otherwise Omari and his family will be evicted from their little patch of land for failure to remit their quota of farm produce to Zuberi's storehouses. 'I want Mboga [Omari's daughter] to be my guest tonight,' demands Zuberi flatly, reducing the grovelling old man to tears of desperation and bitterness (22–23).

This incident, in fact, ingeniously pulls all the ropes of perverted masculinity into a tight condemnatory knot. In Zuberi's outrageous demand we see not only macho man's abuse of power but also the use of feudal possession (*umwinyi*) to degrade the powerless by asserting his 'strength' over them by imposing his rapacious virility/sexuality on the most defenceless among them. Nor is this incident of sexual plunder, taken by Zuberi and his ilk to be a display of their strength, isolated in the narrative. Indeed, it is anticipated in the detailed narrative of Zuberi's rape of Semeni, who has struggled in all possible ways to ward off his advances. In order to underline the ugliness of Zuberi's perverted concept of masculine sexuality, the author uses symbols and metaphors of voracious predators as Zuberi stalks his prey. Symbolically, he is seen looking at a painting he had bought from a studio on the mainland: 'a grey wolf is bending over and devouring its prey, a rabbit—he has already torn out one of its sides; it is bleeding profusely and some of the blood is splattered on the leaves of the surrounding shrubs' (9).

Although the omniscient narrator says that Zuberi 'did not know why he was attracted to that painting,' the reader does not miss its significance when, as Zuberi readies himself for his nefarious act, he tells himself that 'he had to be a lion' (10). Now, the lion (*simba* in Kiswahili) is frequently invoked as a symbol of masculinity, again vaguely, without spelling out which of its characteristics— pride, strength, voraciousness, ruthless killer-instinct, love of blood—men should emulate.

But even when men like Zuberi think they are emulating the lion's positive trait of pride, their execution of it can be revoltingly depraved. Their line of action is to break down resistance at all costs and by any means available. Thus, the main motive behind Zuberi's rape of Semeni, for example, is to humiliate her and punish her for hurting his pride by rejecting his advances: 'He had, so he told himself, saved himself the shame of being overcome by her whom he now regarded as a mere finch' (74).

Earlier he had articulated this thought to his opportunistic accomplice, *Biti* ('Ms') Daudi, as he continues to gloat over his 'conquest': 'I sent you to her, my lady, an elder like you and she sent you back empty-handed. I called her over myself and she put on airs before me. Then I realised how humiliating it would be for you and me to be defeated' (29).

In the worst scenario cases, as in that of Zuberi in *Asali Chungu*, the worst of the *simba* characteristics tend to be the ones selected. The reader may be intrigued to note that the lion metaphor is invoked again in the seduction scene between Dude and his sister-in-law, Latifa: 'Do not play with a lion and put your hand in his mouth! A sudden animality enveloped him and he was seized by excitement' (194).

That animality (*unyama* in Kiswahili) is probably what the author criticises particularly in the 'lion-men' of *Asali Chungu*. Fortunately, he has normative standards in Swahili society against which this *unyama* can be judged. First, there is *dini*, the Islamic faith and ethic frequently referred to (e.g., 6, 32, 113–115), though not particularly emphasised in the novel. Second and most important, is *utu*, the Swahili-bantu concept of humanity, humanism or human decency (107). Any kind of behaviour that transgresses this decency, whether by men or women, is *unyama* (animality or animalism). Soon after Zuberi demands to have Mboga sacrificed at the altar of his lust, the narrator reflects that he has 'turned into a *weevil* that moves from one young plant to another, destroying their leaves' (24; emphasis added). Later in the novel the narrator states a general principle, familiar to Swahili society: transgressing or overstepping the bounds (*kukiuka mipaka*) of humanity is the unforgivable sin and it is punished with demotion from humanity—'He wants to go on acting, to do things and overstep the bounds of humanness and in the course of his actions he turns into a crab: mud is its habitat' (67).

A superb symbolisation of the degradation of those who transgress human decency, extending the leitmotif of animal imagery, is Dude's dream of the four copulating frogs, one male and three female, representing himself and Amina and her daughters, Shemsa and Latifa, all involved in a depraved sexual mess (196–197).

However, it is not only in sexual excesses that the men of *Asali Chungu* transgress the bounds of humanity. In their pursuit of possessions, for example, their aim is not decent comfort and provision for those in their care but ostentation and intimidation of the *wanyonge*.[8] Thus, for example, the celebrations of the *maulidi*, in honour of the birth of the Prophet, turn into a competition of profligate parties and banquets thrown by the rich anxious to demonstrate their importance (read 'manhood') in society (32–33). Their residences are designed not only for comfort but also 'to heckle and tease the poor and the destitute' (66). The manly command (i.e., being in charge) that they crave repeatedly manifests itself as unilateral and high-handed dictatorship, which, in Zuberi's career in *Asali Chungu*, culminates in his insistent and most disastrous order, against his wife's objections, that Shemsa should marry Dude ('Karimu'): 'Listen, woman,' Zuberi barks (note the persistence of the animal motif). Amina had never heard him speak so harshly, even in his youthful days. 'I am the father of the child and I am also the owner of this house. Whether you like it or not, Shemsa will marry Karimu' (171).

Amina, Zuberi's wife, who has been dating Dude/'Karimu' and wants to prevent the impending incest, is obviously the immediate victim of Zuberi's masculine arrogance. But, as will be seen later, the whole family, including Zuberi himself is about to be engulfed in devastating scandal and misery because of this exaggerated presumption of command. Indeed, as can be gathered from what has been said in passing so far, the perverted display of masculinity by characters such as Zuberi leaves a litter of victims along its trail, until it finally catches up with its perpetrators. The unattended petitioners at the doorstep of Zuberi's office are obvious victims of his *dhuluma* (oppressive conduct) and are left wondering whether the district commissioner would ever be 'at their service' (7). Pili, regarded as 'gutter trash' (*kisabaluu*) by Zuberi, who throws her unceremoniously out of his office, is another bitter victim of his irresponsible arrogance. The case of old Omari and his family, who face certain ruin unless they submit to Zuberi's depraved demands (21–23) has already been mentioned. In fact, we gather from the narrative that Omari is not a unique victim of Zuberi's *umwinyi*. It appears that nearly half the petitioners at Zuberi's office are the victims of misdoings, ranging from releasing livestock into people's crop fields to burning their orchards of clove and palm trees, committed by Zuberi or his agents (2–4). Their collective cry is: 'What can we do, my sister and we are *wanyonge* without a voice?' (3).

Indeed, the system, both feudal and colonial, run by the likes of Zuberi, is quietly but roundly lambasted in *Asali Chungu* for its victimisation of the powerless. The Ng'ambo ghetto, for example, is described in ways that leave the reader in no doubt that its inhabitants are condemned to a life with neither material decency nor prospects for self-improvement.[9] Most significantly in the novel, several of the people condemned to live (and even die) in the Ng'ambo are direct victims of the voracious excesses of men like Zuberi.

Semeni and Dude are of course the worst cases of Zuberi's victimisation in the novel. The drugging and raping of Semeni would have been crime enough.

But when Zuberi refuses to accept responsibility for Semeni's ensuing pregnancy and child, Dude, even when pressed to do so (5–6), condemns them to a life of misery and destitution in the *Ng'ambo*, where Semeni dies (56–57) and from where Dude, denied parenthood, eventually emerges to torment Zuberi and his family to near-extinction.

Indeed, Dude, as a Frankensteinian monster reflecting Zuberi's chauvinism, poses the greatest challenge to his father's outrageous masculinity. But Dude is not alone in challenging Zuberi. Nearly all the victims of his oppression, greed, imperiousness, arrogance and lust—the expressions of his misconceived masculinity—pose or express some kind of challenge to him. The challenges range from verbal protests through uncooperative or rebellious responses to direct attacks on Zuberi's property, personality and family. An aggravating factor to these challenges is Zuberi's deteriorating health in the later stages of the narrative. Though relevant to our topic and plausibly interpretable as poetic justice for the excesses of his earlier life, this development will not be discussed in detail here.

Verbal challenges run through the novel. In the opening chapter, for example, we have Pili's bold confrontation with Zuberi, ending in her prophecy in which she suggests that Zuberi will not get away with his misdeeds: 'You have eaten your neighbour's chicken: its legs will point at you.' There is also the collective protest of the neglected petitioners: 'Even though we cannot take action, we will speak out. We will speak out, come what may' (3).

Semeni's humble but earnest pleadings with Zuberi not to impose himself on her —pleas that Zuberi takes for pride—are also a challenge. Amina's desperate protests against Dude's match with Shemsa (168–171), despite ulterior motives, are also a challenge, as indeed are several other exchanges between her and her husband (e.g., 14–15, 116–117). The last of the verbal challenges to Zuberi is ironically found in the gossip of the servants about the mess of incestuous scandals in which his family is entangled (205–209). Zuberi's overhearing of the servants' derisive banter leads to his final realisation—'It is obvious that I myself am the cause of all this'—before he collapses and eventually dies. It is as if the violated and dead servant girl, Semeni, returns and takes her revenge on Zuberi through her representatives, the serving women.

There is, however, another way in which Semeni defies Zuberi. After she is raped, Semeni leaves Zuberi's homestead, never to return, contrary to Zuberi's naïve expectation that now that he has humiliated her, she will meekly submit to him. Indeed, the more Zuberi tries to assert his predatory power, the more he provokes resistance and rebellion from his victims. The case of Pili, for example, who gatecrashes his office and roundly tells him off over his mistreatment of Semeni (5–6) has been noted in passing. The narrative also hints that the seemingly helpless Omari, who Zuberi requires to donate his daughter to him in exchange for his continued tenancy on Zuberi's land, refuses to comply: 'He would very much rather starve to death than strip himself naked by sending his daughter to that beastly creature' (23).

The most decisive act of rebellion against Zuberi, which in turn leads to the assault on his person and family, is Amina's flagrant adultery, first with various unnamed young men and finally with Dude, Zuberi's unacknowledged son and thus her stepson (66–75, 111–150). Amina's conduct could be read as mere wilful waywardness, the desperate antics of a sex-starved middle-aged woman seeking to reassure herself of her continuing attractiveness and sex appeal (72–73). A closer look reveals, however, that an element of revenge on the now-ageing and ailing Zuberi looms large in her actions. Apparently Amina has been either aware or suspicious of Zuberi's misdoings all along. The narrator's laconic comment on a conversation between husband and wife the morning after Zuberi sneaks out of bed and goes on his rape errand is significant: 'There were days when Zuberi and his wife exchanged words which each of them interpreted in his or her own way . . . that is the common behaviour of thieves. . . . And one would have wondered how fourteen years of their marriage had passed without a quarrel leading to divorce (15).

Another indication that there is more to Amina's behaviour than a search for mere sexual gratification is the way she brings Dude (whom she introduces as 'Karimu') into her matrimonial home and persuades Zuberi to make him his business manager. This is obviously Amina's ploy to exert control over Zuberi and his affairs and maybe eventually replace him altogether with Dude, to whom she proposes marriage, rather preposterously, in the expressed hope that the 'old dodderer's days' would soon be over (139).

Dude could, to a certain extent, be regarded as a relatively accidental scourge of Zuberi, at least in the initial stages. But his role is far more complex than that. His acceptance of Bushiri's invitation to act as Amina's gigolo as a way out of his destitution may be understandable, if not acceptable. The reader should not underestimate the importance of Baya's inebriated assessment of Dude. Baya, Dude's childhood companion, now a wreck from the buffets of the Ng'ambo, states that Dude has betrayed himself: 'And you, even you, Dude, look, you're no longer a human being. You're not a man. You've been ruined. You've been bought by this woman. Ugh! You're utterly shameless, incapable of recognising filth, accursed wretch that you are. You're a slave' (149).

The recurrence of these utterances in Dude's conscience as he agonises about his future and comes to terms with his break with Amina underlines their significance to the character and to the reader. We surmise from these bizarre reflections that the lifelong neglect to which Dude has been subjected has turned him into a creature (remember that 'Dude' means 'Thingummy') totally devoid of self-respect, ready to seize on any opportunity for his survival and comfort. Of course he could defend himself with sentiments like those expressed in Bushiri's words that 'even if we were to talk of human decency [utu], there's nothing that human decency can do to change anything about my state of powerlessness [*unyonge*]' (107). He thus readily agrees to perform, to 'sing for his supper,' through the virile/masculine satisfaction of Amina's needs. At this stage, none of the three characters in the triangle is aware of the true relationship among them. Zuberi's startled discernment of a striking resemblance between Dude's features and those of his own photograph taken twenty-five years earlier (116), as well as his growing inclination to accept Dude/'Karimu' as his adoptive son, in lieu of the son he 'unfortunately' never had (117–118) can still be attributed to the profusion of coincidences and dramatic ironies with which the narrative is replete. The most intriguing point about this situation, however, is the contrast between Zuberi's and Amina's interest in Dude. Zuberi sees in him the prospect of alleviating his disappointment with his inability to beget a son, a disappointment he feels in startlingly strong terms: 'He is not his own begotten son. *It does not matter,* Zuberi decided. *If I have missed Mother's breast, I will suck at a dog's*' (118; emphases in original).

Male chauvinist to the last, Zuberi regards having two daughters but no son as 'missing Mother's breast' and he is willing to go to any length ('suck at a dog's breast') to attenuate the 'deficiency.' The reader should note that in Islam, Swahili dogs are dirty, untouchable creatures.[10] To Amina, on the other hand, Dude's attraction lies in his fragility and vulnerability. As she confides to *Biti Daudi*: 'See what he's like: weak of constitution, helpless and without any possessions but with a certain charm and male handsomeness.'

Although Amina's assessment of Dude may not be accurate, its importance as a hint towards an alternative form of masculinity can hardly be overemphasised. In it we see all the qualities that are lacking in Zuberi's brand of masculinity, which made him a loser, as far as she is concerned, probably long before his physical and sexual debility. Indeed, it is revealing that the qualities Zuberi admires in Dude are nothing like what we see of Zuberi at the height of his powers: 'Poor boy, Karimu was humorous, respectful and a diligent worker. Truth to tell, he was a blessing' (161). One could even argue that Zuberi's over-concentration on power, strength and virility aggravates his predicament when these qualities desert him (161).

Dude, however, is a curious mixture of gentleness and charm, on the one hand and ruthless and voracious opportunism on the other. Although his acceptance of Amina's advances—in spite of his awareness of their perversity—is understandable in view of his destitution, his connivance with her to insinuate himself into Zuberi's home and business affairs raises serious doubts about his 'victim' status. His behaviour on his reappearance as Shemsa's suitor (and later husband) reveals a man who is every bit as cunning, avaricious and rapacious as Zuberi was in his heyday. He not only clings to his relationship with Shemsa despite his realisation that she is Amina's daughter ('In the end he would eat the hen and its pullets'[11]) but he also goes on to humiliate Amina by pretending to bargain with her over a financial inducement, which he contemptuously rejects in exchange for her marriage to Shemsa (180–181). His perversity culminates in the seduction of his sister-in-law, Latifa (who, like his wife Shemsa, turns out to be his half-sister).

Perhaps this final ugly twist in the story gives the best clue to Dude's role in the thematic framework of the novel. It seems that in the Swahili moral narrative (*kisa na maana*, meaning the tale and its meaning) Dude is a nemesis visited on both Amina and Zuberi for their transgressions of *utu*. The indictment is made in a wry remark about halfway through the novel: 'Zuberi and Amina had the same kind of lust although their excuses were different. Zuberi kept complaining that Amina had not satisfied his natural expectations and Amina that Zuberi was too old for her... Their animality [*unyama*] kept growing until it fully ripened in their hearts.'[12]

By treating Dude as an object for her adulterous pleasure Amina dehumanises herself and Dude. Her embarrassment and horror at Dude's involvement with Shemsa may thus be seen as deserved punishment. But it is to be noted, as suggested earlier, that Amina can be justifiably regarded as a victim of Zuberi's excesses. The final responsibility for the disastrous mess of his family thus rests squarely with Zuberi. Even Dude's excesses, which are acknowledged in the narrative as transgressions, are traceable to his upbringing, or lack of it: 'This waywardness of his might perhaps have been traced to the foundation of his origin. Otherwise we could say that his upbringing and the impact of the environment in which he had been raised since his tenderest years, had crippled him.'[13]

This is where the wheel seems to come full circle. For Dude's 'origin' is Zuberi's rape of Semeni and it is Zuberi's arrogant refusal to accept paternity that condemns Dude to the crippling environment in which he is raised, the *Ngambo* ghetto.

11. Masculinity in Chinua Achebe's *Anthills of the Savannah*

Clement A. Okafor

The man who visits only his friend's *obi* drinks palm wine on an
empty stomach.
But the man who also visits *mkpuke*, the house of his friend's wife,
eats food and delicious fish as well.

Igbo proverb

Gender is a social construction and communities around the world use various
cultural practices to teach their young people the norms of acceptable gender
roles. Among the Igbo people of Nigeria, proverbs are cardinal strategies for
acculturating youngsters into what society expects of them. Igbo notions about
masculinity are encapsulated in the proverb above, which will serve as the
theoretical underpinning for the present analysis of the portrait of masculinity
in Chinua Achebe's *Anthills of the Savannah*.

The proverb is informed by traditional Igbo architecture, wherein the
domicile of the patriarch, his *obi*, is located at the entrance to his walled
compound, whereas his wife's dwelling, the *mkpuke*, is situated within the walled
enclosure. In this proverb, the patriarch is clearly the head and ruler of his
household; yet there are limitations to the sphere of his authority. The proverb
shows that although he may provide palm wine, he does not cook; hence, he
may not serve food to his guest. This is a reflection of the situation in real Igbo
family life, where gender roles are complementary rather than antagonistic.
Indeed, in Igbo life, when the male members of a family find a problem too
intractable, they usually invite their sisters to intervene and often the women's
agency helps to solve the problem.

By the same token, the guest in the proverb, who does not fully appreciate
the complex dynamics of the Igbo household and cultivates only the patriarch,
loses in the end. The wise visitor, on the other hand, who recognises the role

of the woman in the home, enjoys not only the hospitality of the patriarch but also the largesse of his spouse.

The image of masculinity portrayed in Chinua Achebe's *Anthills of the Savannah* is essentially an inter-textual continuation of the project of constructing masculinity that Achebe began in *Things Fall Apart*. There is internal evidence to support this view. For example, Beatrice, the heroine of *Anthills of the Savannah*, says that she feels like Chielo in *Things Fall Apart*: 'As a matter of fact I do sometimes feel like Chielo in the novel, the priestess of the Hills and Caves. It comes and goes, I imagine' (114). This affirmation is surprising, given that Beatrice has not been exposed to much of her people's culture on account of her Christian upbringing and long sojourn in England, studying for her university degree.

Additional internal evidence comes from Ikem's discourse in *Anthills of the Savannah* on the popularity of the name 'Nneka' among his people. In *Things Fall Apart*, Uchendu teaches Okonkwo that 'Nneka' is a popular name because it affirms the dominant role a mother plays in the life of her child. She is there for her child, especially during difficult times. However, Ikem argues in *Anthills of the Savannah* that his people use the name merely to assuage their consciences over their oppression of women.

Yet there is other evidence that, during critical moments of her life, Beatrice is aware that she has two different personalities: the modern educated woman and the village priestess:

> Perhaps Ikem alone came close to sensing the village priestess who will prophesy when her divinity rides her abandoning if need be her soup-pot on the fire, but returning again when the god departs to the domesticity of kitchen or the bargaining market-stool behind her little display of peppers and dry fish and green vegetables. He knew it better than Beatrice herself (105).

Thus, an exploration of the image of masculinity in the earlier novel is critical for a deep appreciation of Achebe's portrayal of masculinity in *Anthills of the Savannah*. Although *Things Fall Apart* depicts masculinity in Africa at the onset of colonialism, *Anthills of the Savannah* paints a picture of masculinity in the continent during the postcolonial era.

In *Things Fall Apart*, masculinity is represented by the protagonist, Okonkwo, who embodies Umuofia's martial ethos, but is propelled by subconscious drives that he barely understands. Okonkwo's major phobias—his fear of being a failure and his fear of being considered weak—are the affective filters through which he views everything that happens to him.

These fears colour his relationships with members of his family. He is the patriarch and he rules his household with a firm hand. Thus, he exercises unchallenged authority over the members of his household. Indeed, not even the prohibition of violence during the holy week of peace can protect his wife Ojiugo from his wrath.

These drives also colour his relationships with his kinsmen, who consider him abrupt and inconsiderate, especially when he calls his kinsman a woman simply because the man has not taken a title: 'Okonkwo knew how to kill a man's spirit' (26).

These same drives colour his relationships with the hostage boy, Ikemefuna, who lives in Okonkwo's household. Okonkwo sees the youngster as a wholesome influence on his own son, Nwoye, who views Ikemefuna as a good role model. With the passage of time, Okonkwo bonds with this young boy and shows him great affection by letting Ikemefuna carry Okonkwo's stool to the meeting of elders. Yet when the oracle demands that the boy be sacrificed, Okonkwo goes along needlessly—against good advice—and is put in a position where he kills Ikemefuna himself, just to prove that he is not afraid.

Okonkwo's phobias also colour his relationship with his son, Nwoye. Because Umuofia is a patriarchal society, succession here is along the male line; hence, Nwoye is Okonkwo's heir. To ensure that Nwoye has the right spirit, Okonkwo regales him with heroic tales of warfare when his son would rather be with his mother, listening to her telling folktales. Ironically, the more Okonkwo tries to fashion his son in his own image of what a man should be, the more he drives a wedge between himself and Nwoye, whose temperament bears an uncanny resemblance to Unoka's. The final break between father and son occurs at a dramatic moment after Okonkwo has learned that his own son was seen in the company of the Christians, whom he despises:

It was late afternoon before Nwoye returned. He went into the obi and saluted his father, but he did not answer. Nwoye turned round to walk into the inner compound when his father, suddenly overcome with fury, sprang to his feet and gripped him by the neck.

'Where have you been?' he stammered.

Nwoye struggled to free himself from the choking grip.

'Answer me,' roared Okonkwo, 'before I kill you.' He seized a heavy stick that lay by the dwarf wall and hit him two or three savage blows.

'Answer me,' he roared again.

Nwoye stood looking at him and did not say a word. The women were screaming outside, afraid to go in.

'Leave that boy at once!' said a voice in the outer compound. It was Okonkwo's uncle, Uchendu. 'Are you mad?'

Okonkwo did not answer. But he left hold of Nwoye, who walked away and never returned (151–152).

The nearly fatal combat between father and son portrays two antagonistic concepts of masculinity: one that is tough on the outside and lives up to the expectations of traditional patriarchal society and one that is gentle and shows emotion. Okonkwo epitomises the former and considers the latter 'degenerate and effeminate.' He sees the two forms as representing the dichotomy between roaring flame and cold, impotent ash.

Okonkwo opts to be the roaring flame and strives at all times to live up to what he considers to be the appropriate image of a man in his patriarchal society. By so doing, he turns out to be an ace wrestler, an awesome warrior, a successful farmer, a good provider for his large and prosperous family and a man who surmounts the penury of his childhood to become one of the leaders of his community. Thus, he embodies a type of successful masculinity.

Yet the novelist subverts this form of abrasive masculinity by introducing elements which show that Okonkwo does not fully understand the intricacies of his culture. For instance, he does not understand why his people believe that Mother is supreme (nneka) and does not learn this cardinal principle until late in life.

The novelist further subverts this form of masculinity by showing us the romantic marital bliss between Ndulue and his wife Ozoemena. The couple bond so closely that their community composes a song about their feelings for one another. Ozoemena is so heartbroken on learning of the death of her husband that she dies the same day:

Ozoemena was, as you know, too old to attend Ndulue during his illness. His younger wives did that. When he died this morning, one of these women went to Ozoemena's hut and told her. She rose from her mat, took her stick and walked over to the obi. She knelt on her knees and hands at the threshold and called her husband, who was laid on a mat. 'Ogbuefi Ndulue,' she called three times and went back to her hut. When the youngest wife went to call her again to be present at the washing of the body, she found her lying on the mat, dead (68).

Okonkwo's insensitivity is highlighted further by his refusal to understand how such a famous warrior as Ndulue could be emotionally dependent on his wife.

By endowing Okonkwo with both admirable and not-so-admirable qualities, the novelist succeeds in portraying a complex male figure who is essentially amiable and heroic, but has a formidable tragic flaw. Thus, the novel explores the outcome of abrasive masculinity in a traditional society at the onset of colonialism. This brand of masculinity considers femininity a handicap and may be likened to the guest in the Igbo proverb who limits his visit only to the obi of his friend and pays a price for it.

This is the canvas to which Chinua Achebe returns in Anthills of the Savannah. In this instance, however, although he focuses on masculinity in postcolonial

Africa, he expands the field of vision to include the activities of Beatrice, whose role in the novel is comparable to that of the spouse in the Igbo proverb. Here, Achebe highlights power and authority as symbols of masculinity. Specifically, he portrays masculinity in *Anthills of the Savannah* through the dialogues and activities of the three dominant male characters: Sam, who later becomes the head of state and his two secondary school classmates at Lord Lugard College— Ikem and Chris. At school, Sam is a good student academically and had excellent social skills. He is '... captain of the Cricket Team, Victor Ludorum in athletics and in our last year, School Captain. And Girls worshipped at his feet from every Girls' School in the province. But strangely enough there was a kind of spiritual purity about Sam in those days despite his great weakness for girls' (65–66). He succeeds in every endeavour and initially wishes to study medicine, but is persuaded by their English headmaster and World War II veteran John Williams to join the school cadet corps and from there he is on his way to the British military academy, Sandhurst. On his return, he becomes the first in his nation to hold numerous senior positions: 'Second Lieutenant in the Army; ADC to the Governor-General; Royal Equerry during the Queen's visit and Officer Commanding at Independence.' Indeed, it appears that his only personality flaw is his colonial mentality that makes him ape the British, especially their upper classes.

Ikem is the most brilliant student in their class and is first in everything throughout their secondary school career. Later he studies in England and becomes an excellent journalist and writer and is eventually appointed editor of the *National Gazette*.

Of the three classmates, Chris has the charmed life of being the one in the middle; he is neither the brightest nor the most sociable. He graduates from the London School of Economics and marries an American, Louise, but the marriage lasts only six months.

A military *coup d'état* by junior officers suddenly makes Sam the head of state of this African nation, Kangan and at the beginning of his regime he solicits Chris's assistance in selecting the members of his Cabinet. The new situation provides an opportunity for these friends and classmates to work together. Sadly, Lord Lugard College trains her students to grow up to become lone rangers, i.e., 'leaders in separate remote places' (66), rather than team players. Thus, the stage is set for the conflict of these rival masculine egos.

Even in the traditional African society portrayed in *Anthills of the Savannah*, masculinity symbolises power and authority. However, one may discern from the novel that the nature and process of acquiring power and authority in a traditional African society differs radically from the acquisition of power in a state. In a traditional African society, the exercise of authority has its roots *in illo tempore*—the very beginnings of society itself. It locates authority within the creative activities of the cosmogons, who established order out of the initial and primordial chaos. As Mircea Eliade has argued, the aim of such narratives is to show that the order, which a culture's heroes established here on earth, is a reflection of divine, cosmic order. In the traditional society depicted in *Anthills of the Savannah*, power is quintessentially dangerous; hence, it needs to be guided and directed by moral authority, which establishes the framework for its appropriate operation. In this society, Idemili—God's own daughter—is the divine agent, who establishes the parameters that govern the moral exercise of power:

> She came down in the resplendent Pillar of Water, remembered now in legend only, but stumbled upon, some say, by the most fortunate in rare conditions of sunlight rarer than the eighteen-year cycle of Odunke festivals and their richly arrayed celebrants leading garlanded cattle in procession through village pathways to sacrifice (102).

In this traditional society, those who seek to exercise authority over fellow human beings must first join the hierarchy of leaders who have taken the title of *ozo*. However, a prerequisite for taking the title is that any aspiring leader must first present himself to Idemili and be found worthy by this divine arbiter of moral behaviour:

> If she finds him unworthy to carry the authority of *ozo* she simply sends death to smite him and save her sacred hierarchy from contamination and scandal. If, however, she approves of him the only sign she condescends to give—grudgingly and by indirection—is that he will still be about after three years. Such is Idemili's contempt for man's unquenchable thirst to sit in authority over his fellows (104).

Thus, the exercise of power in this society is a sacred trust leaders dare not subvert and masculinity is represented by restrained collective leadership. This is the template against which the exercise of power in Kangan is compared.

In Kangan, a military dictatorship has supplanted the open discussion and collective governance that characterised masculinity in the pre-colonial system. At the inception of this regime, the state is ruled by a triumvirate comprising His Excellency, the general and military head of state and his two childhood friends and collaborators, Christopher Okiro, the commissioner for information and Ikem Osodi, the editor of the *National Gazette*. Their relationship, which is mediated by their mutual friend, Beatrice Okoh, senior assistant secretary in the Ministry of Finance, prospers during the early days of the military government. However, this cordial relationship deteriorates sharply in the wake of the failure of the national referendum, in which the military head of state's attempts to transform himself into a president-for-life. The general is particularly angered by the negative vote of the Abazon region, Ikem's home district and he interprets it as an act of betrayal.

Unlike the collective leadership of the male elders in the traditional template described above, the government of Kangan is a dictatorship in which state power is objectified and embodied in the person of the military head of state. The head of state is not answerable to anybody and uses the power of his office to dismiss Ikem from his job and to punish the people of Abazon. Having earlier cancelled the government projects in the territory, he now imprisons their elders for leading a delegation to the presidential mansion, even though the elders are not subversive. On the contrary, they have come to Bassa because they understand that there has been a profound change in the power structure of their country. Initially, they imagined that they were free to express their preference during the referendum, but they now know better. They now know that autocratic rule has replaced traditional consensus in Kangan national affairs. Moreover, they have seen the institutional vehicles of oppression that have been mobilised against their people. As a result, they have come to Bassa to recant and to renounce their previous opposition to the president's ambition:

So we came to Bassa to say our own yes and perhaps the work on our bore-holes will start again and we will not all perish from the anger of the sun. We did not know before but we know now that yes does not cause trouble. We do not fully understand the ways of today yet but we are learning (127).

They have learned to be pragmatic (or perhaps cynical). The real motivation for their *volte-face* is the catastrophic drought that threatens to decimate their people. The intensity of the drought is reflected in Ikem's 'Hymn to the Sun':

The birds that sang the morning in had melted away even before the last butterfly fell roasted to the ground. And when songbirds disappeared, morning herself went into the seclusion of a widow's penance in soot and ashes, her ornaments and fineries taken from her—velvet of soft elusive light and necklaces of pure sound lying coil upon coil down to her resplendent breasts: corals and blue chalcedonies, jaspers and agates veined like rainbow. So the songbirds let no void, no empty hour when they fled because the hour itself had died before them. Morning no longer existed (31).

In this elegy that laments the incineration of a people' environment and their civilisation, the only person who survives the catastrophe is a madman. However, even this last remnant of humanity does not live long: he is torn apart by the dogs that fight with vultures in a desperate and macabre battle for pieces of the dead man's carcass.

Although Ikem's elegy alludes to a similar legendary drought, it suggests that the present catastrophe is worse than any previous disaster in the people's history. Indeed, the elegy refers to a previous drought that forced the people to abandon their sick and dying relatives in search of their present and more hospitable territory. During that migration, when the ancestors of the people of Abazon arrived at Ose, they massacred its inhabitants and renamed their territory Abazon. Thus, the very foundation of their homeland is steeped in devastation and death. Nevertheless, even the legendary calamity was better than the present situation—in the past, there was a way out. In the past, it was possible for their ancestors to abandon their home and conquer and settle in a new territory. Such an option does not seem to be available during the present disaster, which is a paradigm for Kangan.

Indeed, Kangan is like the scorched earth of Abazon because its government wields almost godlike authority and its president exercises arbitrary and autocratic power over his fellow citizens. He terrorises his cabinet officers and surrounds himself with sycophants. In that paranoid environment, anyone who has an independent view is considered dangerous and should be eliminated. This leads to the brutal assassination of Ikem and the hounding of Chris. Even so, these measures do not save the president or his regime. The president is shot by a drunken police officer for coming to the aid of a girl he is intent on raping. As a result, the trio who ruled Kangan at the inception of the regime are completely decimated. In the end, the men—who imagined they owned Kangan—are consumed by the revolution that they initiated. This is the pitiful outcome of egotistic and unbridled masculinity in postcolonial Africa.

Trying to find an explanation for the dismal failure of this form of masculinity leads us to a consideration of the theology encoded in the inscription on the back of the bus that transports Chris and his companions to the north. The calligraphy addresses the far-reaching consequence of egocentric masculinity and the issue of why modern African states are saddled with tyrannical governments. In addition, it provides an explanation as to why most modern African states have betrayed their people's dreams about independence and have become nightmares instead. The inscription suggests that the emergence of such monsters as His Excellency, the military president of Kangan—and by extension, Presidents Idi Amin and Mobutu Sese Seko—is explicable within African theology. Within this theology, there is an inevitable link between cause and effect. Thus, whatever fate befalls someone is believed to be the just retribution for that person's previous actions. Seen from this perspective, it follows that the African people are themselves responsible for whatever ogres and monsters they permit to emerge as the rulers of their postcolonial countries:

So those body decorations and beauty marks on *Luxurious* rose to occupy his mind. The Christian and quasi-Christian calligraphy posed no problem and held no terror. But not so that other one: *Ife onye metalu*, a statement unclear and menacing in its very inconclusiveness. What a man commits...Follows him? (203)

The answer to the haunting question above suggests that the people of Africa are collectively guilty for the hell that modern African governments have created here on earth for their compatriots. In which case, Africans have nobody but themselves to blame for the terrible governments that rule postcolonial African states.

After establishing culpability for the failure of egotistical masculinity, the novelist elevates the discussion to another level, specifically the remedy to the seemingly intractable problems that bedevil modern African political systems. Here, the novel addresses the issue of how to solve the problems created by the autocratic regimes that have destroyed the hopes and aspirations of a continent. More specifically, it attempts to answer the question, 'What must a people do to appease an embittered history?' (220)

Indeed, the last 400 years of African history have been terribly bitter. They began with the Trans-Atlantic Slave Trade, which destroyed virtually all the Sub Saharan states, depopulated the continent and enslaved its ablest people in the Americas and elsewhere. This was followed by the colonial period, when the various European nations enslaved the Africans on the African continent itself. The decolonisation of the continent was expected to give the Africans the opportunity to use the tremendous resources of their land for the benefit of their own people. Regrettably, the Africans who succeeded the colonial masters were not truly interested in the welfare of their compatriots. Most of them were concerned only with their personal aggrandisement and the perpetuation of their administrations. As a result, they squandered their national resources, maintaining themselves in power and eliminating their real and imagined enemies. The resulting police states these rulers created made them very unpopular; hence, whenever the military overthrew them, the populace welcomed the generals, who became the new rulers. In most instances, however, the generals soon compounded the economic incompetence of the politicians with brutal suppression of all dissenting views, leaving the people not only impoverished but embittered as well. The net result is that the high hopes for independence have been betrayed throughout the modern African states. The frustration generated by the disastrous outcome of independence prompted the former vice president of Kenya, Oginga Odinga, to declare that Africa has not attained true independence as yet.

The challenge, then, is how such an impoverished and embittered people can escape the dehumanising environment in which their leaders have incarcerated them. In the lecture that Ikem gives to the students of Kangan, he states that the duty of a writer is to make society aware of its problems, rather than to provide solutions.

A discernible solution in the novel calls for deploying the strategy of the wise guest in the Igbo proverb, who avails himself of the resources of the spouse, in addition to those of the patriarch. Beatrice takes over the mantle of leadership after the slaughter of the men who imagined that they owned Kangan. In the wake of the catastrophic failure of egotistical masculinity, the men leave the reconstruction of Kangan society to a woman: Beatrice, *Nwanyibuife* (A female is also something). The irony is that this fifth girl born to a family that desperately wanted sons will now take over the task of rebuilding the community that the men have destroyed. She is indeed like the biblical stone that is initially rejected by the builders but eventually became the cornerstone of the house. She is the person who is left to answer the query of the songbird, the chief servant of the king in the folktale. It is her sad duty to inform the diligent chamberlain that the king's property is not correct and that the king's treasury, as well as his entire domain, had been laid waste by the reckless actions of the menfolk.

In her new role as leader, Beatrice draws on her resource as the priestess of Idemili—who came to earth to establish the rules that govern the moral exercise of power—to restructure her shattered community. Hence, Beatrice bears her personal bereavement with fortitude and remains strong enough to nurse Elewa until she gives birth to Ikem's daughter. Even as Beatrice grieves over her personal tragedy, she is the rallying point for the various fractured segments of her traumatised society. Thus, she turns her apartment into a forum for discussing the deepening crises in her nation and the venue for reconciling the antagonistic segments of her society, such as Emmanuel, the student leader and Captain Abdul Medani, a member of the dreaded and loathed state security forces. In addition, she engineers an ecumenical union between Christians and Muslims that takes place in the same residence. In this manner, Beatrice's role in the postcolonial state resembles that of Idemili's in the mythic past.

The new leader's most revolutionary innovation, however, remains her restructuring of gender roles in her society. Traditionally, it had been the duty of a father (or his representative) to name a child during the naming ceremony. The naming ceremony that Beatrice organises for Elewa's baby, however, is far from traditional. Firstly, it is held in the section of the city previously preserved for the habitation of European colonialists, an anomalous setting for a traditional ceremony. Second, there is no father (or his representative) to give a name to the child. Rather, Beatrice herself names the baby. Even more significantly, she gives the girl a name—'Amaechina' (May the path never close)—traditionally reserved for boys. With this singular act, Beatrice seems to imply that her society should eliminate its traditionally stratified gender roles. Indeed, she argues, albeit humorously, that because only a woman knows the identity of the real father of her child, she should be the person to name her offspring, rather than her husband. In any case, the approval given by Elewa's uncle to these innovations indicates that such restructuring may not do violent damage to the spirit of the tradition.

If anything, the actions of the new leader parallel those that Igbo women would take in real life if their community were threatened by disaster. Indeed, by wielding the 'spear thrust into the ground by the men in their hour of defeat,' Beatrice merely assumes the traditional role of women in Igbo as well as in many other African societies: the court of last resort. Her role in the novel is, after all, akin to that performed by the women during the historic Aba Women's War of 1929. During that event, to which the novel alludes, men were either unable or unwilling to challenge the authority of the British colonial government. As a result, the womenfolk mobilised themselves and confronted the might of the alien oppressors in the eastern Nigerian city of Aba in 1929. Fearing that the Women's War would precipitate a general uprising in the entire colony, the colonial rulers capitulated and annulled the odious taxes that triggered the courageous action of the women.

The heroic role of these fearless women is merely a reminder that traditionally African women take over the leadership of society from their menfolk whenever the entire society is threatened by monumental disaster. The women assume such leadership roles especially when the men do not have viable strategies for warding off the impending calamity. The political initiative taken by the women during the Women's War is, then, the paradigm that guides the actions of the heroine of *Anthills of the Savannah*: the heroic women of Aba are like the legendary 'anthills surviving to tell the new grass of the savannah about last year's brush fires' (31).

The portrait of masculinity that is discernible in *Anthills of the Savannah* is a continuation of the construction of masculinity Chinua Achebe began in *Things Fall Apart*. *Things Fall Apart* explores the outcome of the abrasive masculinity that considers femininity a handicap. The masculinity presented in this novel may be likened to the guest in the proverb at the beginning of the chapter who limits his visit only to the *obi* of his friend and pays a price for it. Masculinity in *Anthills of the Savannah*, on the other hand, may be likened to the wise guest in the proverb, who visits both the *obi* of the patriarch and the house of his spouse and benefits from their largesse. Thus, *Anthills of the Savannah* elevates the construction of masculinity to another level by considering what comes after egocentric masculinity has exhausted itself, namely the complementary and redemptive potentials of womanhood in postcolonial Africa.

12. Dark Bodies/White Masks: African Masculinities and Visual Culture in *Graceland, The Joys of Motherhood* and *Things Fall Apart*

Gwendolyn Etter-Lewis

> With a defeated sigh, he turned to the small tin of talcum powder stuck in one of the pockets of his bag. He shook out a handful and applied a thick layer, peering into the mirror. He was dissatisfied: this was not how white people looked. If only he could use makeup, he thought, the things he could do.
>
> Chris Abani, *Graceland*.

The spectacle of Elvis Presley performed in white face by a Black teenager situates Chris Abani's *Graceland* in a miasma of conflicting masculine images. From Elvis Oke and Sunday, his father, to the King of Beggars, the Colonel, Redemption and others, male characters enact a variety of African masculinities that contradict and reinforce prescribed norms. This coming-of-age narrative, set in Lagos in the 1970s and through the 1980s, focuses on Elvis Oke, a motherless son seeking validation from a father he despises. The unrelenting tension between father and son entangles Elvis's precarious transition from childhood to adulthood in what Abani describes as a 'solid impermanence' (49)—an unstable state of being retarded by a complex intersection of poverty, violence, displacement and unrealised dreams.[1] Coming to manhood in such turmoil unsettles Elvis in fundamental ways. Yet this is more than an account of son versus father, younger generation versus older generation, or modern versus traditional. Embedded in the text is a subtle critique of African masculinities that brings into sharp relief long-standing assumptions about what it means to be a man. Drawing on earlier male icons depicted in the African literary classics,

Things Fall Apart by Chinua Achebe and *The Joys of Motherhood* by Buchi Emecheta, as background for my discussion of *Graceland*, I focus on the intersection of word and image in the (re)creation of African masculinities.

In particular, I am interested in the way that representations of masculine identities, especially non-mainstream varieties, are mediated by visual cues. How does narrative inscribe manly virtues in male (and sometimes female) characters? The process necessarily involves a conjoining of visual and verbal signs in a merger that creates a space where opposing traits vie for dominance and expression. As a result, these sites of engagement employ language that 'opens up the conflicts that inform society.'[2] Examining fictional depictions of African masculinities allows readers to pinpoint specific areas of cultural disruption. Hence, I argue that it is the seeing of difference that evokes the strongest reactions to unorthodox ways of being male.

The Joys of Being a Man

'Nwoye knew that it was right to be masculine and to be violent, but somehow he still preferred the stories of his mother...'

'Did I not pay your bride price? Am I not your owner?'

Things Fall Apart

Portrayals of male characters in *Things Fall Part* and *The Joys of Motherhood* illustrate several of the most salient models of African masculinities that inform later representations by other Nigerian writers. As the above quotes suggest, *being* a man is defined by a cluster of traits (e.g., strength, stoicism, violence, control) that secure the primacy of men within an *ideally* stable social hierarchy. According to Desiree Lewis, 'Patriarchal scripts of identity and culture are entrenched in the icons that give shape to our hopes, in the literary traditions that inspire us and in the very words that we use.' Thus, examining images behind the words establishes a mechanism for deciphering layers of meaning otherwise not readily apparent. It allows us to witness what Richard Candida Smith calls a translation: 'Usually, the interpretation of images involves a translation of visual impressions into words.' Working backwards from this concept and doing a kind of simultaneous translation, we can uncover the ways that words and images work together to create specific embodiments of male identity.

African masculinities in *Things Fall Apart* are situated in a pre-colonial context. Okonkwo is a 'Big Man,'[3] one who is wealthy in people, yams and power. Early on, his physical description is presented as central to his identity:

He was tall and huge and his bushy eyebrows and wide nose gave him a very severe look. He breathed heavily... When he walked, his heels hardly touched the ground and he seemed to walk on springs, as if he was going to pounce on somebody. And he did pounce on people quite often. He had a slight stammer and whenever he was angry and could not get his words out quickly enough, he would use his fists (8).

Okonkwo appears strong and feline. His stern countenance is bolstered by a violent nature expressed in his 'pouncing' on strangers, friends and family. Even though he may be inarticulate, his notoriety is not based on his words, but on his physical strength and force of personality. In contrast, Unoka, his father, is the direct opposite. He has not acquired any titles and prefers palm wine to hard work. Just as his son is widely known for self-made success, Unoka is reputed to be lazy and capable of living only for the moment: '[H]e was tall but very thin and had a slight stoop. He wore a haggard and mournful look except when he was drinking or playing his flute' (8). This is the *look* of weakness and failure to thrive as a man. His thinness is a metaphor for deficiency, a lack of both material and spiritual substance. Unoka is stooped, bowed down beneath the weight of his debt and irresponsibility. He is intimately connected to his music, but concerned about little else. These verbal descriptions provide readers with visual images associated with men's success and failure respectively. Each character's approximation of manliness is directly tied to his physical appearance and his ability to conform to societal expectations.

There is evidence elsewhere in the text that Okonkwo's psychological indoctrination into manhood developed partly with his awareness of how men are *not* to *be*. Reflecting on his fear of failure, he recalls how he learned to abhor his father's deficiencies: ' . . . and even now he still remembered how he had suffered when a playmate had told him that his father was *agbala*. That was how Okonkwo first came to know that *agbala* was not only another name for a woman, it could also mean a man who had taken no title' (17). From this humiliating encounter grows Okonkwo's hatred of 'everything that his father Unoka had loved. One of those things was gentleness and another was idleness' (17). The implications are clear—Okonkwo equates masculinity with brawn, force and an industrious work ethic. This attitude fortifies his personal belief that 'To show affection was a sign of weakness; the only thing worth demonstrating was strength' (30). So when his first son, Nwoye, indicates vague signs of laziness, Okonkwo corrects him by 'nagging and beating' him.

Estranged from both his father and his oldest son, Okonkwo further demonstrates the penalties that individuals provoke when they subscribe to unconventional behaviours. Upon his discovery that Nwoye has forsaken traditional beliefs for Christianity, Okonkwo launches into a tirade, unprecedented in its ferocity: 'You have all seen the great abomination of your brother. Now he is no longer my son or your brother. I will only have a son who is a man, who will hold his head up among my people. If any one of you prefers to be a woman, let him follow Nwoye now while I am alive so that I can curse him' (158). At this moment, Okonkwo exercises a kind of social censorship by expelling Nwoye from the family. He associates Nwoye's actions with the most degrading and insulting contradiction of a man—that of being a woman. Although being idle and unproductive is objectionable, one may still be called a man, a weak man, but nonetheless, a man. However, the most grievous humiliation is for a man to be cited for his alleged display of womanly qualities. Being branded with such appellation implies that a man is totally dominated, unfit to be considered male.

In *Things Fall Apart* African masculinities are constructed in an oppositional framework.[4] Okonkwo, a model of hegemonic or dominant masculinity, is the binary opposite of Unoka. He lives his entire life striving to be different from his father and dispenses severe punishment to men who do not conform. This characterisation reinforces Morrell's suggestion that 'in addition to oppressing women, hegemonic masculinity silences or subordinates other masculinities, positioning these in relation to itself such that the values expressed by these other masculinities are not those that have currency or legitimacy.'[5] The softness and lack of drive exhibited by Unoke and Nwoye, for example, are worthless qualities that have no bearing in men of substance.

Finally, Nwoye's conversion to Christianity marks a significant departure from the life Okonkwo desires for him. Although he has admitted that his children are not like him in personality or motivation—'my children do not resemble me' (63)—he still firmly expects that his eldest son will uphold the family tradition: 'He wanted Nwoye to grow into a tough young man capable of ruling his father's household when he was dead and gone . . . he was always happy when he heard him grumbling about women. That showed that in time he would be able to control his women-folk' (52). From Okonkwo's point of view, oppositional relationships are the natural order of the social hierarchy and a man's place is superior to that of women, children and subordinate males.[6] So Nwoye's turning away from his community (i.e., family) and beliefs is also a rejection of the masculine identity that is his birthright. Okonkwo's reflection on the situation yields a sour taste of betrayal: 'Now that he had time to think of it, his son's crime stood out in its stark enormity. To abandon the gods of one's father and go about with a lot of effeminate men clucking like old hens was the very depth of abomination' (142). Although scholars such as Morrell and Connell argue that in any given society, masculinities shift and change over time, *Things Fall Apart* makes clear that indigenous masculinities, though embattled, continued to exert significant influence on the performance of African masculinity. In later periods characters continue to be portrayed as constrained by their adherence to or departure from the normative male standard. As we observe in *The Joys of Motherhood* and *Graceland*, men who do not look or behave according to the prescribed standard of male identity are ostracised and as noted above, showered with the worst appellation of all—they are not real men, but women.

The central narrative in *The Joys of Motherhood* takes place during the colonial period and expands on several themes (e.g., the clash of cultures, the individual versus the community) explored in *Things Fall Apart*, but with a feminist twist. The main female character, Nnu Ego, is drawn against the male characters who govern her life. The 'Big Man' in this text is her father, a local chief, Nwokocha Agbadi. He benefits from the so-called 'patriarchal dividend' by virtue of his status as head *man*. He lives in a compound consisting of seven wives, two mistresses, numerous children and relatives. He is a well respected 'son of the soil' (11). 'Nwokocha Agbadi was a very wealthy local chief. He was a great wrestler and was glib and gifted in oratory. His speeches were highly spiced with sharp anecdotes and thoughtful proverbs. He was taller than most and since he was born in an age when physical prowess determined one's role in life, people naturally accepted him as a leader. Like most handsome men who are aware of their charismatic image, he had many women in his time' (10).

Nwokocha Agbadi has several qualities in common with Okonkwo in *Things Fall Apart*. Both are taller than the average man and both are skilled wrestlers. However, unlike Okonkwo, Agbadi is a man of words, an accomplished orator known for his provocative speeches. Nonetheless, oratory simply enhances his appeal because it is his physical attributes that actually secure his place in the community: '[H]e was born in an age when physical prowess determined one's role in life, people naturally accepted him as a leader' (10). His physical features accommodate his personality, which is described as arrogant, sarcastic and cruel, but sometimes also kind and tender. These divergent qualities create an image of a man whose physical strength is offset by genuine compassion. It is as if his intellectual qualities dilute the potential brute force of his physical attributes.

In measured distinction from her father, the paragon of African masculinity, Nnu Ego's mother, Ona, is atypical. She is set apart from other women because of several conditions, including her physical appearance: '[S]he was of medium height and had skin like that of half-ripe palm nuts, smooth, light coffee in colour... Though she was always scantily dressed, she frequently made people aware of being a conservative, haughty presence, cold as steel and remote as any woman royally born' (12). The majority of community members agree that Ona is rude, spoiled, egocentric, troublesome and impetuous. Needless to say, she is not well liked by Agabadi's people, but 'they respected her as the only woman who could make Agbadi really happy' (15). In short, she is tolerated because of her value to Agbadi, her link to a Big Man and nothing else.

Another aspect of difference is the fact that Ona's father has no living sons and not many children. As a result, he lavishes his attention and resources on Ona and ensures that she will be his exclusively. This state of living for the benefit of her father affords her privileges that other women do not enjoy and simultaneously exempts her from a normal life. According to Agabadi: 'He had maintained that she must never marry: his daughter was never going to stoop to any man. She was free to have men, however, if she bore a son, he would take her father's name thereby rectifying the omission that nature had made' (12). Unquestionably a man is in charge of the women in his life and to that end Agbadi utilises his patriarchal privileges by specifying how and under what conditions his daughter will have a relationship (or not) with a man. He permits Ona to live with Agbadi, but not to marry him. And as fate would dictate, their only child is a girl—Nnu Ego, who inherits none of her mother's spunk and all of her father's conservatism. It should be noted that Ona dies in childbirth, which implies, in a symbolic way, that there is no place for a non-traditional, masculinised woman: '[Y]ou see, you won't even allow yourself to be a woman. You are in the first weeks of motherhood and all you can do is to think like a man' (24–25).

Later in the narrative, when Agbadi betroths Nnu Ego to Nnaife (her second husband), readers encounter a different kind of male, one who is separated from the land and in close contact with White colonials. Nnu Ego relocates from rural Ibuza to bustling Lagos, where her husband-to-be is employed. The first time Nnu Ego sees Nnaife, she is less than pleased with his appearance.

Nnu Ego...was just falling asleep with a full stomach when in walked a man with a belly like a pregnant cow, wobbling first to this side and then to that. The belly, coupled with the fact that he was short, made him look like a barrel. His hair, unlike that of men at home in Ibuza, was not closely shaved; he left a lot on his head, like that of a woman mourning for her husband. His skin was pale, the skin of someone who had for a long time worked in the shade and not in the open air. His cheeks were puffy and looked as if he had pieces of hot yam inside them and they seemed to have pushed his mouth into a smaller size above his weak jaw... Why, marrying such a jelly of a man would be like living with a middle-aged woman! (42).

Not only is Nnaife's build the direct opposite of her father's, he does not display the physical signs of hard work valued by her people, the people of the soil: '[S]he fought back tears of frustration. She was used to tall, wiry farmers, with rough blackened hands from farming, long, lean legs and very dark skin' (43). Nnaife's roundness, lack of stature and pale skin are completely unattractive. In Nnu Ego's mind, Nnaife's physical appearance makes him seem less than a man and more like a woman. She (mis)interprets his gendered identity based on the shape of his body. Richard Candida Smith remarks that to read a body is 'to inscribe it with an imagined interiority, an essence that linked one to a specific position in a social hierarchy' (4). In this case, by contemplating life with Nnaife in the context of life 'with a middle-aged woman,' Nno Ego inadvertently assigns herself a lowly position in the hierarchy in which being old and female are supreme disadvantages. Here, it is the woman and not the man who clings to standards of male identity that do not apply. As such, Nno Ego's complicity reinforces the gender oppression that overwhelms her life. She sums it up when she testifies in court that: "'Nnaife is the head of our family. He owns me, just like God in the sky owns us'"(217).

African masculinities in *The Joys of Motherhood* are subordinated to feminine models of African womanhood within the narrative framework. They are no less powerful, but are situated in the background of the storyline. This too is a kind of oppositional rendering of gendered identities, but in this case the primary focus is on differences between women and men. Nnaife is deficient or weak in physique and moral convictions, but because of his male privilege as head of the family, he freely dominates those 'under his roof.' In one respect this seems to be the crux of Emecheta's argument—that the prescribed social roles of women and men create an effective mechanism for the oppression of women. Several characters explain how this works: 'You are to give her children and food, she is to cook and bear the children and look after you and them' (71). The only exception to the rule is in the city where women's and men's roles shift according to the rigorous demands of urban survival and the dictates of Christianity: '[I]n Ibuza, women made a contribution [to supplement the husband's income], but in urban Lagos, men had to be the sole providers' (81). Thus, given the pervasiveness of colonial rule and the harsh consequences for non-compliance, African men's sphere of authority shrank considerably. The home and family became a place where Black men could freely exercise the power invested in them by the ancestors. Amatokwu, Nnu Ego's first husband, for example, makes clear their relative positions with regard to the importance of producing children: 'I am a busy man. I have no time to waste my precious male seed on a woman who is infertile' (32). As expected, he soon takes a second wife and immediately impregnates her. Nnu Ego's rapid displacement within the marriage suggests that wives are dispensable commodities traded and changed at the discretion of their husbands. Nnu Ego's second husband, Nnaife, also comments on their asymmetrical positioning: '[D]id I not pay your bride price? Am I not your owner?' (48) Implicit in these comments are notions of entitlement that only men enjoy. The male–female relationships in the text are indicative of an oppositional continuum that situates masculine identity on one extreme end and feminine identity on the other. These binary oppositions are grounded in women's and men's materiality. That is, their roles are based on qualities of the body: men's ability to impregnate women and women's capacities to carry and bear children. Again, Emecheta implies that this kind of biological determinism is harmful to women, but constructs a narrative that conveys the idea that even though men's and women's social roles may be slowly changing, the dominance of men over women remains a crucial component of male identity.

I use these scenarios to illustrate several points. First, there is attention to physical details that anchor the texts to gendered male identities characteristic of the respective time periods and to particular societal values. As we see in the last example, Nnu Ego, reflecting the conventional expectations of her kinsmen and women, prefers in men thinness rather than obesity, short rather than long hair and dark rather than light skin. These qualities are more than a patterned collection of physical traits. They are material exemplars of dominant masculinities. Correctly or incorrectly, these characters' bodily traits are assigned value according to prevailing standards of masculine identity. Those who differ suffer the consequences.

Second, physical contrasts represent oppositional masculine identities. That is, they are not just different, but antithetic to one another. The flourishing of one ensures the demise or silencing of the other. As Lisa Lindsay and Stephan Miescher point out in *Men and Masculinities in Modern Africa*, at any point in time, 'one form of masculinity rather than others is culturally exalted' (6). In *Things Fall Apart*, for example, the masculine identity manifested in Okonkwo overpowers that of the other characters. And even though Okonkwo comes to a tragic end, his physical image endures. In the case of Nnaife in *The Joys of Motherhood*, masculine identity is in a state of flux. There is a transformation taking place between rural and urban masculinities. Nnaife and his contemporaries are unlike Agbadi and men of the previous generation. They survive in an environment unknown to their fathers. Their masculine identities are in revision, whereas older expressions of African manhood are restricted to rural communities. Both versions cannot exist in the same location at the same time. Cordelia, Nnu Ego's friend, best sums it up when she remarks on the impact of city life on African men: '[T]hey stopped being men long ago. Now they are machines' (53).

In essence, visual images of African masculinities in these texts suggest that a character's identity is defined almost exclusively by gender. Details about the look of a man are intertwined with the ways he acts out or performs his gendered identity and this, in turn, determines how he is perceived by others. Even in a transitional condition of existence there are rarely neutral states. There are no unspecified in-between male identities.[7] Either a particular character is a man, in every loaded sense of the cultural construct, or he is deemed a woman.[8]

'It's Not Easy to Be a Man': Coming of Age in a State of Flux

This is a journey to manhood, to life: it cannot be easy. The old Igbo adage is: Manhood is not achieved in a day.

Chris Abani, *Graceland*.

Graceland represents a significant departure from the more traditional models of male identities portrayed in *Things Fall Apart* and *The Joys of Motherhood*. In this text we find complex, alternative masculinities (including the forbidden domain of homosexuality) that co-exist uneasily and in constantly fluctuating positions of dominance and subordination. Elvis, the main character, is situated between extreme versions of African masculinities. He occupies a fluid space that is perpetually renegotiated, but never discrete or firm. The central narrative shifts back and forth between Elvis's childhood in Afikpo in the 1970s and his teenage years in Lagos in the 1980s. Each location represents a different lifestyle that Elvis does not live out completely. This fragmentation of daily living is further exacerbated by a series of devastating events: the death of his mother, his own rape as well as that of his young female cousin, physical abuse, grinding poverty and imprisonment. Loss permeates every corner of his life and Elvis is reduced to finding his own way, becoming a man in the midst of trauma.

As a male, Elvis inherits status and privilege established long before he was conceived. Marilyn Thompson notes that, '[i]n all cultures and societies, gender stereotypes begin from the moment we are born and are identified as either a boy or a girl. This label determines how we will be treated, how we are expected to behave and our view of the world.'[9] By virtue of his gender, Elvis is entitled to enjoy the patriarchal dividend at his leisure. Even so, not all members of the community embrace these predetermined values without question. When Beatrice, Elvis's mother, discusses her illness and impending death with her own mother, Oye, she acknowledges the importance of being male. Beatrice confesses that she wants to become a part of the masculine elite for several good reasons and will do so by being reborn in the lineage as a boy:

> ...remember de songs dat de women would sing when a boy was born? Ringing from hamlet to hamlet, dropped by one voice, picked up by another until it had circled de town. And de ring of white powder we would wear around de neck to signify de boy's place as head of de family. [for girls]...a dirge. Mournful, carried by solo voices until all de town was alerted of de sadness of de family. And de ring of powder we wore was around de elbow to show the flexibility and willingness to work hard of de woman. When I come back, it will be as a boy. You know that dat's the only reason Sunday hasn't taken another wife. Because I bore him a son (37).

In addition to the difference in songs, strategic parts of the body are marked with white powder connoting the higher province of men (the neck) and the lower one of women (the elbow). Here, the construction of masculinity as well as femininity is represented by an acknowledgment of women's and men's unequal societal positions. Furthermore, Beatrice's awareness of these contradictions sparks her motivation to take action even though it may be largely symbolic at this point in her prematurely shortened life.

At the age of 5, Elvis experiences a customary ritual that punctuates his eventual coming to manhood. In Afikpo it is natural and expected that certain stages in this process are observed, in part, to ensure that the future generation continues the same tradition. Even though the ceremony has been streamlined for the convenience of modern life, it is still an important gesture.

Elvis had no idea why his father had summoned him to the backyard, away from the toy fire engine he was playing with. He had no idea why he had been asked to strip down to his underwear, or why Uncle Joseph first strapped a grass skirt on him and then began to paint strange designs in red and white dye all over his body. But he was 5 years old and had learned not only that no one explained much to him, but that it was safest not to ask (17).

This event illustrates White's idea that masculinity is constructed on different parts of men's bodies rather than on the body as an undifferentiated whole: 'not just on genitals but on faces, arms and backs.'[10] In this instance, acknowledgment of readiness for manhood is marked by specific cultural symbols. Elvis's body is adorned with a grass skirt and certain colours.[11] In addition, he is expected to display the bravery/instinct of a warrior by killing his first eagle. Elvis, still very much a child, is dismayed by the prospect of taking a life, so Uncle Joseph explains: '[I]t is the first step into manhood for you. When you are older, de next step is to kill a goat and den from dere we begin your manhood rites. But dis is de first step'(19). Although the bird that is killed is a chick and not an eagle and even though someone else other than Elvis does the actual killing, this early indoctrination into manhood indicates that the making of boys into men is a gradual process accentuated by various milestones (e.g., killing an eagle, then a goat) and reinforced by the community. After the ceremony, Elvis celebrates with his male teenage cousins and embraces the idea without question: '[S]itting on the counter in his grass skirt, drinking his Fanta and watching Godfrey and Innocent tease the girl behind the counter, Elvis felt like a man' (21). At this moment Elvis is a spectator learning the script that he has been given permission to act out. He is taught how to be a man by custom, examples, values and expectations. He gradually learns that this privilege is accompanied by responsibilities that he may not easily refuse.

On the other hand, Elvis's mother has different ideas about what kind of knowledge he would best benefit from. Beatrice has no investment in book learning, but takes a more practical approach to skills needed for survival after her death: 'I am preparing him, Mama. I am teaching him things dat useless school cannot. I have taught him to sew, to iron, to cook, to read and to write at a level beyond his age' (38). Even though Oye argues that this is not enough,

Beatrice is not dissuaded. The issue, however, is that sewing, cooking, ironing and perhaps even reading, are outside of men's traditional domain. Elvis may be able to successfully employ these skills, but how does this affect his masculine identity? Reading, perhaps, is the least suspect of these skills and Elvis is never without several books even though he lives in dire poverty. Ironically, his love of reading makes him appear to be well educated even though he did not finish high school. He selects from a wide range of African, African-American and European books, the majority by male authors. The types of books, their respective themes and the significance to Elvis's life are beyond the scope of this chapter, but suffice it to say that masculine ideals implied by the titles and themes must play some small role in Elvis's expanding consciousness.

The first manhood ritual (e.g., killing an eagle) is just one of the many ways Elvis learns how to (be)come a man. This initial phase is supervised by kin and elders who essentially are Elvis's initial male role models. In essence, he is nurtured by his immediate community. However, as Elvis grows older, he ventures more frequently outside of the compound and comes into contact with a greater range of role models. At 13, Elvis looks up to the older, non-kin males he encounters at the local motor park where he watches silent Westerns and Indian films:

> While he waited for the main film to come on, Elvis wandered over to where some of the older boys were playing a game of checkers for money. At fifteen and sixteen, with no parents or interested relatives, these boys eked out a living, either as apprentice mechanics or motor-park thugs. Elvis idolised them and wished he could live their lives (146).

At this point in his life, Elvis is disillusioned by the males in his compound. His mother is dead and he is both a witness to and victim of rape, as well as a casualty of physical abuse at the hands of his father. The brutal violence he sees in the masculinities that surround him is overwhelming. As an alternative, he finds solace in the local teenage and film heroes. He admires them because of the defiance and rebellion that they habitually enact. It is worth noting that the boys all agree that John Wayne and a persona simply referred to as 'Actor,' who usually plays a villain, are their favourites. These screen idols, including others such as James Bond and Dr. No, represent hegemonic masculinity in a most convincing format. With no adults to counterbalance the fantasy of the rogue/hero who cannot be killed and always wins, the boys are left to their own imaginations: 'and there was a power in the words that elevated them, made them part of something bigger' (150).

The Measure of a Man: Leopards, Butterflies and Homos

Opposition to dominant masculinities in *Graceland* is acted out both overtly and covertly. The masculine ideal is represented imperfectly by Sunday and to some extent, the King of Beggars. Both men are members of an older generation whose traditional upbringing in the village did not adequately prepare them for the rigours of urban the life they experience as adults. Both men try to act as father to Elvis under less than favourable conditions and both come to an untimely demise. Driven to violence by events they cannot control—death/murder of family members, political sabotage and corruption and government/military abuse of power—Sunday and the King of Beggars engage in desperate acts of resistance for the sake of honour and vengeance, respectively. The fact that their actions result in their own deaths and that their overt challenge to the dominant order is met with lethal force, suggests that older, traditional African masculinities may be in decline or at least in a critical condition.

Sunday, unable to recover from the death of his wife, the loss of a local election and in turn, the loss of his livelihood, takes a final stand. He wants to 'die like a man' even though he has not lived like one. In order to save his neighbourhood from demolition by government order and forsaken by cowardly fellow protestors, Sunday faces the troops alone. He attacks their bulldozer with a cutlass and is immediately gunned down.

> Sunday fell in a slump before the 'dozer, its metal threads cracking his chest like a timber box as it went straight into the wall of his home. Sunday roared, leapt out of his body and charged the back of the policeman, his paw delivering a fatal blow to the back of the policeman's head. With a rasping cough, Sunday disappeared into the night (287).

Sunday gives up his life for a noble cause and by so doing restores his tarnished reputation and manly image. Whether or not this is an act of bravery, madness or suicide is questionable. However, the mystical description of his death implies that Sunday returns to his ancestors honourably via the leopard totem that whispers to him shortly before the confrontation. And in the true spirit of a brave warrior, in some small way he avenges the government's injustice by killing one of their men. The policeman that Sunday slays 'looked like he had been mauled by some large predator. This was strange because there were no animals of that size anywhere near Lagos or Maroko' (305).

In a parallel death scene, the King of Beggars experiences a similar fate during the same protest. When the King confronts the Colonel he realises that this officer is the one who killed his entire family long ago. The King's search for revenge comes to a dramatic end: '[W]hat happened next would be described differently later. Some would mention butterflies surrounding the King; others, cats; others still, dogs; others said eagles. Some also said that a hand reached down from heaven and handed him a sword with which to smite the unjust army' (302). The King of Beggars kills the Colonel with a dagger and is in turn shot to death by soldiers. He too 'dies like a man' in retaliation for the murder of his family. Unlike Sunday, whose body is lost in the rubble of the ghetto, the King of Beggars receives a posthumous bonus. He is made a legend: 'deified, turned into a prophet, an advance guard, like John the Baptist, for the arrival of the Messiah' (303). Accounts of both deaths include descriptions of mysterious events that cannot be fully explained or rationalised. This touch of magical realism dissolves the boundaries between competing masculinities and is a reminder of the underlying significance of traditional beliefs. As Brenda Cooper observed, magical realism captures 'the paradox of the unity of opposites; it contests polarities such as history versus magic . . . life versus death.'[12]

From an entirely different perspective, a covert challenge to dominant masculinities occurs in the form of homosexuality. The mere hint of same-sex relations and/or desire precipitates the most excessive reactions. The mainstream backlash that ensues may not be random, but a systematic way of extinguishing or nullifying opposition. According to Janet Bujra, 'A denial of homosexuality may extend to a denial of the implied diversity of masculinities.'[13] In other words, within the varieties of African masculinities, homosexuality usually is not considered a legitimate expression of male identity, although there is a faint hint to the contrary in this narrative. Specifically, it is visual cues that agitate much of the homophobia in *Graceland*. Seeing displays of anti-male identity (e.g., men or boys in drag) is the spark that ignites the flame of retaliation, especially among self-appointed guardians of male supremacy. As a nine-year-old, for example, Elvis has a brutal encounter with his father because social codes that regulate adornment of the male body are violated in an act of pretend play. At no point does Sunday consider that what he sees is a collective imaginative performance rather than a reflection of an underlying sinister reality.

> Elvis longed to try on their makeup and have his hair plaited. Aunt Felicia finally gave in to his badgering and wove his hair into lovely cornrows. One of the other girls put lipstick on him. Giggling and getting into the game, another pulled a minidress over his head. On Elvis, it fell nearly to the floor, like an evening gown. He stepped into a pair of Aunt Felicia's too-big platforms and pranced about, happy, proud, chest stuck out (61).

At this same moment Elvis's father returns home and 'squinted as Elvis approached, face changing in slow degrees from amusement to shock and finally to rage' (61). He sees his boy in drag and responds with excessive force. Sunday beats Elvis until he is unconscious and rants that: 'No son of mine is going to grow up as a homosexual! Do you hear me! . . . Elvis is my son. Son, not daughter' (62). Once Elvis regains consciousness Sunday shaves his head in order to get rid of the decorative cornrows. It is as if Sunday is trying to restore Elvis's maleness by removing all signs of femininity. During this arduous process

Sunday remarks: 'It's not easy to be a man. Dese are trying times. Not easy' (63). In this situation Sunday may be referring to any number of issues, including the difficulties within his own family (e.g., lack of money, illness and subsequent death of his spouse), political unrest in the region, or a general concern about the role of men in the rapidly changing community. Whatever the case may be, his comment implies that there is an added burden that men must take on at this time. Thus, fuelled by the stress of extra responsibility, Sunday's intense reaction to Elvis in make-up and a dress illustrates Robert Morrell's citing of some of the characteristics of hegemonic/dominant masculinity: 'among its defining features are misogyny, homophobia, racism and compulsory heterosexuality.'[14] Within this arena of tightly controlled behaviour, strict social codes do not allow for exceptions. Sunday targets Elvis for retribution instead of the women and attempts to beat him into submission, to hammer him into conformity with acceptable male behaviour.

Another factor that further complicates Elvis Oke's situation is the fact that he does not look masculine. Instead, there is a softness to his facial features that outwardly mutes his battle for survival: '[H]is hair was closely cropped, almost shaved clean. His eyebrows were two perfect arcs, as though they had been shaped in a salon' (6). Like his namesake, Elvis's face could be read as either masculine *or* feminine. These incongruities in his appearance make him suspicious in many ways. Accusations of homosexuality plague his teenage years. Again, the prevailing masculine system of social codes enforces a constant vigilance by all members of the community. It does not matter whether or not an allegation has substance. The fact that a certain behaviour or look is so labelled gives momentum and concreteness to the idea that homosexuality is indeed a viable alternative to prevailing masculine identities.

> With the tip of his index finger, he applied a hint of blue to his eyes, barely noticeable, but enough to lift them off the white of his face. Admiring himself from many angles, he thought it was a shame he couldn't wear makeup in public. That's not true, he mentally corrected himself. He could, like the transvestites that haunted the car parks of hotels favored by rich locals and visiting whites. But like them, he would be a target of some insult, or worse, physical beatings . . . It was exasperating that he couldn't appear in public looking as much like the real Elvis Presley as possible (77).

Even though Elvis does not equate transvestites with homosexuality, he realises that others easily make this assumption. His recognition of this dilemma and his own position within it, suggests that he is keenly aware of the strict confines of dominant masculinity. Forbidden to wear make-up in public by uncompromising male codes of conduct, Elvis submerges his infatuation with cosmetics in his Elvis impersonation act, wholeheartedly believing that face powder, eye shadow and lipstick will transform him visually into Elvis Presley.

Although Elvis Oke tries to concede to the prevailing male standards, he cannot escape the homophobia rampant in his environment. On several occasions he is accused of being a homosexual. In one situation Elvis rides on the back of a motorcycle driven by his friend Redemption. Elvis apparently holds on too tight and Redemption objects: 'Hey, Elvis, are you homo? Release me small' (192). One could argue that the comment may have been made in jest, but the fact that Redemption chooses this particular wording rather than any other suggests otherwise. Another incident occurs when Elvis and his teenage peers discuss oral sex and the possibility of 'experimenting' on one another. Elvis finds this idea appealing but, contrary to his inner feelings, makes the charge: 'Dat is homo. It is taboo, forbidden' (197). Rather than give in to sexual desire, he chooses a safer path and exercises the censorship that heterosexual male privilege requires. The last episode takes place when Elvis is in prison. He is tortured by a soldier who rubs a chemical compound all over his body, including his penis. Despite this substance burning his flesh, Elvis has an erection and subsequently ejaculates. The torturer responds cruelly: "'So you be homo," Jerome said, laughing breathlessly' (295). Elvis can neither defend himself nor understand his body's automatic reaction to stimuli. Yet his shame seems to give the insinuation a ring of truth. These encounters reveal an underlying and active homophobia that saturates both public and private life. Undoubtedly, allegations of inappropriate conduct (i.e., homosexuality) are a means of keeping men in check while simultaneously contaminating the social environment with ignorance and bias. Desiree Lewis observes that 'Homophobia therefore symbolizes a profound resistance to surrendering the identities, ritualised behavior and social codes that cultures prescribe for us.'[15] To that end, hegemonic African masculinities give no ground to alternate identities that pose threats to the prevailing order.

Writing on the Body

An Elvis Presley impersonator in Nigeria may seem odd, out of place. In this context the crossover of an American icon symbolises the United States as a place of freedom and individual creative expression. Eric Lott suggests, 'Like baseball and the Statue of Liberty, the figure of Elvis guards the way into America.'[16] Connect this to Elvis Oke's dream of the United States as a place where he can practice his craft without restraint and we have a perfect fit. Furthermore, Elvis Oke's imitation of Elvis Presley, not James Brown or even Fela Kuti, is linked to his audience—White tourists, as well as to his inheritance of Elvis Presley records from his mother.[17] Combined with his passion for dancing and the ever-pressing need for income, this seems like a practical option. Yet the Elvis that Oke creates is heavily made up, distinctly feminine and more symbolic of American culture than anything else.[18] At the heart of the matter is Elvis's desire to use make-up. Extending beyond a childhood quirk, his obsession with cosmetics precariously situates him outside of the typical domain of men. Thus, within the province of women, he learns techniques of applying make-up early in his life. Observing his Aunt Felicia's ritual of dressing up to go out partying with her friends, he discovers that the process of painting one's face transforms the human body:

'Okay,' he said sitting on the edge of the bed, watching her putting on her makeup, fascinated by the deep flake of her powder-patted cheeks, the cherry pout of her lips and the heavy blue eye shadow that made her look older. He was amazed not just at how much makeup made her aware of herself, but by how much he wanted to wear that mask. It would be a perfect remedy for his painful shyness (173).

Elvis's impression of make-up as a kind of mask is much more than an adolescent fantasy. The process of decorating the body with colours and ornaments in order to create a fictional persona is connected to Igbo masquerade: 'a performance and a practice . . . in which illusion is created through the use of some combination of facial disguise, costume, body decoration, props, movement.'[19] Certainly one can argue that women's use of cosmetics is a kind of modern day masquerade wherein a woman puts on a disguise and plays certain roles for a particular audience (i.e., men). Elvis himself engages in the same kind of masquerade when he puts on a costume and assumes a different personality in an attempt to impersonate Elvis Presley and when he tries to be a petty criminal (e.g., a gigolo, drug runner, human body parts distributor) under the tutelage of Redemption. So Elvis's life involves many layers of masking, each with disparate and sometimes unpredictable results.

From another angle, Elvis perceives unique opportunities in the art of using cosmetics. It is a means of both revealing and camouflaging the body. He realises, however, that make-up is a regular part of a process of self-actualisation for women, but not for men: '[H]e envied her this ability to prepare a face for the world. To change it any time she liked. Be different people just by a gentle hint of shadow here, a dash of color there. She could even change her hair to suit her mood' (173). So lacking a legitimate means of doing the same thing, of being able to prepare 'a face for the world,' Elvis indulges in make-up for his Elvis Presley impersonation. He diligently applies heavy make-up for each performance:

Drawing quickly and expertly with the black eye pencil, he outlined his eyes, the tip of the pencil dancing dangerously close to his cornea. Pulling the mascara brush free, he knocked the dried goop off before dragging it through his already dense lashes. Again he examined his hard work intently before selecting a deep red lipstick. Not satisfied with its shine, he rubbed some petroleum jelly over his lips and then smacked them. Much better, he thought (78–79).

Elvis Oke constructs a mask for himself by virtue of his Elvis Presley impersonation. In this mode of being he presents a face to the world that is simultaneously feminine and masculine, native and other. One can visualise such a face, but not necessarily link it to Elvis Presley. Clearly the tourists for whom he performs do not immediately make that association: '[H]e doesn't look like any Elvis I know' (12). Oke fails to establish his intended connection with the tourists, but perhaps he inadvertently recreates an image deeply embedded in Nigerian culture. The white talcum powder, the dark wig and the red lipstick may make Elvis Oke look less like Elvis Presley and more like a *mmuo*, an icon most likely outside the purview of the foreign visitors. According to Esther Dagan, the 'best-known masks of the Igbo are the *mmuo* ... elegant white masks with elaborate hairstyles, representing the pretty maiden Mmuo and symbolizing physical and mental beauty.'[20] This unconscious association with his ancestral past restores, if only briefly, a relationship with kin that previously has been dormant. So his performance of Elvis Presley is more than an act; it is an ancient rehearsal, 'a means by which people reflect on their current conditions, define and/or reinvent themselves and their social world and either reinforce, resist, or subvert prevailing social orders.'[21]

In addition to performing Elvis Presley, the process of becoming Elvis by applying make-up establishes another psychic connection to family. The bonds between Elvis and the women in his life are broken when Beatrice and Oye die. Shortly thereafter Aunt Felicia marries and moves to the United States. Thus, Elvis has no significant female kin in his immediate environment during his later teenage years. His personal ritual of putting on make-up changes the situation profoundly:

Elvis nodded along, singing under his breath as he mixed the pressed powder with the talc. The lumpy powder crumbled in cakes of beige, reminding him of the henna cakes Oye ground to make the dye she used to paint designs all over her body. Satisfied with the mix, he began to apply it to his face with soft, almost sensual strokes of the sponge... Finishing he ran his fingertips along his cheek. Smooth, like the silk of Aunt Felicia's stockings (77).

These physical sensations and visual images (re)connect Elvis to his grandmother and aunt, long absent from his life. For Elvis, preparation for his act brings with it a bridge to a female presence that is more than fond memories. Whether or not he recognises the deeper meanings of his masking, the metamorphosis it entails allows Elvis another level of existence wherein he is both a participant in and observer of his own illusion. With regard to Elvis's mother, there is no connection in this context. In an ironic twist of circumstance, Beatrice does not wear make-up: 'Beatrice was a stubborn one, like you... But she was beautiful, even more so than a mermaid and dark. Probably as dark as the antimony women use to draw patterns on themselves. She never could wear makeup, your mother. She was so dark it never showed. I always said she was like a photo negative.' (104) Oye's description of her daughter suggests that Beatrice's physical appearance is extraordinary in that her attractiveness and skin colour exempt her from the cosmetic enhancement that other women commonly practice. Her natural beauty cancels out any potential benefit that make-up could accomplish. She does not need to participate in the masquerade. Oye's use of a mermaid analogy endows Beatrice with a mystical aura that is further complicated by her comparison to a photo negative—an inversion of a positive image. Even when she is living, Beatrice is more spirit than body. Elvis, just barely alive, is the opposite—more body than spirit.

Ultimately Elvis and his friend Redemption acknowledge that Elvis's chances of survival in Lagos are minimal at best. His 'Elvis' act is all but finished, the majority of his family members are dead or absent; he has no gainful employment or other trappings of life to indicate that he is indeed an honourable Igbo man. In effect, his tenuous existence cannot withstand the present crisis of abject poverty. So the unexpected solution that these childhood friends contrive propels Elvis into an unfamiliar world where once again he will have to reinvent himself: 'Nothing is ever resolved, he thought. It just changes' (320).

Conclusion

Graceland, *Things Fall Apart* and *The Joys of Motherhood* are tied together by several commonalities, including visual models of African masculinities embedded in the respective cultural settings. However, *Graceland* is distinct from the other two novels in its vivid representation of African masculinities as complex and shifting states of existence anchored to specific versions of masculine embodiment. Thus, the meaning of being and becoming an Igbo man is locked in the reciprocal gaze of the performers as well as the audience: '[S]he paused in front of him, taking in his clothes and wig and the talcum powder running in sweaty rivulets down his face. "Who do dis to you?" she asked' (13).

13. Sexual Impotence as Metonymy for Political Failure: Interrogating Hegemonic Masculinities in Ama Ata Aidoo's *Anowa*

Naana Banyiwa Horne

Ama Ata Aidoo's play, *Anowa*, has frequently been submitted to feminist analyses. Although the female protagonist, Anowa, has been the focus of many feminist readings, little attention has been devoted to exploring the life of the male protagonist, Kofi Ako, through the lens of gender. The many feminist analyses of *Anowa* provide strong evidence of Aidoo's play being a primarily female-centred drama, one that explores issues of African womanhood, femininity and sexuality; nonetheless, the author also gives considerable attention to issues of manhood, masculinity and hegemony. Thus, she impresses upon us the symbiotic nature of the relationship between femininity and masculinity and womanhood and manhood—femaleness and maleness corresponding to each other like the feet, the left foot following the right foot instinctively in a well-choreographed dance. Ultimately, Aidoo makes us recognise that an exploration of the life of the male protagonist as a gendered subject is necessary if we are to fully understand the gender issues undergirding her play.

Anowa is the story of a young woman who marries a man disapproved of by her elders. What starts off as a potentially great love story and a quest for fulfilment for both husband and wife, disintegrates into a nightmarish struggle involving oppression, dehumanisation and resistance that eventually claims the lives of the lovers. The central issues explored include polygamy, which hinges on male sexual prowess and fathering children and typically figures strongly as a marker of masculinity—hegemonic masculinity to be precise—and wifehood, with its associated roles of childbearing and childrearing, which are typically projected as indices of ideal femininity and womanhood. Aidoo's play affirms that gender identities are consciously constructed. She redefines notions of gender and sexuality, particularly within the historical, political and economic context and interrogates indigenous constructions of femininity, masculinity and sexuality against the backdrop of slavery (domestic and transatlantic) and Western political, economic and cultural encroachments into nineteenth-century Ghana. Her interrogation of gender constructions encourages us to recognise that 'understandings of masculinity [and femininity] are linked to histories of institutions and economic structures.'[1]

In an environment in which sexual potency for men and childbearing for women are imperatives, the playwright depicts a female protagonist who does not have children and a male protagonist who is sexually impotent, thus challenging normative notions of masculinity and femininity. By challenging the sexual underpinnings of normative masculinity, Aidoo asserts that sexual potency figures powerfully in hegemonic masculinity. Her male protagonist, Kofi Ako, is not only sexually impotent and openly confronted by his wife as responsible for the childlessness of their life, but Anowa also links her husband's inability to engender life with his ruthless exploitation and dehumanisation of the fruit of other women's wombs in his quest for hegemonic masculinity. In a context in which African males collaborate with White exploiters of the African people, the sexual impotence suffered by Kofi Ako serves as metonymy for political failure, specifically the failure of African male leadership. Conversely, that Anowa does not have children is perceived as an assertion of female agency, an act of resistance in the form of a woman withholding her productive capabilities in a socio-economic context in which the fruit of the female womb is abused by unscrupulous males.[2]

Anowa, however, has deep significances beyond the symbolic level. The playwright consciously engages gender ideologies while exploring, in intricate ways, issues that cut to the heart of normative masculinities and femininities in her depiction of the two main characters and in underscoring the symbiotic nature of the relationship between them. Not only is the subject of male sexual impotence—sexual dysfunction and the failure to impregnate women—introduced; it constitutes the central conflict in the play and is explored in a public manner that underscores the threat that the condition poses to hegemonic masculinity. Anowa's open confrontation of her husband is a transgressive act. It compels him to shoot himself, in spite of the fact that he, at that point in his life, has already established a firm reputation as the richest and one of the most powerful men on the Guinea Coast, an accomplishment that garnered for him the status of a 'Big Man.' This configuration of masculinity will be explored more fully below.

An essay by Marcia C. Inhorn, on the subject of masculinity and sexuality in Egypt, provides support for the significance of sexual prowess in the construction of hegemonic masculinity:

No matter the cause, male sexual dysfunction is profoundly threatening to Egyptian notions of hegemonic masculinity...in a society where masculinity is homosocially competitive and the same Arabic term is often employed for both sexual 'virility' and 'manhood'...Infertility is a 'sexual' condition, one that implicates and deeply challenges normative male sexuality, masculinity and paternity in places like Egypt, where 'to be a man' means to be a virile patriarch who begets children, particularly sons.[3]

The tendency to employ the same Arabic term in reference to both sexual virility and manhood is not only common in Egypt. In fact, among the Akan, the same term (banyin/barima, in Mfantse and Twi, respectively) references both manhood and the penis in sexually virile contexts. In fact, most societies popularly conflate problems of sexual potency and male infertility, associating both with the loss of virility and manhood. Stephan Miescher notes that among the Akan, because the attainment of fatherhood status remains crucial to adult masculinity, men who have no children are neither perceived as full adults nor can they aspire to senior masculinity.[4]

Kofi Ako has been given some attention in an earlier article by Naana Banyiwa Horne that explores issues of female subject identities and agency in Ama Ata Aidoo's plays. However, the attention he receives in that article is on the exploration of the specific oppressive factors in Anowa's life, stemming from patriarchy, rather than on studying Kofi Ako as a gendered subject. The approach in that article is consistent with the theorising of men in feminism and emanates out of the understanding of feminism 'as a set of theories [that] both explains women's fear of men and empowers women to confront it both publicly and privately.'[5] That acknowledgment notwithstanding, the article's limitation is that it emphasises Anowa's 'experiences of the consequences of men's domination rather than the focused theorising of men and masculinities.'[6] This chapter makes up for that deficit by giving Kofi Ako the same critical scrutiny Anowa is given as a gendered subject. It turns the critical lens fully on Aidoo's male protagonist as a gendered subject. It focuses on issues of manhood and masculinity, especially Kofi Ako's climb from a 'good-for-nothing-cassava-man' (75), i.e., a male of questionable masculinity, to his attainment of hegemonic stature as a 'Big Man' by becoming the richest and most powerful man on the Guinea Coast. We follow him in his quest to accumulate those cultural symbols that denote manhood, particularly what can be constructed into hegemonic masculinity.[7] The objective of this chapter is to affirm that the most promising approach to understanding Anowa entails the focused theorising of not only the gendered subjectivities of the female protagonist but that of the male as well.

Although Aidoo's Anowa is the main focus of this analysis, introductory observations regarding Chinua Achebe's Things Fall Apart and Mariama Bâ's So

Long a Letter help to map the critical terrain to the male subject identities of manhood and masculinities traversed. Achebe's novel can be perceived as the prototypical male-authored text. Even as the novelist problematises the male protagonist's strive to attain hegemonic masculinity in his society, Achebe, nonetheless, underscores Umuofia society's valorisation of such masculine attributes as sexual and physical prowess, strength, fearlessness in doing battle or shedding blood.[8] We watch the male protagonist, Okonkwo, embark on a frenzied climb from being the son of an *agbala*, a man with no redeeming attributes of masculinity, hence, derogatorily regarded as a woman, to become one of the men who epitomise hegemonic masculinity.[9] His reputation as one of the leading men of Umuofia culminates in his acquisition of three wives and significant titles; Nwakibie, possibly the wealthiest and highest titled man in Umuofia, has nine wives. Manly men, therefore, are recognised by their ability to marry many wives and accomplish acts of valour.

Not surprisingly, Okonkwo's emergence as a man among men is underscored by his throwing the renowned wrestler, Amalinze the Cat, in a wrestling match that memorialises his physical prowess. Ekwefi, who becomes Okonkwo's second wife and is also recognised as the one woman for whom Okonkwo harbours strong emotions (though he has a problem with showing his tender side) falls in love with him upon witnessing the legendary wrestling match. It is significant that Ekwefi, who ends up marrying someone else because, at the time, Okonkwo is too poor to afford the dowry, runs away from her husband and moves into Okonkwo's household to become his second wife once he proves himself capable of refunding her first husband's dowry and supporting her: i.e., once Okonkwo proves himself a man among men by his growing wealth and valorous accomplishments. Ekwefi's move fosters the perception that it is preferable even to be a second wife of a man whose manhood rests on publicly acclaimed acts of valour than to be the first wife of a man whose manhood is not publicly recognised.

Conversely, Mariama Bâ's *So Long a Letter* is a novel that can be perceived as a prototypical female-authored text. In it, polygamy is interrogated; it is problematised. Polygamous marriages are not shown as a boost to male ego. On the one hand, polygamy is presented as a tempting choice for men who are experiencing a mid-life crisis as a way to upgrade their public standing as virile men. On the other hand, they are shown paying a high price for that choice, a price that ultimately diminishes them in stature. Mawdo Ba, who marries Aissatou, his college sweetheart, against his mother's wishes, eventually succumbs to taking young Nabou, who has been groomed by his mother to be her replica, as his second wife. Of course, Aissatou leaves him. She makes the choice to wear the mantle of her dignity and strip herself of the love of a man who chooses to separate his emotional needs from his physical desires, one who draws 'a line between heartfelt love and physical love' (31). Aissatou's action—

choosing divorce over being part of a polygamous marriage—challenges one of the foundation stones of hegemonic masculinity in her world. She rejects the commodification of women by a marriage institution (polygamy) that pegs a man's enhanced sense of his masculinity (his financial acumen and sexual prowess) to his accumulation of women as trophy wives. Likewise, Modou Fall, Ramatoulaye's husband, takes Binetou, the classmate of his own daughter, for a second wife. Instead of sealing his claim to hegemonic masculinity by attesting to his sexual potency, he dies from a heart attack undoubtedly brought on by the stress of meeting the sexual and other demands of his young wife. Mariama Bâ's novel suggests that male hypersexuality comes with a price tag that can exact a heavy toll not only on women and children but on men too.

It is in light of challenging the normative notions of gender and sexuality that *Anowa* acquires significance in this chapter. Like Mariama Bâ in *So Long a Letter*, Aidoo deflates hegemonic masculinities in this play. From the beginning of the play, the playwright starts interrogating and undermining traditional notions of femininity and masculinity. In the Prologue, two prominent male institutions, the army and political leadership, are brought under scrutiny within the context of notions of feminisation and masculinisation. It is significant that a male character who has attained senior masculinity (i.e., elderhood) is the one who takes on the burden of deflating the male ego by scrutinising male military and political performance.[10] In order to interrogate these institutions with some authenticity, Aidoo turns her attention to historical events that played a major role in the colonial history of the Gold Coast—the role of the Mfantse leadership in the eventual British defeat of the Asante and the total colonisation of the Gold Coast. Set in the historical period that marks the official dating of British colonisation of the Gold Coast in 1874, it is pertinent that the Opanyin (elder) in this play—the Old-Man-Mouth-That-Eats-Salt-and-Pepper—is endowed with wisdom in addition to having knowledge of the relevant historical events and their impact on the society and its people.[11]

Historically, the Mfantse leadership, in its myopic desire to curb Asante aggression and advance its own economic ambitions, solicited the help of the British. The Mfantse army collaborated with the British in defeating the Asante, ironically providing the British not only with a springboard for colonising the Gold Coast but an elevation in power that attributed a hegemonic masculinity to the British as colonial masters and a subordinate masculinity to the Gold Coast male leadership as the colonised. In its naïveté, the Mfantse leadership did not recognise that the British had an agenda of their own—of political and economic domination—for which they were seeking local allies. In Aidoo's play, both the army and the leadership of the Mfantse people are shown to be ineffectual. She draws attention to the inefficacy of both these institutions early in the play. It is with tongue in cheek and embarrassment that both the army and the leadership of the Mfantse are spoken of in the Prologue. The Old Man Mouth-That-Eats-Salt-and-Pepper[12] confides conspiratorially to his imagined audience: 'But bring your ears, nearer, my friends, so I can whisper you a secret. / Our armies, well-organised though they be, / Are more skilled in quenching fires than in the art of war!' (66). It is a well-known fact that an army that is worthy of its name leaves its mark on the world, not by quenching fires but by winning wars. Strength and valour are normative markers of manhood; men are revered for their courage, their effectiveness in protecting their lands and people and for winning wars that often lead to an expansion of their territory. In this sense, the Asante prove themselves real men by acquiring a reputation for their warlike nature and for empire-building. Miescher affirms the high esteem in which militaristic values are held among the Asante. The Mfantse army, on the other hand, is shown in the play to be incapable of accomplishing comparable manly feats.

By implication, if the men constituting the Mfantse army are lacking in significant manly qualities, then they are effeminate; they are women; they are *agbala* (borrowing the concept from Chinua Achebe's *Things Fall Apart*). Okonkwo's father, Unoka, an artist who loves peace, hates war, is afraid of bloodshed and has won no titles, is called an *agbala*. In Aidoo's play, the 'lords of our Houses,' the leaders of the land, are shown to be no manlier that the men designated *agbala* in Achebe's *Things Fall Apart*. The Old Man Mouth-That-Eats-Salt-and-Pepper pleads on behalf of the 'lords of the Houses.'

> So please,
> Let not posterity judge it too bitterly
> That in a dangerous moment, the lords of our Houses
> Sought the protection of those that-came-from-beyond-
> the-horizon
> Against our more active kinsmen from the north (66).

The 'lords of the Houses' are portrayed as cowards who are cognisant of their cowardice. Recognising that they are no match for their more warlike neighbours and therefore, need protection from them, they take an unmanly action: they turn for protection to the White men and thereby become feminised in relation to them. They are impotent and get around their impotence by subordinating themselves to the British through political alliances.

> ... [T]he lords of our Houses
> Signed that piece of paper—
> The bond of 1844 they call it—
> Binding us to the white men
> Who came from beyond the horizon (68).

The Mfantse leadership is bound to the White men in a manner that renders the men women's protectors. The signing of the Bond of 1844 places them in a relationship of women to men—White men, in this case—thus feminising the Mfantse leadership in a manner that mirrors the feminising of Africa through European colonialism.

There is also an economic dimension to this arrangement that recalls conventional marriages in which women traditionally attach themselves to men for protection and economic gain. The 'lords of the Houses,' in collaborating with the Whites, become dependent on them for their economic well-being. They come to find 'a common sauce-bowl / In which they play a game of dipping with the stranger' (66). The Old Man Mouth-That-Eats-Salt-and-Pepper laments:

> . . . [L]et it not surprise us then
> That this-One and That-One
> Depend for their well-being on the presence of
> The pale stranger in our midst:
> Kofi was, is and shall always be
> One of us (67).

Kofi Ako, the male protagonist of Aidoo's play, is singled out as one such man who depends on the Whites for his well-being. In fact, it is through trading with the White men on the coast and controlling the palm oil trade that he becomes the richest man on the Guinea Coast and establishes his reputation as a 'Big Man.'[13] The irony that this African Big Man's big man status emanates from his dependence on the White man is not lost on us.

In *Anowa*, notions of normative masculinity and femininity—an understanding of what constitutes society's sense of 'true' manhood and womanhood—unfold throughout the play. With Badua (Anowa's mother) and the Old Woman Mouth-That-Eats-Salt-and-Pepper serving as judge and jury, they project the society's gender norms through the expectations they hold of Kofi Ako and Anowa. In Aidoo's depiction of her female and male protagonists, however, she always gives an indication of what the expected gender norms are only to subvert them. Anowa is a case in point. She possesses legendary Ghanaian feminine beauty, yet she does not epitomise normative femininity. She defies the traditional expectations her society holds of women. The playwright's description of her heroine employs traditional Ghanaian imagery of beauty.

> Beautiful as Korado Ahima,
> Someone's-Thin-Thread.
> A dainty little pot
> Well-baked,

And polished smooth
To set in a nobleman's corner (67).

What stands out about this description is Anowa's exquisite beauty that makes her a fitting wife for the best of men—the nobility, the upper classes. Perceptively, the limiting nature of life for upper-class women—as decorative pieces to be acquired by noblemen to enhance their own image, which evidently is not limited to particular cultures—is hinted at here.

At a poignant moment in the play, Badua articulates her aspirations for her daughter, thereby giving expression to the more conventional expectations of ordinary women in the society.

> I want my child
> To be a human woman
> Marry a man
> Tend her farm
> And be happy to see her
> Peppers and her onions grow.
> A woman like her
> Should bear children
> Many children (72).

The image of womanhood that is upheld here, in addition to valourising motherhood, presents women in a work environment. Thus the typical Ghanaian woman, as depicted by Badua, is a gendered human subject whose work-horse image contrasts starkly with that of the aristocratic image of woman as a dainty little pot set in a nobleman's corner, which makes woman merely decorative. In the play, these two images of womanhood, derived from two distinct classes, stay in contestation. Anowa considers a life committed to work as the productive, fulfilling choice for herself as a woman, but once they start to attain prosperity, Kofi Ako prefers her to be a decorative piece who will deck herself out to flaunt her husband's wealth thereby enhancing his image as a 'Big Man.' But Anowa stubbornly persists in wearing her old clothes, the mark of her resistance of the exploitation that has produced her husband's wealth as well as her identification with the exploited masses whose labour has produced that wealth.

Aidoo's play is full of ironies. When the play opens, we learn that Anowa has 'refused to get married six years after her puberty' (70), an action that is a great source of concern for her mother and the community because it poses a threat to motherhood. Instead of settling down, like a good woman, 'she goes around wild, making everyone talk about her' (70). The Old Woman Mouth-That-Eats-Salt-and-Pepper expresses the popular sentiment regarding Anowa: 'That Anowa is something else! Like the beautiful maidens in the tales, she has refused to marry any of the sturdy men who have asked for her hand in marriage. No one knows what is wrong with her!' (67). That Anowa's transgressiveness has mythic significance is implied in her being likened to 'the beautiful maidens in the tales' (67). These maidens typically go against the grain by refusing to marry suitors chosen for them or preferred by parents and/or elders. When they finally marry, they make their marriages their personal responsibility by choosing their own husbands.[14] Like these legendary maidens, Anowa is not against marriage *per se*, though she rejects all the suitors approved of by her family. She does, indeed, choose her own husband and she does go against the established norms by making her marriage her individual affair instead of an event involving the entire family. When her society seems to have given up all hope of her marrying, she runs in one day and unexpectedly announces to her parents that not only has she 'met the man' she wants to marry, but that Kofi Ako has proposed marriage to her and she has accepted his proposal, thus single-handedly handling her own marriage. In addition, she bases her choice on love—'I have found someone I like very much'—rather than on society's indices of what constitutes a good husband. When her mother persists in denigrating the suitor Anowa has chosen, she does not hesitate to shut her up.

In Akan society, the man's family typically will 'knock on the door' of the woman's family to ask, on his behalf, for her hand in marriage. When a woman's hand is sought in marriage by a prospective husband's family, the consent of the woman's people to the union hinges on the conviction that the prospective husband will be able to ensure economic stability for the woman and the children who will come into the union. Stephan Miescher's study of Kwawu, which is a part of the larger Akan society of which Yebi, the location of the play, forms a part, gives an indication of the expectations of Anowa's society regarding adult masculinity:

> In Kwawu, adult masculinity was signified by marriage. As in other Akan societies, men reached adult masculinity by taking [on] 'the role of material providers and protectors of families.' Kwawu elders expected a married man to 'look after the health of his wife, to clothe and feed her and to farm for her and house her.' As a father, he should 'rear (his children) till they come of age'... (124).

Ironically, Kofi Ako, the man Anowa chooses for her husband, falls far short of meeting the normative attributes of manhood presented above. Badua's reaction when Anowa breaks the news of her having accepted to marry Kofi Ako is telling.

> Of all the mothers that are here in Yebi, should I be the one whose daughter would want to marry this fool, this good-for-nothing-cassava-

man, this watery male of all watery males? This I-am-the-handsome- one-with-a-stick-between-my-teeth-in-the-market-place . . . (74–75).

Badua publicly questions Kofi Ako's manhood, rejecting him as a potential son-in-law because he 'will not put a blow into a thicket or at least learn a trade'(76). She questions what he was 'able to make of the plantation of palm trees his grandfather gave him . . . [a]nd the virgin land his uncles gave him' (78). Her anger is fuelled by his not having shown promise as a burgeoning 'real man' who is capable of attaining stature in society by acquiring wealth and becoming a good provider for his family—spousal as well as matrilineal. The society Badua represents cherishes strength and hard work in men; a man is known by the strength of his arm and Kofi Ako's arm bears no testimony to strength; he has no recognisable accomplishments. Aidoo's Kofi Ako contrasts rather sharply with Chinua Achebe's Okonkwo, whose 'fame rested on solid personal achievements.'

The images Badua projects of Kofi Ako are highly damaging to his manhood. For one thing, she holds it against him that he considers himself 'the-handsome-one-with-a-stick-between-my-teeth-in-the-market-place.' The market place is a place of serious commerce, not a place for showing off one's looks. A man who dwells too obviously on his good looks rather than on solid accomplishments is considered not just vain, but a fool. Indeed, she questions everything from Kofi Ako's intelligence to his sexual prowess. It is not only his ability to work hard and be a good provider but his very manhood that is called into question by Badua calling him a 'good-for-nothing-cassava-man.' As Achebe points out in *Things Fall Apart*, yam is a man's crop and cassava is a woman's. Therefore, the yam becomes a synecdoche for manhood and the cassava for womanhood. Badua's association of cassava with Kofi Ako's personality feminises him and undermines his manhood. His manhood is further compromised by the nomenclature 'watery male,' insinuating that Kofi Ako's manhood is weak and diluted.

Badua is not the only one who disapproves strongly of Anowa's choice of a spouse. The Old Woman Mouth-That-Eats-Salt-and-Pepper is openly hostile towards her for choosing Kofi Ako and rejecting all the seemingly deserving men who have sought her hand in marriage. The two women are so vested in the normative configurations of manhood that they are blinded to the problematics inherent in that configuration. Anowa, on the other hand, seems keenly aware of the hegemonic nature of normative masculinity. As the play unveils later, normative masculinity is hegemonic and can be devastating, especially to women and even to men themselves. It is domineering; it is oppressive; it precludes equality between the man and woman in a relationship; it thrives on the wife subordinating herself to the husband. Power in the relationship is not equally shared; power rests in the hands of the man. For her part, Anowa does not perceive marriage as an occasion for compromising female self-determination and so, in her own marriage, she seeks to build a partnership based on equality—a relationship in which power is shared along with responsibility. Where Badua and the Old Woman Mouth only see failure, Anowa sees possibility. The Kofi Ako she chooses for her life partner is not a ready-made man. He has no prior accomplishments on which to base his authority. As a result, she sees marriage to him as an opportunity to have a hand in the shaping of her marital life, to build a life together. It is this vision that is expressed in her desire 'to help him do something with this life' (77–78), because she is the spouse with focus and drive in the relationship.

In the beginning of their marriage, Anowa does achieve her dream of attaining marital bliss without losing her personhood. Because of the constricting nature of her society and its intolerance for individuality, she and Kofi Ako leave Yebi, rejecting farming, the designated work/productive activity established by her society for attaining adulthood for both males and females, because it is too confining for her 'roving spirit'—and Kofi Ako has already failed miserably at it. Instead, the couple enters into a marital and business partnership, outside of the constricting gender norms of the society, integrating their private and work lives. They engage in commerce with the coastal Whites. In the beginning, they have a good relationship and appear happy together, working and building a life. Despite the popular conception of Kofi Ako as a failure, the couple attains an enviable degree of prosperity and even respectability. However, once they start accumulating wealth, the harmony in their marital and business relationship starts to erode. Kofi Ako grows increasingly hegemonic.

At this point, it is imperative to examine the fundamental factors underlying the harmonious marital relationship between Anowa and Kofi Ako at the early stages of their marriage and the drastic turn the relationship suddenly takes, which not only alienates the one-time lovers from each other but eventually causes their demise. Aidoo affirms that gender configurations are indelibly 'linked to histories of institutions and economic structures.'[15] Thus it is by understanding how constructions of masculinity and femininity have been challenged by historical events and the concomitant shifts in the meanings of gender, that we can gain an understanding of how Kofi Ako, a young man who clearly fails to meet the normative male gendered attributes of his society, comes to rise in stature to acquire the compelling attributes of manhood—wealth and power—that publicly define hegemonic masculinity. The compelling factors are embedded in the challenges history poses to the lives of the individuals and groups who are caught in its tide.

The society Aidoo depicts is a society in transition. Although it is recognised that African societies are not static and they have always been confronted by their share of flux, the culmination of the European intrusion into the African world, marked by the Trans-Atlantic Slave Trade, followed by European colonialism, introduced dramatically alien ideals that affected the African world in unfathomable ways. At the time of Anowa and Kofi Ako's marriage, Western political, economic and social institutions had encroached on the Gold Coast, particularly the coastal towns. The Trans-Atlantic Slave Trade had, by this time, given way to European colonial domination of the African continent. With European designs to colonise came opportunities for economic and social advancement. Patriarchal and colonial ideals were becoming entrenched in marital relationships and society as a whole. Therefore, even as contact with the coastal Whites was opening up opportunities for upward mobility and economic success, Western imperial and patriarchal values were gaining equally firm roots.

Anowa and Kofi Ako are among the early beneficiaries of this historical legacy, hence they did not feel confined by their society's sanctioned mode of productive activity for the attainment of adult status, or by the limited definitions of success. Once Anowa and Kofi Ako leave Yebi, they seize the opportunity to explore new lucrative economic avenues for becoming productive as well as successful by going on the road, travelling inland to buy leather and other goods and returning to the coast to sell them to the White men. It is arduous work, but it provides Anowa with an outlet for productivity, leadership and fulfilment of her adventurous spirit and Kofi Ako a chance at prosperity. Anowa plays an active part in both the decision-making and the daily operations of the business; and though Kofi Ako hates hard work, the prospect of making money keeps him interested and feeds his masculine desire for public acclaim. Although the mere act of working does not automatically acquire Kofi Ako a hegemonic stature, nonetheless, it brings him a level of wealth and acknowledgment that he had not had before. Ironically, these entitlements arouse in him not just a desire to be a man but a desperate need to be *The Man*. Along with this need develops resentment against Anowa's leadership acumen which undergirds the couple's economic success. It is this obsession with becoming *The Man* that catapults Kofi Ako on a journey towards hegemonic masculinity. What factors could have compelled him to submit completely to hegemonic masculine ideals? Earlier assaults on his manhood may have sparked a desire to reclaim his masculinity by submitting to normative gender expectations; nonetheless, it seems the greatest influences come from White patriarchal and colonial ideals. People like Kofi Ako who travel to the coast to trade with the Whites evidently become exposed to White ideologies of gender and class and with time, start mimicking them, thereby underscoring the transforming impact of history on gender constructs, a phenomenon of which Ama Ata Aidoo, the playwright, is strongly cognisant. *Anowa* is a text that is committed to the exploration of both female and male gendered subjectivities. Aidoo explores more than one form of masculinity, juxtaposing a gentler, less aggressive masculinity—what Arthur Flannigan Saint-Aubin[16] calls testicular/testerical masculinity—against a domineering, power-grabbing, abusive masculinity that is hegemonic, designated phallic masculinity. The Kofi Ako we encounter in the early phase of the play, I contend, manifests testicular/testerical masculinity whereas, in the latter phases of the play, he develops distinctly phallic attributes to attain hegemonic masculinity.

In an essay in which Saint-Aubin addresses the issue of over-identification with hegemonic masculine characteristics, he decries patriarchy's tendency to privilege the phallus/penis over the testicular/testicles as the defining matrix in masculinity. He draws on G. P. Haddon's ideas in her book, *Body Metaphors: Releasing God-Feminine in All of Us:*

> The testicular component of a man's sexuality has very different qualities than the penis or phallus. Physiologically, the testicle is a reservoir, a holding place, where seed is nurtured to maturation. Unlike the penis, whose power manifests itself through intermittent erection and ejaculation, the testicle is stable and abiding. It quietly and steadily undergirds the man's sexuality. It 'hangs in there.' The testicle is the germinal source, the vessel from which is poured forth the sap or water of life.[17]

Building on Haddon's ideas regarding the testicles, Saint-Aubin differentiates positive from negative attributes emanating from the testicles. He turns to etymology, to extract out of the Latin origins of 'testicles' associations of protectiveness as well as testiness; upon these associations, he develops the negative and positive potentials of that male organ.[18] A man is considered to be experiencing the testicular mode of masculinity, the positive potential deriving from the testicles, 'when he is nurturing, incubating, containing and protecting. The testicular masculine is characterised by patience, stability and endurance.' Conversely, the negative propensity deriving from the testicles, labelled 'testerical,' is characterised by testiness in its various forms and a lack of direction, as well as inertia.[19]

The testicular/testerical masculine, I contend, is more conducive to the experience of males from Akan societal constructs. In effect, the Kofi Ako with whom Anowa falls in love manifests testicular and testerical masculinity. Akan societies are based on matrilineal kinship systems that are more sympathetic to female ingenuity and are conducive to engendering female personhood.[20] As a result, such societies tend to foster a gentler, less aggressive masculinity in males from that kinship system. It is my conviction that the prominence of female centredness in matrilineages encourages male members of that societal set-up to become less inhibited in embracing character traits that are akin to the feminine, which are seated in the testicles and tend to be suppressed through over-identification with phallic genitality in patriarchal ideology. Saint-Aubin points out that:

[M]ost of the testerical, like the testicular, is considered effeminate and is therefore usually considered undesirable in man. It is important, however, to resist conceiving or theorising the testicular/testerical as nonmasculine by subsuming it under the feminine. The patriarchal ideal is unequivocally phallic; there are few nonphallic role models . . . [I]n fact within patriarchy, the construction of a masculine identity and the experience of masculinity are indeed contingent upon a denial of the testicular/testerical; they are contingent on a man's projecting this aspect of the self onto woman (250).

Although I agree with this perspective, I want to affirm that the so-called feminine is an integral component of man. The male XY chromosome bears witness to that phenomenon by retaining the female X chromosome.

Kofi Ako straddles the spectrum of testicular and testerical masculinity. The character traits he manifests at the time Anowa falls in love with him are clearly in tune with testicular masculinity. He is gentle, fun-loving and so happy in love that he appears unflustered by Badua and the Old Woman Mouth's negative evaluation of his manhood; he even seems to value Anowa's ingenuity and to appreciate her leadership qualities. However, even at that stage in the relationship he displays testerical characteristics. He is lazy, lacks direction and seems to be afflicted by inertia; hence Badua's dismissal of him as 'a good-for-nothing-cassava-man.' In his early marital life, under the magical influence of love, he falls under the 'spell' of Anowa's spiritedness; thus, under her tutelage, he gains enough direction to work alongside her long enough to attain a level of success and prosperity. However, with time, he becomes more testerically masculine, regressing to his old laziness and becoming cantankerous prior to finally making a transition into phallic masculinity—the form of hegemonic masculinity that patriarchy privileges.[21] By the last phase of the play, Kofi Ako, who has bought completely into the Victorian patriarchal values of the coastal Whites, seems particularly seduced by their aristocratic lifestyle—a lifestyle that thrives on leisure, the exploitation of the labour of others, lavish living and the reduction of women from efficient workers to decorative pieces.

In the play, Aidoo marks the specific point in time when her male protagonist determines to become *The Man*. On a particularly frightening night on their journeys, when a fierce storm is brewing, Kofi Ako waits for Anowa to fall asleep and then announces ominously to the elements and the sleeping woman: 'Anowa, I shall be the new husband and you the new wife' (87). Being the new husband translates into making himself the dominant one in the marriage and reducing his wife to subordinate status so he can acquire the power to make unilateral decisions. Kofi Ako does not suddenly attain hegemonic masculinity but systematically builds himself into a powerful patriarch. He embarks on his journey into hegemonic masculinity by developing a three-tiered plan— contracting potions for prosperity and inoculation against enemies; procuring slaves to exploit their labour and coercing Anowa into giving up work to become a stay-at-home wife. In the initial stages of his journey into hegemonic masculinity, during what is clearly a transitional phase, he becomes highly testerical, acting testy in all its manifestations. The moment they start prospering, he regresses to his old lazy self and becomes contentious and manipulative, complaining constantly about how difficult and dangerous their line of work is and how detrimental it is to Anowa's feminine health.

Phase two of the play is set on the highway and it is in this phase that we catch a glimpse of the couple in their marital and work life. It is also in this phase that Kofi Ako's penchant for consulting medicine men, his desire for protective potions and his intentions to acquire slaves are revealed. They have been on the road for about a fortnight and have more travelling to do to get to their destination. They have bought leather they are carrying to the coast to sell. That they have been battling inclement weather is evidenced by their appearance, the wetness of their merchandise and the fact that a few of the leather goods are too wet and stinking to survive the trip. Yet notwithstanding these problems, Anowa stays optimistic and encourageing, whereas Kofi Ako complains ceaselessly about their hard line of work. From him we learn that they have to travel 'over two hundred miles to the coast' (83). But the eternally optimistic Anowa, like a troop leader, assures him that 'if we are not too tired to go a little further, we shall be there tomorrow' (84). It is worth exploring, in some detail, the specific indications the playwright provides us with for reading the changing gender dynamics in the couple's life. As they break their arduous journey to rest for the night, they talk, as most married couple's do, once they settle down for the night. Given Kofi Ako's persistent complaints about the hazards inherent in their occupation, Anowa suggests an expansion of their family and labour force through marriage. What Anowa proposes is the conventional solution to such issues in their world. Not having had children of her own, she sees a prospective co-wife as an asset—a companion and co-worker with a potential to expand their labour force by bearing children for the family. But the moment Anowa suggests to Kofi Ako, 'Why don't you marry another woman?' it is indicated 'Kofi Ako registers alarm.' When he tells her, 'You know you are annoying me' and she jokingly adds, 'Perhaps it is your medicine's taboo?' his reaction forces Anowa to ask, 'Ah Kofi, why has your voice gone fearfully down so quickly?' Though this interchange and Kofi Ako's over-reaction overshadows his impotence, which is eventually forced to the fore by Anowa in the concluding segment of the play, they accentuate the testerical masculine characteristics fanning his insecurities. He reproaches Anowa for 'saying something about medicines and taboos' when she is 'the same person who said we didn't need anything of that kind' (84). Kofi Ako conflates a genuine discussion of medical concerns with references to potions and taboos. The skewed nature of his argument is revealing of his testiness. As the conversation proceeds, however, the husband and wife's divergent views on the subject of potions emerge. Kofi Ako's obsession with potions is evident in his insistence, 'We need to do something to protect us.' For her part, Anowa is convinced 'a shrine has to be worshipped however small its size. And a kind god angered is a thousand times more evil than a mean god unknown. To have a little something to eat and a rag on our back is not a matter to approach a god about.' When it becomes evident to Kofi Ako that Anowa will not budge, he resorts to underhanded tactics. His retort—'Maybe you feel confident enough to trust yourself in dealing with all the problems of life. I think I am different, my wife' (85)—is calculated to make Anowa appear overly confident in her own resourcefulness and disparaging towards needing spiritual intervention.

In Kofi Ako's altercations with his wife over contracting potions, he pretends he is only concerned with potions for protection; however, Anowa's objection indicates that his dabbling in potions is not limited to protection. It is common lore in Ghana that one can contract potions that can draw prosperity, with help from medicine-men. However, everything has a cost. The tricky part is that this process often entails trading something valuable, such as a man's sexual potency or a woman's ability to have children, for the power to 'attract' or 'draw' wealth. We later learn from Badua that people in Yebi 'have been saying it for a long time . . . that she and her husband sold her birth-seeds to acquire their wealth' (92). However, knowing the aversion Anowa has to potions and shrines and Kofi Ako's attraction to them, the more plausible assumption is that it is Kofi Ako who has 'sold' something—possibly his wife's birth-seeds and his own sexual potency—for not only wealth but power. Growing from 'a good for nothing cassava man' into one of the wealthiest and most powerful men of his time definitely does not come cheap.

It is worth noting that it is after the disagreement over potions that he stands menacingly over the sleeping Anowa to proclaim he 'shall be the new husband' and Anowa 'the new wife.' The morning following this proclamation, he starts pressuring Anowa to quit working altogether and also unveils his intentions to procure slaves. Kofi Ako times his broaching of this subject in order to make it appear as a legitimate solution to the compelling problems confronting them. He pushes his unethical agenda of buying slaves by taking advantage of Anowa asking him what the medicine man he has been consulting about her prospects of having children has told him. First telling her in a hesitant manner that the doctor finds nothing wrong with her womb, he adds in a ponderous tone that the doctor believes the problem lies in Anowa's restlessness (i.e., hyperactivity) which prevents her blood from settling. (Among the Akan, it is believed that it is out of the mother's blood (mogya) that the human body is formed during conception.)[22] Therefore, if Anowa's blood is not settling because she is taxing her body too much through her line of work, then she is risking her chance at motherhood, the most significantly gendered adult role for women. 'Perhaps this work is too much for you' (88), Kofi Ako intones, insinuating that Anowa is selfishly putting the pursuit of materiality over parenthood—the most spiritual and significant of life-choices—by persisting in a hostile working environment. Given such a situation, asking Anowa to give up work makes Kofi Ako the sensible, considerate and even mature spouse, whose actions are fuelled by his concern for the well-being of a wife who is too headstrong or foolish to do what is in her best interest. However, upon critical examination, we see the hand of a master manipulator at work.

Right after hinting at the detrimental impact strenuous work is having on Anowa's womb, Kofi Ako declares that 'the time has come . . . to think about looking for one or two men to help.' The great show of concern for Anowa's health seems calculated to make what is clearly an unethical proposition acquire the veneer of a logical solution to a problem. He even attempts to make his declaration sound like a good business proposition, by indicating that 'they [slaves] are not expensive' (89). Anowa protests her husband's decision to buy human beings on moral and humane grounds, expressing her belief that 'no man made a slave of his friend and came to much himself. It is wrong. It is evil.' But Kofi Ako callously counters her protest with 'What is wrong with buying one or two people to help us? They are cheap' (90)—as if the only worthy consideration is economic. There is a stark difference between the Kofi Ako with whom Anowa left Yebi and the Kofi Ako who displays such hunger for prosperity and power. His testicular traits wear thin, rendering him increasingly testerical. He turns domineering and ruthless, descending into hegemonic masculinity with its propensity to exploit and dehumanise. Throughout the play, Anowa's philosophy of life and work are expressed unequivocally. Life as she sees it is lived purposefully and work is an instrument that lends purpose to life. Kofi Ako, on the other hand, embraces feudal and capitalistic notions regarding work. To him, work is drudgery; the only value he sees in it is as a means to wealth and power; and the fastest way of attaining his ends is to exploit the labour of others by making slaves of them so that he can reap the fruits of their labour. Being a physically weak man himself, he fortifies himself by consorting with medicine men for 'a little something' in aid of prosperity and protection and buys the strength of other men to exploit for personal gain. Though he does not believe in soiling his own hands, he believes firmly in owning the productivity of others. Therefore, buying slaves cheaply becomes his pathway to owning their productivity. It is through the exploitation of slave labour that he grows into possibly the wealthiest man on the Guinea Coast and one of the most powerful.

Kofi Ako harnesses his hegemonic image by buttressing the feudal/capitalist ideals with Western patriarchy. Having acquired slaves to exploit, in spite of Anowa's vehement protests, he moves to forcibly retire Anowa from work. Her open declaration of the love she has for work and the fulfilment she derives from it notwithstanding, he uses his veto as *The Man*, i.e., as the one with the authority to make and enforce the rules, as happens to be the case in patriarchies, to render her redundant so that he can install her in the home as a woman of leisure, as a decorative piece that will speak to the man's power to control and his ability to possess. He attempts to persuade her to find satisfaction in their overflowing wealth and in her being his wife:

> Enhance this beauty nature gave you with the best of craftsmanship in cloth and stone. Be happy with that which countless women would give their lives to enjoy for a day. Be happy in being my wife and maybe we shall have our own children. *Be my glorious wife, Anowa and the contented mother of my children* (99: emphasis added).

This attempt to turn Anowa into 'A dainty little pot / Well-baked, / And polished smooth / To set in a nobleman's corner,' an aspiration that is aristocratic rather than normative to the indigenous society, is Kofi Ako's final thrust towards hegemonic masculinity. As Badua makes evident in the beginning when she expresses her aspirations for her daughter, women work to build their community and contribute to the upkeep of their families. It is only women of the upper classes—white women and mostly those indigenous women mimicking white upper-class values—who live as decorative pieces and women of leisure. For her part, Anowa makes a conscious choice to live her life in resistance to oppression and human exploitation by openly protesting the means by which her husband acquires his riches and power. In resistance to Kofi Ako's patriarchal impositions on her, she suggests he marry a woman who has bought into those materialist values: 'One of those plump Oguaa mulatto women. With a skin so smooth as shea-butter and golden like fresh palm-oil on yam' (96). She refuses to avail herself of any of the riches her husband accumulates from exploiting other human beings. She goes around in her old clothes and wanders restlessly, like a ghost, about the mansion Kofi Ako has constructed from slave labour and furnished with Victorian emblems of patriarchy and aristocracy, which causes her affluent and powerful husband great distress because her appearance and demeanour throw a pall over his newly acquired stature of power.

It is my conviction that Anowa does not only dissociate herself physically from Kofi Ako's wealth by continuing to wear her old rags, but strikes directly at his complicity in the dehumanisation of the fruit of woman's womb by not having children. Though Anowa's lack of children has commonly been construed as barrenness on her part, I urge her condition to be read as an act of resistance, of conscious withholding. In a context in which Africa's male leadership teams up with White enslavers to abuse the fruits of the African woman's womb, the African woman resists this dehumanisation by withholding the fruits of her womb. Read in this context, Anowa's condition transforms from a lack and a tragedy into a conscious act of resistance, empowerment and triumph for the oppressed and the exploited. Though the Trans-Atlantic Slave Trade takes place before Anowa's time, she is endowed with racial memory of this horrendous event, as her childhood dream and subsequent dialogue with her grandmother affirms. It is fitting that the African mother, the one who produces the human beings who become the victims of this dehumanising process, is also the one who shuts down production by withholding her childbearing capabilities.

Through Kofi Ako's interaction with the coastal Whites, the once 'good-for-nothing cassava man' comes to master the power dynamics embedded in human exploitation for material gain. It is one of the ironies of history that the man Anowa marries becomes one of those Africans who help perpetuate slavery on the continent. He builds a whole 'empire' by exploiting slave labour, thus symbolising the African leadership that collaborates with Whites in the exploitation of African people by choosing to be stooges in the interest of personal aggrandisement, rather than revolutionaries who will join forces with the masses to combat colonial exploitation and oppression. It is significant that in his quest for hegemonic masculinity, he draws on both Western and indigenous institutions for attaining his objective. He models not just Western patriarchal and feudalist/capitalist ideologies but revamps some of the indigenous institutions for attaining dominant masculine status. The outcome is the attainment of an identity that blends the 'benevolent' Western slave patriarch with the African 'Big Man.' In theorising African masculinities, the African 'Big Man' has been offered as a model that 'provides perhaps the most enduring image of African masculinity.'[23] Kofi Ako redefines this model by tempering indigenous practices of communality with Western ideologies of wealth production and power consolidation. Miescher and Lindsay explore this institution in various historical contexts. 'Across the continent[,] and for a long sweep of history, ambitious people (usually men) have worked to enlarge their households and use their 'wealth in people' for political and material advancement.' Turning her attention to colonial Nigeria, Lindsay points to Yoruba men in the early nineteenth century who through 'competing with each other for followers, wealth and reputation' became prosperous and influential enough to attain the status of 'big men.' Men aspiring to this status would strive to surround themselves with people willing to provide labour for 'the expansion of ... [the aspirants'] farms or trading enterprises'—to help them develop into big men.[24]

Recognising that 'wealth in people' is central to the status of 'Big Man,' Kofi Ako resorts to buying slaves in order to surround himself with people whose labour he exploits for political and economic gain. His model for attaining power and wealth, however, maintains the form but not the heart of the indigenous institution. Most traditional 'Big Man' set-ups consisted of kinfolk:

'[T]he large complex households headed by a Big Man surrounded by his wives, married and unmarried sons, younger brothers, poor relatives, dependents and swarming children.²⁵ Reciprocity is integral to the 'Big Man' dynamic. 'A large household and wealth thus reinforced each other: a Big Man attracted dependents by his ability to provide for and protect them; in turn, they supported his claims to be "big" by contributing labour or productive resources, serving him personally, or enhancing his reputation for generosity.²⁶

When we encounter Kofi Ako in the final phase of the play, he has built himself into a chief, a role that commands Big Man status. Though the title *obirempon* is not used in the play, it is an indigenous Akan term that befits his hegemonic status, even as his brand of hegemony brings out the divergences within appropriations of this indigenous institution. Miescher notes that the *obirempon* ideal, which originated with the founding of Akan settlements in the forests, has enjoyed a sustaining, alluring appeal in the history of southern Ghana. The Kofi Ako we encounter in Phase Three is hailed as a chief and has a settlement made up of the men, women and children he has bought to work for him. His entrance is accompanied by the pomp and circumstance associated with royalty. He is decked out in opulence, carried by his subjects (slaves) and hailed as a powerful man. Clearly, his acquisition of the *obirempon*/Big Man status taints an indigenous institution conceived within a spiritual, communal context with the inhumanity at the heart of slavery and the acquisitiveness and materialism that drives feudalism and capitalism, its modern derivative. Miescher draws attention to the deviations of the colonial/postcolonial derivative of the original institution. 'Originally a chiefly title, by the late nineteenth century, the [*obirempon*] big-man status related to men who had amassed fortunes trading items like kola nut and rubber' (11). Like these newly emerging *obirempon*, Kofi Ako amasses tremendous wealth through controlling the palm oil trade on the Guinea Coast. 'Big men were expected to share their wealth and act like the pre-colonial *obirempon*, famous for their generosity and conspicuous display of wealth' (11). Conversely, Kofi Ako replaces the communal ethos of reciprocity at the heart of the traditional Big Man model with a Western individualist, feudalistic/capitalistic ethos based on exploitation. Not even his insistence that his slaves address him as 'Father' and Anowa as 'Mother' mitigates the exploitative and dehumanising blunt of the means he chooses for pursuing wealth and power. One of the most telling images in the play is that of the young twin slaves, Panyin and Kakra, who are wasting their childhood fanning Kofi Ako's throne to keep the seat cool for when he sits on it. Anowa's resistive spirit reveals itself when she stumbles upon them in her wanderings through the mansion. She vocalises the pathos in their disenfranchisement by lamenting the plight of the mother who carries her children for nine months and goes through birth pangs only to have them snatched away from her protective love to be reduced to a life of drudgery. She relieves them from the ridiculous task they have been assigned and sends them off to play, a more fitting activity for children. Kofi Ako is an embodiment of those African Big Men who emerged in the wake of European colonialism who 'have honed the attributes and perquisites of dominant masculinity in much of postcolonial Africa'[27] and have 'gained their hyper-masculine status through wealth, followers and connections to political power—attributes which in turn supported each other.'[28]

Ironically, Kofi Ako's journey into hegemonic masculinity results in sexual impotence, the loss of the most defining element of manhood and masculinity. The ostentatious display of material wealth and power serves as the fulcrum upon which his publicly acquired status of hyper-masculinity rests; nonetheless, the ultimate seal of manhood, of his Big Man stature, is his presumed sexual potency, the test of which lies in his marrying many wives and having many children who will immortalise him as a Big Man. The Old Woman Mouth-That-Eats-Salt-and-Pepper—the fiercest denigrator of the young Kofi Ako's manhood, who later becomes his most ardent praise-singer—affirms that the phallus is, indeed, the ultimate definer of hegemonic masculinity. Calling on the 'people of Yebi [to] rejoice, / for Kofi Ako has prospered' (101–102), she broadcasts loudly for the whole world to hear that 'Kofi Ako can stand / On his two feet to dress up fifty brides / And without moving a step, / Dress up fifty more' (102). But, truth be told, although the ability to afford marrying many wives is seen as a public indicator of hegemonic masculinity, the ultimate signifier of virile manhood is the evidence of children who are begotten through sexual prowess. It is significant that any intercourse reminiscent of virility engenders fear and discomfiture in Kofi Ako. On such occasions, he is shown examining his limbs intently.[29] Given the definitive nature of sexual virility in constructions of manhood and masculinity, it comes as no surprise that once Anowa confronts him with his impotence and openly declares that her 'husband is a woman now . . . He is a corpse. He is dead wood. But less than dead wood because at least, that sometimes grows mushrooms' (122), Kofi Ako kills himself. In his ruthless pursuit of hegemonic masculine ideals, he sacrifices his humanity; hence his forfeiture of the ability to engender life by fathering children.

In her play, Ama Ata Aidoo joins ranks with African writers like Chinua Achebe, Mariama Bâ and Ousmane Sembène to reveal the magnitude of the cost to humanity that can result from men's pursuit of hegemonic masculinity, by exploring the multiplicity of symbols embedded in male sexual impotence. Kofi Ako's sexual impotence ultimately serves as a metonymy for the political failure of postcolonial African male leadership that often sacrifices the welfare of the people in the pursuit of power and wealth—the crowning symbols of hegemonic masculinity. When that failure of leadership results in the dehumanisation of the children of Mother Africa, what better signification of this dehumanisation than the imagery of sexual impotence? It is doubly fitting that, at the end of the play, Anowa, the symbol of African women's resistance to such dehumanisation, offers her profound insight—that Kofi Ako has exhausted his masculinity acquiring slaves and wealth (121)—gained as eye-witness to her husband's journey into hegemonic masculinity, a journey that cost him his very humanity. It is the knowledge she gains, regarding the connection between hegemonic masculinity and human degradation through exploitation, that makes Anowa announce, at the end of the play, that she has grown wiser than the wise ones she originally counted on to enlighten her.

14. Virility and Emasculation in Ahmadou Kourouma's Novels[1]

Siendou A. Konate

Manding society has an enormous presence in Ahmadou Kourouma's fiction, lending both credibility and complexity to the narratives of political, social and gender hierarchies that permeate his writing. Underlying these multiple arenas are the competing instincts of gender difference, which are intended to bolster the image of men and diminish that of women. However, Kourouma complicates the gender divide by drawing attention to the paradoxes of masculinity. The goal of this chapter is to explore the internal contradictions in the author's representation of manliness in three of his novels: *Les Soleils des indépendences* (1968), *Monnè, outrages et défis* (1998) and *En attendant le vote des bêtes sauvages* (2001). They have been translated, respectively, as *The Suns of Independence* by Adrian Adam (1981), *Monnew* by Nidra Poller (1993), *Waiting for the Vote of Wild Animals* by Carrol F. Coates (2001) and *Waiting for the Vote of Wild Beasts* by Franck Wynne (2003).[2] I use the terms 'virility' and 'emasculation' to express the clash of masculine experiences that challenge conventional notions of manhood in Manding society. This chapter attempts to demonstrate how virility and/or masculinity spread through Kourouma's representations.

Kourouma's works are set in Africa and although he addresses issues that pertain to the African continent as a whole, he focuses on the life experiences of the Manding. Moreover, when Kourouma does not specifically represent the Manding, the style of the novel is drawn from their culture, which is riddled with verbal and physical gestures of gendered self-assertion. Although men assert their manliness and/or masculinity, women contribute to the same thing by instilling a sense of manliness in young boys and extolling female social roles to young girls. The novels discussed in this chapter portray common forms of identity affirmation among males and females in Manding society. Whether it is the case of Fama, who attempts to value the purity of his royal blood despite his inevitable fall into namelessness and oblivion, Djigui, who stays in control until he is overthrown and/or disempowered by French colonial forces, or Koyaga, who is a traditional hunter turned head of state, one notices that the sword (and/or 'force') is a major cultural idiom of Manding society because it produces manliness, virility and/or masculinity, which the Manding call *tchêyaa*. None of these characters want to be associated with an action or an attitude indicative of femininity. Each asserts his masculinity by any means possible. In other words, central to all three novels is the idea of virility, a concept that is dear to each character. Although these characters distance themselves from anything feminine, there seems to be a force that draws them into a vortex of disempowerment or unmanliness (i.e., emasculation). Those who hold onto manhood are eventually emasculated. This chapter demonstrates how emasculation unfolds in the novels; that is, how the process goes hand-in-hand with the affirmation of virility among the Manding.

The Suns of Independence is the story of Fama Doumbouya, who expects to be treated with the respect due his social rank and yet becomes disillusioned with the era of African independence. Independence is not what Fama has thought it would be. He is demoted to the rank of a beggar, one who ekes out his existence from the funeral ceremonies of other Malinke and Muslims in the capital of the newly independent republic. Fama, a true Malinke prince, ends up being a 'vulture,' as the Malinke call those who were ruined by independence and who became 'funeral chasers' in the capital. He becomes a burden for his wife, who is the one who brings food to the household when the opposite is supposed to be the norm. Independence has meant disaster and debacle for Fama and everything he represents.

In *Monnew*, Kourouma portrays the declining reign of Djigui, another Malinke noble. Djigui, the King of Soba, rules and enjoys all the privileges and honour attached to his status, until one day a series of messengers arrive to announce the advent of a new rule, that of the 'French, the French white Christian Toubabs, the Christians Nazarenes...The Nazaras are avowed enemies of Islam' (9). Colonisation means the end of Djigui's reign and possibly, the end of the Soba kingdom. Therefore, to ward off the coming danger, Djigui performs all sorts of sacrifices, including human, only to realise that this gets him nowhere. His collaboration with the colonial forces at the close of the story is one of the many signs of both his disillusionment and the end of African chieftaincies and kingdoms.

Waiting for the Vote of Wild Animals builds on Malinke society and culture to describe the African condition in general and the failure of African leadership in the Cold War era in particular. Koyaga is the hero of the story. He is a traditional hunter who fought in the Indo-China and Algerian wars on behalf of the French only to end up unemployed in his country, the newly independent Republic of the Gulf. Being a war veteran, Koyaga believes he ought to be treated with special attention by the new administration, which is far from the case. Disappointed and furious, he organises various social and military movements. Through blackmail, ruse and the use of force he succeeds in staging a military coup, deposing the president and becoming the first military head of state of the country. Koyaga's emergence as a head of state, chief and master of the country is not only attributable to violence, but is also due to a woman, his mother, who is well-versed in occultism.

The stories of Fama, Djigui and Koyaga are inspired by the structure of Manding society, where manliness is the social barometer. All three characters come from a rigidly hierarchical society where the free-born wield political power, which is connected to manly prowess and virile feats. Fama is royalty: he is 'of Dumbuya father and Dumbuya mother, the last legitimate descendant of the Dumbuya princes of Horodugu, whose totem was the panther...' (4). Djigui is the embodiment of the kingly lineage in *Monnew*. Although Djigui's power is equalled by his wife's presence as well as her intrigues in the palace, he exemplifies the dominance of male power among the Manding. If, like any king in his part of the world, he weds many women, the King of Soba remains faithful to his status of hunter, which is the only quality required of a leader in old Manding society. During the first years of Djigui's reign, '[l]ike all young Malinke princes he often went hunting in the bush. He could retrieve the game faster than the hunting dogs. And those were the only works that he bothered about' (5). As far as Koyaga is concerned, his social title—master-hunter—places him on a par with Fama and Djigui: the status of master-hunter is synonymous with might and royalty. Although nobility and royalty supersede the gender barrier, the major characters of the novels are noble males, thereby indicating that power is masculine in their society.

Kourouma bases the style of the novels on the function of the *griot* and the technique that *griots* employ in Manding society. Praise-singer, genealogist, historian and advisor to kings and regents, the *griot* describes the past in order to influence the behaviour of the descendants of the kings and great historical figures. Kourouma takes on the role of a *griot*. He recounts and explains the deeds of the past to affect the present. By setting the stories in Manding society, Kourouma uncovers the unbreakable link between Manding masculine values and the naturalised violence that shapes it. It is not an exaggeration to state that violence is the norm because a society that expresses fear of femininity will masculinise when it can. Thus, Manding epic stories appear as the background against which *The Suns of Independence*, *Monnew* and *Waiting for the Vote of Wild Animals* are cast. Such stories inspired Kourouma because they extol masculine and virile values, which not only reveal that the founding of Old Mali was possible only by force, violence and manliness (*tchêyaa*) but also speak to political issues of today. *Griots* past and present have remained constant in extolling the resources that nurtured Sundiata and his masculine and virile achievements. Through war and violence he created a bigger Manding society and rose to glory and prominence. This resonates with Samory Touré in the 1880s, when he sought to reconstitute the Manding Empire in the face of growing French colonialism in

West Africa. The stories of Sundiata and Samory Touré and the violence he celebrates, seem to be a palimpsest for the novels. Thus, using the epic of Sundiata as background is both warranted and illuminating.

Djibril Tamsir Niane first brought to the academy the story, as told by the *griot* Mamadou Kouyate. The story recounts the circumstances that precede the birth of the hero. Sundiata frees his people from Sumanguru Kante, the blacksmith and Susu king, who put them in a bondage that literally turned men into women. Through successive wars Sundidata liberated Manding and thus remasculinised its men. Sundiata was born to Maghan Fata and Sogolon, in most stories considered the ugliest woman in the land. In spite of everything, her son Sundiata was the *naa'ngama*—the one who would save and expand the kingdom after the demise of Maghan. Like any epic hero, his birth was announced by supernatural signs, such as a storm, heavy rain and other 'divine' manifestations. The hero endures the mischievousness of his half-brothers and was even cast out of the kingdom only to return and become the ruler, as was his destiny.

To assert his worth, masculine force and authority, Sundiata must prove himself. He wages many wars, chief of which is the battle of Kirina, where he defeats Sumanguru, his arch enemy. Jeli Kouyate graphically describes the violence that makes Sumanguru's troops lose to Sundiata's:

> The Sossos were surprised by this sudden attack for they all thought that the battle would be joined the next time. The lightening that flashes across the sky is slower, the thunderbolts less frightening and the flood-waters less surprising than Sundiata swooping down on Sosso Balla and his smiths. In a trice, Sundiata was in the middle of the Sossos like a lion in the sheepfold. The Sossos, trampled under the hooves of his fiery charger, cried out. When he turned to the right the smiths of Soumaoro fell in their tens and when he turned to the left his sword made heads fall as when someone shakes a tree of ripe fruit. The horsemen of Mea wrought a frightful slaughter and their long lances pierced flesh like a knife sunk into a paw-paw.[3]

Sundiata and his fellows had to clear their enemies off the land in order to allow for a new day to dawn. The feats of the hunter-king of the Manding carry the potential of boosting the pride and confidence of his descendants. Their achievements and the degree of their manliness are measured by the strength and statesmanship of the forefather. Admittedly, the mother of Sundiata is central to his political edification—most versions of his story accord her a huge panegyric. However, storytellers highlight his political achievement and *tchêyaa*, thereby positing these as the things that any Manding person must emulate.

Everyday speech revolves around virility and audacity. It is worth noting that the idea takes real form when it is executed through coercion and violence, as described by Kourouma. Men affirm their manhood through power over their peers and their women. They speak violently, maintaining that such is the way of men. However, the masculinity of a man, his maleness, can be destroyed if he is overpowered by a man or woman who uses the same means more effectively. Therefore, the virility, along with the violence (verbal or physical), that makes and consolidates power is the foundation of society. It is a gendered power; i.e., virility or male power regulates every part of life. However, the secondary role of the female in Kourouma's works seems to belie the concept of the weaker sex. As argued above, the language of the people testifies to the influence of their heroic past, which permeates and even dictates their daily interactions. Evoking the ways of the 'real' man, defeating other men, or women defeating men or their kindred are all instances of the deployment of virility and its counterpoint, emasculation. According to the dictionary, 'emasculation' is the process of depriving someone of virile or procreative power by way of castration. It also means to weaken someone by curtailing their vigour, strength or spirit. In other words, emasculation is about the symbols and instruments of virility: the masculine sexual attributes and its power and prerogatives.

Kourouma appropriates 'emasculation' to show tumultuous inter- and intra-gender exchanges. In the novels, emasculation can be approached as literal or metaphoric. In a literal sense, emasculation operates along the line of the rituals of hunters. Among this community, there is a belief that all animals possesses a *nyama* (evil spirit). When the animal is slain, it releases a spell, either against the hunter or the people around it. If the hunter is trained in bush values, he can ward off the spell by neutralising it and making the power his own. When a hunter slays an animal he must show evidence to the community: the tail of the animal. This is not merely proof of the kill. The power of animals resides in their tails, through which it releases its destructive energy in the bush. Thus, a good hunter cuts the tail of the animal and shoves it in its mouth. A dangerous cycle remains open if the tail is not put in the mouth of the animal.

'Tailing' the game is the emasculation of the animal. In Manding culture and more importantly the daily speech of the Manding people, emasculation is constantly referred to by both men and women. Men and women refer to the male sexual organ as a tail. The Manding threaten to cut the tail off their enemies. The use of this pattern of speech is not exclusive to men. Women also engage in the same kind of rhetoric. A woman may threaten to cut the tail off another woman. In short, the phallic attributes—the clitoris and the penis—are the embodiment of male or female power and their annihilation results in taking the power of the adversary.

In *Waiting for the Vote of Wild Animals*, a fictionalisation of the inner life of Manding traditional hunters, Kourouma reinforces the role of emasculation, not only among Manding hunters, but as a technique used in African politics. He recommends emasculation for politicians who do everything to maintain their grip on power. As he adapts emasculation to the political, Kourouma illuminates the charlatanism and mystical forces in African politics. Some politicians believe that the life of their country hinges on their power. Koyaga embraces such a belief. He depends on Nadjouma, his mother and his Muslim charlatans as he rises to prominence, seizes power and strives to hold on to it for as long as possible. To remove them from power, which stands as a form of virility, means stripping them of that virility and rendering them effeminate. In addition, emasculation—in Kourouma's use—is deployed in the physical elimination of the enemy, which Koyaga the hero does.

When, as general president and hunter, Koyaga realises that his popularity and political power are waning, he worries that he is losing his manliness as well. To stop such a draining—synonymous with becoming a woman—he needs to build up occult power, which only a hunter can do. Kourouma delves into the sacred practices of hunters and appropriates their peculiar storytelling technique—the *donsomana*:

> ... a type of discourse, a literary genre for the purpose of celebrating the deeds of the hunter-heroes and all sort of heroes. Before introducing a hero in a *donsomana*, the genre requires that his praises be sung. A hero is a tall mountain and the performing sere is a traveller. The traveller perceives the mountain from far away, before approaching it, walking around it and getting to know it (19).

Kourouma explains his reasons for adapting the hunter's storytelling technique to the novelistic genre. He attempts to retrieve the technique from oblivion, because 'At night, in Malinke villages, the griots of hunters tell the *donsomana*: the life of hunters, their struggles with wild animals supposed to have magical power. Hunting is therefore a fight between magicians.'[4] As the hunter's mystical power fades, he seeks vigour through catharsis. He increases his power by freeing himself from the negative memory of his misdeeds by re-enacting his feats.

This technique of narration allows Kourouma to satirise the failure of post-independence leaders in African nation states. Instead of peace, economic stability and freedom, the masses are served the dish of violence and dictatorship. Parodying a West African state—most likely the Republic of Togo—and various African heads of states, Kourouma shows a Koyaga who reaches the presidential palace by killing his adversaries. What is more, he literally emasculates them after he kills them. In fact, when Koyaga and his *lycaons* (wild dogs) kill President Fricassa Santos, they symbolically turn him into a traditional hunter's game: they unbutton his trousers, cut off his genitals and stuff them in his mouth. Cutting the 'tail' of Fricassa Santos is meant not only to nullify his virility, but also to benefit them: the emasculator receives the power of the emasculated. In order to maintain himself in power, Koyaga eliminates his rivals. However, the act of killing is insufficient; it needs to be followed by emasculation, as with game.

It is clear that emasculation as an act has remained the same, although the object of the ritual has changed and the space where the emasculation takes place has shifted from the hunting ground to the political arena, which is like the bush, where wild animals attack those who are not careful, strong or do not possess magical powers. Koyaga deals with his adversaries in this manner because they would kill him, given the chance, just as wild animals would. The political sphere is where the strongest reigns and prevails.

Emasculation can also be metaphorical at times, in the sense that it does not actually involve mutilation of the genitalia. Instead, it involves the use of power and determination on a figurative level, in the politics of power among males and between males and females. Outsmarting male rivals can be construed as emasculation. So is the overpowering of a female who has all the masculine physical strengths, such as the mother of the hero of *Waiting for the Vote of Wild Animals*. As a matter of fact, among the *paleonegritics*—the ethnic people to whom the hero belongs—the figure of the mother is special because she has the real power.

> Black traditions hold that all hardships endured by the mother in marriage are transformed into vital energy and merit—into success for the son. The son of a rich man is not necessarily rich. The son of a man who is exceptional in knowledge may be an idiot. While the child always becomes like his mother and always possesses what belongs to his mother (24).

For the mountain *paleos*, the concept of manhood goes hand-in-hand with motherhood. Admittedly, the hardships that the mother goes through in marriage are usually caused by men. Nevertheless, the success of a man seems to hinge on the woman he stands by.

In addition to the traditional values attached to the mother figure among the *paleos*—and the romanticisation of the mother to mask her ancillary position— it is clear that Koyaga's case is exceptional, inasmuch as his mother is reputed to be a strong breed. Not only is she well versed in mysticism, but 'she was the champion of combat among the mountain girls and she will die without any other woman managing to force her nape to the ground' (25). All through his career in the military and in politics, plots and other schemes are foiled by his mother, Nadjuma. However, this strong woman with the characteristics of a man, according to the *paleonigritic* worldview, had to pass through the tradition of marriage in order to be fully socialised.

Marriage among the *paleos* is contracted only through abduction. The suitor abducts and rapes the girl while she is still a virgin. The girl must resist in order not to be the laughing stock of the community, for it would be rumoured that she did not stand up to her abductor and that she 'let herself be carried away like a dead doe' (25). Tchao, a wrestling champion from the village of Tchaotchi, has his eyes on Nadjuma. He plans to abduct her. The memory remains with Tchao forever. She does not fake resistance as other girls usually do. Kourouma thus describes Nadjuma's resistance:

> She refuses to pretend she defends herself with all her muscular strength, all her technique. Tchao, during the final days of his life in prison, was to recount once more that the combat in which he had engaged to possess Nadjuma was the roughest fight of his career. A combat of giants, a combat of professionals. Beneath the feet of champions, grass is uprooted and the earth is plowed deeply (26).

Of course, the mother of the hero is a strong one, one that rubs elbows with men, thereby showing that she is their equal. However, she is 'unmanned' or overpowered by Tchao in order for the latter to have her as a wife and to be the father of Koyaga, the hero. Although Nadjuma is not a man, she does have the characteristics that make her a man in the eyes of men: Tchao brings himself to her level when he relates the story of their wrestling like giants. As argued above, emasculation, albeit dealing fundamentally with the phallus, is not utterly reserved for the male. Women also avail themselves of it so as to gather power, strength and recognition in society. Women 'unman' their adversaries by threatening to cut off their clitoris, which is a form of neutralisation of the adversary, because it is a common belief that sex is power, both literally and symbolically, for males and females alike. In men, sex is the power to subdue the 'weaker sex.' In women, it is a magnet in the sense that it demobilises the serenity and self-control of the man.

Kourouma uses the metaphor of emasculation to express the sense of loss that the privileged in traditional societies felt in the early days of African independence. The era of independence emasculated people of princely stature like Fama. As he is walking through the market square the protagonist is seized by the memories of grandeur of his people's past. Being a *jula*, or Manding trader, even colonialism could not preclude the freedom of his occupation. Come independence, Fama is out of work. He feels some remorse. However:

> let no one take Fama for a colonialist mind. For he had seen the colonial era, had known the French administrators who meant many and many troubles: forced labour in the wood-cutting camps, on the roads and bridges; taxes and more taxes and fifty other levies such as every conqueror demands, not to forget the lash of the whip and other torments. But what matters most to a Malinke is freedom of trade. And the French, also and above all, stood for

the freedom of trade that enabled the Jula, the big Malinke race, like one man, heard, saw, walked and breathed; these two things were at once its eyes, its ears, its feet, its loins (5).

Independence turns Fama into anything but the contrary of what he claims to be, i.e., a man. And yet any man who fails to deliver the manly prowess expected of him by other men (or the community at large) is accused of effeminacy. An effeminate man is one who seems weaker than the average or regular man, according to the standards of patriarchal societies. In fact, masculinity among the Manding is the expression of power, potency and fear of failure and its subsequently aggressive or violent compensations. Masculinity seems to be associated with strength, the ability to overcome obstacles and mostly, the ability to do things better than any other man.

In *The Suns*, one can see that the values and belief systems of the Manding have collapsed. Independence stripped the nobles of their social standing. The princes have lost their subjects. Fama, the prototype of those princes, has lost the substance and value attached to his name, which he flaunts in people's faces without success. The prince he is has become useless and only fit for the underclass. From being 'born to gold, food in plenty, honour and women' (5), which all point to his princely status, Fama, the Prince of Horodugu, walks through the capital, from one funeral ceremony to another, in order to gather money and food for his household. He is now less than the shadow of his former self. The true blood prince, as Fama calls himself, now competes with the *griots* as their equal, because they all swarm in the capital city: 'all "work" the burials and funeral rites. Real professionals' (4).

He is so devalued that he brawls with beggars over leftovers and small sacrificial packages of food given out during funeral ceremonies. In these circumstances the people who are looking for something to feed on do not pay attention to Fama, 'the last legitimate Dumbuya' (9). A *griot* and therefore someone of a lower social status than Fama, insults the prince. Thus, Fama thinks that the shadow of a dead man, for whom the Malinke are officiating funeral sacrifices, should 'inform the ancestors that under the suns of Independence, Malinke insulted their prince and even went so far as to strike him' (8). Fama's nostalgia for the past is sparked by the collapse of old values. One can see the extent of Fama's social demotion. Unable to take the humiliation of independence, Fama decides to go where he commands respect—to his kingdom: 'He was now the incumbent leader of the Dumbuya tribe. What honour, what power that had meant before the European conquest! All the Dumbuya mothers had poured libations and offered sacrifices, that their womb might bring forth the child that would be chief of the dynasty' (61).

In reality, there is not much reason to rejoice. The former incumbent of the seat Fama is about to fill has passed away and only left 'four widows, the four most substantial items of his estate, two of them old women that the deceased himself had inherited' (61). He is unaware that 'to be a chief of a starving tribe means only famine and a gourdful of worries' (61). On his way to Togobala, as he reaches the last village of the Ebony Coast before entering the Socialist Republic of Nikinai, a customs officer singles him out and asks him to show his identity card. It is unbearable for Fama to have to interact with those whom he deems inferior. By way of reciprocation, he calls the agent the worst name a Manding can possibly call a man of substance and honour: 'A bastard, a real one, a shameless forest brat whose mother surely never knew a scrap of loincloth nor the married state, dared to stand there on his own two testicles and say that Fama, a foreigner, could not pass without an identity card!' (69).

In the new republic, identity has become a matter of the utmost importance because colonisation reconfigured the native space, which became a new geopolitical entity when the colonists left. Fama denies this new reality. Thus, he loses his temper. The pain he experiences is mostly due to his relegation to the status of a *griot*. A prince does not announce himself. His *griot* carries out this duty.

Fama is even more emasculated when he fails to provide for himself and his wife, Salimata. Instead, he is taken care of by Salimata, contrary to the way gender roles are designated among his people. The man provides for the family whereas the woman does housework. However, Salimata is the one who sells food and takes care of her husband, which denotes his devaluation/emasculation. What is more, Fama is unable to impregnate Salimata, who runs from one charlatan to the other in search of a remedy for her supposed barrenness. Even when Fama marries Mariam, he is unable to impregnate her. This shows that Fama is the unhealthy one, not Salimata. One negative event after another leads to Fama's downfall, which Kourouma attributes to independence. His sterility and the meaninglessness of the Dumbuya throne he brags about are all the results of independence.

Like Fama Dumbuya, the *fama* of Soba, Djigui Keita, testifies to the collapse of the Keita-led kingdom through external factors. In lieu of independence— although it implies freedom from the colonial yoke, it has come to mean the opposite for Fama–Djigui is beaten by the forces of Nazerenes he attempts to antagonise. Asked to put down his weapons and submit to the French he retorts: 'We built this tata against them, against the Nazaras, against the uncircumcised. I am a Keita, an authentic totem hippopotamus, a Muslim, a true believer who would rather die than live in irreligion' (23). Djigui finally realises that the war is over as Samory Touré, his ally, friend and brother in Islam has been defeated by the French colonial forces. His own warriors are routed. The Nazarenes, those who the Keita deem unfit to stand next to them because they did not sustain the pain of circumcision and virility, inflict '*monnè* and shame' upon Djigui, thereby castrating him. His castration happens on two levels: taking an oath of allegiance and doing so on a Friday. When Manding warriors win a battle they force the defeated to drink the *Deguê,* a porridge of millet or rice flour with curdled milk. It is 'a public ceremony, with regulatory ritual, which takes place on the battlefield where the combat had been fought and won' (32). To acknowledge his defeat to the 'foreigners' he despises so much, Djigui must partake of the *Deguê.* As he does not walk the way of the honourable men by committing suicide (as his two generals did), he is forced to submit to an unavowed but discernible bondage: 'You, Djigui, will not be dethroned. You are requested to ride up to the camp next Friday after the main prayer [and] you will renew the oath of allegiance of the Keita to France by a visit to the captain in command of the Kebi. During these visits the captain will dictate to you his wishes' (33).

Djigui is demoted. He is not the man he claims to be. Instead, he is among the dregs of his community no matter how he now stands in it. He may be called 'king,' but he is one under the uncircumcised Christian Nazerene's rule. No wonder Samory Touré's *griot*, Djeliba Diabate, 'a great panegyrist, a learned historian, a talented kora player whose fame has gone beyond the frontiers of the Mandingo,' (29) renounces Djigui's hospitality. This is all the more important because Djigui is the Keita king and Diabate is a *griot* that the Keita of the upper caste interact with. Yet the *griot* declines the King's offer, retorting:

> I have made a vow to give up praise-making. I have renounced griotery. The voice of that told heroes such as Samory Touré and his sofas, heroes such as you, Keita, will not be honoured and will not honour you in telling the ones who will come after you, the ones who will live in a conquered land. With the end of the era of Samory Touré, valiance is finished and griotery with it. The submission, slavery and cowardice whose era now opens will not need praises. Silence, regret, nostalgia will sing them better than the kora of the griot ... The chords of my kora don't vibrate anymore, I have forgotten the genealogies of the great families, my voice also is extinguished. All that is left to me is my strength in my arms; all that suits me is labor (30).

The *griot* tells the free-born not only of his failure, but also of the end of his glory. Moreover, he shows the way to go: 'When the horon and the fama cease to be heroes, we go back to the land. I will go till the soil until new exploits by those who were praised by my ancestors many long centuries call me from my lougan' (30). Djeliba Diabate is forced to stay in Soba to serve the king, as if to save his face. The *griot* makes his point: Djigui is nothing but an empty shell, the shadow of the name he bears. One can see that as the end for the Keita because Djigui and his subjects have become slaves of the colonials, who force them to build train tracks in the savannah. Worse, the occupation has turned Djigui's son Bema into a traitor and a rebel, starved his people and ultimately the son dies in dishonour. The emasculation for the king could not be any worse.

Introducing an equilibrium, Kourouma gives women their share of justice: he portrays them as having the upper hand in an environment where they are not likely to amount to anything. Of course, like all the characters in *The Suns of Independence* and *Monnew*, women are affected by both colonialism and independence. Women suffer the same pain as Djigui and Fama. Yet a closer look at characters like Salimata, Moussokoro and Nadjouma reveals their force and the hidden salience in the stories. If independence emaciated and emasculated Fama, Salimata is empowered. Beyond her new role of breadwinner, she seems to gather strength and speaks up for herself. She defends herself when she is about to relive the bitter experience of her early girlhood. In fact, Salimata almost literally emasculates a man—she uses her knife to chase the charlatan who promises to help rid her of her infecundity and yet tries to rape her. In fact, the courage of Fama's wife is not rewarded. She remains childless. As she solicits the help of Chekura, the latter recommends that Salimata perform sacrifices to the gods that grant children. She must slaughter a ram or a rooster: such was revealed to the charlatan in a vision during his retreat:

> During last night's retreat, in the midst of my prayers and incantations, I saw things concerning you. First the weight of your sadness, then yourself and then blood, much blood, flowing over my arms and staining my robe. A raised knife, red with blood, was running like a hare. Shouts and cries of astonishment slowed its pace. And someone murmured: 'He will strike and kill without sacrifice' (44).

Chekura abuses Salimata's belief in both the existence of *nyama* (spell) and the sacrifice to ward it off, which makes her stay with the charlatan. Unfortunately, Chekura lusts after her. When she is sure of Chekura's intentions, Salimata grabs a knife and chases him. Salimata cannot accept further abuse: she had been 'emasculated' once already and the 'memories [of her excision] rose to assault her. Proud and smiling she had gone forth to the field of excision. Torn by pain, she had met misfortune and shed blood like the [sacrificed] cock' (51). Moreover, she had been raped on the night of her excision while she was still bleeding profusely. These memories impel her to pursue Chekura. It is interesting to see a woman cornering a man in this community, because the opportunity does not often arise. Salimata vents her vengeance on Chekura, who represents the system that violated and raped her. The fact that she strikes him with a knife may be construed as her regaining the virile-like power that excision took from her. Kourouma's portrayal of Salimata, first as a powerless woman and in the end as a 'virile' combatant is perhaps his way of empowering a gender that is kept subjugated among his people.

Salimata's plight is comparable to Moussokoro's in *Monnew*, which is set in traditional Manding society, where gender relations are expressed in a way that puts females at a disadvantage. Women must be prepared for wifehood and motherhood. To achieve that end, they are educated by an old lady, as in *Monnew*, whose task it is to perpetuate traditional practices by seeing to it that young girls know their social role in traditional communities. The old lady tells young Moussokoro that '[t]here are three words for women's lot in this world and they all have the same meaning: resignation, silence and submission' (117).

Maude Adjarian captures the predicament of women in communities described in the kingdom of Soba in *Monnew*. She writes that 'female desires and impulses that go against or transgress the social norm are immediately contained and held in check by external agents, both physical and verbal.'[5] To prevent female rebellion in their patriarchal society, men seek women's help to keep their gender 'in its right place.' The collusion of women with the patriarchal social structure is more plausible when one takes a closer look at the female rite of passage or socialisation, i.e., female genital ablation. The practice partakes of the rigid mentality of role division by gender. It is an extension of male control of female sexuality and it only celebrates motherhood as pain, endurance and self-sacrifice. In this context, it is understandable that a man would express his sexual desires and fantasies and ensure that they are satisfied. Conversely, a woman who openly expresses her biological needs is tagged as frivolous, promiscuous and a danger to the socio-moral order.

In the process of female socialisation, the clitoris of the young girl is removed in order to prepare her for a more responsible and moral role: the subservience and docility of the woman and the subsequent endorsement of male supremacy. It is believed that if a girl is not incised, her sexuality will be uncontrollable because the clitoris is thought to be that which makes a woman more assertive, promiscuous and prone to overstepping the bounds of the place carved out for her by customs and culture. The ablation of the clitoris is deemed to foreclose any such situations. In short, the excision of the woman's erectile organ plays the function of damming or even curtailing her hyper-sexuality and thereby making her 'really feminine,' i.e., having her abide by the customs and rules that regulate social life. One might also say that the ablation of the clitoris, which can be construed as the counterpart of the penis because of its erectile nature, is the neutralisation of any masculine tendency in the female.

Moussokoro seems not to have undergone patriarchal attempts to curb her urges and as a result she attempts on numerous occasions to escape the threefold web of silence, submissiveness and resignation. Notwithstanding that her world is organised in such a way that she must not antagonise the social role cut out for her gender, she displays signs contrary to what society expects. When she senses the anti-conformist attitudes of the young girl and wife-to-be, the old lady watching over her advises conformity: 'a future good wife and mother must learn how to hold back, to control herself . . . To weaken is a crime and a sin.'⁶ And yet Moussokoro does not comply. She is named after the mother of Djigui. According to custom, a Manding should not address his or her mother's or father's namesake by their name. He or she should be addressed as 'Mother' or 'Father.' Thus, Djigui calls Moussokoro 'Mother,' thereby defusing any fear the young girl may have of interacting with the king. However, little does she know that the king harbours the intention of adding her to his harem, which 'was swarming with young women offered by the village chiefs for his [Djigui's] coronation along with cattle, sheep and measures of grain' (116). Moussokoro refuses to be part of Djigui's pack of women. She is free-minded and a 'born fabulator'—someone who dictates her own versions of stories to the griots. When she was born, her father taught her both the Qur'an and the secrets of sorcery. Moreover, 'her mother taught her the little secrets used by northern women to make themselves favorites: the art of love and recipes for that succulent northern cooking that we Malinke love so much and our wives don't know how to do' (114).

Perhaps the secrets Moussokoro was taught predisposed her to rebel against century-long sexual norms. The knowledge she acquires is usually meant for men. As if her knowledge turned her into a man who could not bear another one, she rejects the idea of being Djigui's wife, which would be considered an honour to many families in the kingdom. She 'was born wanton. At the age of 11 she was already running away, sleeping around and telling lies' (123), which contrasts starkly with the lot of Manding woman (resignation, silence and submission.). She 'was tied up, beaten and packed off with a class of girls who went into the sacred grove the next day for initiation and excision' (121). It is clear that female circumcision is meant to resocialise a girl who is intent upon smashing the old table of laws. Initiation is a way of fully preparing boys and girls to submit to the gender identity roles designed by their culture. It comes late for Moussokoro, because in her escape she sleeps wherever she can and she is deflowered by her friend Abdoulaye. Her strong sexual urge must be curbed. Excision takes care of that. Despite the trials she undergoes, Moussokro's pain is nowhere near its end when Djigui discovers that she is not 'a woman,' as the Manding say when a girl is not a virgin. He has a choice: 'He could stifle the affair, have a chicken slaughtered on the street the matron would display the next day. He wouldn't let himself do that. But neither did he order the guilty girl to be done away with or sold to someone beyond the frontiers of Soba to recuperate the dowry by the Keita' (123).

In a case like this, the punishment that Moussokoro deserves is death; however, she is sent off to Toukoro, a holy town where the widows of the Keita kings live and where 'all the first kings were buried with their servants and all the women they had honoured who were still in condition to procreate' (125). Her husband has not died, but she must face an isolation meant for old menopausal women. What is worth retaining is that happy denouement of the story of the Keita of Soba. Moussokoro ends being pardoned by Djigui and becomes the Queen Mother who makes decisions on all the political matters of the Soba Kingdom. Despite the anathema cast on Moussokoro, she is reinstated in the royal court. What is more, 'Djigui made it a habit to question Moussokoro about the conformity of his decisions with the precepts of the *Qur'an*; he would do so for the rest of his life. Once he questioned her on the value of the prophecies of the official soothsayers; all his life he would continue' (130). Every act of the Queen Mother is institutionalised: 'After the official meals she offered him special dishes; it became a tradition. One evening, after he had officially honoured the designated wives, he went and slept with Moussokoro; this practice was institutionalized' (130).

Moussokoro holds the reins of power: she makes decisions about the political orientations of the kingdom. More importantly, she makes decisions about the representation of the kingdom for both insiders and outsiders. Her versions of fact are what *griot*–historians use to give accounts of happenings in Soba (132). It is therefore correct to state that Moussokoro emasculates Djigui and obliquely, the whole kingdom: she posits herself as the centre of Manding society. Perhaps such a move by Kourouma at the end of a story that concedes but a tiny place of pride to the female gender is a redemptive one inasmuch as it can be construed as the author's call for a change among men and women. Both genders are concerned here because one makes the rules and the other enforces them. Initiation and the attending excision, which consecrates the division of gender roles, are carried out by women. Whether it is Salimata, Moussokoro or Nadjouma, these women are represented as they really appear in the cultural contexts parodied by the author. Yet the end of each story shows that the woman is empowered substantially and thus stands as equal, if not superior, to the man.

To conclude, it should be emphasised that the sociocultural context— Manding imagination and experience—the author is most familiar with is aptly appropriated. Using his people and their culture, deeply informed by masculine power, physical force and death as the backdrop of his representation, Kourouma shows the logic of power among the Manding people, where men have the upper hand. Historical and factual subversion aside, the three works show what the Manding past looked like. The interspersing of the stories with the *griotic* tradition is meant not only to ascribe more credibility to the content but also pillory the practices in which the stories are grounded. Extreme belief in past glory, which keeps the Manding people prisoners, the condition of women and the use of violence as a means of social mobility and visibility serve Kourouma's purpose, which is to confront the gangrenes that eat at Africa. The condition of women, despite the positive and fictional contrast, is alarming.

The political situation on the continent is not any better than what the stories depict. The emasculation of Fama is indicative of the violence the colonised have suffered. Yet it goes beyond that, as it also foretells the failure of the leadership. The story of Djigui is a patchwork that displays the collusion of African chieftains with the colonial forces that mapped out the continent. Koyaga is a parody of the leaders who brought disillusionment after independence, dictatorship and the attending moral deliquescence of the African elite. But despite Kourouma's justified pessimism with regard to Africa's future, it can reasonably be believed that the works display the African woman as a force for change, good or bad. Fama's Salimata changes the order of role division in post-independence Ebony Coast, whereas the Dumbuya Dynasty means nothing except as an old memory; Nadjouma helps install a dictator even if she proves her occult power and Moussokoro holds the actual reins of power in the background after she is disgraced and rehabilitated by Djigui.

Mostly known for perpetrating violence on the French language, knowingly and/or out of ideological decision—some critics accuse him of having inadequate literary knowledge, whereas others see a solid and well-designed linguistic strategy—it ought to be said that Kourouma's works are representative of the past, present and future of Africa in crisis, not only due to the former colonial masters, but also because of the collusion of Africans with the aforementioned masters today. The consequence of such collusion is the failure of the African postcolonial state.

15. Women, Men and Exotopy: On the Politics of Scale in Nuruddin Farah's *Maps*

Peter Hitchcock

A place on the map is also a place in history.

Adrienne Rich

It is a commonplace in Nuruddin Farah's fiction that he subsumes form to character as metaphor. Even if Farah had not consistently invoked the substance of metaphor in talking of his fiction, critics have not had to look far to reveal metaphoricity at the heart of his endeavours. Whether exploring the fate of Misra's vexed affiliation in *Maps* (1986), the novel that is the focus of this essay, or Soyaan's search for an explanation for the death of his twin brother in *Sweet and Sour Milk* (1979), the first novel in his trilogy *Variations on the Theme of an African Dictatorship*, one finds characters who appear to be at one with the agon of Africa in general, or the conflictual emergence of Somalia as a postcolonial state in particular. But the longer one looks at these correspondences the more problematic they become. Despite the heartfelt nuances in Farah's representations of women, for instance, metaphorising their condition can easily be misread as reproducing the very conditions of harmful masculinist discourse their characterisation is meant to deflate and call into question. Similarly, although certainly not apologising for the violence of colonialism, Farah's searing investigations of the dysfunctions in the family that is his Somalia can appear to be blaming the victims for the paroxysms of the state in colonialism's aftermath. One is tempted to correlate these excesses of characterisation with the ambiguities of national identity itself and indeed this theme will re-emerge in the following pages. Certainly the texture of Farah's formal engagement with the predicaments of postcoloniality are profound and disturbing in equal measure, as if the artist's purview is itself symptomatic of the eruptions and disruptions of form in the postcolonial state. Yet we would have to qualify this connection, not just to allow for the brilliance of Farah's capacious imagination, but also to track the complex logic of identification and disavowal that structures a specific form of exile in constructions of the long space.[1] Indeed, what is striking about Farah's language is the numerous ways in which he stretches it as a measure of the outsideness that is its very possibility. Such a postcolonial exotopy not only confounds the somewhat peremptory and even obligatory narratives of exile trumpeted by world literature as currently construed, but questions in an innovatory and perhaps insoluble manner compulsive metaphoricity in the understanding of the writer's relationship to nation and gender as fiction

Because I write here of symptoms, I want to note first something of the consonance between Farah's literal and aesthetic outsideness before exploring in more detail how gender and nation interrupt this neat synergy, producing a logic of space that both qualifies the idiosyncracies of the transnational and rethinks Farah's fulcrum of feminine and masculine in understanding the postcolonial state. In the work of Mikhail Bakhtin, *vnenakhodimost'* (outsideness, outsidedeness, or what Tsvetan Todorov terms 'exotopy') operates in several registers (in part because of the logic at stake and in part because of Mikhail Bakhtin's shifting terminology).[2] In *Toward a Philosophy of the Act* the oughtness of the acting 'I' is predicated on its unique subjectivity: there are other 'I's in general but these are 'theoretical' and 'are not I for me.'[3] Bakhtin believes that by specifying the 'I' rather than abstracting it, one can account for deeds or acts that are responsible or answerable. The twist is this individuation is insufficient in itself—the same specification is required of the Other in order for an act to be both 'once-occurrent' and answerable. Indeed, just as Being is tied to the act as 'answerable cognition' so it becomes increasingly influenced by the uniqueness of an Other.[4] The special implications this has for postcolonial exotopy and 'Being in the world' will emerge in a moment, but here one should note Bakhtin offers another taxonomy for specifying the 'I' in its uniqueness via aesthetic coordinates. The problem is not so much that in 'Author and Hero in Aesthetic Activity' Bakhtin discovers an aesthetic solution to a properly philosophical impasse (literary theory, after all, is littered with these tenacious acts of hubris), but that the substitution of Author and Hero for I and Other tends to emphasise historical events, that which gives to time and space its specificity, its uniqueness, its unrepeatability. If Bakhtin posits a first philosophy as a response to a contemporary crisis of action and authorship, he increasingly admits that the logic of contemporary context itself informs the theoretical framework, so that even aesthetics has an oughtness not just to itself but to historical processes that cannot subsume categories of the social or political, for instance. When one adds 'historicity' to 'individuality' all coordinates of I and Other are radically and substantially particularised.[5] This is why, for instance, places on maps are also places in history.

The border at this level is not an integer of a binary or a hierarchy that descends from I to Other. The borders of the individual and that of a culture are less the sign of exclusion but of socialisation itself. Feminine and masculine, for instance, are not polarities along the same axis but variable markers in a field of socialisation edged by space and time. The boundaries mark a condition for cognition, not an absolute separation or an assumption of the whole. This is the 'ness' in outsideness: exotopy is more about cognitive processes than an always already cognicised division between female and male, author and hero, life and art, self and society and even the universal and the particular (Bakhtin's revisions notwithstanding). Thus, it is not enough to suggest that an author opens perspective on a discreet cultural domain or bounded space (the latter would include, of course, both psychic zones and border scales from the skin to the nation and beyond); rather, her or his outsideness would figure a taxonomy of space, or what Bakhtin describes as 'an intense axiological atmosphere of responsible interdetermination.'[6] It is this, I would argue, that grounds not just the answerability to nation, but also articulates the perspicacity of the 'trans' in transnational.

This is one way of assessing the difference between Farah's actual exile, convoluted as it is and the principle of the exilic in his narration. It also suggests a strong counter both to the suggestion that Farah seeks to stabilise identities *vis-à-vis* his imaginary state (Somalia, or what he calls the 'country of my imagination'[7]) and to the justifiable urge to enlist Farah into the postmodern pantheon of the forever in flux, where the nexus of realism and nation can be approvingly jettisoned. The exotopy of responsible interdetermination does not cancel postmodern subjectivity, but neither does it cede the identity gambit to the chimera of the realist nation (this places Farah at some remove from the cultural nationalism of Soyinka, Ngugi, or Armah). The space of negotiation between the individual and the state is immanent to the logic of outsideness that binds the author to the substance of form. Characters are less mischievous metaphors for such form-giving complexity than symptoms of an impasse in the imagination of nation itself. The nation 'appears' in the displacement afforded by the individuation of characters.

Farah figures this difficulty in a number of surprising and innovative ways, most prominently in the association of gender and desire as a kind of deep conscience of the nation. One could, of course, read this primarily as an authorial compensation, however well meaning, for the conditions of exile itself: a dogged and intricate psychic redress for living beyond home. Having been identified as an ardent critic of Somali dictators, chief among them Siyad Barre, one could hardly blame Farah for his exile (He was sentenced to death and survived three assassination attempts. He eventually visited Somalia in 1996, after twenty-two years of absence.) Indeed, Farah rarely refers to his outsideness as exile, preferring instead the designation of a writer 'living and working abroad,'⁸ which now is technically accurate because he may return as he chooses. Because of Farah's own insistence on the psychic taxonomy of this relation, criticism of his writing identifies a postcolonial analysand for whom words form an eminently literary version of Somalia, 'a new country and a new logic, another reality, born of psychic necessity.'⁹ One cannot discount this logic of affiliation for such 'interstitial intimacy,' as Homi Bhabha calls it, provides a crucial interpretive key to the writer's role in nation and narration. Yet the exilic has all manner of manifestations that do not necessarily afford the prescriptions of Other used in relation to 'Third World' authors. As Kwame Anthony Appiah notes in his appreciation of Farah: 'writing is always more about identification than identity: the work of the imagination is never simply to express our selves.'¹⁰ What I would like to emphasise here are some of the symptomatic articulations of masculinity and femininity that do not resolve themselves into heady expressions of the author as a postcolonial exile, nor indeed as some preternatural soothsayer on the sexual proclivities of The African Male or The African Female. The exotopic function does not return meaning to the author as ultimate arbiter, but pinpoints the logic of relation itself in the form giving properties of specific writing. By this I mean Somali cultural practices work to fashion the novel as it cannot fashion itself, a process of identification that stretches boundaries (sexual, national, political and cultural) in provocative and necessarily problematic ways.

The *Blood in the Sun* trilogy (*Maps, Gifts* and *Secrets*) is at once the sign of postcolonial distress, Somalia as a kind of archetypal failed state and the site of an intense meditation over the lived relations of gender and national identification. Farah's gambit has clearly sought a link (pointedly, his novel of 2003 is called *Links* and features an epigraph from Freud on the link as a double life) between these levels of social being as an index of what must change for Somalia to be at home in the world. In *Maps*, the first novel of the trilogy, this link is explored primarily through the character of Askar, a Somali boy who grows up in the Ogaden, itself a space of contestation that is ethnically Somali but politically Ethiopian. In a versatile and far-reaching critique of the novel, Rhonda Cobham has suggested that in the three forms of pronoun used to tell Askar's story (I, you and he), in particular, his relationship to his surrogate mother, the Oromo servant Misra, we can trace the kernel of crisis in Somalia's sense of self as divided, as dis-identified, as 'misgendered': 'The inability of the narrative voices that define Askar to differentiate between Askar and Misra, between maleness and femaleness and between age and youth or accuser and accused works also as a metaphor for the shifting status of the signifier "nation" within the Ogaden and for Somalia as a whole.'¹¹ The term 'misgendering' comes from a discussion in the novel (168) about how non-native speakers of Somali and people like Askar who are at the edge of Somalia's ethnic reach, replace the masculine third person singular with the feminine third person singular (this often occurs when moving from a language in which the third person singular is not gendered except by context, although here it measures a misaligned affiliation). Cobham argues that the term usefully characterises the unstable nature of national and sexual identities in the novel and that the linguistic slippages that punctuate the content and style of the narrative are challenges both to ethnographic essentialism and a Somali nationalism that to date has only served to accentuate clannish incommensurability. What happens, however, if we take these important elements of Farah's novel as symptoms rather than metaphors, as signs of material and mental flux less secured by the marvels of linguistic competence or authorial intent?

The central relationship of Askar and Misra is continually entwined with an ethnicist assessment of Somalia's postcolonial statehood, as if the border disputes over the Ogaden (the story is set around the Somalia–Ethiopia war of 1976 over this territory) might yet be resolved through an understanding of the erotic and the adoptive. Askar's mother dies as a result of giving birth to him, whereas his father dies in the nationalist struggle the day before Askar's birth. Misra, a servant in the extended family takes up the charge of Askar's care and there follows several sequences in which Askar's selves dissolve into an identification with Misra, his surrogate mother. They become blood relatives not from a revelation in the family tree but from consanguine intimacy. Blood would not be spilled nationally, these scenes seem to say, if blood were shared incestuously. As Derek Wright notes, Askar as 'the human analogue of Ogaden' is subject to a sexual 'confusion' about his origins, just as the parenting of Somalia as nation has been riddled by the coupling of warring imperialist states (Britain, Italy and France), Cold War geopolitics and postcolonial feuding.[12] In this biological fantasy as political fiction Askar's identification bleeds into Misra's, not just in assuming an outsider relationship to the being of Somalia, but by internalising the norms of a bodily feminine. Identification here is prosthetic and supplementary: at one point Askar believes he is menstruating, which is later linked to a constant taste of blood in his mouth. Lest we unproblematically believe Askar's assumption that a 'woman [is] living inside him' he continually projects an image of masculinity onto Misra, assuming the position of a 'third leg' between hers in bed, as if this might guarantee his own. In attaching himself to Misra as a phallus, Askar effectively claims the space of her perceived femininity. Yet by making Misra male and by seeing himself as the logical extension of that maleness, Askar constructs a kind of auto-erotic Oedipal dynamic in which he can simultaneously desire to kill the father in her while claiming the mother for himself and to a degree, *as* himself. Askar tells her one day that if she does not continue to look like a corpse he would have to kill her (38) so she would remain like his deceased mother, a telling displacement (and perhaps premonition, as the story unfolds) forged by untimely absence. At one point, Misra suggests that Askar imagine that he is a blind man and that she is his 'stick' (16), a statement more about his imagination than hers. This phallic economy encompasses Aw-Adan, one of Misra's lovers (and Askar's teachers), who removes his wooden leg before climbing into bed with her. Askar recalls this prosthesis when Misra is explaining how the body turns stiff after death, which serves to remind Misra of Aw-Adan's visits and to equate phallic certitude with lifelessness and virility at the same time (the erect penis as *rigor mortis*). Askar then remembers or fantasises (much of the tension in the novel is attained through this ambiguity) watching Aw-Adan gain his erection, having lost his leg, a metonymic moment punctuated by Misra's cries of 'my man, my man, my man' (32). Whatever 'secrets' Misra and Askar share beneath the sheets (their 'games' are only suggested) the reader is left in no doubt that the terms of femininity and masculinity are critically in play in the novel and that to understand the body's signifiers, by thesis and prosthesis, one is drawn to connect its blood to the flow of nation, the blood and guts of affiliation, or kinship and religion as Benedict Anderson puts it in his theory of nation as an imagined community.[13]

The problem for Farah's novel is not that these signifiers do not work in terms of sexuality and nation but that they work too well, as if the connection between the erotic reverie of Askar and Misra to the fate of Somalia is only one of scale along the same axis: trope on their bodies and one has a logic for nation. There are clear advantages to scaling of this kind, not least of which is that bodies do make nations so it behooves us to examine how nations are made in the body image of its participants. Yet there is a particular danger when the subject is the postcolonial nation, whose failures and corrupt excesses assume the form of a pathology for Western observers, who are all too willing to elide the role of former empires in what a nation can become in favour of emasculating or infantilising narratives of Third World syndromes where emerging post-imperial states must seek the tender mercies and psychic ministrations of their former colonisers (the Real Men of History). Farah, of course, wants to save Somalia from itself, not prepare it for adoptive hegemony, but that is why one must attempt to distinguish fiction's formal explorations of identification and scale, its spatial relations, from the nation's lived contradictions that, however much they permit isomorphic correspondences, are not best reduced to individual sex or personal desire. The danger with unproblematic scaling is one loses the nuance of what Askar calls 'notional truth' (228) in relation to a national one. The problem of *Maps* is indeed in differentiating these imaginary spaces, these sexually charged bodies of correspondence as something other than the delusional dreams of simultaneity or simply the hope, 'as dreamers do, that the dreamt dream will match the dreamt reality' (228). In what ways might we hold to Farah's acute observations of male and female desire without reconstructing what is otherwise a restorative masculinist fantasy of anchoring the state with phallic sutures?

Farah, not surprisingly, reads Somalia as a literary experiment (In 'Why I Write' he goes as far as saying it is a badly written play by Siyad Barre) and for criticism this is a wonderfully apposite vocation. Hilarie Kelly, for instance, describes *Maps* as 'a Somali tragedy of political and sexual confusion' and finds a fatal flaw or two in Askar's waywardness. In truth she remains critical of the ways in which this confusion is manifest in the novel and suspends judgement on whether Askar actually figures Somalia's unsure identification. The point would be, however, that the invocation of the tragic itself confirms not just a literary distance but the logic of narration afforded by transnational commentary. The text, at this level, invites an engagement that subsequently permits the logic of scale mentioned above foregrounding the notional as national. Again, the tendency is to read off the minutiae of character as the notional truth of nation or, still more controversially, as the fateful compulsion of the African male. If indeed Farah creatively valorises the narrative strategy of mapping the truth of form it is in its centrifugal logic *vis-à-vis* Somalia, a poetics of transgression, rather than in that more studied and by all means tragic, map of nation that merely requires a tinkering with the borders established by colonial fiat.

Even Derek Wright, who is one of Farah's most astute commentators, interrogates the scale of *Maps*, the personal and the national, only to confirm such a relation sets the stage for the subversion of the latter by the former. In *Maps:*

> The relations between a nation and its members are expressed through the roles of parents, or guardians and children. The postcolonial nation is parented or, more precisely, foster-parented. Nationality categories are most accurately read through the positions assumed by the novel's various surrogate parents towards their charges. Conversely, the destabilization of these categories is perceived through a series of pseudo incestuous role-reversals that subvert these positions. The postcolonial territory of Askar's birth is, like Askar himself, without natural parentage. Neither is it self-creating, as Askar fancies himself to be—'I had made myself, as though I was my own creation' (23)—though it may have the opportunity to take charge of its own destiny. Such territories are, in reality, the imaginative constructs of colonial and postcolonial cartographers (British, Italian, Ethiopian, Somali), conceived not biologically but intellectually: Askar, who is the human analogue of the Somali Ogaden, describes himself as 'a creature given birth to by notions formulated in heads, a creature brought into being by ideas' (3). Such creatures are adopted beings with adopted identities defined by adoptive parents and Farah sustains the analogues between the child's ties with the family and the individual's more artificial ties with the nation only by replacing Askar's real parents with a range of surrogates and guardians.[14]

Wright correctly pinpoints Farah's own analogical insistence which questions who is appropriately Somali Ogaden (Askar believes it to be himself, of course, but the truth of the hybridised territory actually favours the Oromo-Amhara Misra who, as the object of patriarchal assignation, nevertheless has her affiliation pinned to Ethiopia). At this level, Askar appears to represent not so much a dream of nation deferred but an ethnicist identification violently exotopic to the substance of difference in the region. Those in the novel who embrace some form of purity in Somali identity, Uncle Hilaal for instance, ironically accentuate the conditions for dispersal and fragmentation. Itemising what constitutes a Somali only seems to undermine the ethnicist claims to territory and this *misunderstanding*, a pattern of blood as the space of nation, permits a reversion to tribe, to specific traditions, to a desperately masculinist conviction. The critic, for the most part, will favour Farah's scaling because of its contrasting ambiguity and elusive allusion. Such destabilising tendencies are to be applauded but when Farah suggests of the colonial maps of Africa 'we should redraw [them] according to our economic and psychological and social needs and not accept the nonsensical frontiers carved out of our regions' the 'we' falls less on Somalis or indeed Africans and more on the outsideness of the imaginative writer whose capacity for troubling borders can then be read to solve the riddle before transnational eyes, Africa's propensity for 'failed nations.'

Farah's aesthetic necessity for redrawing maps is not the same as a geopolitical strategy for reconfiguration, but this does not mean we should bracket the power of his imagination when the actual running of a state is at stake. The idea is to maintain some perspective on the political efficacy of the exotopic imagination without taking analogy as truth. Nobody doubts the intriguing possibilities suggested by Askar's sexual identifications, for instance, but these might work better to question the logic of analogy itself rather than the failings of this nation or that. Certainly Farah has insistently argued against formations of patriarchal masculinity in his fiction, from his first novel *From a Crooked Rib* (1970) to his most recent, *Knots* (2007) and there is an unflinching dedication to unmasking the complex ideological and practical political constraints on the women of Somalia. Yet this feminist solidarity often works within the terms of analogy, even as it questions the image of the victimised woman as emblematic of nation, so a measure of scepticism must be maintained. Analogically, the novel as form also tends to stand in for the narrative of nation and for the epic nature of African traditions (particularly where orality is concerned), which only compounds the wariness at issue.[15] As is well known, Somalis have long traditions of oral poetry, including those that are held to be gender specific (for instance, classical verse like *gabay*, *jiifto* and *geeraar* assume a masculine concern for heady affairs of state, whereas *buraambur* is held to be a woman's poetry inclined to themes of life, death and marriage). In the figuring, rather than figures, of Askar and Misra I would suggest that the status of gender is radically particularised, whereas the form of exotopy spatialises this specificity. Farah thus offers the perplexing formula that Somalia is outside or beside itself, whereas the propensity for exorbitance is actually found in assigned gender and sexual roles. The invitation to analogy is in fact the affirmation of non-coincidence. This, I believe, lies at the root of Farah's opacity.

Askar seems to epitomise a peculiarly masculine capacity for self misrecognition, so much so that he is willing to affirm Misra's sense that he has made himself, that he was the midwife at his own birth. Doyens of the study of national ideology will here note a familiar trope: the subject, faced with a founding ambivalence born of definition through the other, resorts to a self presence anchored by auto-genesis. Obviously gender and nation are relational terms but here I will maintain the difference between a national subject and the nation as subject. Askar, for his part, wants to rationalise the meaning of his birth and the circumstances of his childhood. His lack of self assurance contrasts with his belief in Misra's sense of self which generally exudes conviction and resolute understanding. I have suggested earlier such observations often depend upon projections and the case can be made that each doubt in Askar's self identity facilitates a corresponding condition of objecthood in Misra. Keep in mind the aura of doubt surrounding the text, from the Aristotle epigraph, Hilaal's letter ('all is doubt'), the Conradian epigraph that begins the second part of the novel ('Every image floats vaguely in a sea of doubt') to the issue of Askar's involvement in Misra's death, which questions the veracity of identities and borders so that, despite the orderly split in forms of narration, (judge, audience and witness) the actual parameters of adjudication shift continuously. And yet the process of objecthood for Misra intensifies to the point where her life and body are ripped apart. Whatever the doubt in the meaning of Askar and by analogical extension, Somalia, there seems much less vacillation on the question of Misra's womanhood and affiliation.

Obviously, Farah does not favour this victimhood but, given the agency one sees in many of his other women characters (e.g., Margaritta, Medina, Ubax and Sagal in the *Variations on the Theme of an African Dictatorship* trilogy, Duniya in *Gifts*, Sholoongo in *Secrets*) one cannot help feeling Misra's character is more sharply constrained, more obstinately fettered with the baggage of patriarchal lore. True, she may well have been operative in the Ethiopian–Somali war (particularly during the so-called 'tragic weekend' when Soviet-backed Ethiopian forces retook the Ogaden), providing intelligence that led Ethiopian security forces to a hiding place of the Western Somali Liberation Front, but her strengths seem absorbed by Askar's obsessions and waywardness as if she is not only a surrogate mother but is indeed that prosthetic extension of Askar's logic of identification. The lure is to read this logic as a veritable parable of Somali possession, because Misra's name (at least in the Somali version) comes from the Ethiopian 'Misrat' meaning 'foundation of the earth.' Here is woman as territory once more, 'taken' by force, raped by colonialism and now by postcolonial border disputes. Metaphors of violent attachment abound in *Maps* but their patriarchal logic is over-determined in ways that complicate Askar's passage from culturally ambiguous boy to nationalist and masculinist Somali man. However Misra is associated with earth (and it is important to note that her dead body is fished from the sea and returned to the earth) her foil to Askar's becoming Somali conjures a myriad set of cultural ascriptions and inscriptions. Misra, Askar explains to Uncle Hilaal, as an Oromo belongs to 'a peripheral people' (170), a statement that calms Hilaal's disappointment with Askar's desire to append Misra's identity to his, despite his official dependency on Hilaal and Salaado. Yet Misra's exotopic function is linked to Askar's selfhood not just by her foreignness but by how this outsideness is culturally articulated. Two points are salient here.

First, if nations are the space of languages, whichever languages are used bear witness to specific trajectories of nation formation. Although Misra might define herself as Ethiopian, Ethiopia's written culture does not think much of her Oromo oral traditions and she is possessed by Amharic. As Wright points out, Misra's Ethiopian association might place her at odds with the Somali but her Oromo identity shares with the Somali an oral heritage patronised by Ethiopian literacy. Individuals can choose languages, but in terms of the state, languages choose you (that Farah has some five languages and writes in English places him closer to Misra than Askar regarding Somali identity and largely defines the nature of his exile and exotopy. The politics of language in Farah is a huge issue requiring a separate essay addressing both the link of language and postcoloniality and the culpability of the critic in that regard). But obviously the state is not necessarily coincident with its citizens on this score. According to Uncle Hilaal, a Somali is a man or woman whose 'mother tongue' is Somali: this is the substance of their identity, 'no matter how many borders may divide them, no matter what flag flies in the skies above them or what the bureaucratic language of the country is' (174). When we hyphenate identities we mark this non-coincidence, as if acknowledging such an act might erase its import for the borders that putatively embrace it. Because Misra speaks Somali, Askar wonders whether she, like him, might be afforded Somali identity papers. Hilaal answers in the affirmative but adds she might require two male witnesses to sign an affidavit to say that they have known her for a long time and she is indeed Somali (despite Hilaal's progressive views on women's rights here he recognises identity in Somali culture requires male affirmation).

The second point links to the first politically. Askar knows Somali, Amharic and Arabic. His tutor in Mogadiscio, Cusmaan, also encourages him in English as part of the knowledge he must use to liberate his people from colonialism (interestingly, he does not read Italian, the language of his biological mother's notebooks). Hilaal concurs, by stating that 'History has proven that whoever is supported by the written metaphysics of a tradition wins, in the long run, the fight to power' (176). Perhaps, but this does not mean the 'master's tools' are the royal road to independence, particularly now that Somali has its own orthography. The issue of Askar's language acquisition is also accentuated by Cusmaan's proclivity for pornography. When Cusmaan is teaching Askar his first sentence in English, 'This is a pen' is rendered by a phallic complement, a *Playboy* centrefold. If the joke is on Askar, Farah's criticism is both broader and pronounced. Askar connects these words to those dictated by the Archangel Gabriel to Mohammed, the Prophet: 'Read, read in the name of Allah who created you out of clots of blood, read!' (176–177) and to a Qur'anic verse, 'The Pen,' that exhorts, 'By the pen and what it writes, you are not mad' (177). In this 'divine design' Askar also remembers being held naked by an unclothed Misra while learning the sentences 'That is the sky' and 'This is the earth' (177). There is enough of the erotic and the sensual in these passages to inspire the kind of 'satanic' inference that earned Rushdie a *fatwa* (my edition of the novel includes a blurb from Rushdie, who is a friend of Farah). When told of these experiences Hilaal suggests both the 'pen' and the 'book' are indices of power, 'metaphors of material and spiritual power' (178) flaunted both by Arab imperialism and by the Europeans in the form of technology. Few doubt the power of inscription but what can this mean for Askar's identification when the erotic and the spiritual are so obviously juxtaposed and where Arabic, the language of the *Qur'an*, is described as 'an alien language with its alien concepts and thoughts imposed forcefully on the mind of a child'? (88) And what can this mean for Somali identification when its most prominent religion is described in this way? Aw-Adan is both Askar's *Qur'an* teacher and Misra's lover. Because Aw-Adan beats Askar so hard for mispronouncing the Word and because Askar has to listen to Aw-Adan's enthusiastic lovemaking with Misra one might expect him to have a less than enthusiastic view of either Arabic or Islam. Yet one feels here the scale of identification skews the question of Somali affiliation at stake, not because a secular view is impermissible but because the equation of pornography and English in Askar's learning does not quite extend to the language in which the story is told. The problem here is specifically with the responsibility of scale and not with some realist objectivity (after all, 'all is in doubt').

If Misra, already of the 'earth,' enables Askar (whose name means 'soldier' or the 'bearer of arms') to distinguish the land from the sky, she also symbolises a more deadly separation, permitting Somali as a violent signifier to emerge. This is, of course, the danger of any metaphorisation of woman in the discourse of man, but it has a particular valence in the manner of mapping, in providing a topography on which the nation can be drawn. Aw-Adan comments that from a very early age Misra for Askar was a 'space' (12), something to be traversed, explored. For Misra, Askar seemed both space and time, offering up a chronotopic presence that, in Aw-Adan's opinion at least, substituted the role of Allah for Muslims (this will permit her subjugation and violation as well as sanction Aw-Adan's beatings of Askar). Askar territorialises Misra, annexes her being to his under the guise of adding himself to her (at one point 'third leg,' at another 'third breast'). Yet the cost of this topographical and masculinist self-presencing is not addition, or surplus, but all too literal subtraction and extraction. Even before Misra 'adopts' Askar her story embodies the sexist cartography of virgin earth to be penetrated and possessed. Although this is sifted through the uneven fabric of Askar's memory and to be sure, Misra's rationalisations, her tale is one of incessant normative masculine machination.

Misra's very conception was contractual: her mother, an Oromo, agreed to provide procreative services to an Amhara nobleman seeking male issue. Because Misra was the result, both mother and child were abandoned. Later, Misra was abducted by a warrior who claimed her in a skirmish then fled with her to avoid recriminations. They are taken in by a wealthy family but the warrior dies soon after and Misra is adopted, first as a daughter and then as the lover and wife of the man of the household. Misra resists her guardian's passage from 'father' to 'husband' and eventually kills the man in 'an excessive orgy of copulation' (72). The theme of sex and death, however, does not end there. Misra is taken in by another wealthy family and quickly moves from servant to lover to wife. She divorces the man but not before two miscarriages and the birth of a baby, who dies at 18 months (a baby who she initially describes as dead within her). And all this before she meets Askar!

One could make the argument that Misra is guilty of giving too much rather than just being taken, but the weight of her victimisation seems to displace both her foibles and her resistance. Thanks to Qorrax's insistent attention Misra is soon with child again but this time aborts it as if the possibility of family is crossed out. What is not in doubt is that once she has nurtured Askar in his manliness (which here is tantamount to Somaliness) and he is imbued with that Fanonian spirit to always question, Misra is subsumed by Askar's subjectivity. After he moves to Mogadiscio to live with Uncle Hilaal and Auntie Salaado he not only enters the maelstrom of Somali urban identity but also learns mapping, which necessitates both incorporation (to some, the absorption of Misra's body) and division, borders and separation. Askar believes he has killed his mother in order to live and by suggestion, if not admission, he repeats the process with Misra. And just as Misra first points out Somalia on a map (another heavily symbolic moment, because her finger is bloody from preparing a chicken, a dead hen inevitably containing an egg that Askar seeks to preserve) so Askar will come to define his Somali identification by realising this presence, this being, as separate from Misra. In part this is accentuated by his circumcision, a trauma promoting all kinds of existential questions but eventually precipitating an ominous resolve:

...now he was at last a man...totally detached from his mother-figure Misra and weaned. In the process of looking for a substitute, he had found another—Somalia, his mother country...a generous mother, a many-breasted mother, a many-nippled mother, a mother who gave plenty of herself and demanded loyalty of one, loyalty to an ideal, allegiance to an idea, the notion of a nationhood (100).

Fostered by Misra's outsideness, Askar's Somali identity congeals into national allegiance and from here Misra is not only detached but the space of her being begins to disintegrate.

When Misra comes to Mogadiscio in search of Askar he believes her to be half her original size and he wants this missing half, perhaps that which he has himself previously taken, to reassert itself (at the time of her arrival Askar is dreaming of being caged inside a woman, wishing to be born whole). Misra fled the Ogaden because she was suspected of being a traitor (she had spoken to an Ethiopian soldier, who turns out to be a half-brother from her Amhara side and she had sold milk to other soldiers), but not before her house was burned down and she was gang-raped. Hilaal and Salaado have no sooner registered Misra as a family member than she is diagnosed with cancer and has her left breast removed. Misra fights the disease with a passion 'lodged in the centre of her heart—the passion to live!' so it is perhaps small wonder that when her lifeless body is found she has not only been killed but mutilated, her heart cut out. Misra appears to have been reduced to the kind of carcass she often prepared; she is nothing more than meat in the Somali imaginary. This is the tragedy of metaphoricity. The instances of Misra's oppression are part of the materialisation of patriarchy: she is not oppressed as a metaphor but as a woman, performatively and biologically. Yet the psychic schema of the novel insists, albeit through misplaced and misremembered instances, that this narrative of the maimed and mutilated is somehow the condition of Somalia's becoming: 'stories with fragmented bodies!/Bodies which told fragmented stories!/Tales about broken hearts and fractured souls!'[16] I am not suggesting that Farah simply endorses this all too familiar tale in which the possibility of woman's signification is struck through by a masculinist national allegory. I would question, however, whether doubt is a sufficient alternative to the process by which Askar's self-questioning necessitates, by gender and national affiliation, the evisceration of all that Misra can be.

That *Maps* foregrounds the violence of cartography in postcolonial statehood is both necessary and salutary. Farah understands all too well that imperialism lives on in the 'Horn of Africa' in the logic of geopolitical borders. To underline the prescience and vitality of his intervention, commentators often distinguish the feminist inclinations of his narration from those of other African male writers, but let us consider for a moment the parameters of Farah's feminist mapping in terms of postcolonial women's writing. Two examples are salient here. The first is the figure of Firdaus in Nawal El Saadawi's novel, *Woman at Point Zero*. The form of the narrative is testimonial, an account of a woman facing execution for the murder of a pimp, framed by the thoughts of her interlocutor, a psychiatrist doing research on female killers. The litany of abuse that Firdaus suffers, from her father, from the act of clitoridectomy, from lovers who betray her, from male co-workers, from her customers once she becomes a prostitute, is delivered in a hard-edged realism punctuated by dreams and thoughts of revenge. As I have argued elsewhere, the impact of this text comes not simply from identification through revenge but from the context in which the narrative is delivered: a monologue by a prisoner that is dialogised by the presence of the doctor. 'Let me speak. Do not interrupt me,' says Firdaus and perhaps for the only time in her life she slips objecthood in the power of her voicing and in the company of her female listener. After her testimonial the doctor resumes the story and informs the reader that Firdaus was hanged. Perhaps the reader assumes the position of the doctor, but the form of this fiction stresses the process of positioning itself which must, of necessity, account for the different contexts in which the story is taken up, including that of a Western audience who may have their suspicions of Arab Muslim males' brutalisation of their women confirmed by a translation of El Saadawi's stark rendering. Thus, the narrative does not elude the moment of metaphor but it raises significant questions about the necessity for metaphor in its reading. El Saadawi is indeed critical of Islamic masculinism but she is not out to satisfy pre-existing assumptions in her international audience (even when her works have been banned in Egypt her primary readership remains Arabic). What are the lessons here for our understanding of Misra's fate?

Certainly the fact that Askar's recollections of his and Misra's love and her life dominate the text vitiates one's sense of her dialogism even as it largely supports Farah's feminist stand on her subjection. Stylistically, the dependence on doubt has a noble postmodern air about it but this cancels through every level of the text, not just Askar's consciousness (or not) of Misra's objectification. Interestingly, despite the careful switching between first, second and third person in the narrative, the level of subjective displacement in Askar's memories remains fairly constant so even when Misra says simply 'I was raped' we expect him to diminish her voice by relativising it (in this case, by reminding her of all the brutality in war). But it is the trope of mapping itself that clearly distinguishes Misra's story from that of Firdaus. Time and time again the constituents of Misra's character are used to score points about the weakness in Somali nationalism, as if the return of her heart might undo the impasse of nation formation, as if it might plug the pitfalls of Hilaal's disquisition on the 'generification of Africa,' punctuated as it is by a 'but'—the uniqueness of the Somali case. It is not the failure of character to approximate the needs of expansive scaling, but whether metaphor, Misra's sad lot, can do the work of politics the fiction demands. In effect, Hilaal's plea for specificity over the generic insistence of the imperialist and transnational powers must be levelled at the logic of characterisation which, in the case of Misra, weighs her down with generic attributes and associations. But surely this is not the correlative of Firdaus who, by introjecting the masculine reverie of her objecthood as whore, goes on to murder this logic's most obvious advocate?

The second intertext comes from Mahasweta Devi's extraordinary story, 'Douloti the Bountiful.' Like Misra, Douloti's exotopic relationship to the state is doubly over-determined. She is a tribal, long-standing inhabitant of South Asia whose territory neither nominally nor actually fits the contours of the modern Indian postcolonial state. Douloti is a bonded servant, dutifully paying off a debt that will always exceed her claims to subjecthood within a patriarchy that sutures and sustains ethnic, caste and class hierarchies. Devi carefully traces the conditions that maintain this inequity so the 'sub' in subaltern comes to figure what is 'sub'tracted (Douloti is 'con'tracted yet this is always in the form of a deduction) from the algorithm of postcoloniality. As Gayatri Spivak argues in her classic essay, 'Woman in Difference' (the political thrust of the title lies in three words becoming two) Devi's attention to the subaltern displaces the colonial/postcolonial binary by offering an alternative topography, decolonisation itself as the space of alterity. What are the consequences of this imaginary map?

For one, the responsibility of metaphor disrupts the compulsive formula of scaling up to nation. Douloti's steady decline through abuse and venereal disease does not stand in for the sickness of nation that is India; she is not its metonymic guarantee. Instead her ravaged body marks the constitutive process of decolonisation itself which cannot ingest national longing without cost to the metaphor of nation at its heart. Perhaps in support of Farah we might say that Misra's missing heart is indicative of this complex sorcery of taking as giving (recall the other two volumes of the trilogy are *Gifts* and *Secrets*), but the point would be to emphasise the reduction to scale in Devi's intervention by which internal colonisation threatens to envelop the logic of nation and the process of decolonisation, therefore, 'maps' elsewhere. Like El Saadawi, Devi is a social realist, so even if the body is read as a platform for misogynistic and patriarchal principles, the body remains. At the end of Devi's story the remains of Douloti's body lie spread-eagled over a clay facsimile of India that a teacher, Mohan, has been using to inspire nationalism in his students. Selfish Douloti died on 15 August, Indian Independence Day and takes up the space where the Indian flag was to be planted: 'What will Mohan do now? Douloti is all over India' (93). Both El Saadawi and Devi use names to sharpen their feminist irony (Firdaus means 'honourable' and Douloti, as Spivak points out, can be made to mean 'traffic in wealth') so when the bonded labourer Douloti ends up obscuring India this agency in death calls the circumstances of Douloti's life into question. However secure India's borders might be (and this, of course, is debatable) it is difference that riddles its internal identity. Douloti is not finally the metaphor displacing the metaphor of nation that is India; rather, she returns to herself in death as that which India cannot represent.

Perhaps Farah's feminist critique in *Maps* adds up to the same thing but it seems to me that he wants to scale up the metaphor of Misra's miserable life as a comment on the wrong-headedness in the Somali national idea rather than bring this mapping down to size, to the scale of difference that is the country's very possibility. At least for Misra, this indeed is the difference between 'woman in difference' and 'woman indifference.' In point of fact, Farah is precisely attentive to the difficulty in negotiating the scale of nation in his work that must, because of his transnational interpellation, impact the way Somalia is read:

> Years ago, whenever I was asked what country I came from and I responded, 'Somalia,' most of my interlocutors would then rejoin rather dryly, 'Oh, Siyad Barre,' a linkage which irritated me no end. I used to harangue anyone who made the metonymy, anyone who mistook the part for the whole. Nowadays, with pity on their faces, my interlocutors first recite a string of warlords' names, then talk about the Somali refugee communities in their respective countries. So that is how Somalia is seen: refugees on the run, starving babies with drones of flies gathered around their eyes and gun-toting gangsters on a technico-battlewagon creating havoc. Somalia has become synonymous with strife.[17]

There can be no doubt that the Western eyes that hold such images of Somalia in their gaze might satisfy the guilty conscience cast by the long shadow, still present, of the colonial episteme by reading Farah. How can we save Somalia from itself, they say, from its infantile dreams of nation (that we indeed fostered by conquering it)? The point here is not to invest exotopy with culpability, for they are already mutually constitutive. Nor is the lamentable tactic to handle correctly the contradictions of metaphoricity and characterisation as if, once more, White men, as Spivak once famously remarked, might deign to save Brown women from Brown men. The issue here is the responsibility of forms in which the space of nation becomes imaginable, a space that might overcome what is extant in nation itself. It is here Misra is not only 'outside' but exorbitant, she exceeds in her specificity the general demand, the patriarchs' generic demand, that the earth is theirs for the taking, for in-stating.

Maps hints at this non-coincidence through the sheer weight of its doubt. That is, whether the liberal Western reader sees it or not, the ambivalence cancels through even the conviction of his gaze so that the Western epigraphs on doubt in the text (Socrates, Dickens, Kierkegaard, Conrad and the Bible) are reflexively undermined by the parts they divide.[18] Spatially, the narrative pivots on the appropriateness of thirds and although this is not a subject position where either Misra or Somalia might rest easy, it throws some light on Farah's alternative sense of postcolonial cartography. It is a tribute to Farah's irrepressible storytelling that he has Askar ask, 'Misra, where precisely is Somalia?' (116). In all the blurring of their gender and sexual energies the relationship of Askar and Misra is meant logically to problematise what is extant as Somalia. True, the metaphoric link is more about hierarchy than the minutiae of what is assigned in either gender or sexual roles, but, the thinking goes, if you cannot place your country how can you seek solace in national identification? Maps are an alibi, an excuse for non-coincidence in the being of a nation. We think of them as settling border disputes, but in fact the substance of cartography is what grounds such disagreements in the first place. As we follow Askar's growing attachment to maps (piqued initially by Misra) he seems to become more secure in his sense of Somaliness. Eventually, however, with the experience of the war over the Ogaden and with his greater understanding of cartographic history, his convictions dissolve. Askar's maps may copy a 'given reality' but their 'notional truth' renders them relatively inconsequential. Who is more important, Hilaal asks, 'the truth or its finder?' (228) This is where the substance of Somalia, like the trace of Misra's being, exists on different scales.

Spatially, the narrative pivots on the appropriateness of thirds and although this is not a subject position where either Misra or Somalia might rest easy, it throws some light on Farah's alternative sense of postcolonial cartography. In terms of national identity, the schism between Ethiopia and Somalia produces the Ogaden as a third space: it is a zone of the Other that must be claimed and kept separate simultaneously. There is an actual land at stake, but the nation idea is its reality as abstraction and this determines its claims on national subjecthood. As a logical component of Farah's narrative, the Ogaden is an exotopic zone where I and Other negotiate, sometimes violently, the constituents of national being. It is first a space, then a place whose meanings are attached to a 'notional truth,' the map (with a history, as Rich reminds us). The problem of scale suggests the map of Somalia is always its people and never its people: the subject is the bar on its abstraction and the very product of the nation idea. We psychologise and anthropomorphise the nation not out of mistaken identity but because it is a spatial extension of our relationship to the Other. We can delight, therefore, in the fact that the borders of self are never coterminous with Being, in the same way that national borders never fit the subject to whom they are addressed. When Askar receives his Somali identity papers his solemn assurance of their content quickly turns into a grudging acceptance of their implication 'I did think that I was expected, from that moment onwards, to perceive myself in the identity created for me' (173). All identity papers are forgeries to some degree. The otherness that enables

Somalia is not just about its comparative ethnic homogeneity in contra-distinction to Ethiopian heterogeneity but its relationship to its own signification. Because of the timely intervention of Benedict Anderson's *Imagined Communities* we are used to reading this nationness as already read, that Somalia is predicated on a print culture that dutifully supplies Somali identity papers. Here again the question of scale is vital because the nation idea in Somalia is not just the fact of its eventual orthography but the overlapping of its vast and intricate oral traditions (particularly, as we have noted, in poetry) with the cultural archetypes of colonialism and imperialism. This time/space contains individuals and individual tales but these are only allegories of its scale, not the coordinates of the scale itself. The answer to the patronising logic of failed nations lies in broadening cartography to the scale of history and politics, not by collapsing it into an otherwise necessary Other, the national subject.

Hilaal, the intellectual conscience of the novel, asks Askar 'Where is *the third*, where is *the other*?' (144) and the answer depends upon exotopic scale. It is clear that thirdness, in terms of Askar's identity, connects to the mutually determining outsideness of him and Misra, a zone of engagement that touchingly and sometimes erotically supplants his lost triangulation of mother and father (Hilaal, in promoting Askar's separation from Misra, also means to conjure the prescience of Askar's adoptive family in the form of his aunt and uncle). This spatial embrace, with its references to third breasts and third legs has a body map all of its own in which Askar figures himself as 'woman' (even to the point of an imagined menstruation), with a secret language that frees him, however problematically, from the thirdness of masculinist identification found in Hilaal's veritable Hyde, his brother, the ignominious Qorrax. I have suggested that Askar's body mapping, delivered in an ambivalent trio of voices (first, second and third person) projects onto Misra, although idealistically believing that he is her extension (the thesis of the prosthesis is masculine). Note the hesitancy in the following declaration, where the reader herself is asked to conspire in this supposition: 'I was part of the shadow she [Misra] cast—in a sense, I was her extended self. I was, you might even say, the space surrounding the geography of her body' (78). The doubt is not necessarily a ruse of aesthetics; the premise is integral to Farah's acute understanding of human identification. What happens, however, if we mistake this geography for the vexed cartography of the region, if the outsideness of body and nation is simply synonymous? If Misra is nominally Ethiopian, then does Askar the Somali surround her? Is Somalia the extended self of Ethiopia? If indeed Misra is best understood in relation to the Ogaden itself, who is casting the shadow in this affiliation? Askar's personal geography speaks to geopolitics but one should resist making it its substance.

In fact, although *Maps* is suffused with all manner of tropological thirdness, Farah motivates doubt to circumscribe the conditions of exotopy in play. In a culture with long traditions of pastoral nomadism and an adherence to tribal genealogy, a national border is always going to seem outside itself. True, in the riverrine south of Somalia, cultivation historically has led to a tribal concern for land as property, but even these borders do not provide the rationalised edge of extant Somaliness. Commentators are rather too hasty to label Farah 'nomadic,' a convenient and largely romantic version of rootlessness consonant with postcolonial cosmopolitanism. Exile, however, is not nomadism: it is conditioned by an outsideness dependent on borders, not their absence or irrelevance. If nomadism is useful in understanding Farah it is as a more volatile feature of non-coincidence; it does not square with the traditional association between the subject as nation and a national subject. It is a symptom of identification's ambivalence rather than subject certitude. On this level, Askar's story clearly questions the logic of identification with doubts about gender, maps, family and national allegiance. Yet even this correlation connecting author to hero (in the Bakhtinian sense) is neither the knot in Somalia as nation nor its aesthetic meaning for Farah. As Farah points out, 'Although one often links a person in exile to a faraway locality, the fact is I felt joined more to my writing than to any country with a specific territoriality.'[19] In other words, Farah often tropes on Somalia as a creative impetus in *his* imagination rather than beginning with the concept of the imaginary state, the very idea of nation itself.[20] Here the space of form betrays an exotopy in which Farah can believe, as he says, that he is not in exile precisely because that would mean referencing 'specific territoriality,' a necessary displacement in the face of social upheaval that defies the form of nation that Somalia should fit.

Bakhtin believed that aesthetic creation could only begin when the author returned to, in this case, himself, that the Other could be engaged first by 'sympathetic co-experiencing' but then, necessarily, by a return to a constitutive outside, a measure of distance indeed as disjunction. At one point he advocated exotopy as a kind of 'transgredient completion' that simultaneously guaranteed meaning and the god-like status of the writer (usually Dostoevsky). Yet he also argued for outsideness within an aesthetics of unfinalisability, not in the service of metaphysics or idealised relativism but conjoined to an understanding of the aesthetic act as dynamic and fluid as the social in which it is enmeshed. It is certainly easier to read *Maps* in terms of the first injunction, as if some combination of three voices finalises what is given to Somalia from the outside. Here, the metaphor of mapping is not free from complexity but nevertheless draws a Somalia according to the nation idea. And better to trust the author's cartographic skills in this endeavour than rely on the nationalist pronouncements of dodgy despots like Siyad Barre or the five-year plans of socialists and communists (many of whom are also in exile) with their dreams of engineered social reciprocity. The second notion of exotopy does not exclude the characters of the first, but also inscribes the culpability of the author in the process and thus produces a map much more ambivalent about its own capacity to represent. Farah's postmodern and postcolonial predilections are conjoined in this exotopic open-endedness, which is as cogently articulated as it is politically obtuse (you believe that you are not building a nation on doubt but on its displacement). What works at the level of signifier cannot secure reason's interest in the state. What are the implications of this aesthetics of non-coincidence for gender in *Maps*? Is Misra, for instance, bound by the externality of masculine certitude or does the phallus as signifier float beyond its own grasp so that even in death the hole where the heart should be, a quintessential lack of lack, decentres the prescribed pretension of patriarchy for nation?

Farah, perhaps more so than Bakhtin, knows that aesthetic outsideness is a luxury compared to the outside requisite of oppressive hierarchisation. It is true that the majority of his women protagonists fight this malevolent othering at every turn. All we have been considering here is whether the critique of Somali identification disables or displaces the analysis of masculinist gender hierarchy at play in *Maps*. The problem of scale is not solved by wily metaphors or shifting pronouns. Similarly, if feminism rightly challenges governing assumptions of the state, Farah's clearly stated belief in the connection of authoritarianism and the oppression of women still requires clarification in terms of fiction writing and his particular perspective on exile. *Maps* demonstrates the difficulty of distance more than its opening of perspective. Whenever we believe that Askar traces the deracination of the masculine and thus a new prospect for the notional truth of Somalia as nation, what remains of Misra, literally and figuratively in Askar's *raison d'être*, returns as a conditional displacement for masculine power. Farah signals this at various moments, but it is in Askar's reveries this more regressive outside asserts itself and his heroic desire is at odds with feminist solidarity.

Near the end of the novel, for instance and just after an eclipse, Askar slips into a dream. Misra has disappeared and in remembering her, Askar's mouth becomes bitter with the taste of blood, 'as bitter as guilt' (248). Other recognisable figures appear in the dream but it is Misra who is most prominent. She sits upon a throne and is the ruler of a 'land of games, of maps telling one's past and future' (249). Just before Askar wakes up, Misra, now a ghost in the land of the dead, says to him: 'All that one hopes to remain of one is a memory dwelling in someone's head. In whose will I reside? Those who brought about my death, or yours?' (250). The police who take Askar in for questioning about Misra's murder could no doubt make much of this dream if told it. Guilty conscience aside, one wonders about the function of Misra's remainder as memory? To some extent we can read this as Misra's final gift to Askar, as that which triggers so much of his past and development. Yet this dream of Misra as the Queen of Askar's maps of memory can hardly be much consolation to her and neither can his gesture 'Do the dead dream?' (250). In a quiet, existential moment in front of the mirror just prior to his arrest Askar tries to fit this memory with his sense of self, to return to himself in relation to Misra. Predictably, his thoughts on his face as a mask extend to Misra: 'Who was Misra? A woman, or more than just a woman?' (256). On the one hand, Misra is no more just a woman than he is just a man; but on the other hand, Askar's interrogative gesture remains consistent with a general will to metaphoricity in which the terms of the masculine are articulated through the othering of the perceived feminine as object (Misra, obviously, does not have the luxury of voice in this way). There are, then, forms of exotopy that attempt to maintain externality as an absolute guarantee over subjecthood and here again Askar interpellates Misra in this vein. If Farah attempts to render this relation more fluid, more open to dialogic interaction and formation, the denouement of the narrative seems to close off this possibility with the suspect analogy that, after all, Misra was a victim of an untenable Somali nationalism. Take out the heart of the Other, this logic says and the Lacanian hole in the Other appears in its place, permitting the symbolic emergence of the Somali nation. 'Dreams dreaming dreams' indeed (257).

Farah is an unflinching critic of patriarchal traditions within Somali culture, but in attempting to displace them in *Maps* a certain deleterious masculinism remains. This is not due to malevolence or some Freudian (or Lacanian) slip; it is indicative both of the importance of scale in using a map as a metaphor and of the formal difference of exotopy between an exile and his country, an author and his hero, the imaginary state and the state of the imagination and the tenuous borders between masculine and feminine. The author is hardly at one with Askar's identity crisis and does not believe, like Askar, that Somalia would have been secured had it authorised a map of the country during its brief occupation of the Ogaden in 1977–1978. The text says simply 'Truth. Maps' (256) and the difference between the two conjures a complex history of struggle in the formation of postcolonial states. Certainly an imaginary map of Somalia without oppressive constructions of the masculine is desirable, but drawing maps to scale (gender, nation) complicates this need, as does the form of exotopy or outsideness through which such acts become possible. In the end, Askar tells the story of his relationship to Misra to himself, which is both a revelation of truth and of maps: they enclose, they divide. Yet this narration may not be enough either to save his life or to rethink the masculine and the feminine that have shaped it.

16. Killing the Pimp: Firdaus's Challenge to Masculine Authority in Nawal El Saadawi's *Woman at Point Zero*

Marilyn Slutzky Zucker

It is my truth that frightens them.
Let me speak. Do not interrupt me. I have no time to listen to you.
Nawal El Saadwai, Woman at Point Zero.

Firdaus, the hero of Nawal El Saadawi's 1975 novel/fictional (auto)biography, *Woman at Point Zero*, offers a scathing indictment of her culture's masculinities that damage political, religious, social and family life. About to be hung for the murder of her pimp, Firdaus attacks all men of her society for their pervasive and corrupting power-driven attitudes and behaviours. El Saadawi's multi-generic text provides detail and perspective on masculinist principles organising Egyptian culture, principles that directly influence the way people conduct their lives. Though Firdaus is incarcerated and condemned ostensibly for a criminal act, we might nevertheless see her as a political prisoner, hated and feared because she tells the truth about the horrific effects of her culture's patriarchal control over herself, over other women and girls and indirectly over the lives of men as well.[1]

Firdaus becomes an early speaker in the growing body of narratives of Arab women's lives.[2] These narratives have become a primary source of information about the tyrannies of private life and suggest their general manifestations in public life, which both support and generate local enactments in family dynamics. Bouthaina Shabaan discusses the tremendous power of heretofore silent women in Arab cultures now 'speak[ing] for themselves.'[3] The details of their personal stories, she says, tell us about the men in their lives, men who set the parameters for women's activities and who would even 'kill them to save family honour.' In her efforts to collect Arab women's stories, Shabaan notes that ten years prior, 'perhaps none of the women interviewed would have said any-thing against their husbands or fathers, because that would have been deemed dishonourable to the family' (3). Yet more than ten years earlier, we find fearless El Sadaawi, offering, with relentless clarity, commentary on the masculinities that structure her culture through the voice of the truth teller, Firdaus.

Firdaus is relentless in exposing the abuses she suffers from the various men with whom she comes in contact, as I discuss below. She experiences humiliations at the hands of men who we think should rather care for and protect her: father, lover and a revolutionary leader, men who could be committed to recasting traditional woman-hating social and political structures. Moving from private enactments to culturally sanctioned systems of abuse, Firdaus's critique shatters the self-satisfied face of patriarchal entitlement. Thus, it is worthy, though not difficult, to specify the multiple violences and betrayals that victimise women, as projected in *Woman at Point Zero*. In the thirty-five years since the novel was first published, however, we have read account after account of this kind of oppression through the growing body of women's autobiographical stories and the lenses of feminist and postcolonial studies. Indeed, Firdaus's story is a prototype for the legion of women's stories that have come forth from her and neighbouring cultures. Something of Firdaus's story, new in its day, has become a familiar one.

Yet El Saadawi's text involves more than the recounting of terrible occurrences in Firdaus's life. The prisoner's story, for example, is framed by the voice of a female physician whose relationship with the prisoner adds complexity to her otherwise straightforward monologue. And Firdaus herself is not what we expect from the female 'victim' of the intense male oppression she suffers. As she tells her own story, she describes her movement from the powerless girl to slowly assuming, as her life progresses, control over money, food and most importantly, her body. Firdaus protects her body and self in a distinctly unwomanly move and kills her pimp. Angry, independent and active, she remains resistant to victimisation, turning her rage onto its appropriate target rather than onto her self. We respond then to the gravitational pull of Firdaus's narrative to reconsider its rendition, to see how El Saadawi, while writing a strong feminist text, appropriates aspects of masculinity for her ferocious female protagonist.

My effort in this essay, then, will be to use the forceful woman-centred nature of *Woman at Point Zero* to comment on the text's construction of masculinity. In addition to noting readily recognisable oppressive acts by men and the embedding social contexts, my reading affirms that it is the woman, Firdaus, who remains central to the text's vision. However, when we look at this story with the newer consciousness of masculinist studies, we see El Saadawi's skill at adapting aspects of masculinity in her female protagonist. Reconceiving the narrative in terms of masculine spaces and behaviours, rather than the female-centred analyses offered thus far, I discuss Firdaus's narration, which sees her taking on some aspects of masculinity in the kinds of things she says and does as she tells her tale and as she relates her story to the woman physician. As the narrative progresses, Firdaus will gain control over each of the text's masculinely inflected entitlements. She will claim a great degree of personal autonomy and authority, transgressing cultural gender codes to create new possibilities for her female life. Finally, El Saadawi gives authorial voice, traditionally reserved for men, to this most abused of women who asks for no sympathy and in a mood of assertive individuality, understands the power she has usurped for herself.

It seems important to begin by locating *Woman at Point Zero* in the context of El Saadawi's lifework. Nawal El Saadawi has been a consistent, brave voice in the face of the powerful patriarchal structures of Egyptian culture; indeed, her writings are responsible for exposing these very structures and their effects on the lives of women. Her biography is well known,[4] yet salient portions of it bear repeating because the text under study is one of her early and most piercing works involving Egyptian social modes. El Saadawi's professional, public and writerly lives remain strongly linked; her activities in the public world integrate with and influence her literary production, bringing her into yet greater controversial positions in her public life.

Nawal was born in a small village near Cairo and educated in 'native Egyptian Arab language schools,'[5] an education tying her ever more closely to the structures organising her own culture. She received her medical training at the University of Cairo, from which she received a degree in psychiatry in 1955. Her choice of specialty shows early focus on the damage of certain upbringings and social structures to mental health, a theme that pervades much of her written work. Appointed to the Ministry of Health in 1958, she became part of the government's effort to attend to the well-being of its people, yet in 1972 was dismissed from her post as Egypt's national public health director as a result of her writings on sexuality. In the early 1970s El Saadawi embarked on a study of women in prison and would publish *Women and Neurosis* in 1976. While working on this study, she began *Woman at Point Zero*, published in 1975, to be followed in 1980 by *The Hidden Face of Eve: Women in the Arab World*. This non-fiction book, aptly subtitled, deals, chapter by chapter, with several of the cultural structures informing women's lives, including 'sexual aggression against the female child' (12–15), 'the circumcision of girls' (33–43), the importance of virginity and the role of prostitution. Imprisoned herself for several months in 1981 by the Sadat regime, El Saadawi soon after founded the Arab Women's Solidarity Association, which was then shut down by the Egyptian government in 1991. El Saadawi published her own prison memoir in 1986. Pushpa Parekh notes the crucial significance of *Memoirs from the Women's Prison*, as it deals with 'specific concepts central to Arab-Islamic cultures, that of woman's sexuality and its control, imprisonment and exploitation in the existing structures of Egyptian society,[6] a theme explored in *Woman at Point Zero*.

In this brief review, we notice an intertwining of El Saadawi's politically active and literary lives, a resonance that echoes again between her non-fiction and fictive works and even more specifically between documentary and fictive modes in *Woman at Point Zero*. Each of these instances manifest cross-pollination between modes of being and modes of writing. In the case of the novel under study, though the particulars of the narrator and Firdaus's stories are fictional and though El Saadawi is clear that the book is fiction, it nevertheless stands as testimonial to the litany of permissions, entitlements and violations of women in male-dominated Arab society.[7]

El Saadawi sets out in her novel/fictional (auto)biography an integration of genres, voices and styles of writing that give textual body to the integrated gendered constructs the novel explores. For example, the author's preface, written as a non-fiction introduction to her novel, begins: 'I wrote this novel after an encounter between me and a woman in Qanatir Prison' (i), firmly locating *Woman at Point Zero* as a fictive work. No doubt, however, the story bears strong resemblance to an actual incident in El Saadawi's life, as the author continues in her preface: 'A few months before, I had started research on neurosis in Egyptian women....' (i), a situation echoed by the framing character of the novel, the female physician, who says, 'This is the story of a real woman. I met her in the Qanatir Prison a few years ago. I was doing research on the personalities of a group of women prisoners and detainees convicted or accused of various offences...' (1). El Saadawi's remarks with overlays of fictive and non-fictive elements set up a merging of voices, making it difficult to tease out precisely who is speaking, (the famous Bahktinian question of narrative) thereby destabilising clarity of genre.[8]

Combining fictive and documentary modes, *Woman at Point Zero* is an early contemporary example of women's prison writings from Arab culture.[9] Barbara Harlow, in her study, 'From the Women's Prison: Third World Women's Narratives of Prison,' notes that a combination of fictive and documentary genres such as we see in El Saadawi's text characterises, in general, women's prison narratives. Harlow discusses Bessie Head's short story, 'The Collector of Treasures,' in which Dikeledi Mokopi has been sentenced to prison for stabbing her husband. Harlow judges the husband's murder 'as a historical action, determined by African history as a challenge to the same history' and 'recasts the protagonist's crime in political terms' (510). She suggests that the combination of genres makes for stunning social commentary, accurately noting that *Woman at Point Zero* 'merges the requirements of fiction and narrative form with the historical and social demands of biography' (511). Thus, along with other such similar narratives, *Woman at Point Zero* constitutes 'an assault on the social order' (509) in which 'writing itself becomes an offense against the state, punishable by law and a prison sentence' (514).[10] Which is where we find Firdaus.

Reading *Woman at Point Zero* as a prison memoir assists our understanding of El Saadawi's presentation of masculinity in both literary and cultural matrices. If we think of the arch-societal expressions of publicly enacted masculine power, we see war, colonialism and prison as the more organised oppressive institutions, which depend on widespread allegiance to masculine codes and values.[11] With the lives of both Firdaus and the female physician who conveys her story immersed in these institutions, the entire novel comments on those codes, telling the truth, albeit telling it through a fictive mode. In the introduction to a more recent collection of non-fiction pieces, *The Nawal El Saadawi Reader*, El Saadawi reconfirms the oppressive nature of masculinity, forwarding the idea of 'prison' as a metaphor for the entrapped, incarcerated lives of women in patriarchy: 'As for women in my country, their husbands are their permanent prisons' (5). So we may see Firdaus in prison as representative of a widespread condition endured by women throughout her culture.

The Firdaus to whom we are indirectly introduced in the brief first section of the book has already lived through the experiences she is about to describe in the longer second section and through which she has come to assume a variety of behaviours generally reserved for men in her culture. And we see that from the outset, El Saadawi presents Firdaus as not an ordinary woman, characterising her at once with qualities nuanced with masculinity. She is rejecting and indifferent and according to the compassionate prison doctor, 'not like the other female murderers held in the prison' (1). El Saadawi's own prison memoir offers a sense of typical female prisoners' behaviour as they develop what Golley calls a 'community of oppressed women'[12]: recognising and acknowledging women from her local communities, developing alliances with other prisoners, working with them for the common good and continuously interacting with prison authorities to better, even slightly, the prisoners' living conditions. Rejecting this 'collective identity' of 'almost utopian solidarity' shown by women prisoners,[13] Firdaus makes no reference to these roles; in fact, we see her actively rejecting connection with the one woman who has come to visit on the eve of the prisoner's execution. The prison doctor enumerates the prisoner's refusals—to see anyone, to answer questions and finally even 'to sign an appeal' (1) that would commute her death sentence. She has been hurt and betrayed by all institutions of her culture and their representatives and thus appealing to one of them, the prison hierarchy, for clemency or even consideration, would without doubt subject her to yet another rejection and betrayal. Thus, rather than signifying a passive withdrawal from life, an emblem of early female resistance to patriarchy, Firdaus's solitary behaviour borders on the arrogant, boasting that she feels 'pride' in her journey. Comparing herself to the most powerful of men, she feels 'superior to everyone else, including kings, princes and rulers' (11).

Firdaus's independent behaviour continues as she refuses to meet with the physician, who seems a 'lady in waiting,' returning again and again for the attentions of the recalcitrant prisoner. The alternation of feelings of desire and rejection on the part of the female physician begins to imitate the duet of lovers, with Firdaus signified as 'male' and the 'active member of the duo.'[14] The narrator convulses with emotion, commenting that the only other time she felt such longing was 'when I loved a man who did not love me' and his refusal felt as a refusal 'of every living thing or being on earth' (4). When Firdaus finally agrees to meet with the woman psychiatrist, the doctor shows physical signs of tremendous excitement:

> My breath in turn quickened...I felt out of breath, for my heart was beating more strongly than it had ever done before...I walked with a rapid effortless pace, as though my legs were no longer carrying a body...I was full of a wonderful feeling, proud, elated, happy...It was a feeling I had known only once before...I was on my way to meet the first man I loved for the first time (6).

What is important to note is NOT that both people are women, but that the doctor is aligned with female coded behaviour as Firdaus is with masculine social traits.[15] Her cold isolation establishes no connection to the doctor, Firdaus's face showing 'not the slightest movement of a lid. Not the smallest twitch of a muscle in the face' (6). Her look then turns aggressive, piercing the physician with eyes that penetrate 'like a knife, probing, cutting deep down inside, their look steady, unwavering' (6). Finally, in adopting a masculine authoritative language pattern, the prisoner begins to command the physician—'Close the window...Sit on the ground'—in an imperative tone that continues as the reader is immersed directly into Firdaus's tale—'Let me speak. Do not interrupt me' (11).

Firdaus has been subjected to multiple manifestations of her culture's punishing masculinities, which El Saadawi presents with unstinting vitriol. As her story winds outward from the home, to an uncle's home, a marriage, work as a secretary and finally a life of prostitution, the circles of abuse widen. The humiliations, sexual aggressions, betrayals and violence meted out by father, uncle, lover, policeman and political activist implicate their associated institutions—familial, religious, political—and their sanctioned female-violating structures. For those who have not read El Saadawi's text, I offer a brief look at her presentation of Firdaus's father to get a taste of El Saadawi's rendition, in tone and content, of Firdaus's story.[16]

The first description of the earliest man in Firdaus's life, told with biting accuracy and ironic fervour, introduces some of the myriad areas of culture controlled by men, areas further developed as the text progresses. Firdaus's father is thieving and deceptive; he knew 'how to sell a buffalo poisoned by his enemy before it died, how to exchange his virgin daughter for a dowry when there was still time, how to be quicker than his neighbor in stealing from the fields once the crop was ripe' (12). He is abusive and sexually violent, knowing 'how to beat his wife and make her bite the dust each night' (12). Physically repellent, with a 'mouth like that of a camel' (19), he eats with animal abandon: 'His tongue kept rolling round and round in his mouth as though it also was chewing, darting out every now and then to lick off some particle of food that had stuck to his lips or dropped to his chin' (19). He belches, noisily expelling air from his 'mouth or belly' and fills the air with his 'coughing, snorting and inhaling,' smoking and snoring (19). The father's dedication to his own food and eating is all-consuming as it were, Firdaus noting that even when one of his children died, he 'would beat my mother, then have his supper and lie down to sleep...My father never went to bed without supper, no matter what happened. Sometimes, when there was no food at home, we would all go to bed with empty stomachs. But he would never fail to have a meal' (180). He is the eater, the beater, the user, demonstrating neglect and arrogance towards wife and children.

The father's public devotion to religion while conducting his private life in an inhumane manner calls into question religion's role in supporting masculine privilege. Firdaus's father and the other men walk home from Friday prayers discussing the imam's sermon, as she comments with irony: 'For was it not verily true that stealing was a sin and killing was a sin and defaming the honour of a woman was a sin and injustice was a sin and beating another human being was a sin...,' all activities well within the scope of the men's daily lives. She describes the unholiness of these 'holy' men, as they

> invoked Allah... or repeated His holy words in a subdued guttural tone. I would observe them nodding their heads, or rubbing their hands one against the other, or coughing, or clearing their throats with a rasping noise, or constantly scratching under the armpits and between the thighs ...they watched what went on around them with wary, doubting, stealthy eyes ready to pounce, full of an aggressiveness...(13).

Firdaus comments that her uncle is a 'respected Sheikh, well versed in the teachings of religion and he, therefore, could not possibly be in the habit of beating his wife.' However, her uncle's wife confirms the 'righteous' habit of religious men: 'It was precisely men well versed in their religion who beat their wives. The precepts of religion permitted such punishment' (44).[17]

Firmly supported by the religious 'patrix,' her father is the tyrant of the house, with control of food, control of money and control of the bodies of women within the family unit. His power over these aspects of Firdaus's life will be replicated by other men throughout the course of her years, with control of her body the prime scene of contest.[18] Most men she has contact with behave as though her body is theirs to do with as they please, which, according to her culture's prevailing constructs, it is. Her uncle, for example, rewards the achievement of her elementary school certificate with his 'great long fingers' fondling her under her nightclothes and feeling their way 'slowly upwards toward [my] thighs' (22). The old Sheikh to whom she's married off comes at her with a suppurating sore on his face, as Firdaus says: 'At night, he could wind his legs and arms around me and let his old, gnarled hand travel all over my body, like the claws of a starving man who has been deprived of real food for many years wipe the bowl of food clean and leave not a single crumb behind' (43).[19] Leaving her husband's home she meets Bayoumi, who seems to care about her, but after Firdaus announces her need to go to work, begins abusing her. He slaps her, locks her in her room, attacks her sexually and violently: 'He sank his teeth into the flesh of my shoulder and bit me several times in the breast and then over my belly. While he was biting me, he kept on repeating: "Slut, bitch"' (50). And so forth with a variety of other men. Firdaus's own body becomes the site of contest and power, a condition echoed in the rest of her society, as Malti-Douglas notes: 'Her reality is indissolubly tied to her body' (3).

In this highly regulated cultural context, with virtually no choice regarding access to her body, Firdaus is fair game to any man who desires her. Thus, she considers prostitution. Sharifa, a high class madam, convinces Firdaus that the life of prostitution allows women control of their bodies and offers new value to their lives. Such value, Sharifa claims, can come only from a woman herself: 'A man does not know a woman's value, Firdaus. She is the one who determines her value' (55). Accepting Sharifa's offer, Firdaus's worldview changes suddenly, completely: 'Can the Nile and the sky and the trees change? I had changed, so why not the Nile and the colour of the trees? . . . I could see the trees, the vivid green light in which everything seemed to bathe, feel the power of life, of my body, of the hot blood in my veins' (55). She soon experiences delights of life she'd never known, wearing beautiful clothes, sleeping on lovely bed linens, her 'nose filled with the fragrance of roses' (56). Before long, however, Firdaus understands that Sharifa makes money from Firdaus's relations with men and escapes from the newest proprietor of her body.[20] With this latest escape, as with each escape from each captor, Firdaus assumes greater responsibility for her own life choices, a developing independence usually reserved for boys and men in her society.

Though she soon moves out from Sharifa's world and continues to have difficult interactions with men, her work affords her some degree of liberty about her body: 'My body was my property alone' (90). Through this newfound activity, she achieves financial freedom, as prostitutes always have, according to El Saadawi, taking advantage of men's sexual urges to address her own financial need.[21] In so doing, Firdaus takes on a financially driven exploitive approach to men, readjusting the sexually exploitative role heretofore enacted by men and perpetrated upon her female body. She is able to find a good apartment for herself, employ an assistant and add monies to a growing bank account. She enjoys the activities of a free person, uncommon for a woman of her lower class of birth and knows material luxuries usually reserved for upper class wives. And given her cultural understanding that men are eventually all powerful over women's bodies, she says she is better off being 'a free prostitute rather than an enslaved wife' (91). Prostitution is her opportunity to achieve economic freedom through a sexual role not much different than that of a married woman, but one far freer than that of women whose actions and behaviours are dictated by, among other things, economic beholdenness to a husband.[22]

In the context of Firdaus's life, then, the choice to become a prostitute makes perfect sense. Because men have used her body freely, to satisfy their own desires, she decides to get paid for what has always been taken from her. The use of her body has been taken with violence and humiliation, rather than being traded for money with which she can begin to manage her own life.[23] Here is Firdaus's attempt in a vigorously controlled environment to exercise some degree of autonomy. And her growing quest for autonomy, in a society where women have little, marks with masculine inflection the contours of Firdaus's journey. Her wilful enactment of selfhood in the face of trapping, tyrannical forces registers to El Saadawi as the kind of rebellion against authority that makes one a hero. Such heroic action exist even in defiance of such bodily attack as Firdaus has endured. Indeed, Firdaus's death by execution hardly erases her self, fulfilling the apex of power generally reserved for men: the telling of her own story.

The turning point for Firdaus in her quest for an autonomy generally reserved for men comes after leaving Sharifa's place and comes in several stages. She first earns her own money, then feels shame and humiliation at the prospect of spending it and finally overcomes that feeling to experience a sense of power and entitlement heretofore unknown to her. Earning her own 'piastre' gives Firdaus a means of dealing with the internalised shame of being an adult woman. She experiences receiving money directly for her sexual services for the first time, without mediation of pimp or madam. She goes with a clean, dignified man, wakes up in an 'elegant bedroom' (63) and after receiving payment feels a new clarity of vision: 'It was as though he lifted a veil from my eyes and I was seeing for the first time' (64). She understands suddenly the power of earning her own money, summoning memories of the small amount earned in childhood from her father for her work in cleaning the animals. In her recounting the event, Firdaus reinforces the tremendous value of wanting and then earning the single piastre as she repeats the unit of currency twelve times in a short passage:

I went to my mother crying loudly 'Give me a piastre.' She answered, 'I have no piastres. It's your father who has the piastres.' So I went in search of my father and asked him for a piastre. He hit me on my hand and shouted, 'I have no piastres.' But a moment later he called me back and said 'I'll give you a piastre if Allah is bountiful to us and we manage to sell the buffalo before it dies.'

The buffalo dies before the father can sell it and Firdaus waits till she sees a pile of sweets before asking again,

'Give me a piastre.' This time he said, 'Do you ask for a piastre, first thing in the morning? Go and clean under the animals . . . and I shall give you a piastre.' And in fact, when I returned from the fields at the end of the day, he gave me the piastre. It was the first piastre he had ever given me, the first piastre that was all mine . . . (64–65).

As a small girl, she was given her first taste of liberty with money and such liberty allowed the otherwise powerless child to buy what she wanted, 'whether sweets or carob, or molasses stick or anything else [I] might choose' (65). Now, with her new ten-pound note, she faces not only the choice of selection, but the suffocating restrictions on an adult woman earning and spending her own money.

Firdaus goes to a restaurant to spend her money and is looked upon with shame by the male waiter. But she does not play the female role by engageing in the duet of victimisation he tries to initiate, a duet that would hardly have taken place were Firdaus a man. The waiter offers 'stolen glances' at Firdaus and her money as she becomes his object of shame: 'He kept his eyes away from my bag, looking all the while in another direction as though avoiding the ten pound note' (66). His furtive looks bring back memories of other experiences as 'object of the gaze': 'I had seen this movement of the eyes . . . it reminded me of my husband, Sheikh Mahmoud, as he kneeled in prayer, his eyes half closed, of the glances he stole now and then' (66) and of her uncle who looked 'with peering eyes' as he surreptitiously fondled her. She wonders if her holding money 'was a shameful thing, made to be hidden, an object of sin which was forbidden to me and yet permissible for others, as though it had been made legitimate only for them' (67). Summoning her courage, she holds her own in the face of the waiter's insinuating looks and bravely gives him the note. Her triumph frees her from the shame associated with having her own money, giving her a sense of independence, control and self-respect: 'From that day onwards I ceased to bend my head or to look away' (67–68).[24]

As Firdaus gathers the kind of financial strength and purpose more common to men in her culture than to women, she also appropriates the power to look directly at others: 'I looked people in the eyes and if I saw someone count his money, I fixed it with an unwinking gaze' (68). As men have done with women, she assumes the objectifying eye of masculinist culture. She sees men as anonymous faces in a generalised group rather than as individuals, a view first offered by a man himself. Bayoumi, the man she lives with in a seemingly loving relationship for many months, learns that she wants to use her secondary school certificate and find work. Infuriated, he beats her with 'the heaviest slap' on the face she had ever received and sends his friend to use Firdaus's body. She recognises suddenly that it is not Bayoumi pressing down on top of her: '"Who are you?" I said. "Bayoumi," he answered. I insisted, "You are not Bayoumi. Who are you?" "What difference does it make? Bayoumi and I are one"' (50). The category, 'men,' forms and is reinforced by Sharifa, as she describes her clients: 'Any one of them, it doesn't make any difference. They're all the same, all sons of dogs, running around under various names . . .' (52). Of course, by the end of her life, Firdaus generalises and stereotypes all men as objects of her hatred as she wishes to do to them the very thing they have done to her throughout her life: 'All the men I did get to know, every single one of them, has filled me with but one desire: to lift my hand and bring it smashing down on his face' (11).

With the murder of her pimp, Firdaus comes full circle in her appropriation of masculinely coded behaviour. She has emerged as an adult woman who has suffered as women in her culture do, but who has slowly assumed some aspects of power associated in her culture with masculinity. She looks men in the eye, earns and spends her own money, speaks in commanding language and in the end, resists relationships that suggest need or connection. Yet it is the precipitous act of killing her pimp that marks Firdaus's evolution to assertive selfhood. She protects herself by attacking the person who is doing her harm; in so doing, she takes on a violently masculine position, refusing the female-nuanced role of victim.

Firdaus does not internalise rage to produce the paralysing constraint of womanly neurosis.[23] Instead she commits murder. That the novel gives value to a woman's violent act against oppression rather than to her victimisation is unsurprising given the moment of the novel's creation. At around the same time El Saadawi was writing *Woman at Point Zero*, she conducted research for her documentary study *Women and Neurosis*, interviewing women in hospitals and prisons suffering from 'mental afflictions" (i). In doing her research on neurosis, El Saadawi came across a woman who she learned had killed someone and never having met 'a woman who has killed' decided to meet with the prisoner. El Saadawi came to admire the prisoner who needed, even as she faced death, 'to challenge and overcome those forces that deprive human beings of their right to live, to love, to real freedom' (iv). As she came to understand that the prisoners' mental afflictions resulted in large part from the rebellion of women trying to live in a world whose rules are made and enforced by men, El Saadawi translated a psychological condition into a social one, thus characterising Firdaus's act of murder in political rather than criminal terms.[25]

A woman committing murder transgresses all cultural codes, for though it is acceptable (and indeed socially valuable) that women subdue themselves neurotically, it is entirely unacceptable for a woman to forcefully subdue another, especially if 'the other' is a man. In this context, Firdaus's murder of the pimp is a political act: a challenge to strict societal codes and the prevailing power structure and a rebellion against the self-subduing processes of neurosis. If we see murder as a complete subduing of the other (in its less extreme form, a characteristic of ordinary masculine culture), we can see 'neurosis' as a subduing of the self, a psychological process in its less extreme form characterising ordinary female life. Women neurotically silence themselves, whereas men ferociously silence the women in their lives. Yet Firdaus does not fulfil the conventional female role, turning her rage in upon herself, but rather enacts it onto a person from the hated category of oppressor: the appropriate 'other.' Firdaus's actions bring about her judgement and execution, given the embedding social structure, with her assertive truth-telling the most dangerous aspect of her crime: "' It is my truth that frightens them. This fearful truth gives me great strength"' (102).

In her defiance of victimhood, Firdaus continues in a line of Third-World women who demonstrate assertions of selfhood in the face of tremendously repressive cultural structures. She wilfully rejects the supplicatory posture required to ask for anything, even her life. In her aggressive refusal of the 'victim' posture, Firdaus exhibits great courage and strength, such as that demonstrated by a progenitor of 'Third World' women's refusal of victimisation. Huma Ibrahim refers to the classic text, the *Mahabharata*, citing Draupadi's story, translated by Gayatri Spivak, in which 'Dopdi' is tortured and brutalised. Yet she refuses to accept her fate as 'victim' and appears naked with her 'mangled breasts' uncovered, in front of the leader, who 'stands before an unarmed target, terribly afraid.' Like Firdaus, with her courageous truth-telling, Dopdi 'throws her victimization into the lap of the victimizer and refuses to be "ashamed" of her humiliation...' (150). Both Dopdi's confronting her abusers and Firdaus's aggression towards hers show us women's heroic actions, as they release themselves from the shame and fear that conspire to hobble their lives.

In *Woman at Point Zero*, El Saadawi shows us what a human being will do in spite of cultural sufferings to feel some degree of personal power and freedom. She has woven a multi-generic tale of a woman whose life embodies an inter-gendered outlook; Firdaus has suffered as women do in her culture and has gradually assumed aspects of masculine power generally off-limits to Egyptian women. Indeed, her coming to power results from her re-authoring her life against the gendered constraints of her society. Firdaus earns her own money and decides how to publicly spend it. She selects the job that avails her of a better lifestyle and chooses with whom she will or will not have sex. And finally she acts out her rage at the appropriate target. El Saadawi re-scripts the death-deferring tales of Shahrazad,[26] constructing a hero in Firdaus who takes for herself some of the gender equality the writer forwards in her stories and in her life's work.[27] Through Firdaus's coming-to-selfhood story, with its masculinely inflected actions, El Saadawi commutes the soulful death sentence, which she sees burdening women in her culture.

17. The Price of Pleasure: K. Sello Duiker's *Thirteen Cents* and the Economics of Homosexuality in South Africa

Timothy Johns

Introduction: 'Homosex is Not Black Culture'?

Winner of the 2001 Commonwealth Writers' Prize for best debut novel in the African region, K. Sello Duiker's *Thirteen Cents* offers a startling, almost counterintuitive portrait of contemporary South African masculinity. Indeed, the novel's depiction of a 13-year-old boy's sexual experiences with men challenges many basic assumptions about the origins of homosexual engagement, both in the novel's immediate setting (South Africa) and across the continent. A variety of political leaders in Africa today denounce homosexuality as the residue of an earlier cultural encounter with Europe—in essence, as a form of neo-colonialism, a cultural hangover from a period polluted by foreign domination and perverted mores. Although more visible vestiges of the colonial order wither, homosexuality continues to flourish. For this reason, perhaps, the rhetoric against homosexuality has been particularly fierce. In Gambia recently, after two Spanish men were arrested for making advances to taxi drivers, President Yahya Jammeh threatened to 'behead gay people at a political rally and said they had 24 hours to leave the country.' Promising 'stricter laws than Iran' on homosexuality,' Jammeh's statement, as reported by the BBC on 3 June 2008, was backed by Gambia's Supreme Islamic Council. But African Muslim clerics are not alone in adopting this homophobic line. As I began to write this chapter on 14 February 2008, Ruth Gledhill, religious correspondent for *The Times* of London, reported:

> The Anglican bishops of the Church in Uganda are to boycott the Lambeth Conference in protest at the liberal direction the Anglican Church is taking on homosexuality. [Uganda], which has more than 30

bishops, joins Nigeria in boycotting the ten-yearly gathering, which takes place in Canterbury this summer... A similar announcement was expected this week from Kenya, also a member of the Commonwealth, but the post-election violence there has postponed the decision until later this year. Rwanda will also stay away.

As these unyielding positions indicate, many postcolonial African leaders see themselves as performing a kind of homosexual exorcism—an activity intended to preserve the African family and African civil society.

As Duiker's *Thirteen Cents* suggests, however, this focus on the heterosexual origins of African culture is facile. Set within a precarious modern global economy, ordinary money problems—as opposed to what is specific to Africa or African culture that motivate the hero's sexual orientation; this novel's emphasis—that is, on economics rather than cultural 'origins'—helps us rethink what is really at stake in the African debate over homosexual practice, particularly as this debate manifests itself in South Africa.

South Africa, the setting for my essay in this collection, would seem to offer a notable exception to the rising homophobic tide on the continent. After the 1994 elections and the end of apartheid, the country's frank legal embrace of homosexuality appeared, even by international standards, truly remarkable. As Mark Gevisser and Edwin Cameron noted in *Defiant Desire*, a pioneering anthology about gay history in the region:

South Africa is the first country in the world to offer gay and lesbian people explicit protection in its constitution. Section 8 of the Chapter on Fundamental Rights outlaws unfair discrimination on the basis of sexual orientation... [I]n his first presidential pronouncement, during his victory speech on the Grand Parade in Cape Town, Nelson Mandela made a point of saying that discrimination against gays and lesbians would no longer be tolerated (ix).

By terminating same-sex discrimination, as well as capital punishment and a variety of other apartheid-era abuses, the Mandela-led African National Congress (ANC) seemed to have hammered through breathtaking legal guarantees, freedoms nearly unprecedented in the world.

Yet as one begins to scratch beneath the surface of Mandela's pronouncement, a more complicated pattern comes into focus—one that exposes an uneasy relationship between the anti-apartheid struggle and the struggle for gay rights. In fact, within the ANC itself, even before the end of White minority rule, contradictory positions about homosexuality abounded. For example, during a 1991 Supreme Court trial in which Winnie Mandela was accused of kidnapping a child from men who allegedly slept with one another, the ANC stalwart and (then) wife of Nelson Mandela 'codified homosexuality as sexual abuse... and characterised homosexual practice as a white, colonising depredation of heterosexual black culture.'[1] Outside the courtroom, at the height of the affair, one of Winnie Mandela's supporters held a sign that read: 'Homosex is not in black culture.'

Today, this type of homophobic position, based on a myth of African cultural purity, appears to be hardening within sectors of the ANC. Speaking at Heritage Day celebrations in KwaDukuza in September 2006, Jacob Zuma, the populist politician many believe will succeed Thabo Mbeki as the country's president, remarked: 'When I was growing up, an *ungqingili* [homosexual] would not have stood in front of me. I would knock him out.' *The Sowetan* quoted Zuma as saying that same-sex marriages were 'a disgrace to the nation and to God.' By peppering the word *ungqingili* into the speech, Zuma effectively distinguished between legitimate insiders (those who understand African 'Heritage Day' and Zulu phrases) and outsiders (those who do not speak Zulu or recognise traditional customs).

One wonders, however, if this inflated nativistic rhetoric, backed by violent posturing, has missed a major point—one that Duiker's novel spells out. *Thirteen Cents* depicts how a banal economic rationale can lie behind forms of sexual experience; which is to say, market forces can have more to do with the determination of sexual orientation than free choice or 'authentic' cultural practice, especially for the most vulnerable. In fact, as the novel indicates, in contemporary South Africa pleasure can only be had at a price: Azure, the hero, a desperate thirteen-year-old street urchin living without any kind of state support or safety net, offers sexual favours to other (usually White and wealthy) men in order to survive. Although, over the course of the novel, the hero explicitly desires women more than men, he must sleep with men to make ends meet. Therefore his sexual orientation appears arbitrary, dependent on the whims of the market. Because men desire him more than women, he bends accordingly. (In Duiker's second novel, *The Quiet Violence of Dreams*, the pendulum often swings the other way: the hero, a prostitute who ordinarily desires men, sleeps with women to pay the bills.) Importantly, however, the gay experience is never coded as 'foreign' in *Thirteen Cents*. Although wealthy White men, living in nice beachside apartments in Cape Town, lure the 13-year-old into prostitution, tough guys on the other side of the tracks, young Black and 'coloured' men who make up the hybrid tapestry of Cape Town, lure the boy into a gang rape. By underscoring, after White minority rule, the mere economics of sexual coupling across the racial spectrum, the need to merely survive or endure or dominate by having sex a certain way, the novel challenges the idea that 'homosex is not black culture'—that is, the idea that African men are somehow more 'naturally' connected to traditional culture than to modern economics.

In what follows, then, I try to show how Duiker's novel aids us in rethinking South African debates over sexual orientation. As we will see, by privileging what is, above all, economically motivated over what is 'traditional' and 'authentic' to South Africa, the novel subtly picks apart not only the homophobic rhetoric brewing in the region today, but the government's failed economic policies as well. It is useful to understand that *Thirteen Cents* is set in Cape Town during the late 1990s, against the backdrop of the ANC's push for a neo-liberal economic system. According to Dennis Altman, this system left South Africans vulnerable to an array of market forces, for it initiated:

> ...an end to restrictions on foreign investment; privatization of government owned enterprises; reduction in the power of unions; corporate deregulation; ...downsizing of the public sector, often through a process of 'out-sourcing'; and steady cuts in public expenditure on health, education and welfare (62).

In essence, the ANC's neo-liberal system left many out in the cold, fending for themselves, without a safety net. Although this political backdrop never receives full treatment, *Thirteen Cents* nevertheless dramatises the state of the nation through the eyes of a subject living without any kind of government cushion, forced into performing sex acts for economic survival. The urchin's sexual vulnerability suggests something about the uncertainty unleashed by the ANC's push for neo-liberal, *laissez-faire* hegemony. Faced with uncertain prospects in a failing public sphere, money concerns dominate the most personal experiences imaginable. Something as private as sexual orientation can be reduced to a price tag.

After an examination of *Thirteen Cents*, which situates the novel against earlier examples of Black masculinity and family life in South African fiction, I unfold a larger claim for what I call, perhaps less delicately than I would like, a history of 'economic homosexuality' in South Africa. I examine how the search for gold in the region helped foster arbitrary homosexual encounters between working class men. In this part of the essay, to debunk the theory of homosexuality as a neo-colonial emblem, I also discuss evidence of pre-colonial homosexuality in Africa.

'The Bank is Very Angry with You'

Written in the wake of White minority rule and a period when a novel without direct political meaning was almost unthinkable, *Thirteen Cents* comes across as strangely detached. Apartheid is never mentioned. In fact, there is very little notice of anything in the news. Current news, together with the politics of the past, seem to exist outside the novel's radar. Azure, the youthful hero, may allude to statues of men on horseback in downtown Cape Town but they are never properly identified. And only a single allusion to a contemporary political figure (Nelson Mandela) finds its way into the novel's pages. But this allusion, filtered through vulgar macho posturing, forecloses the sustained engagement readers of novels written during apartheid came to expect. As Azure walks through one of Cape Town's 'coloured' slums, Richard, his companion and later, one of his sexual predators, reads Afrikaans graffiti on the wall: *Mandela se poes* (Mandela is a pussy) (49). According to the graffiti artist, Mandela, symbol of the 'New South African' government, is effeminate, womanly, a pussy. Politics in post-apartheid society belong to women, or at least to men lacking proper fortitude. The streets, however, belong to real men with no time for the delicacies of legislative rhetoric. For beyond the violence men exact upon one another in the streets and between the sheets, little political vision can emerge. Only the present and one's ability to survive in the present matters.

But if economic decay is a symptom of government negligence, then the stagnant and often desperate state of Duiker's characters offers a pregnant political lesson about the post-apartheid state—and the mismanagement of this state by the governing ANC. The lack of political discussion in the novel is actually telling: foreclosure of direct involvement with politics suggests that many South Africans, such as the urchin hero of the novel or the graffiti artist, remain excluded from any kind of meaningful relationship with the government. Azure and other characters who inhabit *Thirteen Cents*—pimps, prostitutes and gangsters, but also less 'criminal' types, such as a homeless man who sleeps on Table Mountain and various informal labourers—live in a parallel universe, a world that may coexist on the same soil as the South African state but finds itself ignored and overlooked by it. In an odd way, then, the novel's inattention to politics reveals something meaningful about politics: a 'hands off' (*laissez-faire*) political climate produces the 'hands off' social climate of the novel.

Duiker's fiction, though not explicitly political, does however fall within what one might call an 'economic' tradition of South African literature, one that emphasises the poverty of Black agency and Black identity under financial constraints. Narrated in the first person, Azure begins his story just shy of 13 years. His age registers in the reader's mind against the novel's titular associations with money—*Thirteen Cents*. Without a safety net to break the urchin's fall, a year of existence can only be weighed against a bargain basement value. And it is precisely this 'price tag' on Black identity that harkens back to an earlier South African author: Solomon Plaatje (1836–1932). *Mhudi*, Plaatje's major contribution to South African literature, is narrated from the perspective of an early twentieth-century African man, of Tswana-Barolong descent, who is nicknamed 'Half-a-Crown.' The name represents a reduction of Black worth, a reduction that can only appear after decades of White consolidation on South African soil. After the intrusion of Boers and Britons into the interior of southern

Africa; after the resulting escalation of Black landlessness; after the transformation of African peasants into servants and slaves on European farms and later, into wage labourers on European-run mines and factories (events Plaatje's novel both anticipates and fleshes out in various narrative episodes), the identity of the African hero diminishes into an impoverished signifier: 'Half-a-Crown.' As Tim Couzens observes in his preface to the 1978 republication of the novel: 'Symbolically the new name [Half-a-Crown] reflects the advent of a new monetary economy, the new worth of the labourer: the names 'Sixpence' and 'Whiskey' were also common.' What is interesting to note here, in terms of the rising signifier of money, is that this change in African identity and worth came about not during slavery but after it, during what Marx called the emergence of a 'free labour' market. Coming out of slavery, the free labourer 'sells his very self and that by fractions.'[2] Reaffirming something of this relationship in an African literary context, Plaatje, much like Duiker, presents a hero based on the abstraction of numbers, made up of mere fractions: Half-a-Crown.

However, in mapping a Black man's place in the South African family, a major difference distinguishes Plaatje and Duiker. This difference demands some attention here (and a short detour into Plaatje's novel), because it highlights the ongoing correspondence between Black masculinity and a transforming economy. Plaatje's novel conjures the advent, out of 'tribalism,' of a Victorian 'evolutionary' ideal—which is to say Plaatje invents, for the first time in South African literature, a monogamous, patriarchal family unit divorced from an earlier, pre-colonial legacy of African sexual practice.[3] Significantly, even though the narrative is set, for the most part, in the nineteenth century, Plaatje's novel portrays a wholly modern African man and woman breaking from pre-colonial sexual mores. Over the course of Mhudi, after Ndebele (Matabele) soldiers set fire to Tswana-speaking villages, Mhudi, the titular heroine, a young Barolong woman of marriageable age, finds herself wandering alone in the desert. For the first time in her life, she is separated from her community—an experience that transforms not only her consciousness but her sexual conduct with men. Eventually, she wanders into Ra-Thaga, a young man of her own ethnic and linguistic group. Yet by moving beyond the polygamous (or 'tribal') stage of sexual development, the magnetic attraction between the pair reformulates sexual behaviour in decidedly Victorian terms.

Michel Foucault claims that Victorian sexual repression carries 'market value.'[4] Although we tend to think of sexual practice as a private matter, outside economic constraints, Foucault reads the repression of a Victorian model transposing energies in bed into energies on the job, at work, where productivity creates profit. Victorian sexual behaviour thus bleeds into the larger calculus of capitalist reproduction, becoming 'an integral part of the bourgeois order.' Under this Victorian regime: 'The minor chronicle of sex and its trials is transposed into the ceremonious history of the modes of production;

its trifling [private] aspect fades from view.'[5] Following along these lines, the symbolic movement in Plaatje's novel, out of polygamy and into a Victorian family unit, establishes not only a new phase for sexuality, but a new economic phase as well. 'My mother had to share my father's affections with two other wives,' Mhudi recalls. 'Did [the Barolong chiefs] not say that man is by nature polygamous and could never be trusted to be true to only one wife? But here is one as manly as you could wish and I have never, never seen a husband of any number of wives as happy as mine is with me alone!' (61). Ra-Thaga, her partner, 'as manly as you could wish,' lacks the polygamous sexual appetites of earlier times, of an earlier 'tribal' economy. As a consequence, Mhudi feels as if she is 'being born afresh' (43). 'Promise me,' she says to her partner in a stilted Victorian tone, 'you will not again go away and leave me. Will you?' 'Never again,' replies Ra-Thaga, adding, 'My ears shall be open to one call only—the call of your voice' (188).

Raised by Methodist missionaries and marginalised from deeper connections to traditional African political and economic structures, Plaatje's model of the perfect wife and 'manly' husband fulfils something of the repressive, Victorian destiny Foucault spells out. It is believed, rightly, that apartheid and the encroachment of European merchants and missionaries into South Africa led to a certain 'deformation of the African family'; yet Plaatje's absorption in Christian principles also helped construct a vision of the nuclear family as a model of sustainability—paradoxically, a model many African church members champion as 'authentically' African today, regardless of missionary intervention.[6] Perhaps the polygamous male and the earlier brand of 'excessive' masculinity could no longer be maintained within the global market imposed by Victorian Britain. According the rhetoric of Plaatje's novel in order to weather the economic storms of modernity, the African family needed to be broken down into a smaller, more sustainable unit—the nuclear family arising by the novel's end. However, later generations cannot withstand the pressure of profits, as the family structure is inevitably reduced to a lonely 'Half-a-Crown.'

Duiker's novel, written nearly eight decades later, ventures even further: it presents the violent dissolution of the African family under economic duress. Duiker presents his hero not as one half of an idealised couple, much less part of a communitarian group, but as a profoundly atomised wanderer—a loner, an urchin unattached to any single mate or traditional patterns. Perhaps for this reason, his story remains utterly deaf to Victorian pieties.

At the opening of *Thirteen Cents*, the African family implodes. Azure—who seems, at once, naïve, intelligent and fragile—tells the reader about the death of his parents in short order: 'Papa was bad with money and got Mama in trouble. The day they killed them I was away at school. I came back to our shack only to find a pool of blood. That was three years ago. That was the last time I went to school' (2). Although the reader can never be entirely certain who 'they' are (i.e., the murderers of his parents), if the rest of Azure's narrative provides any indication, his parents have been done in because of criminal links—links established because no other jobs were available. In this novel of the 'New South Africa,' because legitimate professional opportunities appear appallingly slim, life often appears worth less than a clip of bills, a collection of cents. If you are poor and 'bad with money' you do not stand much chance of survival—much less a chance to determine your own sexual conduct.

From the very beginning, the reader enters a parallel universe, a criminal underworld that tourists visiting the beautiful spots of Cape Town rarely encounter. Initially, though he is only thirteen (and therefore especially vulnerable in this environment), Azure forges a buffer between himself and the cruelty of the town. 'I am alone,' he confesses. And like Robinson Crusoe, he establishes solitary routines on a beach.

> The streets of Sea Point [a beach strip just beyond downtown Cape Town] are my home... I walk a lot. My feet are tough and rough underneath. But I'm clean. Every morning I take a bath at the beach. I wash with seawater. Sometimes I use a sponge or if I can't find one I use an old rag. It's just as good. Then I rinse off the seawater at the tap. It's not that bad washing with cold water. It's like anything—you can get used to it (1–2).

Ironically, despite the hero's proximity to the hub of an international capital (Cape Town), he lives according to a primitive economy, sleeping and bathing outdoors.

Once Azure figures out how he can make money near the beach (by sleeping with men), he begins to make contacts with various people who, if all works out, can help him multiply his earnings and eventually, move beyond this primitive state. In essence, the people he meets on the streets become his new family, or, put another way, he makes up for his lack of family (who have been murdered) by inventing one on the street. Joyce, a woman 'who only works nights' becomes a mother figure. Allen, a dangerous pimp, becomes his father. This arrangement provides a simulacrum, however unsettling and a parody of a normal family.

But Azure clings to this irregular 'family' because, beyond it, lies a social abyss. Hospitals, clubs, churches, organised sports, unions—all seem completely beyond the urchin's grasp. In essence, South Africa's civil society appears indifferent to Azure's development and apparently out of reach. Even the police, who hover menacingly at the margins of the novel, never enter the hero's life in any meaningful way. Although Azure never seeks protection from the 'New South African' state, the state never intervenes. Disregard appears mutual—an indication, however implicit, of a 'hands off' economy at work. Thus, in a certain sense, one type of oppression replaces another. For if apartheid, with its draconian pass laws, seemed oppressively 'hands on,' then the protagonist of *Thirteen Cents* faces a world that seems oppressively 'hands off.' The helping hand of the state is nowhere to be found.

Living on the streets in Cape Town, on the beaches and under bridges, at the margins of a highly privatised, gated environment, one thing alone connects the parallel universe, the world of prostitutes and pimps and urchins, to the official, bourgeois universe of the state: money. As Azure says of Allen, the local pimp: 'Money is his language. It's the only thing he remembers, everything else is unimportant' (16). Because real teachers and fathers have been replaced by stand-ins, the pimp becomes Azure's principal instructor: 'I've learned something from Allen and this is money is everything' (16). But, ultimately, Azure fails to learn enough. At one point in the novel, after prostituting himself near the beach, he loses his profits to parental predators. Not only does Allen, the pimp, steal from him, ripping off his newly bought sneakers, so does his surrogate mother, Joyce. The closest thing to a 'Mother Africa' figure in *Thirteen Cents*, Joyce functions as Azure's bank: 'Joyce understands banks and how they work,' Azure claims (11). Trusting her powers, he hands Joyce money he has earned turning 'tricks' with men. But here, as on so many levels, the official world of government and financial institutions is replayed through a parodistic criminal lens. The young hero remarks: 'Joyce said you can only take out your money [from the bank] on special days, not on weekends and you must give them a reason why you need the money, *exactly like gangsters work*' (21; emphasis added). Told from the perspective of a child, the underworld and the official designs of the bank appear of a kind. Sadly for Azure, who possesses no adequate defence against the predatory instincts of his 'mother' prostitute, he is no match for the bank and the requirements of brick-and-mortar institutions.

> Me, I have forgotten even how to hold a pen, so how can I go to the bank myself? Grown-ups ask many questions there. You must remember when you were born and exactly how old you are. You must have an address and it must be one that doesn't keep changing. Like you must stay in the same spot for say maybe five years and when you move you must tell the bank. They must know everything about your movements (21).

The bank's cautious pattern of surveillance is only activated, however, if one chooses to belong to the official universe of the status quo; otherwise, the 'bank' of the seedy underworld, run by his 'mother' will take over. One slips without much notice from an official economy into an unofficial one; money rules both spheres. In these ways, the underworld not only mocks the official, proper, bourgeois world above, it also takes over when the other fails. Yet both parts of the bifurcated economy, the underworld and the world above, are susceptible to shake-ups and periodic implosions. For if banks crash and suddenly require government intervention, so too can the fragile economic support for the urchin shatter. As Azure finds out, Joyce, his unofficial 'bank' has been defaulting on him. Returning to her apartment for the money he has given her to hold, she balks:

> 'I need my money,' I tell her.
> 'What do you need it for? I give you food, don't I?'
> 'But I need it. I'm in trouble.'
> 'Get out,' she says, 'you have caused me nothing but trouble. The bank is very angry with you' (76).

What had seemed a gift (Joyce's food offerings) is now understood, at least by Joyce, as a source of payment; and what we assume to be impersonal (a bank) now takes on an increasingly personal tone: 'The bank is very angry with you.' Perhaps this is the most important difference between the official economy and the informal one: the latter is more personal and angry with the urchin and hostile to his grievances.

Azure is stripped of everything. Yet, amazingly, he finds solace in the lovely sound of his given name and in his unusual appearance. 'Ah-zoo-ray,' he effuses, rolling his tongue, again and again, over the three lovely syllables. Duiker appears to make a subtle play here on the adolescent sexuality of another novel: *Lolita*. Just as Humbert lingers over the three-syllable name of a prepubescent girl ('Lolita, light of my life, fire of my loins. My sin, my soul. Lo-lee-ta: the tip of the tongue taking a trip of three steps down the palate to tap, at the three, on the teeth. Lo Lee Ta,'[7] Azure elevates the only 'thing' he truly possesses—his skin and name—with a modicum of this same passion:

> My name is Azure. Ah-zoo-ray. That's how you say it. My [real] mother gave me that name. It's the only thing I have left from her. I have blue eyes and a dark skin. I'm used to people staring at me, mostly grown-ups. When I was at school children used to beat me up because I had blue eyes ... (1).

Only by remembering the singular gifts of his mother can the narrator emphasise ownership over identity, even if he is continually beaten up because of his hybrid racial appearance. Everything else is stolen from him, leaked into the parasitical cash nexus. Abandoned by his adopted family, he begins a dizzying decline in the Cape Town streets.

'Getting to Know Your Own Shadow'

Who was K. Sello Duiker? What kind of social environment did he emerge from? And perhaps more importantly: how can we situate his brand of masculinity within a more recent South African literary tradition, one that moves beyond the Victorian pieties originally expressed by Solomon Plaatje?

Born in Soweto in 1975, Duiker grew up against the backdrop of the Soweto Uprising of 1976; in essence, in a deeply charged political atmosphere, one in which a militant vision of Black masculinity usually reigned. In novels such as Sipho Sepamla's *A Ride on the Whirlwind: A Novel of Soweto*, Black masculinity takes on heroic—and generically heterosexual—idealisation. During this high period of struggle against apartheid, in the fictional construction of Black masculine identity, politics was never far away. The leading man of the age, Nelson Mandela, appears not as some distant, alien figure (as he does in *Thirteen Cents*), but centre stage. In Sepamla's novel, for example, newspaper clippings about Mandela are peppered next to descriptions of potent Black men tortured by White police officers. Immediately after a description of an interrogation scene, Sepamla's narrative offers, in almost haiku form, the following brief: 'News Item / Mandela Becomes Black Pimpernel / Reported Seen in Dobsonville / No Comment Says Police Spokesman' (183). The integration of news blotter connects the fictionalised interrogation on the ground, in the narrative proper, with a greater and previously indifferent, canvas of history. A 'whirlwind' of events may blow through the township, but the men living there also help orchestrate the storm. In order for Sepamla's 'whirlwind' to blow, masculine militancy (of a sort wholly absent in Duiker's) must come to life. Although women may add an important component to the anti-apartheid struggle and though many appear hardened and disciplined in Sepamla's pages, they are sometimes portrayed as victims of the perverse sexual calculus of apartheid, in need of militant Black men to rescue them. In one disturbingly eroticised scene, an African schoolgirl is beaten to a pulp and apparently raped by White cops: 'Nkele's hands were being held behind her back, her breasts bare, dangling like over-ripe fruit, for she was a freedom child in the modern sense.' A hopeless 'freedom child' facing the masochistic punishment of the state, she calls out for one of her male comrades: 'But with bony white hands holding hers in a vice was immobilised and could only cry out for all the gods to hear, for all the right-thinking persons inside the police headquarters to hear and have her pain pierce their hearts' (182). Much like a 'Hottentot' woman burned by a Boer woman with a blazing iron in *Mhudi*, Plaatje's nineteenth-century novel, the act of White torture upon a Black woman fosters a desire, however implicit, for upright male leadership—for African chivalry, for heroes like Nelson Mandela and his grass roots lieutenants and in Plaatje's case, for Ra-Thaga, the idealised Victorian husband.

But Duiker's *Thirteen Cents*, produced well after the rise of Black militancy depicted in Sepamla's *A Ride on the Whirlwind*, highlights sexual encounters across colour lines that would have seemed wholly out of place in apartheid literature. Although a number of White women are depicted as prostitutes in Duiker's novel, their principle pimp Allen is Black. Despite the fact that certain characters, such as Gerald, a gangster, wish to be White ('He thinks he's white because he's got straight hair and a light skin'), a sea change in racial dynamics appears in the works (5). Although nagging racial inequities still obviously persist in South Africa, the multiracial nature of the post-apartheid settlement appears to have significantly tweaked the calculus of sexual behaviour.

How does Duiker's own background fit into this new socio-sexual arrangement? According to Bafana Kumalo, Duiker grew up middle-class, with Roman Catholic origins.[8] Sabine Cessou notes that 'Duiker's life was marked by various identity crises, seen for instance in the very name Duiker itself, a common coloured name adopted by his Black grandfather in order to render himself more employable.'[9] Although it seems impossible to measure the effect of this opportunistic 'identity' scheme on our writer's identity, by young adulthood, we do know that Duiker left greater Johannesburg for Rhodes University in Grahamstown, where he studied journalism. After his time at Rhodes, Duiker moved to Cape Town, the setting for all of his fiction. After *Thirteen Cents*, his second novel, *The Quiet Violence of Dreams*, won the Herman Charles Bosman Prize. Then suddenly in 2005, at the age of 30, after a nervous breakdown, Duiker apparently committed suicide. A literary career already graced with awards, hailed by veteran South African luminaries such as Lewis Nkosi and Zakes Mda had abruptly ended.

There is some speculation that Duiker had been a male prostitute. Whether true or not, the role of the prostitute features prominently in both of his novels. Perhaps this devaluation of love and the pitfalls of prostitution led to Duiker's suicide; one can only speculate. But many prostitutes never kill themselves. Indeed, as passages from Duiker's *Quiet Violence* indicate, despite the degrading condition of prostitution, one can still find pleasure in it—at least with men. In *Quiet Violence*, as I indicated in the opening, the hero's desire for men outweighs his desire for women. As Cheryl Stobie notes, the prostitute's 'sex with men is seen as transcendental'; sex with women on the other hand, appears 'ridiculous.'[10]

Tshepo, the main character of the second novel, is openly gay. As a consequence, he seems to have sex with women simply for sport and of course, for money. Heterosexual sex is for him, oddly spiritless. 'There is something comical about watching a woman having sex,' he remarks:

[Women] let go so completely. Really, it makes me want to laugh. I have to hold myself back as I watch [a woman's] face twisted in comical expressions, moaning about things that only she knows about. I thrust quicker and deeper into her. Her expression becomes too much. I have to hide my laugh by pretending to moan harder (333).

Despite the intense physical proximity, Tsepho seeks no intimacy with women. Heterosexual engagement fosters an almost comically out-of-body experience. A woman's 'moaning about things that only she knows about' is reciprocated with play acting, 'pretending to moan harder.' But because Tshepo must sleep with women to get by, he pretends to enjoy it.

Yet Tshepo (or Angelo as he comes to be known at the brothel) clearly relishes sex with male customers. Pleasure may come at a price, but because he seems to enjoy the experience anyway, payment is the icing on the cake. In a poetic turn, he calls gay sex 'getting to know your own shadow.' After telling us about the banality of sex with women, Tshepo sings 'a long paean of praise to homoerotic desire'[11]:

> To explore a man's body? It is like getting to know your own shadow intimately.
> It is like being a child again. It is like playing with fire safely and not getting burned...
> To love a man is not like loving a woman.
> To love a man, to feel his strength? It is like a road whose twists and bends you know well.
> It is like knowing all the answers to all the questions in an exam.
> It is like being passed before being tested. It is like being in a foreign country but speaking their language.
> It is like being welcomed to carnival.
> It is like singing alone and hearing your echo...
> To know a man? It is like serenading yourself and all men.
> It is like having the choice of all the delicious forbidden fruit in a garden.
> It is like hearing butterflies sing . . .
> It is like having your cake and eating it, scraping the depths of desire and satisfaction . . .
> Oh, the infinite beauty of a man and his penis
> (334–335).

In this elaborate, almost Whitmanesque ode to 'the infinite beauty of a man and his penis,' gay coupling appears to offer a wealth of adventure ('like being in a foreign country'), yet without any of the dangers or surprises of an adventure (like speaking a foreign language). Indeed, contradictions appear flattened, in a peculiar way, by the gay experience. You sing alone but you hear your own echo. You are served 'delicious forbidden fruit' but with no punishment meted out. 'It is like playing with fire and not getting burned,' we are told. The prostitute of *Quiet Violence* may entertain both men and women, but he obviously prefers 'getting to know your own shadow.'

In *Thirteen Cents*, however, a methodical variety of sexual attraction, lacking any poetic value, takes shape. As I have suggested, Azure cultivates fantasises about women to make the attraction work; which is to say, he projects an attraction for women upon homosexual circumstances. In an early scene, after meeting a 'John' on the beach, Azure is asked by to produce an erection in the man's apartment. 'I have to concentrate hard to get excited,' Azure reveals. 'I think of Toni Braxton and Mary J. Blige,' attractive American pop singers. 'They usually do the trick for me' (9). Concentrating on the image of sexy singers, he finally produces the desired result for the customer. Fantasies of women help facilitate his erection and ultimately, the sexual act between man and boy (Azure has just turned thirteen). Later, after going the first instance of copulation, the 'John' lies on top of Azure and grinds into the boy's hips. 'Why aren't you getting an erection?' the John asks. Once again: 'I think of Toni Braxton and my dick rises.' 'That's better,' the John says and the two have anal sex (91). As if flicking on a switch, sexual orientation becomes weirdly arbitrary. Although, clearly, homosexual desire is dramatised with power in Duiker's *Quiet Violence*, here it merely seems invented for the moment, a game played for money. 'I know how to please a man,' Azure reveals. 'I know these bastards. I've done this a thousand times. They all like it if you play with the part between their balls and asshole' (84). However, this performance is methodical, purged of desire or deep feeling: 'I never ask them how [it] feels' (84).

Fantasies are, of course, not always an accurate barometer for measuring sexual orientation. But *Thirteen Cents* makes Azure's inclinations strikingly overt. Indeed, while wandering Table Mountain, the protagonist genuinely seems confused by the idea of a homosexual's free will. Why would a man willingly sleep with another?

Azure meets a homeless man, white and middle-aged, living in a cave on the mountain. Because the man chooses to be gay (*moffie*, in the local Afrikaans slang), Azure is incredulous. However, as we will notice in this exchange, the gay man is equally incredulous about gay prostitution:

'I didn't think you were a moffie,' [Azure] say[s].
'Whatever,' [the homeless man] says.
'I work with them.'
'What do you mean, you work with them?'
I pat my dick.
'Oh I see, that sort of thing. Well, I'm not into that' (116).

The gay man's admission ('Well, I'm not into that') would seem, out of context, a renunciation of homosexuality. However, he is simply renouncing the degradation of gay prostitution, that is, making money for something he considers sublime. For Azure, on the other hand, 'getting to know your own shadow' is configured around seemingly artificial desires—around manu-factured images of pop stars, generated by memory. Sex is essentially rendered a business transaction.

' Economic Homosexuality' on the Gold Mines?

Is it possible then, to discuss a legacy of 'economic homosexuality' in South Africa? As I have stressed, I use the phrase with tremendous trepidation. For what determines sexual orientation is never so easily decided. Which is to say, economics can never stand alone; money problems may forever fail to over-determine a person's intimate sexual proclivities. Although, in our discussion of *Thirteen Cents* so far, I have suggested that economic factors help guide and motivate sexual behaviour, clearly many issues—biological factors, social pressures, something as ordinary as boredom or curiosity—can orient sexual preference. Nevertheless, what I hope to have underscored—and will continue to develop in this short section—is a powerful and oddly arbitrary economic dimension undergirding sexual orientation in South Africa. The rise of European capitalism, globalisation and apartheid may, on the surface, appear to have fostered this type of economic model for sexual behaviour. But there is convincing evidence, at least outside South Africa, to support the idea that pre-colonial African societies were deeply invested in homosexual practice far in advance of European intrusion. In *African Intimacies*, Neville Hoad draws our attention to a case, in 1886, when the 'last indigenous ruler of Buganda execute[d] over thirty pages at his royal court, apparently for refusing to have sex with him following their recent conversion to Christianity' (ix). Hoad's research turns the idea that 'homosex is not black culture' on its head. Indeed, it suggests that, in certain cases, colonial heterosexuality warred with pre-colonial homosexuality. In fact, as Hoad speculates, the sexual orientation of the Buganda ruler may have become yet another 'moral' rationale for empire-building on the continent. Whatever the case, the anecdote about the Bugandan king clearly shows that the origins of homosexuality can never be portrayed as definitively European or African. The idea of settled heterosexual African origins is in my view farcical. For the anecdote of the king of Buganda suggests something else as well: sexual behaviour is always related, at least in some capacity, to greater economic concerns. The feudal African court saw itself threatened by a foreign cultural economy. Faced with the encroachment of capitalism and the reformed sexual behaviour of Christians, the king struck back, killing his newly reformed pages—in his mind, desecrated black men who would no longer sleep with him.

Changing gears in this section, I try to unpack a different kind of historical precedent for black homosexuality. South Africa's gold and diamond mining industries have long been associated with sexual metaphors. In fact, it is possible to sketch a crude paradigm shift, forged during the development of the mining industry, between alternating forms of sexual penetration. If, as I will suggest in a moment, penetration became 'gay' in character under apartheid, then this penetration was once generally considered 'straight.' During the

'Scramble for Africa,' H. Rider Haggard's *King Solomon's Mines* (1885) dramatises the conquest of mineral wealth in the region in distinctly heterosexual terms— that is, as the rape of 'Mother Africa,' the violation of the subcontinent's virginal body by randy European adventurers. In the middle of Haggard's novel, a diamond 'treasure map upside down shows [the] breasts, navel and pudendum' of a naked, unspoiled woman awaiting penetration by foreign men.[12] Mounting the intimate and forbidden spaces of the southern African interior—for profit, for diamonds—allegorises masculine imperial conquest over a feminised African body. Thus a striking 'economics of sexuality' develops out of Haggard's imaginary act of heterosexual coitus. Yet as I will suggest in this section, by the twentieth century, due to the strict division not only of labour but of gender under capitalist mining production, a homosexual model began to reign. Black men working in South Africa's gold mines appear to have performed homosexual acts they may not have performed otherwise—back at home, under a different economy. Homosexual activity simply fit the constraints of the economic model.

If any situation can be said to be 'over-determined,' motivated by a kind of economic totalitarianism, the goldmines fit the bill.

> It has long been argued by sociologists that the compound system [constructed by the architects of the gold and diamond industries in South Africa is] one of the most effective forms of labor control ever invented... [B]lack miners are locked into a total system in which they are little more than puppets of management. Every possibility for effective resistance has been systematically removed, leaving workers exposed to the self-formative effects of a veritable panopticon, a total institution controlling not only their productive but also their personal experiences at the mine.[13]

Thus if economic determinacy can be illustrated anywhere, it was here— under apartheid, digging for the gold that made the White man rich. Arriving out of economic need or simply dragooned from 'homelands' and neighbouring African countries; separated from women, children and community; compounded with other men, many previously strangers and from differing ethnic and linguistic groups, in crowded dormitory quarters on the squalid Witwatersrand; stripped naked before White bosses and fellow workers and monitored by draconian pass laws; forced to work long hours in the dangerous bowels of the mines—the migrant workers of South Africa became part of a system that divorced itself, in breathtaking ways, from older continuities in southern African society. Here men met other men in an entirely new way.

What needs highlighting, above all, is the fact that gold mining was an all-male affair. T. Dunbar Moodie's study, *Going for Gold*, underscores a heightened sense of 'masculine self-formation' in the compounds (17). Yet, interestingly, despite the excessive macho posturing we might expect in this type of environment, a new eroticism of male bonding and role playing came into play. For in the emerging construction of masculinity, in a work site bereft of women, homosexual behaviour often mimicked traditional elements of heterosexual coupling. A fascinating split between male 'wives' and male 'husbands' took hold in the compounds, an arbitrary construction of sexual orientation not entirely unlike what we find in the prostitution episodes in Duiker's novel.

Moodie's book introduces a Tsonga-speaking Shangaan worker named Philemon. Philemon tells an interviewer (Vivienne Ndatshe) that, because women were not available in the compounds of the mines, senior workers made love to mine 'boys.' Role playing games soon became routine and sustained: '[The 'husband'] would 'double his join' [i.e., stay twelve months instead of the normal six] on the mines because of this boy. He would 'make love' with him . . . penetrate his manhood between the boy's thighs' (Moodie, 1994, 121).[14] Male 'wives' were expected to 'look feminine,' Philemon recalls. 'They would [buy] pieces of [cloth] and they would sew [them] together so that [they looked] like real breasts. They would then attach . . . strings that made it look almost like a bra so that at the evening dancing 'she' would dance with the 'husband.' (127). In Moodie's account, this role playing game eventually absorbed the most ordinary forms of economic practice. According to Moodie's informant, 'young men of the miners were not merely sexual partners but were also 'wives' in other ways, providing domestic services for their 'husbands' in exchange for remuneration' (121). Despite the staggeringly autocratic condition of the mines, various men were able, through homosexual behaviour, to negotiate something of an economic division of labour common to many traditional African households. It is the qualified construction of agency that we might call 'dominance without hegemony': although many of the men may not have engaged in sexual activity with other men had they not been compounded, this activity also opened up a necessary space for 'play,' for willed domestic routines that established a modicum of independence within a nearly total disciplinary system of work.

Historians of South Africa, even progressive historians, have generally treated this rise of homosexuality in the mines with a scandalised air. For example, in his introduction to the *Selected Short Stories of R. R. R. Dhlomo*, Tim Couzens refers to such couplings as 'perversions,' behaviour equal to 'bestiality' (3). Even within the Black dormitory culture itself, there seems to have been a moralistic 'don't ask, don't tell' policy in place. As one informant claimed about gay love trysts: 'What is public knowledge is that it goes on. [Yet] the culprits keep it scrupulously discreet . . . It [only] comes into the open . . . when disaffection sets in. But we all know it takes place.'[15]

But why should a response to gay coupling, even under trying circumstances, be so judgemental? The totalitarian atmosphere of the mining culture may have forced workers under strict domination; yet, as we have seen in this division between male 'wives' and male 'husbands,' it never fostered complete hegemony. Homosexual role playing in the compounds can be understood, in my view, as a symbolic re-enactment of free relationships in an un-free context. Remember: one of the reasons men slept with other men had to do with the fact that, for six months or more at a time, there were no women around. Although women arrived in the mining centres and townships to perform domestic and informal labour, including prostitution; and though women began to open *shebeens*, illegal houses of liquor, the apartheid mining system sustained, at its core, a highly masculinised work environment. Certainly, as the 'fake breasts' example above attests, men engaged in role playing and role reversal games with some degree of playful autonomy. However, we should never construe these reactions too romantically. As Philemon noted: 'There was no other way... One could hardly escape [gay sexual engagement]. If somebody wanted you, he would hardly give up. I mean, he would go so far as sending people to come and propose to you on his behalf—until you agreed.'[16] Therefore, within the 'free' space of role playing (which some might interpret according to the senior–junior relationships in a Greek gymnasium), un-free sexual relationships often developed as well. Ironically, as many might expect, practices of domination existed within the dominated group.

Although this sketch of gay unions in the gold mines remains just that (a sketch), I believe it helps contextualise a larger blueprint of 'economic homosexuality' in South African history. As Achille Mbembe and Sarah Nuttall recently observed: 'Beneath the visible landscape' of gold mining and a South African city built on gold (Johannesburg) lie cultures beyond 'orders of visibility.'[17] Much like the culture of the dark, underground mine itself, homosexuality represents one of these more or less 'invisible' orders. The discussion of gay coupling in the compounds, provided by informants, usefully draws our attention to one of these 'invisible' orders. But so does Duiker's novel. Although set in Cape Town, away from the compound system and the profits forged by gold, the blueprint for sexuality remains just the same—off the official radar screen, beyond the care of the state; indeed, ostracised by the party in power— the ANC. In apartheid's gold mines and in Azure's adventurous hustling, a firm sense of gay identity—which is to say, identifying who is gay and who is not— can never be entirely gauged outside economic forces. Moreover, as Duiker's drama suggests, the play acting of 'economic homosexuality' did not end with *apartheid*.

Conclusion

What particularly interests me then, is the fact that even after apartheid, a model of 'economic homosexuality,' somewhat oppressive in nature, can still reign. But let me be very clear: homosexuality should never be considered on its own an oppressive practice. As Duiker's *Quiet Violence* suggests, African men can often be transformed and elevated by having sex with other men, provided that the sex is conducted safely and voluntarily. *Quiet Violence* makes this liberation palpably poetic. In the spirit of the post-apartheid settlement, we should celebrate this freedom, as well as defend gay rights and marriage. Why should one type of oppression be replaced by another? However, my larger argument is that sexual orientation seems in many ways, no less economically determined now, in South Africa's neo-liberal economic climate than it was under apartheid.

Evidence? Perhaps we should return one last time to *Thirteen Cents*. As Azure sinks deeper and deeper below the surface of society, below the absent safety net of a neo-liberal economic system, his story becomes increasingly nightmarish. Tossed from gangster to gangster like a rag doll, he is eventually beaten, gang-raped and sodomised by a stranger named Richard and his friends: 'I do as I'm told. [Richard] stands there and starts rocking his pelvis. My jaws get tired. I take his dick out of my mouth and wank him... The door opens. "Hey, what's going on in here. I want to join the party," one of [Richard's friends] says and laughs. Richard smiles as the other unzips his fly' (53–54). What we find here is a thirteen-year-old boy oppressed not by homosexual practice per se, but by his depressed economic circumstances. An urchin that happened to be a girl might have experienced similar horrors. Both examples of rape should be equally condemned.

Earlier, we find Richard reading graffiti on a wall with a macho swagger, as if he were looking for girls, for 'pussy.' Here however, we find him forcing Azure into the depths of slavery. Without a family, community or sympathetic government to help the hero, an oppressive sexual economy digs in. After the assault, the hero wanders the streets of Cape Town in a daze, trying to put his life and body back together. In need of physical and emotional rescue, he recognises from his experience, that South Africa's institutions remain virtually impenetrable to people of his stature. 'No one's going to help you in Cape Town,' he has been told. 'You must do everything yourself' (98). Because he also knows that gang members hover the streets like vultures, he decides to hike up Table Mountain, the great natural wonder rising high above the city. He sets up camp and towards the end of the novel, the story appears to have set economic development back to the beginning of time, to an economy of primitive accumulation. Making fires and living in the most rudimentary fashion imaginable, above the thrum of city life below, Azure appears to have shed every possible connection with the modern world and global economy. Hungry and dizzy, he begins to suffer from hallucinations: 'Every night I make a big fire in the cave. I burn all sorts of things, mostly arms and legs and lots of monsters' (126).

Set in this earlier framework, making fires and eating lizards, it seems symbolic that in the world below, looking down from Table Mountain, Azure can still see the glimmering lights of the city—emblems of capitalist modernity. If apartheid means 'apart-ness' in Afrikaans, here too ironically, even after White minority rule has been lifted, a tremendous chasm between the 'haves' and the 'have-nots' of economic production remains.

In the last scene, Azure's body is increasingly withered atop Table Mountain. The loss of his family—his real family—becomes, at this point in his suffering, an ever-present mantra: 'My mother is dead. My father is dead, I repeat again.' Apparently, he will soon join them, for his hunger provokes increasingly wild visions:

I put my fingers in my ears and close my eyes tight. The mountain shakes and the wind tears through everything. Insects scorch while the fire rains. Lizards crawl under the rock with me. They jump everywhere on me with fright . . . Soon the whole mountain feels like an oven. I lie there and sweat with fear. When I open my eyes briefly I see hooves, claws and feet running in every direction. A hellish explosion comes from the sky . . . I know what fear is (163).

As I have suggested in this essay, there is little explicit critique of post-apartheid politics in *Thirteen Cents*. And yet the urchin's final 'fear,' the hunger-fuelled visions he endures with no help in sight, speaks volumes about a society with little protection for its most vulnerable. Azure will remain homeless on two counts, without anyone to raise him and without a government to catch his fall. Faced with this type of social Darwinism, it seems significant that by the end of the novel he enters a world of animal hallucinations. It also seems essential to read this type of descent and the arbitrary sexual relations that go along with it as part of a more general economy—lifted as Foucault would say, from the 'trifling aspects' of bedroom manoeuvres. If sex indeed has 'market value' the new economy of South Africa will be certain to exploit it.

18. The Ambivalence of Masculinity in Gorgui Dieng's *A Leap Out of the Dark*

Daouda Loum

In this chapter I will demonstrate that masculinity cannot be dissociated from femininity, for one cannot exist without the other. In *A Leap Out of the Dark*, masculinity is explored in the light of such paradigms as sex and gender and within the spheres of tradition and modernity. Close reading reveals that when masculinity is related to sex, it embodies biological characteristics common to all men (e.g., phallus, physical appearance, virility, generative power). Conversely, when the term pertains to man's social status, sex-attributed roles, behaviour and personal qualities, it is the by-product of gender construction from a masculine perspective, in the interaction between man and woman, in the family, social, cultural, economic and psychological fields. That is why, in *A Leap Out of the Dark*, masculinity suggests a plethora of images because its gendered fabrication does not escape the evolution of Senegalese society from tradition to modernity. An example is that fatherhood or endurance, which is narrowly associated with masculinity, is now and then interpreted differently in the country and in the city.

Introduction

The author's first work of fiction, *A Leap Out of the Dark*, is the first novel ever written in English by a Senegalese scholar. Therein lies the interest of the novel. Innovative and challenging insofar as it uses a medium different from French in a francophone environment, the novel is a major contribution to the literary canon of African literature in general and Senegalese literature in particular.

There are two important reasons relevant to the choice of English as the main vehicle of communication: one is didactic; the other is pragmatic. In fact, as a teacher, Dieng aims to demonstrate that he has a good command of English, which he shows through the correctness of the language and the clarity and concision of his style. He is also conscious that as the most widely spoken language worldwide, only English can permit him to reach a larger readership and hence, make a reputation for himself.

Compared to the European colonial novel, which mainly focuses on themes, *A Leap Out of the Dark* is a real breakthrough in terms of form. It stands as a continuation of the typically African novel, one of the chief characteristics of which is to break from the European literary conventions from which it developed.

The originality of the novel resides in the fact that, like Ahmadou Kourouma's *The Suns of Independence* (1968), it draws its narrative discourse from an African oral tradition that is reputed not to have any boundaries between literary genres. Hence, the strong presence in the novel of a constant blending of English with expressive Wolof words, praise songs, tales, allegorical accounts, references to the elders' wisdom and especially, proverbs, including adages, aphorisms and apophthegms.

This stylistic feature is interesting because it testifies that the African novel mirrors the deep and tight interpenetration between African and European cultures. Therefore, correct deciphering of the text requires that the reader understand Senegalese culture. At this level, it is critical, before going any further, to clarify that culture is interchangeable with civilisation, as Edward B. Taylor remarked: 'that complex whole which includes knowledge, belief, art, morals, law, custom and any other capabilities and habits acquired by man as a member of society.'[1]

In addition, *A Leap Out of the Dark* encompasses many subtypes because it embraces a broad range of subject matter. For example, it meets the definition of a social novel because it brings to the fore some of the most acute daily problems that constitute obstacles to the development of African countries. For instance, the novel is deeply concerned with elements of everyday life, e.g., marriage, bleaching, endless money-consuming family ceremonies, polygamy, poverty and the hardships of rural life.

Next, *A Leap Out of the Dark* takes the shape of an autobiography in the sense that it is a narrative in which memory, introspection and imagination flow together and present remarkable insight into the writer's personality, attitudes, impressions and convictions. Indeed, for African novelists, childhood is a cultural melting pot that no subsequent experience can totally obscure. Ngeech, where an important part of the action takes place, is the author's native village. Through Moodu, the protagonist, the narrator—who is the writer himself—nostalgically relates his early childhood years. He presents a particularly heart-stirring account of his life as a school boy, insisting on his sufferings as preparation for an accomplished manhood.

Finally, *A Leap Out of the Dark* can be read through the lens of postmodernist theory. The author, for whom all art is propaganda, concentrates on sexual politics, using a deconstructive procedure to interpret such interrelated, though different, concepts as gender, sex and culture, out of which a great deal of literature has been produced since the emergence of the feminist movement.

Accordingly, like Nigerian novelist Buchi Emecheta, who might have influenced him, Dieng seeks to point out the contradictions, within different cultures, between masculinist and feminist assumptions in order to display their relativity.

This chapter attempts to demonstrate that masculinity defies one unique definition because it hides a plurality of representations. However, for convenience sake, it is necessary to clarify that 'masculinity,' which bears overtones of sex and gender, refers here to the physical and abstract qualities of being masculine. Thus, 'masculinity' must be examined across biological, historical, geographical, economic, cultural and religious determinants. That is why, in A Leap Out of the Dark, the novelist, who is both a conservative and a reformer, contrasts two images of masculinity in rural and urban Africa. As will be noted, his ultimate purpose is to demonstrate that the similarities and differences between the two pictures are fashioned by culture and consequently, the need to contextualise and reformulate gender roles in Africa.

Definitions of Masculinity

There is almost unanimous agreement that if sex is biological—and thus innate, natural and static—gender is a social and cultural fabrication that occurs through a lengthy dynamic process. Myra Jehlen notes the opposition between sex and gender, asserting that 'from the perspective of gender, identity is a role, character traits are not autonomous qualities but functions and ways of relating. Actions define actors rather than vice versa. Connecting history and not nature, gender is not a category of human nature.'[2]

This position is shared by early American constructivists such as Julie Rivkin and Michael Ryan, e.g., Adrienne Rich, Kate Millet and Germaine Greer, by French feminists from the mid-1980s, such as Julia Kristeva, Luce Irigary and Hélène Cioux and by African-American feminists such as Barbara Smith, Mary Washington and bell hooks, who derive their inspiration from theories of Marxism and post-structuralism and for whom masculinity as gender identification is a construction of civilisation. Most importantly, they lose no time in pointing out that what is unfair about the latter is that it is a male construction which, although favouring male domination and interests, assigns so-called 'appropriate' identities or roles to men and women. The result is the clear-cut division in patriarchal or androcratic societies between masculinity and femininity.

From this perspective, boyhood, manhood and fatherhood are components of masculinity, just as girlhood, womanhood and motherhood are vital constituents of femininity and these images permeate A Leap Out of the Dark.

In the wake of the constructivists, Elsa Jones argues:

Whether we are women or men, all the selves we are and could be are organized and sometimes constrained and warped, by the various layers of the culture in which we live. For most of us, this culture is one which construes difference as an indication that one must be right, or superior and the other wrong, bad or inferior, so that those who find themselves in positions of influence, choice and attributed power often use these to exploit, ignore, diminish and control others.[3]

In contrast, essentialists such as Rivkin and Ryan think of gender as the natural differences between man and woman. They find support in biological, linguistic and psychological factors to opine that womanhood, for example, refers to the specificities that make a woman a woman: the vagina, the womb, ovulation, the breasts, maternity, menstruation, lactation and all reproductive organs. As for masculinity, it evokes first and foremost the penis, erection, coitus, sperm and procreative power. That is why, in *A Leap Out of the Dark*, right at the start of the narrative, Faatu defines herself as a woman and Moodu, her husband, as a man born with male genitals. Obviously, each of these characteristics implies duties, social expectations and suitable behaviour.

Though apparently antagonistic, the viewpoints constitute the two sides of the same coin. One has no precedence over the other and they corroborate the naked truth that masculinity and femininity have their essence in sex first and then in gender, the latter being minutely tailored in such a way that it perfectly fits he or she who holds the power or takes the initiative.

This is why masculinity brings to mind a plethora of images diametrically opposed to that of being female. The term alludes to a set of gendered ideas, speeches, codes, etiquettes and qualities, as well as duties traditionally ascribed to man. Like the concepts of race, nationality or culture, masculinity does not come from a vacuum. It develops in the individual from his or her earliest years within a precise environment and through socialisation. From this standpoint, masculinity can be conceived of as the conditioning or nurturing of a man by civilisation, the structuring of his mind to inculcate in him those characteristics considered manly.

Therefore, because the imagery of masculinity varies from one culture to another, as illustrated in *A Leap Out of the Dark*, especially, on the one hand, through Moodu and Faatu and the inhabitants of Ngeech on the other, it covers a farrago of attributes, including physical power, sexual and functional roles, social status, emotional traits and intellectual qualities.

Representations of Masculinity

In *A Leap Out of the Dark* the author paints different pictures of masculinities to show, as mentioned above, that masculinity encodes a multiplicity of biological attributes, as well as sex-based roles and features. In order to make location fully play its roles, he sets his narrative in two make-believe worlds: Ngeech, a village in the most remote and climatically hostile part of Senegal and Kaada (which is an anagram of 'Dakar' the capital of Senegal). This comparative and contrastive approach demonstrates that the construction of gender, especially the characteristics attached to masculinity, is dependent on such parameters as history, place, people and culture.

Sex and Sexuality as Ferments of Masculinity

The narrator states on the first page that sex is the first foundational symptom of masculinity. In the protagonist's heated discussion with his wife, it appears that masculinity finds its first roots in genes. From a congenital standpoint, one is a man by nature and not by nurture. Thus, to be a man is tantamount to having the male sex, not the female one. Faatu, Moodu's wife, provides a plausible argument in support of this undeniable reality: 'You are a man like the others, aren't you? Are their dangling things heavier than yours?' (57).

The novelist introduces the first meaningful imagery of masculinity through figurative language such as similes and tag questions. Both vehicles serve to define Moodu's character, i.e., his personal characteristics and qualities, including his gender, physical appearance, personality, thoughts, actions, expressions, traits and attitudes. Faatu's questions in the introduction are thus meant to tell more about her husband's masculinity. From this direct description, the reader perceives that for her, one is either a man or a woman— there is no intermediary sex.

The second vehicle of the imagery of masculinity is the use of extensive metaphors. The male sex, i.e., the testicles and the penis, are imaginatively identified with or compared to 'dangling things.' Though implied, the analogy is suggestive and has many implications. One is that manliness symbolises physical strength, virility and bravery. In this respect, masculinity, as Simone de Beauvoir demonstrates in *The Second Sex*, is a characteristic to be proved, measured and tested because it is invested with power: 'The penis has become the symbol of manhood, which is socially valued' (261).

This brings up the imagery of the female sex as a flat and immobile thing. Thus, contrasting with the male sex, the female one, which epitomises femininity, alludes to discretion, passivity, docility and the ability to receive, among other attributes.

Remarkably, sex and sexuality are the backbone, the centre of gravity of masculinity. And it is masculinitity that holds a marriage together. A man who cannot satisfy his wife's sexual desires cannot gain her respect and love. Sexual deficiency is so serious a handicap that it often causes women to divorce or sleep with other men. That is why regular and intensive sexual intercourse is one of the three pillars of marriage, along with providing food and clothes. As the narrator aptly puts it when talking about the main character's parents: 'They could always find out ways and means to play in a civilized way their wedlock game whenever they wanted to' (58).

This shows that in all societies, effective and efficient sexuality is a standard bearer of marriage. It suffices to quote Francis, a virile male character in Emecheta's *Adah's Story* (1983), who makes no bones about stating that 'no marriage succeeds without a good sex life. As far as he was concerned, marriage was sex and lots of it, nothing more.'[4]

Though distant in time and place, one should recall Nathaniel Hawthorne's *The Scarlet Letter* (1850) in order to be sure that in all times and places, marriage implies effective sexuality. Hester Prynne, a married woman, whose husband has been absent for a long time, cannot help committing adultery simply because she needs to satisfy her sexual urges.

Another concrete and no less interesting case is related to emigration. In Senegal many emigrants stay abroad for years, leaving their wives at home. Turning marriage into a virtual relationship and reducing masculinity to the satisfaction of their wives' material needs, they seem to forget that the sexual intercourse they deprive them of is a staple that all the money in the world cannot buy. Consequently, the most faithful and sober among their wives stoically abstain from sexual intercourse. As for the others, who cannot possibly do so, they either cheat or choose to divorce.

Sexuality in which man proves his power is thus to marriage what blood is to the organism. It gives meaning to marriage—nourishes and fortifies it. By way of proof, marriage breaks as the groom is declared impotent. What makes the latter's fate more tragic is that not only does he lose his wife and money, but his honour disintegrates. He is metaphorically pointed at as a man whose 'belt is loose' (i.e., whose testicles are not heavy enough, to paraphrase Faatu in *A Leap Out of the Dark*). Thus, some disrespectful women do not hesitate to make advances, just to poke fun at him.

Actually, in traditional Africa, an impotent man is like a bull that cannot have an erection. What they both have in common is their inability to contribute to the growth and development of their species. The only difference being that the latter is doomed to be sold or slaughtered, whereas the former is stigmatised.

Another barometer of masculinity is bigamy or polygamy. The more wives a man has, the more he evidences his courage, physical strength and sexual potency: 'Many men chose to marry several wives because it was seen as a mark of bravery. If you chose to keep to one wife, people would point at you and label you a henpecked husband' (64). This idea immaculately appears in Achebe's seminal work, *Things Fall Apart* (1959), where the narrator states that to have many wives augurs well for masculinity, but on the condition that the husband succeeds in controlling and ruling all of them.

In the same vein, being polygamous is suggestive of masculinity because it jibes with having a large family to support, which is also proof of courage and industry. As a reservoir of workforce as well, polygamy is all the more determining in a man's life because it guarantees him respect, security and autonomy. This is not the case in the city. In *A Leap Out of the Dark* Moodu confesses that his being monogamous neither reflects alienation nor cowardice. Analysing the problem from a Marxist and deterministic angle, he insists that his economic condition cannot allow him to support many wives and their offspring, because not only is everything expensive, but he is the only breadwinner.

As can be noticed, sexuality intermingles with manhood. It is a skill demanding physical and technical efficiency and a conjugal duty indicative of full-fledged masculinity. In the country, children are initiated from an early age. For this reason, boys often hide in the bush to experiment with their potency, erecting through some form of masturbation. Or, under the guidance of their elders, they learn how to have real sexual intercourse with little girls or, strange as it may seem, with cows or sheep. In *A Leap Out of the Dark* this is particularly the case with Moodu, who 'never forgot the baobab tree root on which he had had his first oiling lessons guided by the elder boys' (64).

Permissiveness then, seems to be inherent in man's nature, sexual power being a mark of his manhood. A good illustration is that when a boy reaches a certain age without being inclined to discover sexuality, his future as a man becomes suspect. It is the same when he puts off being circumcised. The anxiety becomes greater when, being of an age to marry, a man fails to do so. He suddenly becomes the main subject of conversation and everybody starts doubting whether he is sexually potent.

This concern justifies why initiation to sexuality in *A Leap Out of the Dark* is almost a ritual of everyday life. A parallel can be drawn between the Senegalese and African-American societies. Alice Walker, for instance, explains that in the Black community, sexuality is liberated for boys: 'My father expected all of his sons to have sex with women. "Like bulls," he said, 'a man *needs* to have a little something on his stick.'[5]

The word 'stick' is packed with meaning. It causes one to think of an erection, as well as being illustrative of the penis as an instrument meant to be used constantly lest it lose its function. There is no doubt about it: a limb that is not used atrophies. In addition, the emphasis put on the verb 'need' emphasises that masculinity, sex and sexuality are inseparable. Any attempt to separate one from the other would be like trying to separate the soul from the body.

Furthermore, the close association of the stick with the penis is a meaningful metonymy. It suggests that through sexual intercourses a man hits a woman to demonstrate his physical power and superiority. In point of fact, men frequently use sexuality as a weapon to punish or discipline women. When he is angry with his wife, he deprives her of sexual intercourse. Though it is passive, this method proves to be more efficient than physical punishment because it prevents a woman from satisfying biological needs that she cannot control. One can posit that this strategy is even cruel insofar as gender codes strictly forbid women to commit adultery, whereas the codes are more flexible and tolerant with men, who are allowed to satisfy their libidos through marital or extra-marital intercourse.

Note then that in African and Victorian gender codes, boys are encouraged, even coached, for sexual intercourse long before getting married, whereas sexuality is taboo for girls. In *The Bride Price* (1979), for example, Emecheta denounces the imbalance in patriarchal societies' sexual politics. She is indignant that the latter is lenient with men's sexual irregularities and eccentricities, while severely reprimanding women for the same acts.

Even more constraining, girls are expected to keep their virginity until the wedding night. That is why, in *A Leap Out of the Dark*, there is no mention of girls taking 'oiling lessons' like boys. Above all, they are forbidden to beget children on the 'wrong side of the bed,' because women are perceived as vestal flames, preservers of moral values. Referring to her own experience, Alice Walker sums up this idea: 'My father was always warning my sister not to come home if she ever found herself pregnant. My mother constantly reminded her that abortion was a sin.'[6]

In *The Women of Brewster Place* (1982), Gloria Naylor stresses the necessity for girls living in androcratic cultures to understand that chastity and obedience to parents are critical female qualities. Mattie Michael, the main protagonist has learnt, at her expense, that transgressing these societal norms is unacceptable. Her illegitimate pregnancy has enraged her father and made it impossible to share a house with him. Consequently, she leaves for an uncertain new destination where she pays for her sacrilege.

It is important to emphasise that in the Senegalese traditional society, sexuality is pivotal in marital life. For this reason, the bride never joins her groom's house alone. She is always accompanied by a couple of experienced married young women who stay with her for a week. During this period, they teach her the secrets reserved for married women. No less important, they are interested in witnessing the outcome of the couple's first sexual intercourse because it determines the success or failure of the marriage.

This event is awaited impatiently because it gives the bride the opportunity to prove her virginity and consequently, her chastity. If her husband deflowers her, she becomes the pride of her family because it evidences that they have brought her up well. Her in-laws and husband also feel reassured for they realise that they have made a good choice. Finally, the groom is crowned a man because deflowering is an undeniable proof of masculinity, by which is meant sexual power. Thus, *A Leap Out of the Dark* displays evident proofs that masculinity is biological and functional before being a construction by civilisation.

The Gendered Construction of Masculine Traits

As for the construction of masculinity and its opposite, femininity, in *A Leap Out of the Dark*, initiation is a decisive and efficient strategy. The narrator stresses that boys sleep in their fathers' huts, which implies that girls sleep in their mothers' huts. When a boy sleeps in his mother's bed, he is considered to have a womanly nature and therefore becomes the laughingstock of his peers. Not only that, the latter will refuse him admittance to their closed circle, where all initiations to masculinity first take place. A patent example of gender differentiation, this custom serves as a preparation to fatherhood: 'The little Moodu used to sleep in his father's hut' (57).

The fact that boys sleep in their fathers' huts is another glaring illustration of the construction of gender identity. First, at a certain age, the boy distances himself from his mother, which prevents him from acquiring female traits, particularly from being emotional or morally weak. Second, cutting a boy off from his mother is a way of raising his sexual consciousness. It makes him realise the gender differences between males and females and serves as a starting point for the initiation to full masculinity. Finally, one can argue from a psychoanalytical perspective that this separation saves the boy from developing the Oedipus Complex. Julie Rivkin and Michael Ryan discuss how gender fabrication operates for men and women:

> The primary matter they must separate from is the mother, who for them represents the tie to nature that must be overcome by the cut into abstraction that inaugurates civilization as men understand it...women, on the other hand, are not required to separate from the mother as they acquire a gender identity; they simply identify with the closest person to them as they grow up, their own mother.[7]

This leads to another central indicator of manhood in *A Leap Out of the Dark*: being unemotional. A man does not cry, whatever the pain. Unlike women, who are emotional and who weep easily, men are supposed to be stoic. No matter how great the grief or discomfort, a man should never complain openly, let alone shed tears. A typical example is while being circumcised a boy cannot afford to cry. If he does, he becomes a disgrace to himself and his parents. Such is the main reason why parents often let children take the initiative to go through this test. It must be added that, in most cases, boys prepare themselves with their peers, encourageing one another. And once they are sure that they are all psychologically and morally ready, they inform their parents. Very often, parents do not approve of their decision spontaneously. They always take their own time to make sure that children have given the question careful consideration.

Another illustration that crying is not manly is evident in *A Leap Out of the Dark*. The metaphor of the 'weeping willow' Moodu's mates use to label him (because he often wept on his way to school) speaks for itself: 'Moodu was alone on his way to school, more often than not shedding tears of sorrow and bitterness. He was continually in a sour mood and as he was the only child from his village in their school, the other schoolboys used to make fun of him calling him "the weeping willow"' (54). From this point of view, what is expected of a man is self-control, enduranceand perseverance. To prepare himself for life, a man should learn to become hardened to all sufferings, adversities and obstacles. To encourage little Moodu and convince him that the present is a golden moment one must take advantage of in order to be ready for the future, the narrator makes older women resort, in a *griot*-like manner, to praises and popular wisdom: 'It is sour today, but tomorrow will be sweet, Jeng Saala Choro Majigéen; Munal, ku mun, muun . . . ' (55).

Moodu's trip back to Kaada from Ngeech also illustrates that endurance is a capital virtue in man. Ironically enough, while Moodu, the emancipated townsman, is complaining about passengers being packed into the coach like sardines, the latter, most of whom are ignorant countrymen and women, consider that his attitude reflects a lack of endurance. In a solemn and unambiguous tone, an elderly male passenger expresses his conception of masculinity thus:

> My good son, I admit that it is stifling here but it all will end soon; the journey will not last a year, will it? There is an end to anything, whether good or bad, sweet or sour . . . Endurance is supreme for a man worthy of the name; but you young men of today are like women; you can suffer no physical pain! (104).

Giving Moodu advice with a flourish, another elderly man pipes in, insisting on tolerance as a central quality, especially for a man worthy of the name: 'Misfortune never lasts long. And I will tell you the truth and die: if your heart is roomy, any place else will be so for you, be it a needle hole' (105).

Masculinity in *A Leap Out of the Dark* also signals a fundamental trait reminiscent of Cicero, for whom courage is man's virtue. Particularly used in the traditional sense, to be a man means not to yield to fright or flinch before danger. Therefore, to retreat is cowardly and consequently, dishonours one's ancestors, who preferred dying to surrendering or running away. The references to 'Dexxale,' where Lat-Dior Ngoné Latyr Diop,[8] a national hero, triumphantly succumbed to 'worthy ancestors' and 'a great family,' show that masculinity and courage merge into each other. The vivid description and cinematographic dramatisation of the following gladiatorial scene between Moodu's father and Iba, Moodu's father's younger brother and a robber armed with a knife, is eloquent:

The robber...thrust his right hand into his baggy trouser pocket and pulled out a glittering knife. As he raised his arm to strike Iba in the chest, Moodu's father shot in. Just in the nick of time. He threw away his machete and then gave the man a violent kick on the hand holding the knife. The knife flew into the air and fell ten yards away from the scene. The robber made a desperate effort to jump for it but even before the rest of the pursuers came up to give him a helping hand, Moodu's father had already neutralized the robber by fastening his strong arms around his trunk, thus blocking both his arms (59).

This event also discloses that discretion is a male characteristic, as opposed to indiscretion, which is associated with femaleness. When the pursuers realise that the thief is Samba, the son of Moodu's friend from a neighbouring village, they calm down, especially as he confesses that he has tried to rob Moodu's ram in order to abide by tradition. The fact is that Samba has a naming ceremony and thus, custom or Islam requires that he should slaughter a ram. Though reprehensible, his act is understandable for someone aware of the heavy weight of societal pressure in the Wolof community. Therefore, to avoid putting him and his worthy parents to shame, Moodu's father orders everybody to hush up the matter: 'Let none of us unveil what happened, . . . I will disinherit you my sons and you my brother I will cut off the string that ties us together, in other words, we will no longer share the same mother' (61).

It is worth noting that the diction, sentence structure and mood contribute to the tone. An integral part of the tenor, the tone is firm and solid, which is in agreement with the notion of authority and power that the term 'masculinity' conveys.

In addition, Moodu's reaction proves that men rate friendship highly. Indeed, there is no doubt that if he were a woman, Samba would become the butt of the village. However, Moodu's father understands that Samba is a worthy man who has been led to try to steal for the first time in order to hold on to his dignity. Most significantly, he knows that Samba could kill himself if he is humiliated. This fear justifies his solemn call to silence tinged with heavy: 'Remember all: nothing happened, except that my son Samba came to see his father for a ram, for his ugly newborn baby, my impotent rival' (61).

The pact of silence that the pursuers sign is evidence that for a man, a promise is a promise. Once a man commits himself to do something, he can neither change his mind nor draw back. Betrayal is considered unmanly and irresponsible conduct. Likewise, when a man is reputed to be a liar or treacherous, he is automatically labelled a woman. He becomes unworthy of his neighbours' confidence, hence his marginalisation and the loss of his respectability. To command respect a man should never tell lies. Faatu therefore, urges her husband to keep his promise to purchase a house of their own. She makes it clear that what she needs is not endless promises, because, as this apothegm goes, 'With promises, one can build thousands of castles in Spain.'

In addition to the male traits displayed in *A Leap Out of the Dark* as integral symbols of masculinity, there is also the economic status, which is instrumental in defining masculinity.

The Economic Factor in the Fabrication of Masculinity

It should be noted that in *A Leap Out of the Dark* masculinity is closely linked to the economic status of a man. It confers economic responsibilities upon him, one of the most important of which is to get a house of one's own. In the city, man should toil and moil to meet this demand because it is evidence of his masculinity and the guarantee of his authority over his family. This assumption accounts for Moodu's firm promise to his wife: 'We'll soon have a house of our own' (3).

Negatively connoted, renting is perceived in the collective mind as a shameful mark of dependence, failure, indolence and lack of being realistic or thrifty. Talking of that, the dialogue between Moodu and the chief of the village is more than illuminating:

'And whose house is the one you are living in now in the capital city?,' asked the Chief, apparently staggered.

'It belongs to a policeman and I am a mere tenant. I am paying him CFA 20,000 a month for the apartment that I occupy with my family; the other rooms are rented by other people with whom I share the toilets and the kitchen,' answered Moodu, obviously seeking to upset the Chief and the entire audience.

The Chief laughed scornfully, 'our kin is a shame upon his people!' (71).

One must keep in mind that in the traditional or Islam-oriented Senegalese society, the head of the family is the only breadwinner and it is incumbent upon him to provide his wife and underage children with a roof, food and clothing. Therefore, failure to fulfil this duty means to be unmanly, emasculated, effeminate or unconscious. Consistent with this conception, marriage to a man who cannot fend for his family is considered a misalliance. That is why, in *A Leap Out of the Dark*, Faatu never misses the chance to remind Moodu that her descendants owe their praiseworthy past she boasts of to the unreserved fulfilment of their true masculinity:

My worthy ancestors never lagged behind any other family in the past; they were first in every good thing...So why should I accept to be last now, me? Why? If I can add nothing to that glorious past because of a worthless husband, I must do all I can so as not to blemish it (4).

The importance given to property in urban and materialistic areas for the assessment of masculinity can be interpreted in other ways. On the one hand, to have a house of one's own amounts to being free, not being exposed to the whims of shady landlords or landladies. On the other hand, a house of one's own serves as a bedrock: it helps preserve stability, unity and harmony in the family. Finally, it guarantees good living conditions and education of the children.

In terms of a house as an index of fatherhood, there is much to say about urban and Islamic societies where children expect to inherit property from their fathers. Besides, whether it is in the country or in the city, the bigger the wealth left by the departed, the more his masculinity is acknowledged.

Thus, it is pointless to emphasise that wealth is masculinised because it plays a crucial role in the construction of gender. To gain his place in society in general and in his family in particular, a man should strive to acquire wealth in order to pass it on to his children. If he reaches this objective, he enjoys all the privileges attached to fatherhood. In other words, he becomes an Abrahamic patriarch, i.e., 'an old man whose absolute power over wives, children, herds and dependents was an aspect of the institution of fatherhood, as defined in the social group in which he lived.'⁹

This amounts to re-asserting that masculinity cannot be reduced to universal characteristics. For instance, in *A Leap Out of the Dark* there is a close link between masculinity and private property, which is a mark of modernity and individualism. In fact, in the city, land is as valuable as gold or diamonds. That is why speculation is savage and in consequence, getting a house or even a small piece of land demands Herculean efforts and sacrifices, as exemplified by Moodu who has been saving for years with a building company.

Paradoxically, in rural areas, where life is communal, providing a roof does not necessarily imply building a house of one's own. In Ngeech, for instance, heads of families live together in large families and in the same compounds, each of them satisfying himself with the necessary huts. As a house is not a sign of prestige and because land is more accessible, because it has been passed on from generation to generation, acquiring these properties is neither an economic challenge nor a determining sign of masculinity.

Thus, unlike in Kaada, where wealth and welfare are emblems of masculinity, in Ngeech masculinity is judged by different criteria. Unquestionably, industry is one of the most appreciated qualities. Manliness is often determined by the importance of the area to be cultivated. He who does not till many large fields is not considered a man. The reason for this is not difficult to guess: to not have many fields is synonymous with being lazy, which is not a male attribute.

Indeed, in an agricultural society, where people live on their own crops, it is not acceptable for a man not to be self-sufficient. When a man cannot feed his family year round with his own crops, when he is obliged to buy food, he loses the respect to which he is entitled as a man. This is particularly true because the money earned from cash crops like peanuts is not destined to be spent on food. Rather, this money is used to buy cattle, another sign of wealth and masculinity. In *A Leap Out of the Dark* the narrator indicates this when he states that each family has a granary full of millet, sheep and goats in the backyard.

In the countryside depicted in *A Leap out of the Dark* raising animals is not only visible proof of masculinity, but also of class consciousness. In fact, in rural areas only noble people (e.g., Moodu's and Faatu's fathers) invest their time, energy and money in farming and cattle breeding. Those who belong to the lower classes (e.g., the *griots*, jewellers and smiths) are not expected to have land or cattle. As a result, they are totally dependent on noble people, of whose masculine traits they always sing in exchange for staple commodities, clothing and money.

Engels argues in *Origins of the Family* that gender fabrication is a plot against women. He locates masculinity, or the power of domination of men over womanhood, in the system of production that confines women and excludes them from the quest for wealth. In his opinion, it was the custom of inheritance that turned matrilineal societies into patrilineal ones, because 'men acquired wealth in the form of herds and wanting to pass their wealth to their own children, overthrew "mother right" in favour of patrilineal inheritance.'[10] Bringing about the empowerment of men, the overthrow of 'mother right' through wealth has disempowered women, reducing them to ciphers and therefore, to docility, domesticity, motherhood and economic dependence.

Examined from this angle, it is easy to understand that the appropriation by men of wealth has the same motive as their appropriation of practicality, intellectual and physical capabilities, tools, technology and industry. Both are part and parcel of a hegemonic and narcissistic masculine construction by which males are constituted as men well equipped to fulfil themselves in the house and in the rough world outside and females as submissive women confined at home to achieve their routine duties to the best of their ability.

In *A Leap Out of the Dark* this accounts for the pressure urban women put on their husbands for them to become householders. This obsession also reveals that femaleness is, rightly or wrongly, equated with impatience, whereas maleness is associated with patience, perseverance and a sense of organisation. The following aphorism, according to which patience is the key to success and of which Moodu ceaselessly reminds his wife, summarises his vision, as well as giving meaning to the irritating behaviour of the latter: 'Timely events take place smoothly' (3).

Contrary to Faatu, who flares up easily whenever she needs something, Moodu is sedate. This demonstrates that self-control is a quality that is mostly found in men. Thus, the latter's advice to the former: 'Anger makes a human being look little. If you are unable to suppress your anger, then you cannot deserve people's confidence. Self-control makes up a human being . . . not of bone and flesh only, but a soulful and witted one' (4–5).

The centrality of landed property for city-dwellers unmasks other salient features of masculinity: realism and lucidity. The narrator insinuates that when it comes to expenditure, men are more rational than women. Consequently, replying to Faatu, Moodu, an assertive intellectual who does not misjudge his purchasing power, draws an adage from Senegalese culture according to which consistency, humility and moderation are virtues to be developed in men: 'Even though the eye cannot carry any burden, it can gauge it and help the head. . . . They who do what they can, tell what they know well, shall sleep tight and I want to be one of those lucky ones' (7–8).

Quite the opposite of men, their providers, women are unreasonably dominated by their whims most of the time. Having interiorised their roles as Victorian women responsible for managing the household and their social status as the property of their husbands, they believe that the latter have to fully take care of them. As a result, women have a tendency not only to overestimate the financial capacities of their husbands, but not to be able to discern priorities either. This striking paradox is illustrated by the attitude of Faatu who, although urging Moodu to immediately purchase a house, wants him to buy her the latest expensive fashions and jewels:

> Moodu found it impossible to understand how a sane human being could run after two rabbits going in opposite directions. Faatu wanted her family to have a house of their own and a good education for their young children, yet, at the same time, she wanted her husband to give her enough money to keep up with her friends, or, more accurately, her rivals (7).

On that score, it must be stressed that in Senegal nothing is excessive when it comes to dressing with studied elegance. Some women spend all their savings on clothes. Less tolerable, others even go so far as to cut the household budget or borrow money or/and textiles, just to vie in stylishness with their companions. What is ironic about this attitude is that they all intend to demonstrate that they are 'big-boned,' by which is meant they belong to rich and noble families. In most cases, their lives are a lie because they are pretending to be so. Wedding, naming and religious ceremonies are, for example, privileged occasions for women to parade, gossip and spread rumours:

> All her husbands' friends' wives – about seven *xeesalized driankees* wore rich grand-booboos embroidered by Kadaa's top fashion designers, made-in-Italy high-heeled shoes and many other expensive articles secured from the Western world. Worst of all, they seemed to be dripping with gold, ostentatiously twisting it around their necks, their wrists and their fingers. Even their handbag handles were made of the precious metal (5).

This passage is worth focussing on for it indicates that in urban women's minds, masculinity complies with prescribed gender responsibilities considered typically masculine. It is an umbrella term for getting a nice house, a wife who adorns it—especially if she is beautiful and always decked out in all her fineries—and success-oriented, caring and proud of oneself.

Because masculinity is tightly linked with the capacity of a man to take care of a woman in a material sense, it is no wonder that trying to live up to this gender identity entails destructive social, political and economic consequences.

Evil Effects of Masculinity

In light of the degree of manhood gauged by the amount of money a man spends (or wastes) on luxury for him and his wife to flaunt, embezzlement has become common in society, especially among male civil servants and politicians. The frequent occurrence of this theme in *A Leap Out of the Dark* testifies to the seriousness and scope of this evil.

Ironically in Africa, in the context of modernity, misappropriating money is sometimes perceived as an emblem of worth. Of course, this conception is neither rational nor ethical. In people's psyche, to get a good position in government administration or in a company is viewed as the reward for one's mother's work. Correctly decoded, the term 'work' designates a woman's total submissiveness to her husband and her unquestioning acceptance of domesticity.

Perceiving the question in the same light, Waali makes Moodu, his cousin, realise that he does not owe his success solely to his own efforts, because his mother's work is more important. Waali reminds Moodu that Auntie Degen could be set as an example because she 'sowed sturdy seeds' in his father's house.

Another well-established belief among some Africans is that national wealth does not belong to anybody. The reason for this conviction is that those of them who believe this have not yet accepted the notions of state, government and the 'common good,' because they sound like abstractions or alien realities.

Finally, in the collective subconsciousness of some is the notion that the successful or prodigal son is everybody's son. He is not only the pride of his parents but is also the pride of the whole community, which can make claims on him when needs be. The opportunism behind this conception is naked, because when one is a pariah or a failure, he only belongs to his parents.

As a result of this mentality, those who manage national finances are expected to gorge themselves with ill-gotten money. Moreover, they are expected to spend lavishly and be generous towards their parents, relatives and friends. Metaphorically, public finances are regarded as a large and delicious cake or a gift from God to be shared. Thus, not to get a big portion becomes synonymous with worthlessness and cowardice. Instead of being highly valued, not to embezzle is seen as bad for one's reputation. Good management is not viewed as honesty, professional integrity or a sense of patriotism. Rather, it is seen as spiteful obtuseness, wickedness, selfishness and systematic refusal to help one's fellow citizens whose mothers have not worked enough to get hold of the cake:

> What sane man would refuse to dance to God's music? If you don't eat, others will, starting right from the top down to the bottom. And to whom does the State belong? The eating of the ministers and MP'S and their wives and children does not prevent my household from eating their daily meals, so why should I be jealous? That is not religious... Their mothers worked more and far better than ours did: there does the real matter lie (12).

These lines are highly significant. They prove that with the invention of modern life, many standards have changed for the worse. For instance, the criteria according to which gender was traditionally determined has become more materialistic than physical, intellectual, psychological and ethical. In the new environment of Kaada, marked by ostentatious manners, masculinity connotes being bold, ravenous and rotten enough to misappropriate money. As a consequence, material success, which is a male ambition, no longer means excelling in one's domain, rising to the top of the hierarchy through self-confidence, hard work and grace, but being 'plucky,' 'reckless,' and robbing shamelessly and with impunity.

Conclusion

In short, the motif of masculinity is so recurrent in *A Leap Out of the Dark* that at times it eclipses the subject matter, which is basically a satire of society in postcolonial Africa. The author subtly presents the notion of masculinity within the general framework of sex and gender. From his narrative, it is apparent that masculinity crystallises universal attributes when it refers to the biological factors that, on the one hand, constitute the quintessence of a man and on the other hand, differentiate him from a woman.

Thus, when masculinity is articulated in terms of gender, it is grasped as an ensemble of characteristics that far from developing in isolation, are derived from a construction by a dominant civilisation whose particularity fluctuates according to time, milieu, economic and political conditions and mental representations.

What accounts for the originality of *A Leap Out of the Dark* is that, in some respects, it can be read as a deconstruction of the stereotypical images of masculinity and femininity as projected by Westerners. Correlating the two concepts, the novelist successfully shows that it is not always fair to describe the construction of masculinity and femininity as a bargain in which woman is the loser. Wedded to his African ideology, the author strongly believes that reducing masculinity to attributes and roles that systematically marginalise, subjugate and weaken women is an erroneous vision. He opines that in the African context, the forging of masculinity does not totally privilege men to the detriment of women. Although conferring advantages on men, the fabrication of masculinity simultaneously makes men carry enormous burdens with aplomb insofar as it imposes constraining social and economic responsibilities towards their wives, which turn out to be a privilege for the latter. Thus, the author conceives of the interplay between masculinity and femininity as a game where there is no weaker or stronger sex and where all biological features and gender roles are well balanced, valorising and complementary.

Equally subversive is the way in which Dieng links masculinity to politics. He highlights the fact that the masculinisation of politics, leadership and management is the main source of the evils confronting Africa. As a result, though he does not advocate an inversion of gender roles, he is in favour of the reconstruction of those that, to use Adrienne Rich's terminology, 'endanger psychically and physically' woman or are detrimental to men or society as a whole. Hence, his gentle hint on the last page of this avant-garde novel is that women exercise their agency in all fields.

This suggests that women should question the way they picture themselves and are pictured by men. Among other things, the author invites them to challenge the imbedded traditional masculinist assumptions that a woman's natural role is to be an embodiment of motherhood and nothing more, or that her brain is smaller than man's (as Lakunle despotically tries to define her in Soyinka's *The Lion and the Jewel* [1963]). No doubt this can only occur through education, for as Maggie Coats justly asserts, emphasising a universal privilege transcending sex and gender, 'education is about nothing but change, the opportunity to grow, to develop, to enhance one's understanding and possibly, one's place in the world.'[11]

A Retrospective: Looking for 'the African' in the Hybrid: Thoughts on Masculinity in Equiano's *The Interesting Narrative*

Tuzyline Jita Allan

The recent discovery by Vincent Carretta of two archival documents refuting Equiano's claim that he was born in West Africa marks another shift in the fascinating evolution of *The Interesting Narrative of the Life of Olaudah Equiano or Gustavus Vassa, the African, Written by Himself* (1789).[1] Unlike the unproven allegations made by anti-abolitionists three years after the narrative's publication that Equiano's birthplace was the Danish island of Santa Cruz (known today as St. Croix in the US Virgin Islands),[2] the new charges are based on baptismal and naval records showing him to be a native of South Carolina. This revelation has the potential to undermine Equiano's reputation as an important historical figure and disable several decades of historical and literary scholarship based on his life and work. An essay in *The Chronicle of Higher Education* (2005) unambiguously titled 'Unraveling the Narrative' captures the concern voiced by historians regarding the implications of Carretta's findings. 'He is a sleuth of the highest order,' Princeton professor of history Philip D. Morgan remarks in a weighty endorsement of Carretta. 'He has raised fundamental questions about Equiano's birthplace...This is a stunning turnabout.'[3] For Nell Painter, the notable African–American historian, the revelation could have far-reaching consequences for African–American history in which Equiano's recollection of 'an almost Edenic Africa' has functioned as 'a kind of founding myth.'[4]

On the other hand, the issue for scholars like Paul E. Lovejoy, distinguished professor of African Diaspora history at York University in Canada, is not Equiano's veracity but the trustworthiness of the new-found evidence. Lovejoy's defense of Equiano is unequivocal : 'The truth that doesn't fit is the document that says he was born in South Carolina. Everything else fits. The one thing that's odd—that's the one that has to be questioned, not the other way around.'⁵ In a longer article he examines the issue in greater detail and concludes that 'a careful reading of the linguistic, geographical and cultural details provided by Vassa leaves little doubt that he was born in Africa, especially in Igboland.'⁶ Carretta, an esteemed Equiano scholar, editor and biographer, has responded variously to the controversy, sometimes asserting the scholarly imperative to seek the truth, at other times reaffirming Equiano's prodigious talent and further yet, downplaying the question of authenticity and redirecting attention to the representational aspect of the narrative. 'In what way,' he asks, 'is [Equiano] "the African," as he calls himself—the representative of millions of others who have been enslaved?'⁷

While we wait to see what new direction, if any, Equiano scholarship takes, the invitations of Carretta and Lovejoy, two prominent voices in the debate, to read *The Interesting Narrative* in new ways could provoke the desire to re-engage the text 'in quest of a mind more original than our own,'⁸ to borrow Harold Bloom's remark on how and why we read. Indeed, we might be even more appreciative of Equiano's creative capabilities if it turns out that he is a playful genius who invented his African identity.

I agree with Lovejoy that the evidence provided in Equiano's narrative about his African origins is both substantively and emotionally true. In addition, I believe the latest debates about the authenticity of his African identity encapsulate the contradictions that have marked the response to his life and his book since the author asserted his prerogative to call himself an African over two hundred years ago. There is on the one hand undying respect for his pioneering spirit, his originality of mind and his triumph over adversity. On the other hand, the unflattering attention paid to him during periods of controversy undermines his work and what he symbolises. Indeed, it seems as though it matters to many people that Equiano be thought of as an African, as he claimed and at the same time to others that he not be. Either way, in a manner reminiscent of Frederick Douglass' description of himself as 'an American Slave' in the title of his autobiography, something powerful resonates from pairing 'Olaudah Equiano' and 'the African.' What did it mean for Equiano to call himself 'the African?' or to be an 'African man' at the end of the eighteenth century? How does this distinction serve his hybrid imagination in *The Interesting Narrative*? How is 'the African' represented in contemporary discourses on identity? What lessons does Equiano's experience in his homeland and across cultures hold for the artistic representations of African manhood, such as those collected in this critical volume? These are complex issues that require debate and extensive analysis. What I will try to do in this retrospective is to give some indication of why these questions are important.

In *The Interesting Narrative* 'the African' is used self-referentially to identify the author, other enslaved or free Africans and blacks. It also serves as a rhetorical tool to gauge Equiano's estimation of his racial otherness. The term embodies the defining difference that sets him apart from Europeans. Africans were generally thought of as intellectually inferior to whites and therefore lacking in talent, ingenuity and other characteristics linked with a civilised society. A man of many talents, Equiano was determined to recast the conversation to allow a different element of his identity to replace the African. He turned to the parallel reality of being a man.

The narrative marks this shift by highlighting Equiano's steady course of heroic action or manly activities as he transitions from slavery to gentleman status. 'Man' in Enlightenment thought was a highly valued concept that addressed the priority of reimagining the world as an engine of progress with man as both the initiator and subject of scientic inquiry. But the new idea of male dominion over the natural world did not include all men. As Roy Porter notes, '[t]o put . . . aboriginal people's capacity for progess to the test of science, natives were sometimes transported to Paris or London and then exposed to the laboratory of polite society.'[9] Wearing the face of this Eurocentric practice, Equiano certainly understood that in his new environment his racial identity was the primary challenge to his humanity and his future. Mary Wollestonecraft's review of The Interesting Narrative captures the prevailing view of Equiano's difference from the category of superior men considered under the generic category of 'man':

> The life of an African, written by himself, is certainly a curiousity, as it has been a favourite philosophic whim to degrade the numerous nations, on whom the sun-beams more directly dart, below the common level of humanity and hastily conclude that nature, by making them inferior to the rest of the human race, designed to stamp them with a mark of slavery. How they are shaded down, from the fresh colour of northern rustics, to the sable hue seen on the African sands, is not our task to inquire, nor do we intend to draw a parallel between the abilities of the negro and European mechanic; we shall only observe, that if these volumes do not exhibit extraordinary intellectual powers, sufficient to wipe off the stigma, yet the activity and ingenuity, which conspicuously appear in the character of Gustavus, place him on a par with the general mass of men, who fill the subordinate stations in a more civilised society than that which he was thrown into at his birth.[10]

The intense focus on masculinity in The Interesting Narrative represents a strategic repositioning by Equiano from the margins of society to the dominant centre where he acquires an unusual level of access to the systems of knowledge and power in the eighteeth century. Also by assuming a broad range of masculine identities, which working together form a hybridised European masculinity, he lessens the impact of the racial humiliation evident in Wollstonecraft's text. The elements of this hybridised model of masculinity cut across the religious, mercantile and intellectual currencies of the age and draw from a long line of respected male figures, including seaman, slave trader, fighting man, captain, man of letters, man of feeling, businessman, gentleman, Christian, free man and 'almost an Englishman.'[11] Equiano renews himself constantly in these roles as he basks in the glow of masculine prowess.

Commenting on the ethos set by the literary culture of eighteenth-century Britain, Paul Goring writes: 'The growing emphasis upon plausibility, the increasing tendency to treat "familiar" matters and the rise in moral respectability are among the most significant trends concerning prose fiction in the eighteenth century.'[12] The practice is reflected in *The Interesting Narrative* as Equiano tries to 'familiarise' or demystify the racial Other (himself) by adopting hegemonic masculine identities. The familiar tropes of masculine character, running the gamut from bravery, courage in adversity, industry and seamanship to authorship and gentlemanliness are on display throughout Equiano's adult life as assets that rebrand him for entry into British society. Incorporated into this mosaic of conventional masculine types is the man of feeling, '[a] benevolent male character type associated with sentimental fiction.'[13] Combining sensitivity, vulnerability and courage, the role is not out of character for Equiano, as evident not only in the compassionate streak that is part of the tapestry of his life but also his refusal to yield the struggle to end slavery.

The stakes in the narrative's drama of competing identities are high, with real-life consequences. For while the compelling presence in the narrative of a powerful masculine persona works to restore Equiano's sense of manhood, the new configurations of male authority are equally resistant to the incorporation of African identity into the narrative's intercultural matrix. In *The Interesting Narrative* African identity remains outside the triumphant figurations of masculinty. The gap widens between Vassa, the man who is 'almost an Englishman' and Equiano, the African. Citing the example of the Turkey/Europe encounter, Kevin Robins describes this kind of dualism involving a 'choice between assimilation of an alien modernity and reversion to the spurious authenticity of (ethnic or religious) origins' as 'a false choice, an absurd choice.'[14]

'What are the possibilities for transcending this impossible choice,'[15] Robins asks? The contemporary response offers various theoretical and critical practices for creating manoeuvring spaces around entrenched structures of power. Of these, hybridity has been hugely influential. Homi Bhabha, the postcolonial theorist and proponent of the concept of hybridity, provides a useful summarising statement in his definition of the term: '[Hybridity] unsettles the mimetic or narcissistic demands of colonial power but reimplicates its identifications in strategies of subversion that turn the gaze of the discriminated back upon the eye of power.'[16]

As a critical practice, hybridity has drawn both praise and criticism. The consensus view recognises its crucial role in studies of Diaspora, postcolonial and other cultural identities that call for 'thinking beyond exclusionary, fixed, binary notions of identity based on ideas of rootedness and cultural, racial and national purity.'[17] Critics, on the other hand, although excited about the term's theoretical possibility, wonder whether it 'create[s] the false impression of symmetry between unequal terms, cultures and nations, distorting and diluting the persistent power struggle between colonizer and colonized.'[18] It is a disturbing possibility Ella Shohat discerned from the outset, warning against the euphoria surrounding its reception: 'A celebration of syncretism and hybridity per se, if not articulated in questions of hegemony and neo-colonial power relations, runs the risk of appearing to sanctify the *fait accompli* of colonial violence.'[19] Questions about subaltern agency in individual and group struggles against abuses of power continue to haunt speculation about the term's viability in colonial and other power relations.

My concern is that hybridity raises questions about its ability to accommodate African identities and realities. Perhaps it is because the universalising elements of its critique do not take into account the eclectic variety of the African experience in both colonial and national contexts. Or perhaps it has to do with the fact that this reality has been consistently undercut by the idea of a fixed and unchanging African character. The term's racial history provides a clue to the latter problem. In *Colonial Desire: Hybridity in Theory, Culture and Race*, Robert Young has traced its botanical and racial origins; the latter is embedded in the idea of the races as different species, with the Caucasian species being diametrically opposed to the African. Young states that '[t]he question had first been broached in the eighteenth century when the different varieties of human beings had been classed as part of the animal kingdom according to the hierarchical scale of the Great Chain of Being. Predictably, the African was placed at the bottom of the human family.'[20] Hence in its current uses, the term's colonial history of epistemological violence is clearly a target for disruption. Yet doubts persist, including the perception that 'it replicates the binaries it is meant to supersede, perpetuating such dichotomies as colonizer and colonized... even as it attempts to articulate a post-Manichean space of interculturation.'[21]

The Interesting Narrative, replete with hybrid mixing, stands to gain from the insights of hybridity theory. The text's distances and dichotomies and the author's irrepressible state of in-betweenness are all spaces in an imperial landscape supported by structures of difference and inequality. The narrative is the classic border-text, spanning land and marine geographies in West Africa, North and Central America, the West Indies, Europe, the Arctic, the Mediterranean Sea and the Atlantic Ocean. Generically, it straddles auto-biography (both the spiritual and conventional varieties), travel literature, slave narrative, captivity narrative and historical fiction. In addition, as many critics have noted, there is a disjunction in style and tone between the opening chapters in the African section and the rest of the text. In other words, it is double-voiced. Its author is more than 'bicultural;'[22] he is a self-described 'citizen of the world.'[23] Not surprisingly, he has several names, although he used only two to refer to himself—Olaudah Equiano, given to him at birth, signifying the one blessed with a voice and Gustavus Vassa, the slave name that invokes a brave sixteenth-century Swedish king in an attempt to mock Equiano's unfortunate state.

The narrative's multiple identities, imperial landscape and crosscultural experience point to a context set up for the opportunity to utilise the interventions of hybridity theory. However, such a reading would have to take into account the restraints and displacement of the African racial identity. In Equiano's hybrid imagination, manhood is enhanced by its transformative character, while African identity remains trapped in sameness. The narrative's negotiating power is clearly gendered; masculinity, not race, frames the construction of new knowledge in the text. Hybridity is generally perceived as a threat to dominant systems of knowledge and power but in the marginal spaces of the narrative occupied by African subjectivity, there are very few signs of empowerment.

A recent example of the inadequacy of the term to enable agency in African contexts involves two South African women, one black and the other white, in a collaborative venture Anne McClintock describes as 'the scandal of hybridity.'[24] McClintock's nuanced summary of the incident is quoted in full in the notes.[25]

The story brings into relief a 'subaltern' experience in an encounter with the dominant culture of a postcolonial nation in which inherited systems of power erupt to disempower the black woman. The colonial history re-inscribed in this drama of representation is played out along not-so-fluid racial, gender, cultural and ideological lines. McClintock elaborates: The book . . .

> is a political scandal, for it speaks of the life of a very poor black woman, telling of her childhood shuttling from shantytown to shantytown, child labour in a white-owned fish factory, reluctant marriage, the birth of her children in wind and sand, the bad infinity of work for white families, her husband's health broken by poverty and fatigue, the domestic violence of despairing men wedded to drink, the tightening of the influx and pass laws for women, the police raids and evictions, the refusals to leave, the ignominies and ordeals at the pass offices, the forced removal to the desolation of the Ciskei Bantustan, the forbidden returns, the dogged perseverance, the family loyalties and survivals—and finally the nationwide rebellion of 1976, 'the revolt of the children.'[26]

Whether it is Equiano's attempt to fashion a new self at the intersection of the cultures of Africa and Europe, or Poppie Nongena's effort to create new worlds where harmful distinctions are erased, the African experience within cultural intermingling is more drama than substance in terms of the transcendence and subversive agency contemporary identity theories, such as hybridity, offer as viable options in colonial and other systems of domination and control. For Equiano, racial identity is sidelined by fluid forms of masculinity that function synergistically to restore his sense of manhood. Nongena, the African woman, herself a writer, is threatened with erasure by a culture whose disparate elements can easily mobilise around the elimination of one of their own.

The breadth of the problem lies beneath the taxonomies of masculinity offered in this volume. With the growing reality of cultural intermingling, coupled with the chaos of life for many, where does the writer/oral artist stand in relation to power? What kind of social consciousness is emerging in these culturally diverse contexts? How is it expressed – as conflict, difference, affimation, or satiric condemnation? This volume of essays on the many expressions of masculinity on the African creative landscape attests to the impulse to challenge, sanctify, or celebrate difference so that diversity can remain a value.

Afterword
Masculinities in African Literary and Cultural Texts

Simon Gikandi

Although it is only now being recognised as an important problem of investigation and interpretation in literary scholarship, the question of masculinity lies at the centre of the key texts of African literature, defining the natures of cultures, traditions and experiences and signalling the complexity of contexts and texts. Indeed, it is hard to think of a canonical text of African literature that is not informed and haunted by the spectre of masculinity. From the epic traditions of the Sahel and the Swahili coast to the founding folktales of the Baganda and the songs of the Northern Lwo, the struggle between men, often over land, patrimonies and memories, generates the production of oral texts. In the written literatures of the continent, canonical texts such as Thomas Mofolo's *Chaka*, Chinua Achebe's *Things Fall Apart* and Okot p'Bitek's *Song of Lawino* are built around the desire, by the central characters, to affirm forms of masculinity which are then posited as the key to historical consciousness and cultural meaning.

Masculinity has been recognised in these texts as an inescapable part of the social fabric in which they are set and indeed of their structuring mechanisms; but it has rarely been recognised as a theoretical or ethical problem, one worthy of reflection as a condition of possibility of textuality or performance. For this reason, among others, *African Masculinities* must be recognised as a pioneering text in the field of African literary criticism. This collection marks the arrival of the field of men's studies to African literary studies and recognises the complex function of masculinity in performance, texts and cinema.

Central to this project is the editors' and contributors' recognition of the location of different forms of masculinity at the interstices of literature, power and cultural identity. This book opens new areas of research or revises some of the most enduring and controversial questions in the histories and literatures that are pegged on gender relations in an African context. Consider, for example, the question of epic. Once upon a time leading European scholars of African oral literatures, most notably Ruth Finnegan, argued that there was no discernible tradition of epic in Africa. In response, two generations of African scholars spent years in the field, recuperating epic traditions from various cultures, producing works that effectively put the Finnegan hypothesis to rest in peace. But these recuperative gestures were not always attuned to the specific ways in which the figure of the male complicated the nature of epic as a genre and social practice. In this book, however, the play of masculinities is shown to have given African epics their uniqueness, marking out the boundaries of the polity, articulating subjectivities and calibrating the work of language and cultural memory.

A central aspect of this book is the contributors' awareness of the intricate and mutually informative relation between feminism and masculinity. For many years African literary criticism, informed by the best of feminist and womanist theory, seemed uncertain about the place of the masculine trope in its primary texts. The problem here was simple: feminist criticism demanded a recognition of gender difference as a central category in literary production; it demanded that the figure of the African woman be made central to acts of reading and that literary histories be more attuned to the complex role of gender in the African imagination. And yet modes of criticism informed by a feminist sensibility could not escape the fact that the major texts of African literature, from *Sundiata* to *Xala* were essentially masculinist and hence seemed, if only in a semantic sense, to be going against the protocols of reading demanded by feminism. If masculinity informed the African cultural text, how could it be read against the grain, as it were?

Many of the essays in this collection address this question in three significant ways: some address the question of power and the contradictions of masculinity in African folktales, proverbs, songs and film and deconstruct the masculine, pointing to the contradictions that emerge in its performance or textualisation. A second tactic is to rethink the complexity of gender and to show how masculinity is not simply an exercise of power—the depository of patriarchy, as it were—but the consequence of deep anxieties about foundations and identities. What might then appear to be the binary opposition between the feminine and masculine in African literature is now shown to be part of a gender complex in which the meaning of male power can only be performed or textualised through the interplay of the two poles.

A third approach is premised on the fragility of masculinity itself: beneath what appears to be hyper-masculinity, especially in the political theatre of the postcolony, are to be found emasculated male figures and an unprecedented crisis of sexual power. Masculinity is often more important to the African cultural text when it is apprehended in crisis or failure as part of a negative dialectic of identity. Indeed, if we adopt the model of reading promoted by this collection, we will discover this other side of masculinity to be a more useful tool of understanding African cultures than all the discourses on patriarchy that fill our library shelves.

What does a mode of reading that recognises masculinity as a conceptual problem bring to the interpretation of African literature? Obviously it provides a better understanding of gender relations on the continent. It takes us beyond the simplistic notion that masculinity in Africa is part of a retrogressive patriarchal economy and the equally simplistic argument that masculine power functions as a mode of African self-assertion and cultural nationalism. It takes us to a more productive moment of cultural discovery: that the manifest masculinity of Sundiata, or Okonkwo or Chaka is driven by deep anxieties about the meaning of gender and especially the figure of the mother, the quintessential sign of the feminine.

What does it mean to read *Sundiata* not simply as an epic about Malinke masculinities but also perhaps as a meditation on the place of Sogolon, the mother, as part of the culturally repressed? What does it mean to anchor Okonkwo's fatal masculinity to the repressed figure of his mother and daughters, the emblems of the other side that might have enabled his passage into the modern world? Does the narrative of Chaka make sense without the figure of Nandi his mother? To assert his will, Chaka kills his mother Nandi; but this act, far from securing his masculine identity, sends him into a delirium, which, in Thomas Mofolo's version of the story, is marked by an apostrophe, the figure of loss: 'Early in the morning the report began to go round that Nandi was dead. Then Chaka poured dust on himself and wept and cried: "Alas, alas. My mother is dead, dead. Alas, alas. From other huts the smoke goes up, but no smoke from mine."'

A book that puts the problem of men at the centre of gender and literary studies is a welcome addition to the African library; the editors, contributors and the publisher must be commended for undertaking this long overdue project.

Notes

Preface

1. http://www.un.org/events/res-1325.pdf

Notes

Introduction

1. Eagleton, *After Theory*, 74.
2. Okpewho, *African Oral Literature*, 3.
3. Cohen, *Being a Man*, 8.
4. *Ibid.*
5. Kimmel, p.?
6. Connell, *Masculinities*, 3.
7. *Ibid.*, 5.
8. Thackway, 58.

References

Cohen, David. *Being a Man* (London: Routledge, 1990).

Connell, R. W., *Masculinities* (Berkeley and Los Angeles: University of California Press, 1995).

Kimmel, Michael, 'Foreword,' in Gardiner, Judith Kegan, ed., *Masculinity Studies and Feminist Theory: New Directions* (New York: Columbia University Press, 2002).

Lindsay, Lisa A. and Stephan F. Miescher, eds., *Men and Masculinities in Modern Africa*
(Portsmouth, N.H.: Heinemann, 2003).

Okpewho, Isidore, *African Oral Literature: Backgrounds, Character and Continuity* (Bloomington: Indiana University Press, 1992).

Lahoucine, Ouzgane and Morrell, Robert, eds., *African Masculinities: Men in Africa From the Late Nineteenth Century to the Present* (New York: Palgrave Macmillan, 2005).

Thackway, Melissa. *Africa Shoots Back: Alternative Perspectives in Sub-Saharan Francophone African Film.* (Bloomington: Indiana University Press, 2003).

1. Staging Masculinity in the East African Epic

Notes

1. This is a popular Kiswahili proverb.
2. The implied 'transgender' aspects of the masculinity enacted in the epic should not, however, be confused with the Western conception of either female masculinity or masculine femininity, both of which are associated with sexuality and are often considered antithetical to—or in opposition with—heteronormativity. What is at stake in the masculine femininity that is described here is the display of attributes normally ascribed to the opposite gender but not necessarily of a sexual nature. See Win Lunsing's 'What Masculinity? Transgender Practices Among Japanese Men.'
3. Mathias Mnyampala and Shihabuddin Chiraghdin claim that Swahili society is matrilineal in nature. Although it is true that most coastal societies were/are matrilineal—and even the Waswahili name their 'tribes' after matriarchs—Islamic Swahili society is patrilineal. Indeed, the Fumo Liyongo epic grapples with the tension between the indigenous coastal matrilineal system and the rising influence of patrilineal Islam. The epic further problematises the divide by tending to implicitly privilege and celebrate the maternal relationships and complicating and unsettling the paternal ones. (I am indebted to Professor Austin Bukenya of Makerere University for this insight).
4. Heath, 'Male Feminism,' 26.
5. Dirksted-Breen, 'Phallus, Penis and Mental Space,' 649–657.
6. Freud, 'Transformations of Puberty,' 220.
7. Bhabha, 'Are You a Man or a Mouse,' 57.
8. Gilmore, *Manhood in the Making*, 12.
9. For a classic example of a conception of masculinity that hinges on the bifurcation between biologically predetermined sexes, see James Ogola Onyango's essay, 'Masculinities in Kiswahili Children's Literature in Kenya' (517). Onyango reduces criticism to a game of numbers in which he finds fault with almost any literature whose male characters outnumber their female counterparts.
10. Mazrui, *Swahili Beyond the Boundaries*, 16.
11. *Ibid.*, 16.
12. Wamitila, *Archetypal Criticism of Swahili Literature*, 92.
13. *Ibid.*, 37
14. These include I. N. Shariff's The Liyongo Conundrum: Re-Examining the Historicity of Swahili's National Poet-Hero'; Fussi Nagy's 'The Ethnic Situation in East Africa and the Folklore figure of Liongo Fumo'; and K. W. Wamitila's *Archetypal Criticism of Kiswahili Poetry*.
15. Finnegan, *Oral Literature in Africa*, 108.

16. Wamitila, *Archetypal Criticism of Swahili Literature,* 37.
17. These studies include Mbele (*'Women in the African Epic'*), Okpewho (*The Epic in Africa*), Biebuyck (*Hero and Chief*), Johnson, (*The Epic of Son-Jara: According to Fa-Digi Sisoko: A West African Tradition*) and Mulokozi (*'The Nanga Bards of Tanzania'*).
18. Steere, *Swahili Tales as Told by Natives of Zanzibar,* 442.
19. Okpewho, *Epic in Africa,* 34.
20. Steere, *Swahili Tales as Told by Natives of Zanzibar,* 442
21. Mshamu, 'Mother's Advice and Prayer: An Epic,' 77.
22. Mazrui, *Swahili Beyond the Boundaries,* 18.
23. Duncan, *Romantic Outlaws, Beloved Prisons,* 36.
24. Roberts, *Conrad and Masculinity,* 7.
25. Heath, 'Male Feminism,' 26.

References

Bhabha, Homi. 'Are You a Man or a Mouse?,' in Berger, Maurice, Wallis, Brian and Watson, Simon, eds., *Constructing Masculinities* (New York: Routledge, 1995).

Biebuyck, Daniel P., *Hero and Chief: Hero Literature from Banyanga Zaire Republic* (Berkeley and Los Angeles: University of California Press, 1978).

Chiraghdin, Shihabuddin and Nabhany, Ahmed, *Malenga wa Karne Moja* (Nairobi: Longman Kenya, 1987).

Dirksted-Breen, D., 'Phallus, Penis and Mental Space,' in *International Journal of Psychoanalysis* 77 (1996), 649–657.

Duncan, Martha Grace, *Romantic Outlaws, Beloved Prisons. The Unconscious Meanings of Crime and Punishment* (New York: New York University Press, 1996).

Finnegan, Ruth, *Oral Literature in Africa* (Oxford: Clarendon Press, 1970).

Freud, Sigmund, 'Transformations of Puberty,' in Strachey, James, ed., *Three Essays on the Theory of Sexuality,* Vol. 7 (London: Hogarth Press, 1975), 207–30.

Gilmore, David D., *Manhood in the Making: Cultural Concepts of Masculinity.* (New Haven, Conn.: Yale University Press, 1990).

Heath, Stephen, 'Male Feminism' in Smith, Alice and Paul, eds., *Men in Feminism* (New York: Routledge, 1989), 1–32.

Johnson, Johnson. F. et al, *Oral Epics from Africa: Vibrant Voices from the Vast Continent* (Bloomington: Indiana University Press, 1997).

Johnson, John W. *The Epic of Son-Jara: According to Fa-Digi Sisoko: A West African Tradition* (Bloomington: Indiana University Press, 1986).

Lunsing, Win, 'What Masculinity? Transgender Practices Among Japanese Men' in Robertson, James E. and Suzuki, Nobue, eds., *Men and Masculinities in Contemporary Japan: Dislocating the Salaryman Doxa* (New York: Routledge, 2002), 20–26.

Mazrui, Alamin, *Swahili Beyond the Boundaries: Literature, Language and Identity*

(Athens: Ohio University Press, 2007).

Mbele, Joseph, 'Women in the African Epic' In *Research in African Literatures* 37 (2) (2006), 61–67.

——The Hero in the African Epic,' in *Africana Journal* 13 (1–4) (1982), 121–41.

Mshamu, Mwanakupona Binti, 'A Mother's Advice and Prayer: An Epic' In Lihamba, Amandina, Moyo, Fulana L., Mulokozi, M. M., Shitemi, Naomi L. and Yahada-Othman, Saida, eds., *Women Writing Africa: The Eastern Region*, tr. Ann Biesteker and Naomi Shitemi (New York: Feminist Press, 2007), 72–80.

Mulokozi, Mugyabuso, 'The Nanga Bards of Tanzania: Are they Epic Artists?,' in *Research in African Literatures* 14(1983), 283–311.

Mnyampala, Mathias and Chiraghdin, Shihabuddin, *Historia ya Kiswahili* (Oxford: Oxford University Press, 1977).

Naggy, Fussi, 'The Ethnic Situation in East Africa and the Folklore Figure of Liongo Fumo,' in *Artes Pupulares* 10–11 (1984), 499–504.

Okepwho, Isidore, *The Epic in Africa: Toward a Poetics of the Oral Performance* (New York: Columbia University Press, 1979).

Onyanyo, James Ogola, 'Masculinities in Kiswahili Children's Literature in Kenya,' in *Swahili Forum* 14 (2007), 245–254.

Roberts, Andrew Michael, *Conrad and Masculinity* (London: Macmillan, 2000).

Seitel, Peter, *The Powers of Genres: Interpreting Haya Oral Literature* (Oxford: Oxford University Press, 1999).

Shariff, I. N., 'The Liyongo Conundrum: Re-Examining the Historicity of Swahili's National Poet–Hero' in *Research in African Literatures* 22 (1991), 153–157.

Steere, Edward, *Swahili Tales as Told by Natives of Zanzibar* (Nendeln, Liechtenstein: Kraus Reprint, 1970).

Wamitila, K. W., *Archeypal Criticism of Swahili Literature, with Special Reference to Fumo Liyongo* (Bayreuth, Germany: Bayreuth University, 2002).

2. Masculinity in the West African Epic

Notes

1. Berger, Wallis and Watson, 1995.
2. Belcher, 1999.
3. Newton, 1997.
4. Olivier de Sardan, 1984.
5. Niane, 1960.
6. Johnson and Sisòkò 1986.
7. Hale and Malio, 1990; Hale and Malio, 1996
8. Hale and Malio, *The Epic of Askia Mohammed*, line 902.
9. es-Sadi 1898–1900; Kâti, 1912.

10. Hale, 1990, 112.
11. Hale, 1990.
12. Bird and Kendall, 1980.
13. Niane, 1965; Johnson and Sisòkò, 1986.
14. Conrad, lines 358–373, in Johnson, Belcher and Hale, 1997, 54.
15. Conrad, 1976.
16. Hale and Malio, 1997, 17.
17. Hale, 1998.
18. Niane, 1965, 58.
19. Niane, 1965, 59.
20. Hale, 1990.
21. Hoffman, 1995.
22. Innes, 1978, 49, lines 391–392.
23. Innes, 1978, 49–50, lines 409–410.
24. Innes, 1978, 50, lines 442–444.
25. Innes, 1978, 9–11.
26. Belcher, 1999.
27. Dieng, 1993.

References

Belcher, Stephen. *Epic Traditions of Africa*. Bloomington: Indiana University Press, 1999.

Berger, Maurice, Brian Wallis and Simon Watson eds. *Constructing Masculinity*. New York: Routledge, 1995.

Bird, Charles and Martha B. Kendall. "The Mande Hero: Text and Context." In *Explorations in African Systems of Thought* (Edited by Ivan Karp and Charles Bird). Bloomington: Indiana University Press, 1980.

Dieng, Bassirou. *L'Epopée de Lat Dior*. Dakar: Editions Khoudia, 1993.

Es-Sa'di, Abderrahman ben Abdallah ben 'Imran ben'Amir. *Tarîkh es-Soudan*. (Translated by Octave Houdas). Paris: Ecole des Langues Orientales Vivantes, 1898–1900; 2nd edition., Paris: Adrien-Maisonneuve, 1964.

Hale, Thomas A. *Scribe, Griot and Novelist: Narrative Interpreters of the Songhay Empire: Followed by The Epic of Askia Mohammed Recounted by Nouhou Malio*. Gainesville: University Press of Florida, 1990.

—*Griot and Griottes: Masters of Words and Music*: Bloomington: Indiana University Press, 1998.

Hale, Thomas A. and Nouhou Malio: *The Epic of Askia Mohammed*. Bloomington: Indiana University Press, 1997.

Hoffman, Barbara. "Power, Structure and Mande Jeliw." In David Conrad and Barbara Frank, eds., *Status and Identity in West Africa: Nyamakalaw of Mande*. Bloomington: Indiana University Press, 1995.

Innes, Gordon. Ed. *Kelefa Saane: His Career Recounted by Two Mandinka Bards*.

London: School of Oriental and African Studies, University of London, 1978.

Johnson, John William and Fa-Digi Sisòkò. *The Epic of Son-Jara: A West African Tradition.* Bloomington: Indiana University Press, 1986, 1992, 2003.

Johnson, John William, Thomas Hale and Stephen Belcher. *Oral Epics from Africa: Vibrant Voices from a Vast Continent.* Bloomington: Indiana University Press, 1997.

Kâti, Mahmoud. *Tarîkh el-Fattâch ou chronique du chercheur pour servir à l'histoire des villes, des armées, et des principaux personages du Tekrour.* (Translated by Octave Houdas and Maurice Delafosse). Paris: Ernest Leroux, 1913.

Newton, Robert. The Epic Cassette: Technology, Tradition and Imagination in Contemporary Bamana Segou. Ph.D. diss. University of Wisconsin, 1997.

Niane, Djibril Tamsir. *Soundjata ou l'épopée mandingue.* Paris: Présence Africaine, 1960. (Translated by G. D. Pickett as *Sundiata: An Epic of Old Mali,* trans. G. D. Pickett. London: Longman, 1965.)

Olivier de Sardan, Jean Pierre. *Les Sociétés songhay-zarma (Niger-Mali): Chefs, guerriers, esclaves, paysans . . .* Paris: Karthala, 1984.

3. Men and Power: The Folktales and Proverbs of the *Baganda*

English Language Sources

Notes

1. Kabira, 'Images of Women in Gikuyu Narratives,' 77.
2. It was common in a polygamous household for one of the women to be designated 'favourite' and the other 'hated.' In a number of cases these designations were based on the sex of the woman's children.
3. The Luganda tales and proverbs used in this chapter are the result of an extensive field research by the author. Some of them are similar to those already collected and published by previous researchers such as Oluganda (*Engero Amakumi Abiri Mu Ebbiri*), Sseganyi (*Ssebato Bafuma*), Ssekamwa (*Ebisoko N'Engero Ez'Amakulu Amakusike*), Masembe (*Engero Zaffe*), Nsimbi (*Amannya Amaganda N'Ennono Zaago*) and Kagwa (*The Customs of the Baganda*). The translations are all my own.
4. In a tale entitled 'Mukwenda's Dumb Wife and the Baby Boy' the husband promises a big reward to the woman who will give birth to a boy. The senior wife (Kaddulubaale) conspires with the midwife to exchange her baby girl with the baby boy belonging to Kasiru, her young 'dumb' co-wife, with whom she had given birth at the same time. Kaddulubaale and the midwife believe that because Kasiru cannot speak their secret is secure. Unknown to them, Kasiru is not really dumb: she has simply decided not to speak, following her mother's advice to remain silent in order to observe

the vice in the world. On the day of initiating the children into the clan, Kasiru speaks up and reclaims her son—much to the shame and embarrassment of Kaddulubaale and the midwife.

5. Freud actually suggests that the baby girl subconsciously realises that by being female she is denied power and therefore bears her mother a grudge for not making her a boy. See *Feminist Frameworks*, 93–98.

6. It calls to mind the remarks of Okereke on page 32 in 'The Birth Song as a Medium for Communicating Woman's Maternal Destiny in the Traditional Community,' who asserts that as soon as a baby girl is born among the Igbo (of Nigeria), everybody knows that she will grow up, get married and produce children, preferably boys.

7. The Baganda clan system provides for individuals to be given names that originate from the clan of the father.

8. One of our informers in the field actually told us her own family story, which we found significant. Her father had seven daughters and one boy, who was the last born. At the age of 17, when the father was about 65, the boy died. In his mourning, the father kept saying: *'Omwana afudde nsigaliddewo'* (The child has died and I am left alone). His daughters stopped mourning their brother and just looked at him.

9. In traditional Buganda, it was taboo for a boy to engage in feminine acts such as peeling Matoke and cooking. If he did so, it was believed, he ran the risk of remaining unmarried for the rest of his life.

10. Rosaldo, commenting on this situation, observes that: 'Girls are more likely to form ties with female kin who are their seniors; they are integrated vertically through ties with particular people into the adult world of work. This contrasts with young boys who, having few responsibilities in late childhood, may create horizontal and often competitive peer groups, which cross-cut domestic units and establish "public" and over-arching ties. See 'Woman, Culture and Society: A Theoretical Overview,' 17–42.

11. Stories of this kind are also common among the Itesot (see Akello, *Itesot Thought Patterns in Tales*). Among the Bagisu of Eastern Uganda, there are the tales that feature Mwambu as the main characters, in which the brother plays a protective role over the sister. The Nyamwezi story, 'The Four Brothers and the Sister,' also illustrates this theme. The first three brothers fail to protect their sister and it is only the youngest that succeeds. The Kinyankore story of 'Nyangoma and Kaliisa' also has the same theme of the boy protecting his sister. This theme therefore seems to be shared with other African societies.

12. Mill, 'Subjection of Women,' 108.

13. Although some oral literature forms can psychologically undermine one group in its struggle against another, the suggestion that this type of

literature is always authored or transmitted by the opposing group tends to oversimplify the literary process and is not supported by evidence from the field. The question of the authorship of oral literature is a complicated one, because groups of people tend to transmit literatures that depict them unfavourably.

14. Kagwa, *Customs of the Baganda*, 233.

15. Here are some of them: *Abasajja ssubi, erimu lisiba linnaalyo* (Men are like grass, some grass ties its fellow grass); *Bw'ogoba musajja munno, olekamu ezinadda* (When you chase your fellow man, you leave enough strength to run back); *Musajja munno lukolokolo, olusika lukusika* (Your fellow man is like a banana tree stump; as you pull it, it also pulls you); *Musajja munno, omuwerera akuwerera* (Your fellow man, you threaten him as he threatens you); *Atatya musajja munne, tawangaala* (The one who does not fear his fellow man does not live long); *Basajja mabaale, gaasa gannaago* (Men are stone, they break each other); *Omusajja kikere, ky'ejja kyokka mu bunnya* (A man is like a frog, it gets out of the hole by itself); *Musajja munno bw'aswakiira, omweesega* (When your fellow man gets very angry it is wise to retreat).

16. Mugambi develops the theory of silencing from the Kintu myth and it works well for the majority of the tales of the Baganda. Unless a woman is noted for being rebellious, she is mentioned only in association with the several tasks that she performs (see 'Intersections: Gender, Orality, Text and Female Space in Contemporary Kiganda Radio Songs,' 48).

17. Author's personal research collection, unpublished. See note 3 above.

18. *American Heritage Dictionary*, 1969.

19. Although the social system of the Baganda condones the beating of women by men, it would look with horror upon a stronger woman beating a physically weaker husband. Part of the briefing that girls get when they are getting married has to do with being patient if their husbands should beat them.

20. Each wife took a name that corresponded to her status in the home. The senior wife was called Kaddulubaale, while others took on names such as Nassaza or Kabejja.

21. Many proverbs feature a man with two homes. He has to run around to protect each home, he often has to eat twice and sometimes he goes hungry because each wife assumes he has eaten elsewhere, as in the following proverbs: *Namaka abirye, afa njala* (The man with two homesteads dies of hunger); *Amaka abiri musango, olwanira agali e Kyagwe, nga n'age e Ssingo baganyaga* (Having two homes is a big problem, you fight to retain the one in Kyaggwe, while at the same time the one in Ssingo is being taken); *Kufuntuka; ngeyalidde gyatasule* (No alternative but to over-eat, like a man [with two wives] who has eaten at the home where he is not going to sleep [When he gets to the other home, he has to eat again, because the wife

will not accept the explanation that he has already eaten somewhere else].).

22. The background to this proverb is the custom of wife inheritance, which was widely practised among the Baganda in the past. The people who inherited wives were normally the brothers of the deceased, although a distant relative was also eligible. Also, an elder son could inherit a wife from his father, provided that wife had not yet given birth to a baby boy. However, the custom of sons inheriting their fathers' wives died out earlier than the general custom of inheritance and is not known to many people today.

23. The Luo of Western Kenya have a similar story featuring an enterprising woman and a man who is docile to the degree of stupidity. The only difference is that where the Baganda have a monster gorilla, the Luo have hyenas (see Onyango-Ogutu and Roscoe, *Keep My Words*.

24. In the real life of the Baganda, there are no signs that suggest that boys love their mothers any less than girls, as is implied in the tale in which the man kills his mother. Indeed, in some cases, boys have been found to be more attached to their mothers than girls.

25. It was even suggested to the researcher that the impotent man was exempt from paying Graduated Tax. This wasn't written down anywhere, but many elders asserted that it was the case in practice. Haji Kassim Kiggundu of Kiweesa Masaka (interviewed on 3 March 1998) was emphatic in his assertion that if a man came out and openly declared that he was impotent, the tax collectors did not bother him.

26. The most commonly used reference is that of 'the bereaved,' but it is possible for one who is not initiated in the context of discourse at any one particular time to miss the point.

27. In the village of Kalama we were told of two cases of young men who had committed suicide because of the taunts about their impotence.

28. In one incident, a female research assistant I worked with was taken aside by a group of women and was told two stories that explicitly feature impotence. The proverbs about impotence, especially the more direct ones, were collected from one old man who insisted on a private, one-to-one audience. Even my (female) research assistant was excluded.

29. This arrangement began to gradually change with the coming of the Europeans. Later, what was left of the Kingdom of Buganda was abolished by Milton Obote in 1962. What was restored by President Museveni in 1993 is a cultural institution without political power.

30. Several scholars, both foreign and indigenous, record the brutalities that were practised by the Baganda kings on their subjects, especially the killing of them at will. J. S. Kasirye and Semakula Kiwanuka, among others, have detailed records of how the kings used their power to

terrorise their subjects. Kings Suuna II and Mutesa I are particularly memorable in Buganda's history because of their tyrannical acts. Mutesa was initially called Mukaabya (one who makes others cry), but he later changed heart and became Mutesa (one who discusses) (see Kiwanuka, *History of Buganda*, 155).

31. The king is called *Sabasajja* (husband of all men) or Bbaffe (our husband). In real life Buganda, all women were regarded as the king's wives and no man had the right to complain if the king took his wife. If a man was passing near the king's palace, he was not allowed to touch any woman, including his wife, because she was automatically the king's wife by virtue of her proximity to the palace.

References

Akello, Grace, *Itesot Thought Patterns in Tales* (Dar es Salaam, Tanzania: Dar es Salaam University Press, 1981).

Amaduime, Ifi, *Male Daughters, Female Husbands: Gender and Sex in an African Society* (London: Zed Books, 1987).

Bamberger, Joan, 'The Myth of Matriarchy: Why Men Rule in Primitive Society,' in Rosaldo, M. Z. and Lamphere, L., eds., *Woman, Culture and Society* (Stanford, Calif.: Stanford University Press, 1974), 263–280.

Beauvoir, Simone de, *The Second Sex* (New York: Knopf, 1953).

Finnegan, R., *Oral Literature in Africa* (Nairobi, Kenya: Oxford University Press, 1970).

Firestone, Shulamith, 'The Dialectic of Sex,' in Jagger, Alison M. and Rothenberg, Paula, eds., *Feminist Frameworks* (New York: McGraw-Hill, 1984), 23–31.

Freud, Sigmund, 'Femininity,' in Jagger, Alison M. and Rothenberg, Paula, eds., *Feminist Frameworks* (McGraw-Hill, 1984), 127–134.

Kabira, Wanjiku M., 'Images of Women in Gikuyu Narratives' (PhD dissertation, University of Nairobi, 1993).

—'Gender and Politics of Control: An Overview of Images of Women in Gikuyu Narratives,' in Bukenya, A., Kabira, W. M. and Okombo, Okoth, eds., *Understanding Oral Literature* (Nairobi, Kenya: Nairobi University Press, 1994), 77–84.

Kagwa, A., *The Customs of the Baganda* (New York: Columbia University Press, 1934).

Kalibbala, E. B., *The Social Structure of the Baganda Tribe of East Africa* (Cambridge, Mass.: Harvard University Press, 1946).

Kiwanuka, M. S., *A History of Buganda* (New York: African Publishing, 1972).

Lakoff, Robin, *Language and Woman's Place* (New York: Harper and Row, 1975).

Lamphere, Louise, 'Strategies, Cooperation and Conflict Among Women in Domestic Groups,' in Rosaldo, M. Z. and Lamphere, L., eds., *Woman,*

Culture and Society (Stanford, Calif.: Stanford University Press, 1974), 97–112.

Lema, Eliesha, *Parched Earth* (Dar es Salaam, Tanzania: E and D Ltd., 2001).

Lercock, Eleanor Burke, *Myths of Male Dominance* (London: Monthly Review Press, 1981).

Mabala, Richard S., 'Gender Relations in Kiswahili Fiction,' in Mbilinyi, D. A. and Omari, C., eds., *Gender Relations and Women's Images in the Media* (Dar es Salaam, Tanzania: Dar es Salaam University Press, 1995), 134–143.

Mazrui, A. M. and Abala, J. I., 'Sex and Patriachy: Gender Relations in *Mawt al-rajul al-wahid 'ala al-ard* (God Dies by the Nile),' in *Research in African Literatures* 28 (3) (1997), 17–32.

Mill, John Stuart, 'The Subjection of Women,' in Jagger, Alison M. and Rothenberg, Paula, eds., *Feminist Frameworks* (New York: McGraw-Hill, 1984), 104–114.

Mugambi, Helen Nabasuta, 'Intersections: Gender, Orality, Text and Female Space in Contemporary Kiganda Radio Songs,' in *Women as Oral Artists*, a special issue of *Research in African Literatures* 25 (3) (1994), 47–63.

Onyango-Ogutu, B. and Roscoe, A. A., *Keep My Words: Luo Oral Literature* (Nairobi, Kenya: East African Publishing House, 1974).

Ojoade, J. Olowo, 'The Old Woman as Seen Through African Proverbs: Fragmentary Remarks About African Society Through Sayings,' in *Folklore* 26 (6) (1985), 110– 114.

Okereke, Grace Eche, 'The Birth Song as a Medium for Communicating Woman's Maternal Destiny in the Traditional Community,' in *Women as Oral Artists*, special edition of *Research in African Literatures* 25 (3) (1994), 19–32.

Okpewho, Isidore, *African Oral Literature* (Bloomington: Indiana University Press, 1992).

Propp, V., *Morphology of the Folktale* (Austin: University of Texas Press, 1996).

Rosaldo, M. Z., 'Woman, Culture and Society: A Theoretical Overview,' in Rosaldo, M. Z. and Lamphere, L., eds., *Woman, Culture and Society* (Stanford, Calif.: Stanford University Press, 1974), 17–42.

Roscoe, John, *The Baganda: An Account of their Native Customs and Beliefs* (London: Macmillan, 1911).

Safilios-Rothschild, Constantina, *Women and Social Policy* (Englewood Cliffs, N.J.: Prentice Hall, 1974).

Schipper, M., *Source of All Evil: The Woman in African Proverbs* (Nairobi, Kenya: Phoenix Publishers, 1991).

Thompson, Stith, *The Folktale* (New York: Dryden Press, 1979).

Vansina, Jan, *Oral Tradition as History* (London: James Currey, 1985).

Walser, Ferdinand, *Luganda Proverbs* (Kampala, Uganda: Mill Hill Missionaries, 1984).

Wellek, Rene and Warren, Austin, *Theory of Literature* (London: Penguin Books, 1993).

Wittig, Monique, 'One is Not Born a Woman,' in Jagger, Alison M. and Rothenberg, Paula, eds., *Feminist Frameworks* (New York: McGraw-Hill, 1984), 178–182.

Luganda Language Sources

Ekibiina Ky'Olulimi Oluganda, *Engero Amakumi Abiri Mu Ebbiri* (Twenty Two Folktales) (Kuala Lumpur, Malaysia: Longman, 1960).

Kagwa, A., *Ekitabo Ky'Empisa Z'Abaganda* (The Book of the Customs of the Baganda) (Kampala: Uganda Printing and Publishing, 1993).

—*Ebika By'Abaganda N'Ennono Zaabyo* (Ganda Clans and their Origins) (London: Sheldon Press, 1927).

—*Engero Z'Abaganda* (Ganda Tales) (London: Sheldon Press, 1927).

Kasirye, J., *Abateregga ku Namulondo ya Buganda* (London: Macmillan, 1955).

Kawere, Edward K. N., *Zinunula Omunaku* (Kampala, Uganda: East African Literature Bureau, 1954).

Kimala, Adam, *Abaganda Ab'Edda* (The Baganda of the Past) (Kampala, Uganda: Luganda Consultancy Bureau, 1995).

Masembe, Harriet, *Engero Zaffe* (Our Tales) (Kampala, Uganda: Fountain Publishers, 1996).

Mpalanyi, Solomon, *Ndikumma Okulya* (Kampala, Uganda: Crane Publishers, 1977).

Nsimbi, M. B., *Amannya Amaganda N'Ennono Zaago* (Ganda Names and their Origins) (Kampala, Uganda: Longman, 1989).

—*Siwa Muto Lugero* (I Do Not Tell Proverbs to a Young One) (Harlow, England: Longman, 1989).

Sseganyi, E. A. K., *Ssebato Bafuma* (Young Ones Tell Tales) (Kampala, Uganda: East African Literature Bureau, 1959).

Ssekamwa, J. C., *Ebisoko N'Engero Ez'Amakulu Amakusike* (Idioms/Proverbs and Tales with Deep Meanings) (Kampala, Uganda: Fountain Publishers, 1995).

4. 'Ndabaga' Folktale Revisited: (De)constructing the Masculine in Post-Genocide Rwanda

Notes

1. Faludi, *Stiffed*, 48–58.
2. This folktale is from Rwanda. My analysis is based on the French translation by Pierre Smith (*Le recit populaire au Rwanda*, 181–183). The English translations from the tale that appear in this chapter are mine. In

Smith's book, the title of the story is 'La fille dans l'impasse' (The Girl at an Impasse). Throughout the folktale, the protagonist is referred to as 'la jeune fille' (the young woman) because (according to Smith's informant), 'it is not clear in the Rwandan mind whether the name, whose sense is hermetic, refers to the heroine or to her father' (180–181). I have decided to use the Kinyarwanda title 'Ndabaga' and to refer to the protagonist as Ndabaga because in another version of the tale the heroine's father has a different name: Sakindi.

3. Greimas, *Sémantique structurale: recherche de méthode*, 180–185.
4. Smith, *Le recit populaire au Rwanda*, 181.
5. Sartre, *Existentialism and Humanism*, 549.
6. De Beauvoir, *Second Sex*, 301.
7. *Ibid.*, 38.
8. Ntampaka, 'La femme et la fille dans leur famille d'origine,' 24–25, quoted in *Human Rights Watch*, 20 .
9. Lacan, *Female Sexuality*, 1985.
10. Ragland-Sullivan, *Jacques Lacan and the Philosophy of Psychoanalysis*, 264.
11. *Human Rights Watch*, 1996, 19–20.
12. *Ibid.*, 20.
13. Chodorov, *Feminism and Psychoanalytic Theory*, 168.
14. De Beauvoir, *Second Sex*, 308.
15. Kimenyi, 'Why is it that Women in Rwanda Cannot Marry?,' 307.
16. Serubibi, 'L'éducation traditionnelle à travers la littérature orale,' 27–28.
17. Powley, Strengthening Governance,' 4.
18. Taylor, *Sacrifice as Terror*, 154.
19. Batamuliza, 'From Warriors to Peacemakers :The Women of Ndabaga,' <www.internews.org.rw/articles>.
20. This statement was made by Rose Kayumba in her address on the Ndabaga association at the Conference on Women Building Peace through Disarmament, Demobilisation and Reintegration on 9 March 2005, at the United Nations in New York.
21. In 2006, I had the opportunity to travel with Ndabaga women returning from the peacekeeping mission in Darfur. Those I spoke to agreed that integrating women in the peacekeeping forces has given the organisation an important gender dimension. Their service has also given the Ndabaga Association worldwide recognition that has reinforced Rwanda's high ranking on the issue of gender balance in government.

References

Batamuliza, Apophia, 'From Warriors to Peacemakers: The Women of Ndabaga' in *Internews Rwanda Articles* (Retrieved 13 June 2005, from <www.internews.org. rw/articles>).

Beavoir, Simone de, *The Second Sex*, Parshley, H. M., ed. and tr., (New York: Knopf, 1953).

Chodorov, Nancy, *Feminism and Psychonalytic Theory* (New Haven, Conn.: Yale University Press, 1989).

Faludi, Susan, 'The Betrayal of the American Man,' in *Newsweek* (13 September 1999), 48–58.

Government of Rwanda, *Rapport national pour la quatrième conference mondiale sur les femmes* (Bejing, China: September 1995).

Greimas, Algirdas-Julien, *Sémantique structurale: recherche de méthode* (rpt. Paris: Presse Universitaire de France, 1986).

Human Rights Watch, *Shattered Lives: Sexual Violence during the Rwandan Genocide and its Aftermath* (New York: Human Rights Watch, 1996).

Kimenyi, Alexander, 'Why is it that Women in Rwanda Cannot Marry?,' in Hall, Kira, Bucholtz, Mary and Moonwomon, Birch, eds., *Locating Power: Proceedings of the Second Berkeley Women and Language Conference*, Vol. 2 (Berkeley Women and Language Group, 1992).

Lacan, Jacques, *Female Sexuality*, tr. Jacqueline Rose; Juliet Mitchell and Jacqueline Rose, eds. (New York: Norton, 1985).

Ntampaka, Charles, 'La femme et la fille dans leur famille d'origine,' in *Haguruka: Association pour la défense des droits de la femme et de l'enfant* (Kigali, Kenya: United States Embassy, 1993).

Powley, Elizabeth, 'Strengthening Governance: The Role of Women in Rwanda's Transition. A Summary,' in *United Nations Office of the Special Adviser on Gender Issues And Advancement of Women (OSAGI)*, Expert Group Meeting on 'Enhancing Women's Participation in Electoral Processes in Post-Conflict Countries (Glen Cove, Ill.: 19–22 January 2004). Retrieved from <www.un.org/womenwatch/ osagi/meetings/2004/EGMelectoral/EP5 Powley.PDF>

Raglan-Sullivan, Ellie, *Jacques Lacan and the Philosophy of Psychoanalysis* (Urbana: University of Illinois Press, 1987).

Rapport de Haguruka. Retrieved from <www.grandslacs.net/doc/3989.pdf, 2001>.

Sartre, Jean-Paul, *Existentialism and Humanism*, tr. Philip Mairet (New York: Haskell House, 1977).

—*Being and Nothingness*, tr. Hazel E. Barnes (New York: Citadel Press, 1964).

Serubibi, Kayirere wa, 'L'éducation traditionnelle à travers la littérature orale,' in *Rwanda. Mémoire pour l'Obtention du Diplôme de Graduat, I.S.P.* (Bukavu, Congo, 1974).

Smith, Pierre, *Le récit populaire au Rwanda* (Paris: Association Classiques Africains, 1975), 181–83.

Taylor, Christopher, *Sacrifice as Terror. The Rwandan Genocide of 1994* (New York: Oxford, 1999).

Women International for Peace and Freedom, 'Rwanda. Women Ex-combatants Seek Inclusion in Peacekeeping Missions.' Retrieved from <http://allafrica.com/ stories/200411180035.html>.

5. The Man from Udje: African Oral Poetic Performance

Notes

1. Chief Jonathan Mrakpor of Edjophe, in an interview on 6 August 1999 at his Otughievwen home in Ughelli South Local Government, Delta State, Nigeria.
2. Chief Dozen Ogbariemu, a native of Iwhrekan in Ughelli South Local Government, Delta State, Nigeria, told me this in an interview on 26 December 2006 in his house.
3. Ojaide, *Poetry, Performance and Art*, 97.
4. *Ibid.*, 101–102.
5. *Ibid.*
6. *Ibid.*, 31.
7. Darah, *Battles of Songs*, 113.
8. Ojaide, *Poetry, Performance and Art*, 96.
9. *Ibid.*, 105.
10. Darah, *Battles of Songs*, 87.
11. *Ibid.*, 21.
12. Elliott, *Power of Satire*, 69.
13. Ojaide, *Poetry, Performance and Art*, 99–100.
14. When I first met Okitiakpe of Ekakpamre in 1977 he was already very old and he asked his eldest daughter to sing me his songs, nodding his head as she did so.
15. Ojaide, Poetry, Performance and Art, 95.
16. Uto is a quarter of Ekakpamre, a town in Ughelli Local Government Area of Nigeria's Delta State. Okitiakpe belongs to the rival Ekrusierho quarter of the same town.
17. Darah, *Battles of Songs*, 214.
18. *Ibid.*, 102.
19. Ojaide, *Poetry, Performance and Art*, 103.
20. *Ibid.*, 124.
21. *Ibid.*, 139.
22. Darah, *Battles of Songs*, 173.
23. *Ibid.*, 147.
24. Ojaide, *Poetry, Performance and Art*, 146.
25. *Ibid.*, 165.
26. *Ibid.*, 121.

References

Bergson, Henri, *Le Rire* (Paris: Presses Universitaires de France, 2004).

Clark, J. P., 'Poetry of the Urhobo Dance Udje,' in *Nigeria Magazine*, 87 (1965).

Conteh-Morgan, John and Olaniyan, Tejumola, eds., *African Drama and Performance* (Bloomington: Indiana University Press, 2004).

Cope, Trevor, ed., *Izibongo: Zulu Praise Poems* (Oxford: Oxford University Press, 1968).

Darah, G. G., *Battles of Songs: Udje Tradition of the Urhobo* (Lagos, Nigeria: Malthouse, 2005).

D'Azevedo, W. L., *The Traditional Artist in African Societies* (Bloomington: Indiana University Press, 1975).

Elliott, R. C., *The Power of Satire: Magic, Ritual and Art* (Princeton, N.J.: Princeton University Press, 1960).

Finnegan, Ruth, *Oral Literature in Africa* (London: Clarendon Press, 1970).

Ogede, Ode, *Art, Society and Performance: Igede Praise Poetry* (Gainesville: University of Florida Press, 1997).

Ojaide, Tanure, *Poetry, Performance and Art: Udje Dance Songs of the Urhobo People* (Durham, N.C.: Carolina Academic Press, 2003).

—*Poetic Imagination in Black Africa* (Durham, N.C.: Carolina Academic Press, 1996).

Okpewho, Isidore, *African Oral Literature: Background, Character and Continuity* (Bloomington: Indiana University Press, 1992).

Opland, Jeff, *Xhosa Oral Poetry* (Cambridge: Cambridge University Press, 1983).

Otite, Onigu, ed., *The Urhobo People* (Ibadan, Nigeria: Heinemann Nigeria, 1983).

6. Masculinities on Trial: Gender Anxiety in African Song Performances

Notes

1. This epigram and many of the proverbs in this chapter can be found in Bukenya's unpublished collection. The author of this chapter has transcribed and translated all song quotations from artists' Luganda audio cassette tapes. I would like to express my gratitude to Austin Bukenya for illuminating conversations on masculinity in Buganda and for generously sharing his unpublished proverb collection. I am also grateful to the Stanford Humanities Centre whose Fellowship enabled me to consolidate work on this piece.

2. The similarities between the Senegalese school teacher Ramatoulaye and the non-western educated Ugandan Kaddulubaale, (the senior wife in

Nakakaawa), are striking. Both women painfully recall their many years of unrewarded marital devotion as they lament their husbands' decisions to take on second wives.

3. A comprehensive discussion of my assertion that the nature, form and function of *kadongokamu* songs have evolved from those of the traditional folktale is available in *Gendered Encounters*, (205–222). A segment of that chapter was the first ever analysis of the *Kayanda* performance as a serious cultural text.

4. I have structured portions of this chapter to create a dialogue with my previous analyses of feminist texts in the two song performances examined here (see item 3 above as well as my article in *Research in African Literature*, 47-70). In certain instances, identical plot moments, like two sides of the same coin, attest to the male-oriented nature of this Ugandan culture.

5. In *Cassette Culture*, Peter Manuel describes an identical phenomenon in India, where proliferation of cheap portable cassette players during the same time period (1980s) created a revolution in which popular music became available to the masses. As copyright laws were not enforced at the time, anyone could make a list of their favourite songs and have them reproduced on site in market stalls.

6. Kimmel, *Masculinity Studies and Feminist Theory*, xi.

7. *Ibid.*, x.

8. The Baganda also have proverbs that signal a celebration of gender balance in marriage. For instance, Ontuuse: Nnalunga yatuuka Jjuuko (You and I are an ideal match: just like Nalunga and Jjuuko), summons the memory of a blissful mythical marriage. Ferdinand Walser's , *Luganda Proverbs* (Kampala, Uganda: Mill Hill Missionaries, 1984) provides an extensive collection of over 5,000 entries with a wide range of thematic concerns. On a continental scale, pioneering the study of African proverbs in the 21st century, Joseph Healey, M.M. serves as moderator of the 'African Proverbs, Sayings and Stories' which should benefit any comparative study. See Website at http://www.afriprov.

9. In his book, *The Black Renaissance in Francophone African and the Caribbean*, Martial Frindethie creatively described this phenomenon as *griotism*.

10. Roscoe, *Baganda*, 361. One of the earlier books on Buganda, this book attests to Buganda's patriarchal heritage to which many of the proverbs testify.

11. RCs were instituted by Yoweri Museveni's postcolonial government to mimic indigenous mediation institutional structures such as the one summoned by Ssepiria in *Nakakaawa*.

12. Perhaps the ineffectiveness or misuse of the RC's power dramatised in the performances reflects the problems of a new nation still struggling to create its identity.

References

Bukenya, Austin, Unpublished Collection of Proverbs.

Frindethie, Martial K., *The Black Renaissance in Francophone African and Caribbean Literatures* (Jefferson, N.C.: McFarland, 2008).

Kimmel, Michael, 'Foreword,' in Gardiner, Judith Kegan, ed., *Masculinity Studies and Feminist Theory: New Directions* (New York: Columbia University Press, 2002).

Luyima, Matia, *Nakakaawa*, performed by Super Singers (audio cassette) (Producer: Kasajja and Sons Studios, n.d.).

Manuel, Peter, *Cassette Culture: Popular Music and Technology in North India* (Chicago: University of Chicago Press, 1993).

Mugambi, Helen N., 'Reading Masculinities in a Feminist Text: Dangarembga's *Nervous Conditions*,' in Ogunyemi, Chikwenye Okonjo and Allan, Tuzyline Jita, eds., *The Twelve Best Books by African Women: Critical Readings* (Athens: Ohio University Press, 2009), 258–282.

—'From Story to Song: Gender, Nationhood and the Migratory Text,' in Grosz-Ngate, Maria and Kokole, Omari, eds., *Gendered Encounters: Challenging Cultural Boundaries and Social Hierarchies in Africa* (New York: Routledge, 1997), 205–222.

—'Intersections: Gender, Orality, Text and Female Space in Kiganda Radio Songs,' in *Research in African Literatures* 25 (3) (Fall 1994), 47–70.

Mukaabya, Willy, *Kayanda*, performed by Festac Guitar Singers (audio cassette) (Producer: Kampala, Uganda: Kasajja and Sons Studios, 1988).

Roscoe, John, *The Baganda: An Account of Their Customs and Beliefs* (London: Macmillan, 1911).

Walser, Ferdinand, *Luganda Proverbs* (Kampala, Uganda: Mill Hill Missionaries, 1984).

7. Faces of Masculinity in African Cinema: Dani Kouyate's 'Sia: La Rêve du Python'

Notes

1. De Lauretis, 'The Technology of Gender,' 715.
2. 'The Griot Meets the Cinema,' an interview excerpt from Stephane Gobbo, in *La Liberte* (Switzerland: 23 November 2001). Available at <www.sialefilm.com/ en/reviews>.
3. The original source of this story is a seventh-century myth of the Soninke people. Both Kouyate and Diagana were fascinated by this myth and its contemporary relevance to African—and universal—power politics.
4. See <www.sialefilm.com/en/authors>. When it was first screened at FESPACO in 2001, the film won six awards and six distinctions at the various international festivals.

5. This storyline is a recurring theme in the representation of women from this part of Africa, which is often hit by natural disasters such as drought. Moustapha Alassane, the filmmaker from Niger, captures a similar theme in *Toula ou la Genie des Eaux* (1974) where, in exchange for rain, a beautiful virgin is offered to the water snake. This is also a story based on a Fulani myth and the director retells it to reflect a contemporary political situation.

6. De Lauretis, 'Technology of Gender,' 714.
7. Boggs, *Gramsci's Marxism*, 39.
8. Burke, 'Antonio Gramsci and Informal Education,' 1999.
9. Gramsci, 'Hegemony,' 277.
10. Bourdieu, *La Domination Masculine*, 48.
11. O'Sullivan et al., *Key Concepts in Communication and Cultural Studies*, 133–135.
12. See <www.sialefilm.com/en/authors/html>.
13. In the interview, Kouyate underlines the importance of having such 'madmen' in society. The madmen are like the artists who must speak the truth, at whatever cost. His view is that 'madness' itself is important for artists; they cannot achieve consistency without folly. Without folly they remain banal. Also see excerpts from a press conference given by Moussa Diagana and Dani Kouyate during FESPACO, about the film *Sia Le Rêve du Python* (Ouagadougou, Burkina Faso: 27 February 2001).
14. Barlet, 'Interview of Olivier Barlet with Dani Kouyate about *Sia*,' 2001. Available at <www.sialefilm.com/en/authors>.
15. This praise song brings to mind the representation of Mobutu in Thierry Michel's film, *Mobutu: Roi du Zaire* (1999). This makes Kaya Maghan a symbol easily identifiable on the African continent.
16. 'If in this film I denounce the god who devours his own children, I also denounce in the film the griots who betray their society.' Available at <www.sialefilm.com/ en/authors>.
17. Barlet, 'Interview of Olivier Barlet with Dani Kouyate about *Sia*,' 2001, Available at <www.sialefilm.com/en/authors>.
18. Osundare, *Thread in the Loom*, 7.
19. Gramsci, quoted in Rivkin and Ryan, *Literary Theory*, 277.
20. This *griotess* is also a foil to Balla, the official *griot*, who does nothing to challenge the state and its excesses. She, like Kerfa, represents the authentic role of the artist: that of truth-teller.
21. Agacinski, *Politique des Sexes*, 16.
22. Bourdieu, *La Domination Masculine*, 55.
23. *Ibid.*, 63.
24. This is an allusion to what Wakhane later confesses to Mamadi about how he let his own daughter, 'Little Mother,' die. This memory reminds him of his insensitivity and worthlessness as a father. That is why he orders the

immediate release of Sia's parents. In spite of his toughness he is a haunted man with a guilty conscience.

25. See Dipio, *Representation of Women and of the Changing Gender Roles in African Film Narrative*.

References

Agacinski, S., *Politique des Sexes* (Paris: Editions du Seuil, 1998).

Barlet, O., 'Interview of Olivier Barlet with Dani Kouyate about *Sia, Le Rêve du Python*' (Cannes Festival, May 2001). Available at <www.sialefilm.com/en/reviews>.

—'Interview of Olivier Barlet with Dani Kouyate about *Sia, Le Rêve du Python*' (Cannes Festival, May 2001). Available at <www.sialefilm.com/en/reviews>

Boggs, C., *Gramsci's Marxism* (London: Pluto Press, 1976).

Bourdieu, P., *La Domination Masculine* (Paris: Editions du Seuil, 1998).

Burke, B., 'Antonio Gramsci and Informal Education,' in *The Encyclopedia of Informal Education* (<www.infed.org/thinkers/et-gram>, 1999).

De Lauretis, T., 'The Technology of Gender,' in Rivkin, Julie and Ryan, Michael, eds., *Literary Theory: An Anatomy* (Oxford: Blackwell, 1998).

Dipio, D., *The Representation of Women and of the Changing Gender Roles in African Film Narrative: A Feminist Critical Approach* (Rome: Pontificia Universitate Gregoriana, 2003).

Gobbo, S., 'The Griot Meets the Cinema,' an interview excerpt from Stephane Gobbo in *La Liberte* (Switzerland, 23 November 2001). Available at <www.sialefilm.com/en/reviews>.

Gramsci, A., 'Hegemony,' in Rivkin, Julie and Ryan, Michael, eds., *Literary Theory: An Anthology* (Oxford: Blackwell, 1999).

Kouyate, D., 'Pseudo Democracy of Africa,' available at <www.sialefilm.com/en/authors>.

O'Sullivan, T. et al., *Key Concepts in Communication and Cultural Studies* (London: Routledge, 1997).

Osundare, N., *Thread in the Loom* (Trenton, N.J.: African World Press, 2002).

Rivkin, Julie and Ryan, Michael, eds., *Literary Theory: An Anthology* (Oxford: Blackwell, 1999).

8. Masculinity in Selected North African Films

Notes

1. This chapter was originally presented as a paper at the Annual Conference of the African Literature Association in Fez, Morocco on 10–13 March 1999. I thank B. J. and Bob Fernea, Sandra Carter, Ellie Higgins and Anne Morey for their advice and comments.

2. In my judgement, the documentary was much more perceptive and non-judgemental, feminist and non-racist than many of its commentators allowed. It is available from Women Make Movies in New York City.
3. Saddek Rabah has dissected the coverage of Islam in the French political weeklies, *L'Express* and *Le Nouvel Observateur* and found the twin topics of the veil and women's status in Islam to be two of the four obsessions evident, the others being the Khomeini *fatwa* against author Salman Rushdie and the notion of *jihad* (which is in reality much closer to sacred mission or crusade than holy war).
4. Naremore, *Acting in the Cinema*, 5–6.
5. There is no space here for a serious comparative analysis of these US and Arab actors, but it would be a very interesting assignment.
6. Hafez, 'Shifting Identities in Maghrebi Cinema,' 39.
7. Arab Film Distribution, Seattle and August Light Productions, San Francisco, are the two main US distributors at the time of writing.
8. Abbas Fadhil Ibrahim writes, 'we have to acknowledge the fact that Egyptian cinema has always loved to mix genres' (35). Ali Abu Shadi likewise writes, 'It is important to note a central problem . . . the overlapping of different genres and the merging of artistic forms, such as melodrama, with genres, such as realism' (85).
9. The word means 'dream' in Arabic.
10. Sometimes also translated as *The Chain and the Bracelet*.
11. Khayati, *Cinémas Arabes*, 46–51.
12. This is perhaps an unkind allusion to 1967, during the war against Israel a number of Egyptian soldiers—certainly not the majority—fled in terror before the advancing Israeli army in Sinai. The episode is portrayed dramatically in Youssef Chahine's *The Sparrow* (*Al-Usfur*, 1971).
13. The Nubian is played mostly for laughs, a depressing iteration of standard Egyptian stereotypes without dramatic justification.
14. A relatively recent instance of this all-too-familiar nonsense is *Gettysburg* (dir. Ronald Maxwell, 1993), where dying generals at the close of the battle scene send stiff-upper-lip farewells to their counterparts on the other side.
15. See 'Excerpts from the Umm Kulthum Nobody Knows,' in Fernea and Bezirgan, *Middle Eastern Women*, 135–165.
16. Ben Ammar, Abdellatif,, 115–116
17. Merzak Allouache has said that, 'In Omar I wanted to make a film and in no way an illustration of slogans' ('The Necessity of a Cinema Which Interrogates Everyday Life,' 96).
18. cf. Viola Shafik, *Arab Cinema: History and Cultural Identity*, 101–102.
19. Berrah, 'Algerian Cinema and National Identity,' 77.
20. An outstanding close reading of this film is to be found in Sandra G.

Carter's magisterial history of Moroccan cinema ('Moroccan Cinema: What Moroccan Cinema?,' vol. 3, iii).

21. I am grateful to B. J. Fernea for this observation.

References

Allouache, Merzak, 'The necessity of a cinema which interrogates everyday life,' in Downing, John D.H., ed., *Film and Politics in the Third World* (New York: Autonomedia, 1987), 93–99.

Ask, Karin and Tjomsland, Marit, eds., *Women and Islamization: Contemporary Dimensions of Discourse on Gender Relations* (Oxford: Berg, 1998).

Ben Ammar, Abdellatif, 'Putting Forward a Clear View on Life,' in Downing, John D.H., ed., *Film and Politics in the Third World* (New York: Autonomedia, 1987), 109–117.

Berrah, Mouny, 'Algerian Cinema and National Identity,' in Arasoughly, Alia, ed., *Screens of Life: Critical Film Writing from the Arab World* (St. Hyacinthe, Canada: World Heritage Press, 1996), 63–83.

Bingham, Dennis, *Acting Male: Masculinities in the Films of James Stewart, Jack Nicholson and Clint Eastwood* (Piscataway, N.J.: Rutgers University Press, 1994).

Callaway, Barbara and Creevey, Lucy, *Women, Religion and Politics in West Africa* (Boulder, Colo.: Lynne Rienner, 1994).

Carter, Sandra G., 'Moroccan Cinema: What Moroccan cinema?' (PhD dissertation, University of Texas at Austin, 1994).

Caughie, John, ed., *Theories of Authorship: A Reader* (London: British Film Institute, 1981).

Cornwall, Andrea and Lindisfarne, Nancy, eds., *Dislocating Masculinity: Comparative Ethnographies* (London: Routledge, 1994).

Farid, Samir, 'Periodization of Egyptian Cinema,' in Arasoughly, Alia, ed., *Screens of Life: Critical Film Writing from the Arab World* (St. Hyacinthe, Canada: World Heritage Press, 1996), 1–18.

Fernea, Elizabeth Warnock, *In Search of Islamic Feminism: One Woman's Global Journey* (New York: Doubleday, 1988).

Fernea, Elizabeth Warnock and Bezirgan, Basima Qattan, eds., *Middle Eastern Women Speak* (Austin: University of Texas Press, 1977).

Hafez, Sabry, 'Shifting Identities in Maghribi Cinema: The Algerian Paradigm,' in *Alif: Journal of Comparative Poetics* [Special issue on Arab cinematics] 15 (1995), 39–80.

Helmy, Ghada, 'The Plight of Women in Filmic Text and Literary Adaptation,' in *Alif: Journal of Comparative Poetics* [Special issue on Arab cinematics] 15 (1995), 178–201.

Ibrahim, Abbas Fadhil, 'Genres et star-système dans le cinéma égyptien,' in Berrah, Mouny et al., eds., *Les Cinémas Arabes* (Paris: CinémAction and Institut du Monde Arabe, 1986), 34–48.

Khayati, Khémais, *Cinémas Arabes: Topographie d'une Image Éclatée* (Paris: L'Harmattan, 1996).

Naremore, James, *Acting in the Cinema* (Berkeley and Los Angeles: University of California Press, 1988).

Rabah, Saddek, *L'Islam Dans Le Discours Médiatique: Comment les Médias se Représentent l'Islam en France?* (Beirut, Lebanon: Dar Al-Bouraq and Paris: Librairie de l'Orient, 1998).

Shadi, Ali Abu, 'Genres in Egyptian Cinema,' in Arasoughly, Alia, ed., *Screens of Life: Critical Film Writing from the Arab World* (Quebec, Canada: World Heritage Press, 1996), 84–129.

Shafik, Viola, *Arab Cinema: History and Cultural Identity* (Cairo, Egypt: American University in Cairo Press, 1998).

Thoraval, Yves, *Regards sur le Cinéma Égyptien* (2nd ed.) (Paris: L'Harmattan, 1996).

9. Penetrating Xala

Notes

1. Pfaff, *Cinema of Ousmane Sembène*, 160–161.
2. Rosen, 'Inter-nation and Narration in Ousmane Sembène's Films,' 31.

References

Ousmane, Sembène, *Xala* (Westport, CT: Lawrence Hill, 1976).

Pfaff, Françoise, *The Cinema of Ousmane Sembène, a Pioneer of African Film* (Westport, Conn.: Greenwood Press, 1984).

Rosen, Philip, 'Nation, Inter-nation and Narration in Ousmane Sembène's Films,' in Petty, Sheila, ed., *A Call to Action: The Films of Ousmane Sembène* (Westport, Conn.: Praeger, 1996), 27–55.

10. Rapacious Masculinity and Ethno-Colonial Politics in a Swahili Novel

Notes

1. Mazrui, *Beyond the Boundaries*, 16.
2. The Zanzibar Revolution, which overthrew the Arab Sultanate, occurred on 12 January 1964, just a few months after the islands were granted independence from Great Britain. The political leader of the revolution was Sheikh Abeid Karume, who eventually led the islands into a union with what was then called Tanganyika to form the United Republic of Tanzania.
3. Although English tends to use the generalised form 'Swahili,' the accurate forms for the language and the people are *Kiswahili* and *Waswahili* (sing. *Mswahili*) respectively.

4. Unless otherwise indicated, all the translations are by the author of this chapter.
5. District commissioners were top divisional administrators in the British colonial system, in the chain of command made up of the governor, the British monarch's representative top administrator of a colony, through the chief secretary and the provincial commissioners, who were in charge of the major regions of the colony.
6. Himid, *Howani Mwana*, ii.
7. Myers, 'Sticks and Stones: Colonialism and Zanzibari Housing,' 12–13.
8. Njogu, *Uhakiki wa Riwaya za Visiwani Zanzibar*, 58–59.
9. Njogu, *Uhakiki wa Riwaya za Visiwani* Zanzibar, 32–65, 76–96.
10. Reference to the dog's breast is also a literary allusion to the poem 'Kiswahili' by the best-known Swahili poet and novelist, Shaaban Robert, which contains the verse 'Titi la mama li tamu hata likiwa la mbwa' (Mother's breast is sweet even if it is a dog's).
11. Njogu, *Uhakiki wa Riwaya za Visiwani* Zanzibar, 161.
12. *Ibid.*, 120.
13. *Ibid.*, 192–195.

References

Himid, Z., *Howani Mwana* (Dar es Salaam, Tanzania: Institute of Kiswahili Research, 2005).
Mazrui, A., *Swahili Beyond the Boundaries: Literature, Language and Identity* (Athens: Ohio University Press, 2007).
Mohamed, S., *Asali Chungu* (Bitter Honey) (Nairobi, Kenya: Shungwaya, 1978).
Myers, G., 'Sticks and Stones: Colonialism and Zanzibari Housing,' in *Africa* 67 (1997).
Njogu, K., *Uhakiki wa Riwaya za Visiwani Zanzibar* (A Critique of the Zanzibar Island Novels) (Nairobi, Kenya: Nairobi University Press, 1997).

11. Masculinity in Achebe's Anthills of the Savannah

References

Achebe, Chinua, *Anthills of the Savannah* (London: Picador, 1988).
—*Things Fall Apart* (New York: Anchor Books, 1994).
Eliade, Mircea, *The Myth of the Eternal Return or Cosmos and History*, tr. Willard R. Trask (Princeton, N.J.: Princeton University Press, 1991).

12. Dark Bodies/White Masks: African Masculinities and Visual Culture in *Graceland*, *The Joys of Motherhood* and *Things Fall Apart*

Notes

1. I extend Abani's metaphor to the whole of life in the Maroko ghetto. In this locale an atmosphere of unsteady endurance prevails regardless of personal and/or familial relationships.
2. Gikandi, *Reading the African Novel*, 149.
3. The African "Big Man" provides perhaps the most enduring image of African masculinity. Across the continent and for a long sweep of history, ambitious people (usually men) have worked to enlarge their households and use their "wealth in people" for political and material advancement' (Lindsay and Miescher, *Men and Masculinities in Modern* Africa, 3).
4. R. W. Connell suggests in *Masculinities* that there are several kinds of masculinities, including hegemonic, complicitous, marginalised and subordinated (76). Although I do not necessarily agree that African masculinities fit into the same categories, an oppositional form of masculinity seems basic to African male identity.
5. Morrell, 'Of Boys and Men: Masculinity and Gender in Southern African Studies,' 608.
6. 'No matter how prosperous a man was, if he was unable to rule his women and his children (and especially his women) he was not really a man' (Achebe, *Things Fall Apart*, 52).
7. '[A]ll men have access to the patriarchal dividend, the power that being a man gives them to choose to exercise power over women. And this can be extended to the power to control the lives of other men as well.' (Ouzgane and Morrell, *African Masculinites*, 6).
8. Women are not necessarily held to the same standards. Okonkwo favours his daughter, Ezinma and frequently treats her as he would a son. He says, 'She should have been a boy' (*Things Fall Apart*, 62).
9. Thompson, 'Boys Will Be Boys,' 168.
10. Lindsay and Miescher, *Men and Masculinities in Modern Africa*, 250.
11. Even though this ceremony is not a masquerade in the technical sense, Esther Dagan explains the significance of colours. In African masquerades three colours are dominant: 'white, red and black. Their symbolic meanings vary, but are generally references to the triad of birth, life and death. White is often seen as spiritual and joyful, red as heat, blood, fire, aggression and war' (*The Spirit's Image*, 105).
12. Cooper, *Magical Realism in West African Fiction*, 1.
13. Burja, 'Targeting Men for Change,' 217.
14. Morrell, 'Of Boys and Men,' 608.
15. Lewis, *Feminist Africa 2*, <www.feministafrica.org/fa%202/02–2003 /editorial>.

16. Lott, 'All the King's Men:,' 192.
17. "'Anyway, your mother loved music and when your grandfather died, she inherited his gramophone . . . Your mother loved Elvis Presley . . .'" (105).
18. In a discussion of Elvis Presley's hairdo as a form of American youth rebellion, Karal Ann Marling notes that 'Back at Humes High in Memphis, rumour had it that he went to a ladies' beauty parlor, that he had a permanent wave . . . There was something perverse about boys who fussed with their hairdos like girls . . .' (As Seen on TV, 167).
19. Kasfir, 'Elephant Women, Furious and Majestic,' 18.
20. Dagan, Spirit's Image, 206.
21. Ibid., 51.

References

Abani, Chris, Graceland (New York: Farrar, Straus and Giroux, 2004).

Achebe, Chinua, Things Fall Apart (Greenwich, Conn.: Fawcett, 1959).

Bell, Clare, Enwezor, Okwui, Tilkin, Danielle, et al., curators, In/Sight: African Photographers, 1940 to the Present (New York: Guggenheim Museum Foundation, 1996).

Bujra, Janet, 'Targeting Men for Change: AIDS Discourse and Activism in Africa,' in Cleaver, Frances, ed., Masculinities Matter! Men, Gender and Development (London: Zed Books, 2002).

Connell, R. W., Masculinities (2nd ed.) (Berkeley and Los Angeles: University of California Press, 2005).

Cooper, Brenda, Magical Realism in West African Fiction (New York: Routledge, 1988).

Dagan, Esther, The Spirit's Image: The African Masking Tradition—Evolving Continuity (Montréal, Canada: Galerie Amrad African Art, 1992).

Emecheta, Buchi, The Joys of Motherhood (New York: George Braziller, 1979).

Gikandi, Simon, Reading the African Novel (London: JaneCurrey, 1987).

Kasfir, Sidney Littlefield, 'Elephant Women, Furious and Majestic: Women's Masquerades in Africa and the Diaspora,' in African Arts 31(2) (Spring 1998), 18–27, 92.

Lewis, Desiree, ed., Feminist Africa 2 (2003). Retrieved 22 January 2007 from <www.feministafrica.org/fa%202/02–2003/editorial>.

Lindsy, Lisa and Miescher, Stephan, eds., Men and Masculinities in Modern Africa (Portsmouth, N.H.: Heinemann, 2003).

Lott, Eric, 'All the King's Men: Elvis Impersonators and White Working-Class Masculinity,' in Stecopoulos, Harry and Uebel, Michael, eds., Race and the Subject of Masculinities (Durham, N.C.: Duke University Press, 1997).

Marling, Karal Ann, As Seen on TV: The Visual Culture of Everyday Life in the 1950s (Cambridge, Mass.: Harvard University Press, 1994).

Miescher, Stephan, *Making Men in Ghana* (Bloomington: Indiana University Press, 2005).

Morrell, Robert, 'Of Boys and Men: Masculinity and Gender in Southern African Studies,' in *Journal of Southern African Studies* 24 (4) (1998), 605–630.

Ouzgane, Lahoucine and Morrell, Robert, *African Masculinities: Men in Africa from the Late Nineteenth Century to the Present* (New York: Palgrave, 2005).

Smith, Richard Candida, ed., *Art and the Performance of Memory* (New York: Routledge, 2002).

Smith, Shawn Michelle, *American Archives: Gender, Race and Class in Visual Culture* (Princeton, N.J.: Princeton University Press, 1999).

Thompson, Marilyn, 'Boys Will Be Boys: Addressing the Social Construction of Gender,' in Cleaver, Frances, ed., *Masculinities Matter! Men, Gender and Development* (London: Zed Books, 2002).

Williams, Susan, *Confounding Images: Photography and Portraiture in Antebellum American Fiction* (Philadelphia: University of Pennsylvania Press, 1997).

13. Sexual Impotence: Metonymy for Political Failure in Ama Ata Aidoo's Anowa

Notes

1. Miescher, *Making Men in Ghana*, 2.
2. Horne, 'The Politics of Mothering, in Azodo and Wilentz, *Emerging Perspectives on Ama Ata Aidoo*, 303-332.
3. Inhorn, 'Sexuality, Masculinity and Infertility in Egypt,' 344.
4. Miescher, 151.
5. Kimmel, 'Masculinity as Homophobia,' in Brod and Kaufman, Theorising Masculinities.119-140.
6. Hearn and Collinson, 'Theorising Unities and Differences Between Men and Between Masculinities,' 97.
7. In his book, *Masculinities*, R. W. Connell discusses hegemonic masculinity. See especially 76–86 for definitions of hegemonic and marginalised masculinities.
8. The object of the reference to Achebe's depiction of Umuofia society's valorisation of the hegemonic masculine attributes embodied in Okonkwo by no means implies that Achebe sanctions them or that they constitute the ultimate societal ideal. Unoka, Okonkwo's father, who is ridiculed as an *agbala*, a woman, upon close scrutiny is revealed to be modelling a more humane masculinity that is characterised by gentleness, tenderness and an artistic sensibility which, because it is non-phallic, is often cast off as effeminate and hence womanly. Okonkwo's eventual demise results from his over-identification with phallic masculinity and his projection of the

non-phallic attributes, modelled by his father, onto the female. The attention given to Achebe's novel stems from his meticulous exploration of the physical and psychological implications of the attainment of hegemonic masculinity with an African society. Mariama Bâ's novel, *So Long a Letter*, is also referenced here for the same reason.

9. In Achebe's novel, the *agbala* with a lower case 'a,' which means woman, is actually used as an insult to taunt those males who have failed to attain titles, in a world in which the attainment of titles becomes one of the distinct markers of hegemonic masculinity. The following quotation from *Things Fall Apart* situates the word in context: 'Even as a little boy he [Okonkwo] had resented his father's failure and weakness and even now he still remembered how he suffered when a playmate had told him that his father was *agbala*. That was how Okonkwo first came to know that *agbala* was not only another name for a woman, it could also mean a man who had taken no title' (13). In Umuofia society, titles are won by men who have proven themselves to be *real men* through their economic standing, prowess in war and leadership acumen. Paradoxically, the dominant oracle in Umuofia, The Oracle of the Hills and Caves, is called *Agbala* with a capital 'A.' *Agbala*, the oracle, on the other hand, is identified as male and referred to in the novel by the male pronoun. The power of *Agbala* is unparalleled, for we are informed 'no one who had ever crawled into his awful shrine had come out without the fear of his power' (16).

10. Stephan F. Miescher writes: 'Senior masculinity, the position of *opanyin*, did not depend on a person's specific age and wealth but rather on comportment, reputation and the ability to mediate conflicts and provide advice' (11). While the experience and maturity acquired by living renders age significant to the conferment of the status of elderhood, an '*opanyin*'s social position ... [is] not self-acquired but ascribed, the product of accomplishments and qualities acknowledged by a larger community' (194). Aidoo, in her play, endows the Old Man Mouth with the socially significant attributes of the *opanyin*.

11. See Odamtten, *The Art of Ama Ata Aidoo*, 42–79, for a detailed delineation of the historical and political shenanigans which undergird Aidoo's play.

12. The name builds on the Akan phrase 'The mouth that eats salt and pepper' to underscore the potency in the spoken word, that is, the consciousness that words are endowed with life, with potency. It is this potency that links words with prophecy.

13. The 'Big Man' construct in African masculinities has been discussed quite extensively by various scholars. In the introduction to their book *Men and Masculinities in Modern Africa*, Miescher and Lindsay, in cautioning of the 'need to be sensitive not only to innovations and ruptures, but also to the powerful continuities in gender systems that resurfaced in various

situations' (3), draw attention particularly to this concept. The African 'Big Man' provides perhaps the most enduring image of African masculinity (3).

14. The trope of the beautiful maidens in tales, referenced in *Anowa*, is common in African folktales. The most well-known rendition of that trope is in Amos Tutuola's *The Palm-Wine Drunkard* (1952).

15. Miescher, 2.

16. Even though the writer's name appears as Arthur Flannigan-Saint-Aubin, that listing is erroneous. There should be no hyphen between Flannigan and Saint, Flannigan evidently being a middle name and not part of the last name. I will therefore refer to him as Saint-Aubin rather than as Flannigan-Saint-Aubin.

17. Haddon, quoted in Saint-Aubin, 'The Male Body and Literary Metaphors for Masculinity,' 249.

18. 'Because the Latin *testis* is the plural of *testis*, a witness, the testes were thought perhaps to bear witness to the truth—which is the meaning of *testify* and *attest*, and the truth of patriarchy is manhood, virility. *Testicle* derives from *testiculi*, little witness. *Testicle* is also related to *testa*, which designates both an earthen pot for seed storage and the skull that protects the brain. In botany, the testa is the protective outer encasing of a seed. On the other hand ... testes/testicles are also related to contest, testiness and thus to opposition and *agon* in general' (249).

19. Saint-Aubin observes that in the same way that positive phallic genitality traits become negative when exaggerated, the same thing can happen with the non-phallic. Staying power and steadfastness might become stubbornness or intractability and might lead to holding on when letting go would be preferable; incubation might become, in an exaggerated state, stagnation. The testerical masculine then is characterised by testiness and all that being testy implies: petulant, fretful, insolent, temperamental, morose and so forth. It is characterised also by lack of direction and by inertia (250).

20. This issue is discussed at length in Naana Banyiwa Horne's 'The Politics of Mothering: Multiple Subjectivity and Gendered Discourse in Aidoo's plays.'

21. Saint-Aubin again provides both the positive and the negative attributes of phallic masculinity. To be phallic in the positive sense is, for example, to be penetrating: inquisitive, persistent, steady, objective, courageous, discriminating, dominant. To be phallic in the negative sense is, for example, to be intrusive: violent, unyielding, discriminatory, exploitive, domineering (249). I have, however, extrapolated only the negative attributes in defining Kofi Ako's manifestation of phallic masculinity, because it is the predominantly negative traits he emulates in *Anowa*.

22. See Horne, 'Ayi Kwei Armah' (42–48) for a discussion of the Akan conception of the human.

23. Miescher and Lindsay, 3.
24. *Ibid.*, 141.
25. *Ibid.*, 3.
26. Lindsay, 141.
27. Miescher and Lindsay, 18.
28. Lindsay, 141–142.
29. I believe his limbs come to symbolise his sexuality, given the obviously phallic nature of limbs and the fact that one will normally not openly examine ones sexual organs publicly. The first time this behaviour is manifested is when Anowa counters his efforts to reduce her to a decorative piece by suggesting he marry one of the Oguaa mulatto women who epitomize female sexuality and sensuousness. His disconcertedness culminates in him stretching his left arm forward and staring at it intently (96). Also, in the final showdown in which Anowa publicly exposes his sexual impotence, he is shown examining 'his limbs as the funeral music or drums rise and fall' (115). The funeral music that plays in the background, setting the scene, foreshadows his impending suicide. It also undergirds the recognition that the death of his virility constitutes the death of his masculinity.

References

Achebe, Chinua, *Things Fall Apart* (New York: Anchor Books, 1994).

Aidoo, Ama Ata, *The Dilemma of a Ghost and Anowa* (London: Longman, 1987).

Bâ, Mariama, *So Long a Letter,* Tr. Modupe Bode-Thomas (Portsmouth, N.H.: Heinemann, 1981).

Coltrane, Scott, 'Theorising Masculinities in Contemporary Social Science,' in Brod, Harry and Kaufman, Michael, eds., *Theorising Masculinities* (Thousand Oaks, Calif.: Sage, 1994).

Connell, R. W., *Masculinities* (Berkeley and Los Angeles: University of California Press, 1995).

Conway-Long, Don, 'Ethnographies and Masculinities,' in Brod, Harry and Kaufman, Michael, eds., *Theorising Masculinities* (Thousand Oaks, Calif.: Sage, 1994).

Hearn, Jeff and Collinson, David L., 'Theorising Unities and Differences Between Men and Between Masculinities,' in Brod, Harry and Kaufman, Michael, eds., *Theorising Masculinities* (Thousand Oaks, Calif.: Sage, 1994).

Horne, Naana Banyiwa, 'The Politics of Mothering: Multiple Subjectivity and Gendered Discourse in Aidoo's Plays,' in Azodo, Ada Unoamaka and Wilentz, Gay, eds., *Emerging Perspectives on Ama Ata Aidoo* (Trenton, N.J.: Africa World Press, 1999).

—'*Ayi Kwei Armah*: An African Worldview in Fiction' (PhD dissertation, University of Wisconsin-Madison, 1993).

Inhorn, Marcia C., 'Sexuality, Masculinity and Infertility in Egypt: Potent Troubles in the Marital and Medical Encounters,' in *Journal of Men's* Studies 10 (3) (2002), 343–359.

Kimmel, Michael S., 'Masculinity as Homophobia: Fear, Shame and Silence in the Construction of Gender Identity,' in Brod, Harry and Kaufman, Michael, eds., *Theorising Masculinities* (Thousand Oaks, Calif.: Sage, 1994).

Kimmel, Michael and Kaufman, Michael, 'Weekend Warriors: The New Men's Movement,' in Brod, Harry and Kaufman, Michael, eds., *Theorising Masculinities* (Thousand Oaks, Calif.: Sage, 1994).

Lindsay, Lisa A., 'Money, Marriage and Masculinity on the Colonial Nigerian Railway,' in Lindsay, Lisa A. and Miescher, Stephan F., eds., *Men and Masculinities in Modern Africa* (Portsmouth, N.H.: Heinemann, 2003).

Miescher, Stephan F., *Making Men in Ghana* (Bloomington: Indiana University Press, 2005).

Miescher, Stephan F. and Lisa A. Lindsay. 'Introduction: Men and Masculinities in Modern African History,' in Lindsay, Lisa A. and Miescher, Stephan F., eds., *Men and Masculinities in Modern Africa* (Portsmouth, N.H.: Heinemann, 2003).

Odamtten, Vincent, *The Art of Ama Ata Aidoo: Polylectics and Reading Against Neocolonialism* (Gainesville: University of Florida Press, 1994).

Saint-Aubin, Arthur Flannigan, 'The Male Body and Literary Metaphors for Masculinity,' in Brod, Harry and Kaufman, Michael, eds., *Theorising Masculinities* (Thousand Oaks, Calif.: Sage, 1994).

Sembène, Ousmane, *Xala*, tr. Clide Wake (Westport, Conn.: Lawrence Hill, 1976).

14. Virility and Emasculation in Ahmadou Kourouma's Novels

Notes

1. Special thanks to Dr Tuzyline Jita Allan and Dr Helen Mugambi, not only for offering me the opportunity to contribute this chapter, but also for suggestions, comments and generous support. I also thank Dr Maria-Theresia Holub for her remarks on the chapter. Any shortcomings remain my own.
2. I use Coates's 2001 translation in this chapter.
3. Niane, *Soundiata: An Epic of Old Mali*, 49–50.
4. Le Renard and Toulabor, 'Entretien avec Ahmadou Kourouma,' 178.
5. Adjarian, *Allegories of Desire*, 161.
6. Griaule, *Conversations with Ogotemmêli*, 119.

References

Adjarian, Maude M., *Allegories of Desire: Body, Nation and Empire in Modern Caribbean Literature by Women* (Westport, Conn.: Praeger, 2004).

Griaule, Marcel, *Conversations with Ogotemmêli: An Introduction to Dogon Religious Ideas* (London: Oxford University Press, 1965).

Kourouma, Ahmadou, *Monnew*, tr. Nidra Poller 9San Francisco: Mercury House, 1993).

—*The Suns of Independence*, tr. Adrian Adams (New York: Africana Publishing, 1981).

—*Waiting for the Wild Beasts to Vote*, tr. Frank Wynne (London: Heinemann, 2003).

—*Waiting for the Vote of Wild Animals*, tr. Carrol F. Coates (Charlottesville: University Press of Virginia, 2001).

Le Renard, Thibault and Toulabor, Comi M., 'Entretien avec Ahmadou Kourouma,' in *Politique africaine* 75 (1999), 173–83.

Niane, Djibril Tamsir, *Soundiata: An Epic of Old Mali*, tr. G. D. Pickett (London: Longman, 1986).

Person, Yves, *Samori: Une révolution dyula* (Dakar, Senegal : L'Institut Fondamental d'Afrique Noire, 1968).

15. Women, Men and Extopy: On the Politics of Scale in Nuruddin Farah's Maps

Notes

1. I use the 'long space' to describe a specific engagement of postcolonial writing with the exigencies of nation state affiliation. Much of this assignation relates to the question of aesthetic form in the construction of postcolonial difference. In part, the attempt is to examine the politics of the extended literary form (e.g. trilogies and tetralogies, for instance) within the renewed and skewed logic of 'world literature.' The concept is elaborated in more detail in a forthcoming book of the same name.

2. For an earlier interpretation of the philosophical and aesthetic articulation of outsideness see Hitchcock, 'Exotopy and Feminist Critique.' .

3. Bakhtin, *Toward a Philosophy of the* Act, 41.

4. *Ibid.*, 49.

5. *Ibid.*, 28.

6. Bakhtin, *Art and Answerability*, 275.

7. Farah, *Yesterday, Tomorrow*, 48.

8. Riggin, 'Nuruddin Farah's Indelible Country of the Imagination,' 700.

9. Farah, 'Bastards of Empire,' 25.

10. Appiah, 'For Nuruddin Farah,' 703.

11. Cobham, 'Misgendering the Nation,' 52.
12. Wright, 'Parenting the Nation,'176-184.
13. Anderson, *Imagined Communities*, 15.
14. Wright, 'Parenting the Nation,' 178.
15. Farah is clearly aware of this formal tension in African culture. Indeed, his 'Acknowledgments' to *Maps* include a reference to *The Epic of Africa* by Isidore Okpewho. The trilogy as a whole speaks to the formal parameters of epic, although many passages inflect its orality. The differences, however, are even more instructive, especially where they interact with the cultural conditions of colonialism.
16. Farah, *Maps*, 161.
17. Farah, *Yesterday, Tomorrow*, 192.
18. Farah's epigraphs are never innocent, so when Francesca Kazan says of *Maps* in 'Recalling the Other Third World,' 'There are no whites in this textual world' one might at least consider the reach of their insinuation. .
19. Farah, 'A Country in Exile,' 4.
20. I have developed this concept of the imaginary state in relation to postcolonial writing in Hitchcock's *Imaginary States*.

References

Anderson, Benedict, *Imagined Communities* (London: Verso, 2006).
Appiah, Kwame Anthony, 'For Nuruddin Farah,' in *World Literature Today* 72 (4) (1998).
Bakhtin, Mikhail, *Art and Answerability*, tr. Vadim Liapunov; eds. Michael Holquist and Vadim Liapunov (Austin: University of Texas Press, 1990).
—*Toward a Philosophy of the Act*, tr. Vadim Liapunov (Austin: University of Texas Press, 1993).
Bhabha, Homi, *The Location of Culture* (London: Routledge, 1994).
Cobham, Rhonda, 'Misgendering the Nation: African Nationalist Fictions and Nuruddin Farah's *Maps*,' in Parker, Andrew, Russo, Mary, Summer, Doris and Yaeger, Patricia, eds., *Nationalism and Sexualities* (New York: Routledge, 1992).
Devi, Mahasweta, 'Douloti the Bountiful,' in *Imaginary Maps*, tr. Gayatri Chakravorty (London: Routledge, 1994).
Farah, Nuruddin, *From a Crooked Rib* (London: Heinemann, 1970).
—*Sweet and Sour Milk* (London: Allison and Busby, 1979).
—*Sardines* (London: Allison and Busby, 1981).
—*Close Sesame* (London: Allison and Busby, 1983).
—*Maps* (New York: Penguin, 1986).
—'Why I Write,' in *Third World Quarterly* 10 (1988), 1591–1599.
—'A Country in Exile,' in *Transition* 57 (1992), 4–8.
—*Gifts* (New York: Penguin, 1993).

—'Bastards of Empire,' in *Transition* 65 (1995), 26–35.

—*Secrets* (New York: Penguin, 1998).

—*Yesterday, Tomorrow: Voices From the Somali Diaspora* (London: Cassell, 2000).

—*Knots* (New York: Penguin, 2007).

Hitchcock, Peter, *Imaginary States: Studies in Cultural Transnationalism* (Urbana: University of Illinois Press, 2003).

—'Exotopy and Feminist Critique,' in Shepherd, David, ed., *Bakhtin: Carnival and Other Subjects* (Amsterdam, The Netherlands: Rodopi Press, 1993).

Kazan, Francesca, 'Recalling the Other Third World: Nuruddin Farah's *Maps*,' in *Novel* 26 (3) (1993), 253–268.

Kelly, Hilarie, 'A Somali Tragedy of Political and Sexual Confusion: A Critical Analysis of Nuruddin Farah's *Maps*,' in *Ufahamu: Journal of the African Activist Association* 16 (2) (1988), 21–37.

Rich, Adrienne, 'Notes Toward a Politics of Location,' in *Blood, Bread and Poetry: Selected Prose 1979–1985* (New York: Norton, 1994).

Riggin, William, 'Nuruddin Farah's Indelible Country of the Imagination: The 1998 Neustadt International Prize for Literature,' in *World Literature Today* 72: 4 (1998).

Saadawi, Nawal El, *Woman at Point Zero*, tr. Sherif Hetata (London: Zed Press, 1983).

Spivak, Gayatri Chakravorty, 'Woman in Difference,' in *Outside in the Teaching Machine* (London: Routledge, 1993).

Todorov, Tzvetan, *Mikhail Bakhtin: The Dialogical Principle*, tr. Wlad Godzich (Minneapolis: University of Minnesota Press, 1984).

Wright, Derek, 'Parenting the Nation: Some Observations on Nuruddin Farah's *Maps*,' in *College Literature* 19 (3) (1992), 176–184.

16. Killing the Pimp : Firdaus' Challenge to Masculine Authority in Nawal El Saadawi in Woman at Point Zero

Notes

1. In *The Hidden Face of Eve* El Saadawi comments on the effects on men of the cultural contradictions posed by differing views of 'progressive political leaders and religious thinkers and those whose values and attitudes towards society are inspired by narrow class privileges and an orthodox traditionalist interpretation of Islam . . . Men are very often the victims of such contradictions in their attitudes towards women' (viii–ix).

2. See Golley, *Reading Arab Women's Autobiographies* (7–9) for a discussion on the notation 'Arab.'

3. Shabaan, *'Both Right and Left Handed,'* 2. Men had been writing about women for centuries. According to Ahmed: 'The subject of women first surfaced as

a topic of consequence in the writings of Muslim male intellectuals in Egypt and Turkey' (*Women and Gender in Islam*, 128).

4. See, among others, Fedwa Malti-Douglas, *Men, Women and God(s)* (9–12) and Al-Hassan Golley, *Reading Arab Women's Autobiographies* (131–133).

5. Malti-Douglas, 10.

6. Parekh, 'Sanctuary and the Prison,' 94.

7. Such a technique was used effectively by Virginia Woolf in *A Room of One's Own*, as she likewise sets out a fictive tale in her overall non-fiction complaint against the male-dominated British educational system. 'Lies will flow from my lips,' she says and the reader can decide whether or not to believe her narrative. As an aside, Woolf's merging of the fictive and non-fictive genres is so 'seamless' that, as a graduate student reading her work for the first time, I had to check to see if indeed Newnham and Girton Colleges were real or made up places. The merging of fiction and non-fiction both enhances and deflects the truth-telling qualities of a text: 'Tell the truth but tell it slant... The Truth must dazzle gradually Or every man be blind' (Emily Dickinson).

8. Chikwenye Ogunyemi addresses yet another aspect of the mélange of genres presented in *Woman at Point Zero*. She characterises its subversive stylistic quality: 'The hybrid narrative with its oral bent challenges the dominance of classic Arabic, written, read and interpreted mostly by men' (*Juju Fission*, 135).

9. Golley finds that the mixture of fictive and documentary modes are common to most autobiographical forms and it is not 'an exclusive characteristic of "Third World" women's narratives' (150).

10. Angela Y. Davis describes the tendency to see 'women who have been publicly punished by the state for their misbehaviors as significantly more aberrant and far more threatening to society than their numerous male counterparts' (*Are Prisons Obsolete?*, 66).

11. I exclude the more private enactment of patriarchy, the family unit, which for El Saadawi, 'constitutes the core of patriarchal class relations' (*The Hidden Face of Eve*, i).

12. Golley, 153.

13. *Ibid.*, 154.

14. Malti-Douglas, 49.

15. See Malti-Douglas for a lesbian reading of the physician/prisoner relationship (51).

16. For a litany of female violating behaviours in *Woman at Point Zero*, see Royer (*A Critical Study of the Works of Nawal El Saadawi*, 2001 and Malti-Douglas (44–67).

17. Here we find a different attitude towards religious precepts from those expressed in *The Hidden Face of Eve*, where El Saadawi is clear in

distinguishing the religious principles of Islam, which she believes are righteous, from the public enactment of the religion skewed to oppressiveness and tyranny by the men who both lead and follow. Critics are in general careful to make this distinction, not blaming Islam, but men's interpretation of Islam. For example, Ogunyemi agrees that under criticism in *Woman at Point Zero* is 'not Islam but the patriarchal slant given to Islam in praxis, to the detriment of women' (115).

18. Malti-Douglas writes: '. . . one of the most important leitmotifs of *Woman at Point Zero* is woman's body. Who owns it? Who controls it? Does Firdaus have a right to it?' (52).

19. See Malti-Douglas for the 'bi-sociation' of food and sex (54).

20. Of course Sharifa is not acting solely on her own behalf, but as a madam herself working for a pimp. The chain of financial exploitation fans upwards.

21. El Saadawi, *The Hidden Face of Eve*, 56.

22. 'Prostitution in fact is the opposite side of the coin to marriage' (El Saadawi, *The Hidden Face of Eve*, 56).

23. In Western post-Freudian terms we could see Firdaus's actions as a version of 'internalising the aggressor,' doing to herself that which the aggressive forces of culture have done. But my reading suggests a more life-sustaining way of looking at such behaviour.

24. The exploitation of women is built upon the fact that man pays her the lowest wage known for any category of human beasts of burden. It is he who decides what she is paid in the form of a few piastres, some food, a dress, a roof over her head. With this meagre compensation, he can justify the authority he exercises over her' (*The Hidden Face of Eve*, 143).

25. Such 'womanly' neurosis was called 'hysteria' in the nineteenth century.

26. For a full exploration of Shahrazad, see Gauch, *Liberating Shahradad*.

27 'To be a criminal one must be a man' (*Woman at Point Zero*, 100).

References

Ahmed, Laila, *Women and Gender in Islam* (New Haven, Conn.: Yale University Press, 1992).

Davis, Angela Y., *Are Prisons Obsolete?* (New York: Seven Stories Press, 2003).

El Saadawi, Nawal, *The Hidden Face of Eve: Women in the Arab World*, tr. and ed. Sherifa Hetata (London: Zed Books, 1980).

—*The Nawal El Saadawi Reader* (London: Zed Books, 1997).

—*Woman at Point Zero*, tr. Sherifa Hetata (London: Zed Books, 1983).

Gauch, Suzanne, *Liberating Shahrazad: Feminism, Postcolonialism and Islam* (Minneapolis: University of Minnesota Press, 2007).

Golley, Al-Hassan, *Reading Arab Women's Autobiographies* (Austin: University of Texas Press, 2003).

Harlow, Barbara, 'From the Women's Prison: Third World Women's Narratives of Prison,' in *Feminist Studies* 12 (3) (Autumn 1986), 501–524.

Hitchcock, Peter, *Dialogics of the Oppressed* (University of Minnesota Press, 1993).

Ibrahim, Huma, 'Ontological Victimhood,' in Nnaemeka, Obioma, ed., *The Politics of (M)Othering: Womanhood, Identity and Resistance in African Literature* (New York: Routledge, [year]).

Malti-Douglas, Fedwa, *Men, Women and God(s): Nawal El Saadawi and Arab Feminist Poetics* (Berkeley and Los Angeles: University of California Press, 1995).

Ogunyemi, Chikwenye Okonjo, *Juju Fission* (New York: Peter Lang, 2007).

Parekh, Pushpa N., 'The Sanctuary and the Prison: Women's Rites/Rights/Writing and Political Activism,' in Makward, Edris, Lilleleht, Mark and Saber, Ahmed, eds., *North–South Linkages and Connections in Continental and Diaspora African Literatures* (Trenton, N.J.: Africa World, 2005).

Royer, Diana, *A Critical Study of the Works of Nawal El Saadawi, Egyptian Writer and Activist* (Lewiston, N.Y.: Edwin Mellen Press, 2001).

Shabaan, Bouthaina, *Both Right and Left Handed: Arab Women Talk about Their Lives* (London: Women's Press, 1988).

17. The Price of Pleasure: K. Sello Duiker's Thirteen Cents and the Economics of Homosexuality in South Africa

Notes

1. Holmes,'"White Rapists Made Coloureds (and Homosexuals),"' 284.
2. Marx, *Wage-Labour and Capital and Value, Price and Profit*, 463.
3. Hoad, *African Intimacies*, 56.
4. Foucault, *History of Sexuality*, 7.
5. *Ibid.*, 5.
6. Hoad, 78.
7. Nabokov, *Lolita*, 9.
8. Kumalo, quoted in Stobie, *Somewhere in the Double Rainbow*, 201.
9. *Ibid.*
10. Stobie, 203.
11. *Ibid.*, 204.
12. Monsman's introduction to *King Solomon's Mines*, 21.
13. Moodie, *Going for Gold*, 11–12.
14. Moodie, 121.
15. *Ibid.*, 125.
16. *Ibid*, 137.
17. Mbembe and Nuttall, *Johannesburg*, 22–23.

References

Couzens, Tim, *The Selected Stories of R. R. R. Dhlomo* (Grahamstown, South Africa: Institute for the Study of English in Africa. Rhodes University, 1975).

—Introduction in Plaatje, Solomon, *Mhudi* (Oxford: Heinemann Press, 1978).

Duiker, K. Sello, *The Quiet Violence of Dreams* (Cape Town, South Africa: Kwela Books, 2001).

—*Thirteen Cents* (Cape Town, Africa: David Philip, 2002).

Foucault, Michel, *The History of Sexuality, Vol. 1: An Introduction*, tr. Robert Hurley (New York: Vintage Books, 1980).

Gevisser, Mark and Cameron, Edwin, eds., *Defiant Desire* (New York: Routledge, 1995).

Haggard, H. Rider, *King Solomon's Mines* (Oxford: Oxford University Press, 1989).

Hoad, Neville, *African Intimacies: Race, Homosexuality and Globalization* (Minneapolis: University of Minnesota Press, 2007).

Holmes, Rachel, "'White Rapists Made Coloureds (and Homosexuals)": The Winnie Mandela Trial and the Politics of Race and Sexuality,' in Gevisser, Mark and Cameron, Edwin, ed., *Defiant Desire* (New York: Routledge, 1995), 284–294.

Marx, Karl, *Wage-Labour and Capital and Value, Price and Profit*, tr. unknown (New York: International Publishers, 1990).

Mbembe, Achille, *On the Postcolony* (Berkeley and Los Angeles: University of California Press, 2001).

Mbembe, Achille and Nuttall, Sarah, 'Introduction: Afropolis,' in Mbembe, Achille and Nuttall, Sarah, eds., *Johannesburg: The Elusive Metropolis* (Durham, N.C.: Duke University Press, 2008), 1–33.

Monsman, Gerald, 'Introduction,' in Haggard, H. Rider, *King Solomon's Mines* (Peterborough, Canada: Broadview Literary Texts, 2002).

Moodie, T. Dunbar and Ndatshe, Vivienne, *Going for Gold: Men, Mines and Migration* (Berkeley and Los Angeles: University of California Press, 1994).

Morrison, Toni, *The Bluest Eye* (New York: Penguin Books, 1994).

Nabokov, Vladimir, *Lolita* (New York: Vintage International, 1997).

Plaatje, Solomon, *Mhudi* (Oxford: Heinemann Press, 1978).

Sepamla, Sipho, *A Ride on the Whirlwind: A Novel of Soweto* (Nairobi, Kenya: Heinemann Books, 1981).

Stobie, Cheryl, *Somewhere in the Double Rainbow: Representations of Bisexuality in Post-Apartheid Novels* (Scottsville, South Africa: University of KwaZulu-Natal Press, 2007).

18. Naming the Masculine: Gorgui Dieng's *A Leap Out of the Dark*

Notes

1. Quoted in Greenblatt, 'Culture,' 225.
2. Jehlen, 'Gender,' 265.
3. Jones, 'Construction of Gender in Family Therapy,' 18.
4. Kandji, 'Female Sexuality in Buchi Emecheta's Writings,' 17.
5. Walker, 'Brothers and Sisters,' 266.
6. *Ibid.*
7. Rivkin and Ryan, *Literary Theory*, 529.
8. Lat Dior Ngoné Latyr Diop (1842–1886) is a Senegalese national hero. Like Alboury Ndiaye, El Hadji Omar Tall or Samori Touré, he was opposed to French colonial penetration in West Africa. He heroically died on the battlefield at Dexeele on 26 October 1886. Acknowledging his bravery, Faidherbe said that brave people like Lat Dior prefer death to dishonour. These words have become the motto of the Senegalese forces: 'On nous tue, on ne nous déshonoure pas.'
9. Rivkin and Ryan, 539.
10. *Ibid.*
11. Coats, *Women's Education*, 24.

References

Beach, Frank, *Pattern of Sexual Behavior* (New York: Harper, 1972).

Beauvoir, Simone de, *The Second Sex*, tr. and ed.H. M. Parshley (New York: Bantam Books, 1952).

Bhabha, Homi, *The Location of Culture* (London: Routledge, 1994).

Coats, Maggie, *Women's Education* (Buckingham, England: VSHRE and Open University Press, 1994).

Dalla Costa, Mariarosa and James, S., *The Power of Women and the Subversion of the Community* (Bristol, England: Falling Wall Press, 1972).

Dieng, Gorgui, *A Leap Out of the Dark* (Dakar, Senegal: Les Editions du Livre Universel, 2002).

Diouf Kandji, Fatou, 'Female Sexuality in Buchi Emecheta's Writings,' in *Bridges: An African Journal of English Studies. Gender, Sexuality and Literature*, No. 6 Spécial (Dakar, Senegal: Institut Sénégalo Britannique, 1995).

Greenblatt, Stephen, 'Culture,' in Lentrichia, Frank and McLaughlin, Thomas, eds., *Critical Terms for Literary Study* (2nd ed.) (Chicago: University of Chicago Press, 1990).

Jehlen, Myra, 'Gender,' in Lentrichia, Frank and McLaughlin, Thomas, eds., *Critical Terms for Literary Study* (2nd ed.) (Chicago: University of Chicago Press, 1990).

Jones, Elsa, 'The Construction of Gender in Family Therapy,' in Burck, Charlotte and Bebe, Speed, eds., *Gender, Power and Relationships* (New York: Routledge, 1995).

Kandji, Mamadou, ed., *Tradition and the Dynamics of Women's Empowerment* (Dakar, Senegal: Dakar University Press, 2006).

Little, Kenneth, *The Sociology of Urban Women's Image in African Literature* (London: Macmillan, 1980).

Millet, Kate, *Sexual Politics* (London: Virago, 1977).

Nettels, Elsa, *Language and Gender in American Fiction: Howells, James, Wharton and Cather* (Charlottesville: University Press of Virginia, 1997).

Rich, Adrienne, 'When We Dead Awaken: Writing as Re-Vision,' in *On Lies, Secrets, Silence: Selected Prose 1966–1978* (New York: Norton, 1979).

—*Of Woman Born. Motherhood as Experience and Institution* (New York: Norton, 1992)

Rivkin, Julie and Ryan, Michael, *Literary Theory: An Anthology* (Cambridge, Mass.: Blackwell, 1998), 528–529.

Schriber, Mary Suzanne, *Gender and the Writer's Imagination: From Cooper to Wharton* (Lexington: University of Kentucky Press, 1987).

Walker, Alice, 'In Search of Our Mothers' Gardens,' in Stanford, Judith A., ed., *Responding to Literature* (Mountain View, Calif.: Mayfield, 1992).

—'Brothers and Sisters,' in Smart, William, ed., *Eight Modern Essayists* (6th ed.) (New York: St. Martin's Press, 1995).

A Retrospective: Looking for 'the African' in the Hybrid: Thoughts on Maculinity in Equiano's The Interesting Narrative [subheading]

Notes

1. Carretta's discovery consists of a 1759 baptismal record from St. Margaret's Church in London, dated 9 February 1759 and the muster book of the *Racehorse*, a ship from the Arctic expedition of Constantine Phipps in 1773. He first published his findings in 1995 in a footnote in the Penguin Edition of *Olaudah Equiano: The Interesting Narrative and Other Writing.*

2. In a June 1792 written in Edinburgh and addressed 'To the Reader,' Equiano wrote: 'An invidious falsehood having appeared in the Oracle of the 25th and the Star of the 27th of April 1792 . . . with a view to hurt my character and to discredit and prevent the sale of my Narrative, asserting that I was born in the Danish island of Santa Cruz [St. Croix], in the West Indies, it is necessary that, in this edition, I should take notice thereof and it is only needful for me to appeal to those numerous and respectable persons of character who know me when I first arrived in England and could speak no language but that of Africa.'

3. Howard, 'Unraveling the Narrative,' 12.
4. *Ibid,*, 13.
5. *Ibid.*
6. Lovejoy, 'Autobiography and Memory,' 325.
7. Howard, 15.
8. Bloom, *How to Read and Why*, 25.
9. Roy Porter, *The Enlightenment*, p.16.
10. Vincent Carretta, *The Interesting Narrative and Other Writing*, p.xxvi.
11. *Ibid.*, p.77.
12. Paul Goring, *Eighteenth-Century Literature and Culture*, p.105.
13. *Ibid.*, p.136.
14. Kevin Robins, 'Interrupting Identities: Turkey/Europe,' p.63.
15. *Ibid.*
16. Homi Bhabha, 'Signs Taken for Wonders,' pp.34-35
17. John McLeod, *Beginning Colonialism*, p.219.
18. Ella Shohat, quoted in *The Hybrid Muse*, p.180.
19. Shohat, 'Notes on the Postcolonial,' p.109.
20. Robert Young, *Colonial Desire: Hybridity in Theory, Culture and Race*, p.6.
21. Jahan Ramazani, *The Hybrid Muse: Postcolonial Poetry in English*, p.181.
22. Caretta, 'Defining a gentleman, the status of Olaudah Equiano or Gustavus Vassa,' p.385.
23. Caretta, *The Interesting Narrative and Other Writings*, p. 335.
24. Anne McClintock, *Imperial Leather*, p.299.
25. *Ibid.*, pp.299-300.
McClintock's summary of the event reads as follows:

'The day after Christmas during South Africa's 'year of fire,' when the Soweto uprising of 1976 was still shaking the country, a black woman whom we have to call 'Poppie Nongena,' though that is not her real name, arrived at the door of Elsa Joubert, a white Afrikaans writer and mother. Nongena was in great distress. The township from which she had fled was in turmoil. Conservative vigilantes armed by the police were on the rampage and thousands of people had taken flight into the bush and surrounding townships. The police were searching for Nongena's brother on charges of murder and she had spent the night huddled with her children in the windtorn bushes of the Cape flats.

While the black townships burned, Joubert herself was about to go on holiday with her family. For some time, previously, she had cast about for a topic for a new book. During the unsettling days of the rebellion, the idea of writing something about the Bantustans had sent her to pass offices, hospital clinics, schools and churches, interviewing and watching, but nothing had struck her with quite the force of Nongena's story. So the two women came to an agreement. Joubert would transcribe and edit

Nongena's life story and should the book sell, the proceeds would be divided equally between them. Nongena needed money for a house and Joubert's cautious estimate of a couple of thousand rands was an undreamed-of windfall. Over a period of six months, Nongema returned three times a week to tell her story in a series of taped interviews. The story emerged in fragments and patches, pieced together by Nongena's unflagging and extraordinary memory. Two years later it was published in Afrikaans under the title *Die Swerfjare van Poppie Nongena*. Translated by Joubert herself the book reappeared in English in 1980 as *The Long Journey of Poppie Nongena* and became an overnight sensation.

26. McClintock, p.300.

References

Carretta, Vincent, 'Questioning the Identity of Olaudah Equiano, or Gustavus Vassa, the African,' in Nussbaum, Felicity A., ed., *The Global Eighteenth Century* (Baltimore: Johns Hopkins University Press, 2003).

—ed., *Olaudah Equiano: The Interesting Narrative and Other Writings* (New York: Penguin Books, 1995).

—'Defining a gentleman: the status of Olaudah Equiano or Gustavus Vassa.'*Language Sciences* 22 (2000) 385-399.

Bloom, Harold, *How to Read and Why*, New York: Simon & Schuster, 2000).

Howard, Jennifer, 'Unraveling the Narrative,' in *The Chronicle of Higher Education* 52, Issue 3 (9 September 2005), A11–A15.

Goring, Paul, *Eighteenth-Century Literature and Culture* (London: Continuum, 2008).

Lovejoy, Paul E., 'Autobiography and Memory: Gustavus Vassa, alias Olaudah Equiano, the African,' in *Slavery and Abolition* 27, no. 3 (December 2006), 317–347.

McClintock, Anne, *Imperial Leather: Race, Gender and Sexuality in the Colonial Contest* (New York: Routledge, 1995).

McLeod, John, *Beginning Postcolonialism* (Manchester, England: Manchester University Press, 2000).

Porter, Roy. *The Enlightenment*. (New York: Palgrave), 2001.

Ramazani, Jahan, *The Hybrid Muse: Postcolonial Poetry in English* (Chicago: Chicago University Press, 1995).

Robins, Kevin. 'Interrupting Identities: Turkey/Europe.'In Stuart Hall and Paul du Gay, eds. *Questions of Cultural Identity* (London: Sage Publications Inc), 2002.

Shohat, Ella, 'Notes on the "Postcolonial,"' *Social Text* 31/32 (1992),99-113.

Young, Robert, *Colonial Desire: Hybridity in Theory, Culture and Race* (London: Routledge, 1995).

Index

existentialism, 51, 58
Existentialism and Humanism (Sartre),
    53
exotopy (*vnenakhodimost*), 8, 217–19,
    223–25, 227, 231–36
eyaggala amatu (Luganda), 46
eyatomerwa endiga (Luganda), 46
eyetisse ekirevu (Luganda), 46

'Faces of Masculinity in African
    Cinema: A case of Dani Kouyate's
    Sia, Le Rêve du Python' (Dipio), 6–7,
    95–115
fadenya (Mande), 27–29
fahima: (Arabic), 121
Faludi, Susan, 50
family, 59, 253, 256–59, 328n11
Farah, Nuruddin, 216, 218–19,
    222–33, 235–36
femininity, 4–5, 13–14, 20–21,
    91–92, 116–17, 219–21, 272–74,
    286–87, 398n2
feminism, 4, 51, 54–56, 118, 141,
    296
Fernea, Elizabeth Warnock, 117–18
feudalism, 140, 142, 144, 194,
    196–97
Finnegan, Ruth, 17, 296
Finzan (1987), 115
Flight, The (Al-Hurub) (1991), 119–22
footbinding, 117
Foucault, Michel, 116, 255–56, 269
Fourth World Conference on
    Women (Beijing, 1995), 55
France, 203, 220
Freud, Sigmund, 14, 22, 219
From a Crooked Rib (Farah), 223
Fulani epics, 32

Galla people, 16–19
Gallimore, Bangira Béa, xii, 6,
    50–65

'Gbejeriemu' (*udje* song), 74
'Gbogidi' (Oloya), 70–71, 74
gender roles and relations, 3–8, 21,
    25, 50, 53, 78, 110, 116–17, 168,
    214, 272–73, 278, 298–99n2; in
    Baganda society and culture,
    36–43, 49, 52, 64, 80–94, 302n1,
    303n4, 303nn9-10, 304n16,
    304n19, 305n22; in Igbo society,
    7, 149, 303n4; in Rwandan
    society and culture, 6, 53–55, 58,
    60–64; in Somalian poetry, 223.
    See also matrilineal kinship;
    patriarchy; patrilineal kinship
generational and sibling rivalry, 22,
    27–32
Gerima, Haile, 101
Gevisser, Mark, 251
Gifts (Farah), 219, 224
Gikandi, Simon, 295–97
Gilmore, David D., 14
Gledhill, Ruth, 250–51
*Going for Gold: Men, Mines and
    Migration* (Moodie and Ndatsha),
    265–66
gold mines (South Africa), 265–67
Goliath, 18
Golley, Al-Hassan, 241, 328n9
Goring, Paul, 291
Graceland (Abani), 160, 167–77
Gramsci, Antonio, 6, 96, 99–100,
    106
Great Chain of Being, 292
Greer, Germaine, 272
Greimas, Algirdas-Julien, 51
griot, 5, 26, 31, 33–34, 104–5, 202,
    209–10, 314n20

haddad (Arabic), 121
Haddon, G.P., 190
Hafez, Sabry, 119
Haggard, H. Rider, 265

Kagame, Paul (Rwanda), 62
Kagwa, Apolo, 40
'Kalasa the Impotent' (Baganda
  folktale), 46–47
Kalenjin community (Kenya), 14
Kassa, Soumayla, 27
Kayanda (*kadongokamu* song), 78–79,
  81–84, 90–94
'Kayima and his Sister in the Forest'
  (Baganda folktale), 39
Keita, L'Heritage du Griot (1995), 96
Kendall, Martha B., 28
Khan, Mohammed, 119
Kibwana oral tale (Haya people),
  23–24
Kierkegaard, Søren, 231
Kiganda (Luganda), 80
Kijumwa, Muhamed, 17
'Killing the Pimp: Firdaus's
  Challenge to Masculine
  Authority in Nawal El Saadawi's
  Woman at Point Zero' (Zucker), 8,
  237–49
Kimmel, Michael, 81
kingship, 47–49, 77, 305nn29-31
King Solomon's Mines (Haggard), 265
Kintu myth (Luganda), 6, 35,
  40–41, 49, 304n16
Kisii community (Kenya), 14
Kiswahili, 14, 139, 317n3
Kiyimba, Abasi, xiii, 5–6, 35–49
Konate, Siendou A., xiii, 8,
  200–215
Kourouma, Ahmadou, 200–202,
  204–6, 211–15
Kouyaté, Mamadou, 27, 30–31, 96,
  104, 203, 313n3, 313n13
'Kpojiyovwi' (Memerume), 76
'Krekpe' (Memerume), 74
Kristeva, Julia, 272
kuganja (Luganda), 37
Kumalo, Bafana, 261

kusajjalaata (Luganda), 89
Kuti, Fela, 174
Kuyatè, Mamary, 29

Lacan, Jacques, 13, 54, 235
Lambeth Conference of Anglican
  Church (Canterbury, 2008),
  250–51
land ownership, 233, 255, 282–84
language, 215, 224–26, 270–71
Laplanche, Jean, 13
Lat-Dior Ngoné Latyr Diop
  (Senegal), 279, 331n8
Leap Out of the Dark, A (Dieng),
  270–87
*Légende du Wagadu Vue par Sia Yataber,
  La* (Diagana), 96
Lewis, Desiree, 161, 174
Lindfors, Bernth, xiii, 7, 130–34
Lindisfarne, Nancy, 116
Lindsay, Lisa, 3, 167, 196–97,
  319n3, 322n13
Links (Farah), 219
Lion and the Jewel, The (Soyinka), 287
Liyongo epic, 5, 13, 16–24, 299n3
Liyongo, Fumo, 16
Lolita (Nabokov), 259
Lott, Eric, 174
Loum, Daouda, xiii, 9, 270–87
Lovejoy, Paul E., 288–89
Luganda, 80
'Lukomwa's Children' (Baganda
  folktale), 47

mabo, 26
madness, 101–8, 111–12, 114,
  313n3, 313n13
Maghreb. *See* Egypt and North
  Africa
magical realism, 172
Mahabharata epic (India), 248
Majotan (Urhobo), 76

Moodie, T. Dunbar, 265–66
Morgan, Philip D., 288
Morrell, Robert, 3, 163, 173
mother-right, 283. *See also*
  matrilineal kinship
Mrakpor, Jonathan, 68
Mugambi, Helen Nabasuta, vi, 1–9,
  41, 78–94, 304n16
Mukaabya (Luganda), 92–93
mulenzi (Luganda), 37
Muna Moto (1975), 115
Muyaka bin Hajji, 17
Mwana Hashima binti Mataka, 20
Mwanakupona binti Mshamu, 17,
  20–21
Mwengo, Athuman, 17

Nakakaawa (*kadongokamu* song),
  78–79, 81–88, 91–92
'Naluggya and Sempala' (Baganda
  folktale), 42
Naremore, James, 118–19
Nassir, Sayyid Abdalla bin Ali bin,
  17
Nawal El Saadawi Reader, The (El
  Saadawi), 241
Naylor, Gloria, 277
Ndabaga Association (Rwanda),
  63–64, 309n21
'Ndabaga Folktale Revisited:
  (De)constructing Masculinity in
  the Post-Genocide Rwandan
  Society' (Gallimore), 6, 50–65
Ndabaga (Rwandan folktale),
  50–59, 63
Ndatshe, Vivienne, 265–66
neo-liberalism, 9, 253
Ngozi, 15
Ngugi wa Thiong'o, 218
Niane, Djibril Tamsir, 203
Nicholson, Jack, 119
Nkosi, Lewis, 261

Nuttall, Sarah, 267
nyamakala (Mande), 31
nyama (Mande), 31

obi (Igbo), 149
obirempon (Akan), 197
Obote, Milton, 80
occult, 31, 202, 205, 215
Odinga, Oginga, 157
Oedipus complex, 22, 278
Ogaden, 219–20, 231–33
Ogbariemu, Dozen, 68, 73
Ojaide, Tanure, xiv, 6, 66–77
Okafor, Clement, xiv, 1, 7, 149–59
Okitiakpe of Ekakpamre, 73–75,
  310n14, 310n16
Okpewho, Isidore, 3, 17
Oloya, 70–71, 74–75, 77
Omar Gatlato (1976), 119, 126–27
omufiirwa (Luganda), 46
oral cultural tradition, 3–5, 17, 25,
  32, 39, 296
*Origin of the Family, Private Property
  and the State* (Engels), 283
'Osokpro' (*udje* song), 74
Osundare, Niyi, 105–6
Ouedraogo, Idrissa, 115
'Our Husband Went to Sing'
  (Baganda folktale), 43
outsideness. *See* exotopy
  (*vnenakhodimost*)
Ouzgane, Lahoucine, 3
oweffumu eryamenyeka (Luganda), 46

Painter, Nell, 288
paleonegritics, 206–7
Parekh, Pushpa, 239–40
Parmar, Pratibha, 117
patriarchy, 61, 126, 161, 191, 194,
  212, 272, 283, 328n11
patrilineal kinship, 38, 44, 283,
  299n3

195–96, 199, 240–42, 245–46,
328n10; violence against, 41–42,
58, 83, 117, 138, 142–43, 168,
211, 244, 268, 304n19. *See also*
childbearing and childlessness;
femininity; menstruation;
virginity
Women of Brewster Place, The (Naylor),
277
Women and Islamization (Ask and
Tjomsland), 118
'Women, Men and Exotopy: On the
Politics of Scale in Nuruddin
Farah's *Maps*' (Hitchcock), 8,
216–36

Women and Neurosis (El Saadawi),
239, 247
Women's War (Nigeria, 1929), 159
Wright, Derek, 220, 222, 224
Wynne, Franck, 200

Xala (1973), 115, 130–34

Yaaba (1986), 115
Yeelen (1989), 98
Young, Robert, 292

Zanzibar, 7, 137–40, 317n2
Zucker, Marilyn Slutzky, xiv, 8,
237–49
Zuma, Jacob, 252